PLANNING

PLANNING

PLANNING

FOURTH EDITION

NEIL COLLAR, LLB (HONS), LLM, DIP LP, LARTPI
Partner, Brodies LLP

W. GREEN

 THOMSON REUTERS

Published in 2016 by Thomson Reuters (Professional) UK Limited, trading as W. Green, 21 Alva Street, Edinburgh EH2 4PS (Registered in England & Wales, Company No.1679046. Registered Office and address for service: 2nd floor, 1 Mark Square, Leonard Street, London, EC2A 4EG).

For further information on our products and services, visit
http://www.sweetandmaxwell.co.uk/wgreen/

Printed and bound by CPI Group (UK) Ltd, Croydon, CR0 4YY.
No natural forests were destroyed to make this product; only farmed timber was used and re-planted.
A CIP catalogue record of this book is available for the British Library.

ISBN: 9780414019331

PREFACE TO FOURTH EDITION

Planning law does not stand still. There has been a surprising amount of change since the last edition. There have been adjustments to the 2006 Act reforms, and the courts have continued to clarify the law. The law is stated as at December 31, 2015.

I am grateful for the support and inspiration of my colleagues in Brodies' planning team—Alison Polson, Karen Hamilton, Kendra Lennox, Kevin Graham, Lee Murphy, and Victoria Smith—and also to our former colleague Robert Seaton, always notable for his enthusiasm for all matters legal. Particular thanks go to Kieran Shafiq for research, and Jackie McGuire, Paul Marshall and Catherine Reilly for reviewing.

This fourth edition is dedicated to Paula, Jonathan, Thomas and Ben for their support and encouragement.

Neil Collar
Edinburgh
February 2016

PREFACE TO THIRD EDITION

Much has changed since the second edition was published in 1999. The Planning Etc. (Scotland) Act 2006 emerged after a lengthy genesis, resulting in fundamental changes to the planning system, which were introduced in 2009. Practitioners are getting used to lots of new procedures, as well as new terms, such as "planning permission in principle" instead of "outline planning permission". I have learned a lot about the new system from writing this third edition and hope that readers will similarly find it useful.

Inevitably, there are already teething difficulties. Readers should be alert for future Court of Session judgments clarifying aspects of the new legislation.

This edition also takes account of other changes, such as the introduction of climate change duties under the Climate Change (Scotland) Act 2009 and the creation of the National Parks. It also discusses the implications of human rights, which have not had the far-reaching impact on the planning system that some predicted, but nevertheless remain relevant and influential. There have been few, if any, landmark court decisions, but reference is made to various court decisions clarifying areas of the law.

The law is stated as at December 31, 2009. However, I have taken the opportunity to incorporate references to the Scottish Government's *Scottish Planning Policy*, published in February 2010, as well as Circular 1/2010 "Planning Agreements", and the decisions of the Court of Session in *McGinty v The Scottish Ministers* and *Forbes v Aberdeenshire Council*. Mention is also made of forthcoming changes, such as the introduction of planning obligations and good neighbour agreements, and new tree preservation order procedures.

My thanks go to Alison Polson, Catherine Stokes, Jackie McGuire, Karen Hamilton, Monica Nelis and Robert Seaton, my colleagues in Brodies' planning team. We have endured together the rollercoaster ride of planning reform, and their research, comments and observations have assisted the preparation of this edition. I am also grateful to my colleague Christine O'Neill who commented on judicial challenges.

This third edition is dedicated to my wife Paula, for her support and encouragement, and to our sons Jonathan, Thomas and Ben (all born since the second edition was published).

Neil Collar
Edinburgh
March 2010

PREFACE TO SECOND EDITION

The need for a second edition of this book largely arose from the consolidation of the planning legislation into four new Acts of Parliament. This has forced planning practitioners to learn a new set of section numbers, and refer to section 75 agreements instead of section 50 agreements. In the five years since the first edition of this book was published, there have been several other significant legislative changes, including local government reorganisation, and changes to the Use Classes Order and the Planning Inquiries Procedure Rules. The courts have also clarified and developed various legal issues. In particular, a Scottish appeal to the House of Lords has resulted in an explanation of the role of the development plan in determining planning applications. Many new policy documents have also been issued by the Scottish Office.

With the approach of the Millenium, this second edition also reviews the future of planning law, particularly with the arrival of the Scottish Parliament, which has land-use planning among its legislative powers, and the incorporation of the European Convention on Human Rights.

The law is stated as at February 28, 1999. Where possible, subsequent changes have been referred to, such as the establishment of the Scottish Parliament. Mention is also made of various consultation papers, which are likely to result in changes to the law in the next few years.

My thanks go to all those at Brodies and Greens who assisted with the production of the second edition.

This second edition is dedicated to my wife Paula, for her support and understanding.

Neil Collar
Edinburgh
June 1999

PREFACE TO FIRST EDITION

"Does the Englishman still fondly believe that his home is his castle when the Executive has the following powers over it?

(1) To knock it down.
(2) To take possession of it, without notice to the owner, but with 14 days notice to the occupier, and without previous payment of the price.
(3) To close the King's highway which gives access to his house.
(4) To direct the colour with which his doors and fences may be painted.
(5) To confiscate his property illegally if he, for example is fighting in Asia for his country and so unable to appeal to the Courts within 28 days from any illegal act.
(6) To seize it and pay as compensation less than its value." (Mekie & Williams: *Town and Country Planning Law*)

The outrage at the growing power of the Executive felt by the authors of this statement is clear. Yet the basic premise of this statement which was written in 1946 remains valid today: the State has considerable powers over land under private ownership.

Town and country planning, to give its full title, is one of the powers exercised by the State to control building and other work on land · which is in private ownership. Since 1947 any landowner wishing to develop his/her land must seek permission from the State before carrying out that development. If this permission is refused, the landowner is unable to carry out the development but has no right to claim compensation from the State as a result. In such circumstances, how can "the Englishman still fondly believe that his home is his castle"? It is therefore surprising, but perhaps a tribute to the results which it has achieved, that the planning system enjoys almost universal support.

This book is written as an introduction to Scots planning law, a subject which has grown in importance over recent years. It is intended for use by any person coming into contact with the planning system, whether in their professional or private life. In particular, Chapter 10 provides a guide to members of the public on the opportunities for participating in the system. Inevitably some readers will use this book as a general reference text. With this in mind, it is recommended that any reader unfamiliar with the operation of the planning system should first read Chapter 2, which describes the "nuts and bolts", before selectively reading other chapters.

For many years Young and Rowan-Robinson's *Scottish Planning Law and Procedure* has been the bible for those involved in the Scottish planning system. This book is not a replacement for their comprehensive work but is intended as an introduction for those who are unfamiliar with the subject. It should also be of use where a more up-to-date text is required, as many areas of planning law have changed since *Scottish Planning Law and Procedure* was published in 1985.

With one exception, the law is stated as at January 31, 1994. It has been possible to address the introduction of the plan-led system on March 7, 1994, although this change in the law came too late in the publishing process for a detailed discussion on its implications to be included. The existence of other provisions of the Planning and Compensation Act 1991 which have yet to come into force, is also noted.

The starting point for this book was my LL.M. thesis "The Effects of Judicial Intervention on Planning Conditions", for which I owe a continuing debt to my supervisor Sue Nott and the University of Liverpool for the award of a research studentship. I also thank Paul Watchman for guiding my first steps as a practising planning lawyer. Many people have assisted with the production of this book. Particular thanks must go to my parents for their constant encouragement. I am also grateful to the partners of Brodies, W.S. and my colleagues for their support. As a novice to legal publishing, I greatly appreciated the help offered by everyone at Greens. And to all my friends, thank you.

Neil A. Collar
Edinburgh
February 1994

TABLE OF CONTENTS

TABLE OF CASES

TABLE OF CASES

TABLE OF UK STATUTES

TABLE OF SCOTTISH STATUTES

TABLE OF UK STATUTORY INSTRUMENTS

TABLE OF SCOTTISH STATUTORY INSTRUMENTS

TABLE OF ABBREVIATIONS

A.C.	Appeal Cases (Law Reports)
All E.R.	All England Law Reports
AMSC	Approval of Matters Specified in Condition
AQMA	Air Quality Management Area
B.P.P.	British Parliamentary Papers
CAR	Town and Country Planning (Control of Advertisements) (Scotland) Regulations 1984
CLEUD	Certificate of Lawfulness of Existing Use or Development
CLOPUD	Certificate of Lawfulness of Proposed Use or Development
CSIH	Court of Session Inner House
CSOH	Court of Session Outer House
DBE	Directorate for the Built Environment
DMPR	Town and Country Planning (Development Management Procedure) (Scotland) Regulations 2013
DPEA	Directorate of Planning and Environmental Appeals
DPSR	Town and Country Planning (Development Planning) (Scotland) Regulations 2008
E.G.	Estates Gazette
E.G.C.S.	Estates Gazette Case Summaries
EIA	Environmental Impact Assessment
EPA	Environmental Protection Act 1990
ES	Environmental Statement
ESA	Environmentally Sensitive Areas
EZ	Enterprise Zone
F.	Session Cases 1898–1906 (8 Volumes), edited by Fraser
FEI	Further Environmental Information
G.W.D.	Greens Weekly Digest
HES	Historic Environment Scotland
HRA	Habitats Regulations Appraisal
IPC	Integrated Pollution Control
J.L.S.S.	Journal of the Law Society of Scotland
J.P.L.	Journal of Planning Law
K.B.	King's Bench (Law Reports)
LDP	Local Development Plan
L.G.R.	Local Government Reports
L.J. (K.B.)	Law Journal Reports (King's Bench)
LRB	Local Review Body
LRPR	Town and Country Planning (Schemes of Delegation and Local Review Procedure) (Scotland) Regulations 2013
M.L.R.	Modern Law Review

NHA	Natural Heritage Area
NNR	National Nature Reserve
NPA	National Park Authority
NPF	National Planning Framework
NPPG	National Planning Policy Guideline
NSA	National Scenic Area
O.J.L.S.	Oxford Journal of Legal Studies
P. & C.R.	Property and Compensation Reports
PAG	Planning Advisory Group
PAN	Planning Advice Note
PARF	Planning Authority Response Form
PDO	Permitted Development Order
PDO 1992	Town and County Planning (General Permitted Development) (Scotland) Order 1992
PEO	Protective Expenses Order
PLBCASA	Planning (Listed Buildings and Conservation Areas) (Scotland) Act 1997
PLBCCACPSR	Planning (Listed Building Consent and Conservation Area Consent) (Scotland) Regulations 2015
P.L.C.R.	Planning Law Case Reports
P.L.R.	Planning Law Reports
PPP	Planning Permission in Principle
Prop. L.B.	Property Law Bulletin
PSA	Planning Etc. (Scotland) Act 2006
Q.B.	Queen's Bench (Law Reports)
RCS	Act of Sederunt (Rules of the Court of Session 1994) 1994
RTPI	Royal Town Planning Institute
SAC	Special Area of Conservation
S.C.	Session Cases
S.C.L.R.	Scottish Civil Law Reports
SDP	Strategic Development Plan
SDPA	Strategic Development Planning Authority
SEA	Strategic Environmental Assessment
SEI	Supplementary Environmental Information
SHEP	Scottish Historic Environment Policy
SI	Statutory Instrument
S.L.T.	Scots Law Times
S.L.T. (Lands Tr.)	Scots Law Times Lands Tribunal Reports
SNH	Scottish Natural Heritage
SPA	Special Protection Area
S.P.E.L.	Scottish Planning and Environmental Law
S.P.L.P.	Scottish Planning Law and Practice
SPP	Scottish Planning Policy
SPSO	Scottish Public Services Ombudsman

SPZ	Simplified Planning Zone
SSI	Scottish Statutory Instrument
SSSI	Site of Special Scientific Interest
TPOR	Town and Country Planning (Tree Preservation Order and Trees in Conservation Areas) (Scotland) Regulations 2010
TCPASR	Town and Country Planning (Appeals) (Scotland) Regulations 2013
TCPSA	Town and Country Planning (Scotland) Act 1997
TPO	Tree Preservation Order
T.P.Rev.	Town Planning Review
UCO	Use Classes Order
UKSC	United Kingdom Supreme Court
U.L. & P.	Urban Law and Policy
UNESCO	United Nations Education, Scientific and Cultural Organisation
W.L.R.	Weekly Law Reports

CHAPTER 1

EVOLUTION OF PLANNING LAW

Planning law is the creation of statute, unlike many other areas of law. The development of the statutory provisions applicable to town and country planning is traced in the first part of this chapter and provides an historical perspective for the current planning system, which is examined in subsequent chapters. **1.01**

The activity of planning initially evolved in tandem with the planning system, with statute setting out the objectives of planning. However, under the present system, statute provides the framework rather than the objectives for the activity of planning. The evolving planning profession and academic thought has led to many theories of planning. The second part of this chapter examines some of these theories, and considers whether there can ever be an answer to the question: "what is planning?"

PRE-1909—ORIGINS OF PLANNING LAW

Prior to the advent of state control of land use under the planning system, the feudal nature of Scottish land ownership provided an important facility for the private planning of land use. Feudal land tenure allows the feudal superior to impose restrictions on what the landowner may do on his own land. For example, the carrying on of trades and businesses likely to have an injurious effect on neighbouring landowners may be prohibited. One of the greatest feats of town planning—the creation of Edinburgh's New Town—was achieved almost a century before the introduction of statutory planning powers.[1] The uniformity of development was secured through title conditions requiring the consent of the feudal superior to be obtained before development could proceed. However, title restrictions can vary considerably and not all feudal superiors in Scotland could be relied upon to impose such high standards. Events were to show that some form of state control was necessary. **1.02**

The origins of planning law lie in the dramatic changes in nineteenth-century British society caused by the Industrial Revolution, with an influx of people from the countryside into the towns, attracted by employment in the expanding factories. Houses were hurriedly constructed to meet the demand, often close to the factories. There was no control over standards of construction, resulting in houses in close and unregulated proximity with little or no regard to the requirements of proper ventilation and sanitation. People were living in slum conditions.

Model industrial villages, such as New Lanark and Port Sunlight (close to Glasgow and Liverpool, respectively), provided a powerful precedent of how work-

---

[1] A.J. Youngson, *The Making of Classical Edinburgh, 1750–1840* (Edinburgh: Edinburgh University Press, 1966).

ers could be housed in pleasant and healthy surroundings, underlining the need for action to combat the existing slum conditions of many towns and cities. Organisations such as the Garden City Association, formed in 1899, promoted development of well laid out towns, with extensive open spaces and houses with gardens. Well designed and laid out towns were seen as the way to assure human happiness and eradicate social problems.

1.03   Insanitary housing conditions were struck at by the introduction of the Public Health Acts. Local authorities were given powers to secure proper standards of drainage and sewage, and also to make byelaws regulating the size of rooms, space between houses and width of streets.[2] Local authorities also had powers to remove insanitary dwellings and supply new houses for the working classes.[3] However, there was still a need for local authority powers to deal with more general land-use problems, such as the separation of incompatible uses.

By the beginning of the twentieth century, there was an increasing awareness of the ill-effects caused by the physical environment of the industrial towns and cities. With the political trend towards democracy and social equality, marked by the beginnings of the welfare state in the budget of 1909, action was required to improve living conditions. A healthy workforce was required to build the Dreadnoughts, the mighty battleships constructed in great numbers by Britain and Germany during the power struggle in the years leading to the First World War. It was recognised that urban conditions were inimical to health, and that degeneration of the population had led to reduced labour efficiency.[4] There was an increasing realisation that Britain had lagged behind other countries, including Germany, in the guidance of the growth of towns. As war became more likely, memories revived of the ill-health of British men enlisting to fight in the Boer War,[5] such ill-health caused by the squalid dwellings in British cities.

Two explanations therefore underlie the general acceptance of the principle of town planning in 1909.[6] First, it was a logical extension of earlier legislation concerned with housing and public health. Secondly, it was clear that the effect of rapid urban and industrial change required a more comprehensive approach than the public health byelaws.

1909–1939—TOWN PLANNING

1.04   Town planning was born in the Housing, Town Planning etc. Act 1909, which conferred a power upon local authorities to prepare town planning schemes for their area[7]:

> "... [W]ith the general object of securing proper sanitary conditions, amenity, and convenience in connection with the laying-out and use of the land, and of any neighbouring lands."

---

2   Public Health (Scotland) Act 1897 (60 & 61 Vict. c.38) s.181.
3   Artizans and Labourers Dwellings Improvement (Scotland) Act 1875 (38 & 39 Vict. c.49), replaced and repealed by Housing of the Working Classes Act 1890 (53 & 54 Vict. c.70).
4   Inter-Departmental Committee on Physical Deterioration, *Report of the Inter-Departmental Committee on Physical Deterioration* (HMSO, 1904), Cd.2175 (BPP, 1904, xxxiii).
5   Gordon E. Cherry, *The Politics of Town Planning* (London: Longman, 1982), Ch.2.
6   William Ashworth, *The Genesis of Modern British Town Planning: a study in economic and social history of the nineteenth and twentieth centuries* (London: Routledge & Paul, 1954), Ch.7.
7   Housing, Town Planning etc. Act 1909 (9 Edw.7 c.44) s.54—applicable to Scotland by virtue of s.53.

The scope of town planning was therefore wider than that of the old sanitary and housing legislation, covering the additional objects of amenity and convenience.

The power conferred on local authorities by the 1909 Act was discretionary, and the cumbersome procedure for the preparation of town planning schemes provided little incentive for exercise of their powers.[8] Moreover, schemes could only be prepared for land about to be developed or likely to be developed, and the Act did not provide for control of building development in the countryside or redevelopment of built-up areas. Statutory town planning was confined to the physical layout of land and buildings, ensuring standards of amenity and convenience. However, local authorities had the power to take a comprehensive approach to development: where previously new buildings had to satisfy public health byelaws, the impact of those buildings on the amenity and convenience of the surrounding neighbourhood now had to be considered. Town planning was born.

Town planning schemes were the principal instrument of town planning until **1.05** 1947. The provisions of the operative scheme controlled development and the authority ceased to have planning control over individual development, unless zoning provisions required its consent for certain uses. The scheme was essentially a zoning plan, dedicating certain areas or zones to specified uses such as industrial use, open space and residential development. It left no doubts about what forms of development were permitted, but this certainty meant that the scheme was inflexible. To give more flexibility zones were often dedicated to a predominant use which was allowed without consent, while other specified uses were prohibited or required the consent of the local authority.[9] Schemes also provided limits on the number of buildings, the space around them, and their appearance. Planning schemes were entirely regulatory in nature, and did not secure that development would take place, merely providing that if it did take place in any particular part of the area covered by the scheme, it would be controlled in certain ways.

After the First World War, there was a desperate shortage of housing and calls for "homes fit for heroes". Social pacification through improved housing provision was a clear antidote to fears of bolshevism and industrial unrest following the Russian Revolution.[10] This was combined with increased planning powers in the Housing, Town Planning etc. (Scotland) Act 1919.[11] During the war there had been a considerable extension of government powers, and it was felt safe to increase local authority planning powers in that light. The 1919 Act introduced compulsory town planning for the council of every burgh with a population of 20,000 or more. These councils were required to produce town planning schemes by 1 January 1926. Although some of the procedural obstacles to the preparation of schemes were removed, there was no attention paid to the most fundamental criticisms and, in particular, there was still no question of planning a town as a whole.

One innovation of the 1919 Act was the introduction of interim development

---

8   Fewer than 10,000 acres of land in England and Wales had been brought under planning control by 1919—Griffiths, "The Law of Property (Land)" in Morris Ginsberg (ed.), *Law and Opinion in England in the Twentieth Century* (London: Stevens & Sons, 1959), p.127.

9   For detailed discussion, see Sir Patrick Abercrombie, *Town and Country Planning* (London: T. Butterworth, 1933); Eoin C. Mekie and Harold B. Williams, *Town and Country Planning Law* (London: E. & F.N. Spon & Eyre & Spottiswoode, 1946).

10 *Committee on Building Construction in Connection with the Provision of Dwellings for the Working Classes* (HMSO, 1918), Cd.9191 (BPP, 1918, vii).

11 Housing, Town Planning, etc. (Scotland) Act 1919 (9 & 10 Geo.5 c.60).

control[12] for the period between the passing of a resolution to prepare a scheme until the scheme became effective, which could be several years. There was no obligation on developers to apply for permission, but a grant of planning permission under interim development control preserved the right to compensation if the development conflicted with the scheme eventually approved. Thus interim development control was purely negative in character, neither obliging nor assisting anybody to do anything. To avoid any liability to pay compensation, the authority would rely on the projected provisions of the planning scheme when granting planning permission.

1.06   The first statute to deal exclusively with town planning was the Town Planning (Scotland) Act 1925, which consolidated existing planning law.[13] This was followed by the Town and Country Planning (Scotland) Act 1932,[14] which extended the planning powers of local authorities by providing that town planning schemes could be made over any land, urban or rural, containing buildings or not. The objects of town planning schemes now included[15]:

> "... [P]reserving existing buildings or other objects of architectural, historic or artistic interest and places of natural interest or beauty, and generally of protecting amenities whether in urban or rural portions of the area."

However, the 1932 Act also removed any requirement upon authorities to prepare town planning schemes, leaving planning as a voluntary activity. It also reintroduced the cumbersome procedures for preparing or modifying a scheme. The growing complexity of planning law was reflected in the size of the 1932 Act: 55 sections and five Schedules, compared to the 22 sections and four Schedules of the 1925 Act.

POST-1939—THE WAR YEARS

1.07   During the Second World War public opinion swung behind the need for effective town and country planning. As a relief from the struggle for survival, hopes had centred on the drive for reconstruction and it was increasingly expected that bold and imaginative planning would create a better Britain. After all, if the war could be planned, why not peace? State direction was seen as the way forward. At last, public opinion was prepared to subordinate private interests in land to the public interest in a planned environment.

The Blitz saw the heart of many British cities and towns destroyed by bombing. Since extensive rebuilding was inescapable, there was an opportunity to improve cities as a whole. It was realised that unless proper planning was implemented, the end result would be a total lack of improvement. There was a need to treat the city as an entity, and not to concentrate on the devastated areas in isolation. Planning could deal with the enormous demand for housing and redevelop congested and inadequate areas of towns and cities.

---

12   See s.37. See Mekie and Williams, *Town and Country Planning Law* (1946), Ch.V, "Interim Development".

13   Town Planning (Scotland) Act 1925 (15 & 16 Geo.5 c.17). The Housing, etc. Act 1923 (13 & 14 Geo.5 c.49) had extended planning powers to areas of aesthetic or historic interest, whether developed or not.

14   Town and Country Planning (Scotland) Act 1932 (22 & 23 Geo.5 c.49). See *Encyclopaedia of the Laws of Scotland* (1933), Vol.14, "Town and Country Planning".

15   1932 Act s.1.

The Government saw the possibilities of using the planning system as a political tool to achieve reconstruction of society after the war.[16] As a result it commissioned three reports to examine the future role of planning. The Barlow Report[17] recommended decentralisation of industry to allow redevelopment of congested urban areas, and a reasonable balance of industrial development throughout the country. This led to the establishment of the new towns. The Uthwatt Report[18] tackled the problem of compensation. Since planning powers were first conferred, the possible liability to pay compensation to landowners had left many authorities unwilling to control development. The report recommended that rights to development in all land outside built-up areas should be vested in the State on payment of fair compensation. This would allow local authorities in the future to divert land to uses not chosen by the owner, without automatic liability to pay compensation. It also recommended that control over development should be secured by speedy legislation bringing all land within interim development control, to prevent development prejudicial to post-war reconstruction plans. The Scott Report[19] called for local planning to become compulsory rather than permissive, and for the approval of the local authority to be required for any development during the period of interim development control.

Following the recommendation of the Uthwatt Report, the Town and Country **1.08** Planning (Interim Development) (Scotland) Act 1943[20] extended interim control of development throughout the country, through the statutory fiction that all authorities were in the process of preparing a town planning scheme. Local authorities were also given the power to enforce interim development control. Previously, enforcement action could only be taken once a town planning scheme was operative and a development did not conform with its provisions. The 1943 Act enabled the authorities to take enforcement action against development which threatened their planning proposals or was not in accordance with the terms of the grant of permission, before any scheme was approved. However, there was still no requirement for planning permission to be sought from the local authority before development could proceed.

The Town and Country Planning (Scotland) Act 1945,[21] known as the "blitz and blight" Act, empowered local authorities to undertake the actual development of their own areas. For the first time, local authorities could buy land simply and expeditiously for planning purposes, particularly for redeveloping as a whole war-damaged or obsolete and badly laid out areas.

Thus by 1945, local authorities had extensive planning powers unheard of before the war. The 1943 Act extended existing powers, while the 1945 Act introduced

---

[16] See generally J.B. Cullingworth, *Peacetime History of Environmental Planning 1939–69* (HMSO, 1975), Vol.1, "Reconstruction and Land-use Planning 1939–1947".

[17] *Royal Commission on the Distribution of the Industrial Population* (HMSO, 1940), Cmd.6153 (BPP, 1939–40, iv, 263).

[18] Expert Committee on Compensation and Betterment, *Interim Report of the Expert Committee on Compensation and Betterment* (HMSO, 1941), Cmd.6291 (BPP, 1940–41, iv, 205); *Final Report of the Expert Committee on Compensation and Betterment* (HMSO, 1942), Cmd.6386 (BPP, 1941–42, iv, 15).

[19] Committee on Land Utilisation in Rural Areas, *Report of the Committee on Land Utilisation in Rural Areas* (HMSO, 1942), Cmd.6328 (BPP, 1941–42, iv, 421).

[20] Town and Country Planning (Interim Development) (Scotland) Act 1943 (6 & 7 Geo.6 c.43).

[21] Town and Country Planning (Scotland) Act 1945 (8 & 9 Geo.6 c.33).

major new powers. However, a complete overhaul of the planning system was still necessary to allow reconstruction after the war.

1947 ACT AND BEYOND

1.09   In dealing with the principal recommendations of the Uthwatt and Scott Reports, the Town and Country Planning (Scotland) Act 1947[22] heralded a new era of planned society. For the first time, local authorities were given comprehensive planning powers, and the whole country was subjected to planning control. The Act had five main purposes[23]:

(a)   to provide a framework, or pattern, for land use against which day-to-day development could be considered (the development plan);

(b)   to bring all development under control, making it subject to the permission of local authorities or central government;

(c)   to deal with specific problems of amenity, including the preservation of trees and woodlands, and of buildings of special architectural and historic interest, and control of outdoor advertisements;

(d)   to solve the compensation and betterment problem[24]; and

(e)   to extend the powers of authorities to acquire and develop land for planning purposes, and the scale and scope of grants from central funds to local authorities carrying out the acquisition and clearing of land.

Perhaps the most important measure in the 1947 Act was the introduction of a universal requirement to obtain consent from the local authority for any development. This control was created by nationalising all development rights in land, leaving owners with the existing (1947) use rights in their land. As all development rights were vested in the state, its permission had to be obtained for any proposed development. Unlike the non-obligatory nature of interim development control, consent was required before development could commence. This was a considerable extension of the proposals of the Uthwatt Report, which had restricted control to undeveloped land outside town areas. The effect of these provisions cannot be exaggerated. Owners were left with no absolute rights to develop their land, build upon it, or even change its use. This was a radical encroachment on rights of private property.

With the universal requirement for planning permission, the town planning scheme became meaningless, as there was no need to impose specific restrictions on the use of particular land. However, the advantage of the town planning scheme had been that the developer knew with considerable precision what development could be undertaken, and this advantage was retained with the introduction of development plans. Under the 1947 Act, development plans had to be prepared for every area in the country, to outline the way in which each area was to be developed or preserved.

The development plan was conceived essentially as a statement of development proposals and the intentions of the local authority with regard to the development

---

[22] Town and Country Planning (Scotland) Act 1947 (10 & 11 Geo.6 c.53).

[23] Ministry of Town and Country Planning, *Report of the Ministry of Town and Country Planning 1943–51* (HMSO, 1951), Cmd.8204 (BPP, 50–51, xx, 133).

[24] For a brief explanation of this problem, see Victor Moore, *A Practical Approach to Planning Law* (London: Financial Training, 1987), pp.2–3. Also, Malcolm J. Grant, *Urban Planning Law* (London: Sweet & Maxwell, 1982), pp.18–20.

of their area, and was intended to show only broad land-use allocations. Unlike the town planning scheme, the development plan carried no guarantee that planning permission would be granted even if development proposals were in harmony with the plan. However, in considering an application for planning permission, the authority had to consider the provisions of the plan and "any other material considerations". In addition, the plan was not intended to be a final statement, even of the broad intentions of the authority. It was to be reviewed every five years, and amendments could be made at any time. It was hoped that the new system of flexible development plans would cure the rigid and static nature of town planning schemes.

The importance of the 1947 Act cannot be overstated. It made planning a compulsory function of all local authorities. Pre-war Britain had been largely free from any operative planning control, but following the 1947 Act every piece of land in Britain was under development control, with a universal requirement to obtain consent before development could commence. The Act imposed unheard of limitations on the rights of landowners, and conferred unprecedented and largely unfettered discretionary power on local authorities. This was the true birth of planning.

1947–1997—50 Years of Planning Law

Although the 1947 Act introduced the most sweeping planning powers yet conferred upon local authorities, disillusionment soon set in. The system rapidly became bogged down with details and cumbersome procedures. Development plans were too detailed and quickly became out of date. Changes to the system of development plans were proposed, to distinguish policy and strategic issues from detailed tactical issues.[25] This proposal was implemented through the introduction of the new two-part development plan in the Town and Country Planning (Scotland) Act 1969. Structure plans, which would require the approval of the Secretary of State, would set out and justify broad land-use policies for the area, policies for the management of traffic, and measures for the improvement of the physical environment. Structure plans would not contain detailed land allocations, which were left for the local plans to cover. Local plans were to set out the detailed plans for the area within the framework of the structure plans. The 1969 Act also provided for increased public consultation in the planning process.

1.10

The introduction of structure plans was seen as the opportunity for achieving more broadly based types of planning, stressing economic and social ends (theories of social and economic planning are discussed below). However, central Government adopted a restrictive approach to social and economic policies in structure plans.[26] Social policies were rarely permitted to be incorporated as specific policies or proposals, and non-land-use criteria were excluded. Although the structure plan offered an opportunity to lay out broad policies and strategy, that policy and strategy related to land use.

The non-financial provisions of the 1947 Act, and the system of structure and local plans, were consolidated in the Town and Country Planning (Scotland) Act (TCPSA) 1997.[27] The Planning and Compensation Act 1991 improved the enforcement regime (see Ch.7 below), but its principal change was the introduction of the

---

[25] Planning Advisory Group (PAG), *The Future of Development Plans* (HMSO, 1965).

[26] J. Jowell and D. Noble, "Structure Plans as Instruments of Social and Economic Policy" [1981] J.P.L. 466.

[27] Town and Country Planning (Scotland) Act 1997 (c.8). Other provisions are in the Planning (Listed

plan-led system, whereby planning decisions must be made in accordance with the provisions of the structure and local plans unless material considerations indicate otherwise (see Ch.3 below).[28]

Local government reorganisation in 1996 removed the two-tier system of local government by abolishing the regional councils. The new unitary councils are therefore not subject to the checks and balances exercised by the regional councils on the district councils, which included the power of the regional council to call in for determination an application which had been submitted to the district council for their determination. The new structure plan areas designated by the Secretary of State required many of the new unitary authorities to work together in preparing structure plans.

HUMAN RIGHTS ACT 1998

1.11   The Human Rights Act 1998 introduced a rights-based culture into British law. Convention rights apply to all persons, and are not divided into developer and third party/objector rights. In consequence, the Convention rights do not fit neatly or easily into the statutory framework for the planning system.[29] In many instances the decision reached will be the same as it would have been if the 1998 Act did not apply, but different factors may have had to be taken into account.

As Convention rights are expressed very broadly, it is difficult to predict how the courts will apply them to individual planning cases. Prior to the Human Rights Act 1998 the British planning system had received little adverse attention from the European Court of Human Rights.[30] Commentators predicted significant changes to planning practice. Those predictions seemed to be borne out by the initial decision in the *County Properties* case, which held that the Scottish Ministers' decision to call-in for their determination County Properties' application for listed building consent, and the appointment of a reporter to hold an inquiry and report on the application, were incompatible with County Properties' rights under art.6(1) to a hearing by an independent and impartial tribunal.[31] However, the decision was overturned on appeal,[32] following the decision of the House of Lords in the *Alconbury* case that a statutory right of appeal to the courts, or potential for non-statutory judicial review, satisfies the art.6 requirement for an independent and impartial tribunal. [33] Subsequent art.6 based challenges to the planning system were

---

Buildings and Conservation Areas) (Scotland) Act 1997 (c.9); Planning (Hazardous Substances) (Scotland) Act 1997 (c.10); and Planning (Consequential Provisions) (Scotland) Act 1997 (c.11).

28   Town and Country Planning (Scotland) Act 1997 ss.25, 37(2). The force of this provision has been blunted by the decision of the House of Lords in *Edinburgh City Council v Secretary of State for Scotland*, 1998 S.L.T. 120 that the assessment of the material considerations is a matter for the decision-maker (see Ch.3 below).

29   Convention rights are discussed throughout this book. See also Neil Collar, *Planning and Human Rights* (Edinburgh: W. Green, 2001).

30   In *Buckley v United Kingdom* [1996] J.P.L. 1018 and *Bryan v United Kingdom* [1996] 1 P.L.R. 47 the planning enforcement system was held human rights compliant.

31   *County Properties v Scottish Ministers*, 2000 S.L.T. 965.

32   *County Properties v Scottish Ministers*, 2001 S.L.T. 1125.

33   *R. v Secretary of State for the Environment, Transport and the Regions Ex p. Holdings & Barnes Plc* [2001] 2 W.L.R. 1389; [2001] 2 All E.R. 929; [2001] J.P.L. 920. But in *Tsfayo v United Kingdom* (2009) 48 E.H.R.R 18 the European Court held that the Housing Benefit Review Board did not comply with art.6, notwithstanding the judicial review jurisdiction.

unsuccessful.[34] The exceptions are the findings by the Court of Session of breaches of art.6 in respect of delay.[35] Doubts have been expressed whether the new Local Review Bodies are art.6 compliant (see Ch.8 below).[36]

The other Convention rights most relevant to planning are the art.8 right to respect for private and family life[37]; and the First Protocol art.1 protection of property.[38] These have received close attention from the courts in enforcement cases involving gypsies (see Ch.7 below). There have also been unsuccessful arguments that grant of planning permission for liquefied natural gas terminals breached the right to life under art.2,[39] and that the right to freedom of expression under art.10 had been breached by criminal proceedings for displaying a banner without advertisement consent.[40]

THE NEW MILLENNIUM—MODERNISING THE PLANNING SYSTEM

The opening of the Scottish Parliament in 1999 renewed attention on the Scottish planning system. After a lengthy consultation process, the White Paper, *Modernising the Planning System* was published in June 2005. It was followed by the Planning etc. (Scotland) Bill, introduced in the Scottish Parliament on 19 December 2005. The policy memorandum stated that the primary objective of the Bill was to modernise the planning system to make it more efficient and give local people better opportunities to influence the decisions that affect them. The Bill sought to make the planning system:

1.12

- fit for purpose by introducing a clearer sense of priority and allowing different types of application to be addressed in different ways[41];
- more efficient by establishing new requirements for the production of development plans that are at the heart of an efficient system that provides certainty for users, and are kept up-to-date[42];
- inclusive, where local people can be more involved in the decisions that affect them and their communities[43];

---

[34] For example: *McDonald v Scottish Ministers*, 2008 G.W.D. 10-198; *R. (on the application of Brennon) v Bromsgrove DC* [2003] J.P.L. 1444; *R. (on the application of Adlard) v Secretary of State for Transport* [2002] J.P.L. 1379; *British Telecommunications Plc v Gloucester City Council* [2002] J.P.L. 993; *R. (on the application of Friends Provident Life Office) v Secretary of State for the Environment* [2002] J.P.L. 958; *R. (on the application of Kathro) v Rhondda Cynon Taff CBC* [2002] J.P.L. 304; *R. (on the application of Vetterlein) v Hampshire CC* [2002] J.P.L. 289; *R. v Secretary of State for the Environment Ex p. Challenger, The Times*, 11 July 2000.

[35] *Lafarge Redland Aggregates Ltd v Scottish Ministers*, 2000 S.L.T. 1361, *Ramzan Bibi v Scottish Ministers* [2006] CSOH 152.

[36] Although in *Sally Carroll v Scottish Borders Council* [2015] CSIH 73, none of the parties suggested that the statutory provisions relating to Local Review Bodies are incompatible with the Convention.

[37] *Lough v First Secretary of State* [2005] J.P.L 208; *R. (on the application of Gosbee) v First Secretary of State* [2003] J.P.L. 1467; *R. (on the application of Brennon) v Bromsgrove DC* [2003] J.P.L. 1444; *Matthews v Secretary of State for the Environment* [2002] J.P.L. 716; *R. (on the application of Vetterlein) v Hampshire CC* [2002] J.P.L. 289; *R. (on the application of Malster) v Ipswich BC* [2001] EWHC Admin 711.

[38] For example, *di Ciacca v Scottish Ministers* unreported 2 April 2003 OH.

[39] *Hardy v Pembrokeshire CC* [2006] EWCA Civ 240.

[40] *Butler v Derby City Council* [2006] J.P.L. 830.

[41] The hierarchy of development is examined in Ch.5 below.

[42] The new development plan procedures are discussed in Ch.3 below.

[43] For example, pre-application consultation requirements—discussed in Ch.5 below.

- promote development in the most sustainable locations.[44]

The Planning etc. (Scotland) Act 2006 received Royal Assent on 20 December 2006. It has been brought into force in stages, with accompanying regulations and circulars.[45] The 2006 Act is not a free-standing provision, rather it amends the Town and Country Planning (Scotland) Act 1997.

The basic structure of the planning system is largely the same, centered around the activities of development planning and the control of development through the requirement for planning permission. Development plan procedures have been changed, and the National Planning Framework has been put on a statutory footing (see Ch.3 below). Control of development is now known as development management. The new hierarchy of development enables different types of development to be addressed in different ways. For example, there is mandatory pre-application consultation for national and major developments (see Ch.5 below).

1.13   A controversial change is the removal for certain developments of the right of appeal to the Scottish Ministers/reporter, replaced by a right to apply to the local review body for review of the decision (see Ch.8 below).

There have also been fundamental changes to the appeals system, in particular the removal of the right to require a hearing or public inquiry to be held, and the prohibition against the introduction of new evidence when submitting the appeal (see Ch.8 below).

A third party right of appeal was not included in the Bill or Act, because of the inevitable delays and unpredictability, and the risk that it would undermine local authority decision-making. Also, the modernisation proposals were intended to strengthen the participation of local people at an earlier stage in the process, where they can influence the form and content of development plans, and then the detail of development proposals in planning applications.[46]

The modernisation has transferred the final say on some decisions from the Ministers/reporters to local authorities, and vice versa.

Local authorities now have the final say on planning applications for local developments where the initial decision is made by a planning officer acting under delegated powers, because the only right of appeal is to the local review body (see Ch.8 below). The new Local Review Bodies represent a significant transfer of decision-making power to local politicians, but the actual significance depends on the extent to which each individual local authority delegates decision-making powers to their officers.

Also, local authorities can now grant planning permission for a wider range of developments without first notifying the Scottish Ministers, and the Ministers have indicated they will call in fewer planning applications for their decision (see Ch.5 below). Supplementary guidance prepared by local authorities in conjunction with their development plans is given an enhanced status, despite the lack of any requirement for objections to the draft guidance to be examined by an independent reporter (see Ch.3 below).

---

[44] Development plan functions have to be exercised with the objective of contributing to sustainable development—see Ch.3 below.

[45] The new development plan system came into force on 28 February 2009 (see Ch.3 below), and the majority of the changes to development management procedures, including appeals, on 3 August 2009 (see Chs 4, 5, 7 and 8 below).

[46] Scottish Executive, *Modernising the Planning System* (Scottish Executive, 2005), para.5.3.4. If the planning authority decide to grant planning permission, objectors and other third parties have no right of appeal. They can petition the Court of Session for judicial review, but the court can only examine legal issues, not the planning merits of the case (see Ch.8 below).

The Scottish Ministers/reporters have been given a greater role in other areas. The **1.14** National Planning Framework establishes the need for the national developments it lists. Although planning applications for national developments will be submitted to the relevant local authority, the authority cannot revisit the issue of need, and will focus on matters such as siting, design, and the mitigation of environmental impacts (see Ch.3 below). A right of appeal against s.75 planning agreements, entered into by the local authority and the applicant for planning permission, has been introduced (see Ch.6 below). As part of the preparation of local development plans by local authorities, any objections to the draft plan must be heard by a reporter. The local authority has very limited scope for declining to follow the reporter's recommendations (see Ch.3 below). This is in contrast to the previous local plan preparation procedure in which the authority had discretion whether to accept the reporter's recommendations. The Ministers also have various default and step-in powers where local authorities are not fulfilling their planning functions.

The modernisation has been rounded off by the publication of the Scottish Planning Policy. This single policy document replaces the series of Scottish Planning Policy documents (SPPs) and National Planning Policy Guidelines (NPPGs).

2015—Review of the Scottish Planning System

In September 2015, the Scottish Government announced a review of the Scot- **1.15** tish planning system.[47] It appointed an independent panel, which is expected to report in May 2016.

The review is to identify the scope for further reform with a focus on delivering a quicker, more accessible and efficient planning process, in particular increasing delivery of high quality housing developments. The aims are to:

- ensure that planning realises its full potential, unlocking land and sites, supporting more quality housing across all tenures and delivering the infrastructure required to support development;
- streamline, simplify and improve current systems and remove unnecessary blockages in the decision-making process;
- ensure that communities are more engaged in the process;
- continue to meet our statutory and international obligations in protecting and enhancing Scotland's nature and environment.

Objectives of Planning

Since the Town and Country Planning (Scotland) Act 1932 no indication has **1.16** been given in the Planning Acts of the objects for which planning powers are conferred. The Town and Country Planning (Scotland) Act 1997 (TCPSA) does provide guidance on the contents of development plans (see Ch.3 below). When determining applications for planning permission, the planning authority are directed to have regard to the provisions of the development plan and to any other "material considerations", and must determine the application in accordance with the provisions of the plan unless the material considerations indicate otherwise.[48] As the power to determine such applications is conferred by the TCPSA 1997, legal

---

[47] Scottish Government, "*A Stronger Scotland. The Government's Programme For Scotland 2015–16*" (Scottish Government, September 2015).
[48] TCPSA 1997 ss.25, 37(2).

theory states that such considerations must be planning considerations. But what is "planning"?

Throughout the years, writers have suggested a variety of objectives, which have altered as the planning system has developed.[49] Every person involved in the planning process has a different conception of the objective of planning—a personal planning theory. Thus one of the problems of planning is that it promises to be all things to all men and therefore satisfies no one objective. However, the flexibility of the planning system has the advantage of being able to adjust to new philosophies and ideas as they arise, such as the concept of sustainable development, whereby planners may be seen as trustees of the environment for future generations.

In general terms, planning seeks to preserve the environment while improving it by careful control of development, moving towards the ultimate goal of a healthy and civilised life. However, a more detailed analysis is required to explain the purpose of the planning system.

Town and country planning is predominantly about land use. However, writers have argued that interpreting "planning" as being concerned solely with land use is unduly confining, and that social and economic factors should be on a level par with land-use considerations.[50] In the sense that town planning is an activity carried out in the public interest, there must be a social element within it. The "public interest" must be an amalgam of the social values and interests of the population. Furthermore, the social origins of town planning lay in concerns for public health. Man's environment was conceived as the determinant of his happiness and behaviour, and early town planners believed that social problems could be eradicated by engineering the environment. Modern theories are less interventionist, providing a framework not to fashion behaviour, but rather to present the widest range of opportunities to enable individuals to fulfil their social objectives.[51]

1.17   There is also an economic dimension to planning, as it represents government intervention in the land market to correct deficiencies.[52] For example, the factory owner has no incentive to minimise pollution from the smoking factory chimney. The planning system therefore intervenes to balance the social costs of this pollution against the social benefits of the factory development, thereby providing for socially optimal use of land. The planning system also has the ability to change land values. Proposals for major developments such as roads can cause planning blight, with property values in the vicinity of the development plummeting. The reverse is also true: a grant of planning permission for a plot of land invariably increases

---

[49] e.g. Abercrombie, quoted in Peter G. Hall, *The Containment of Urban England* (London: George Allen & Unwin, 1973), Vol.2, Ch.1; Peter G. Hall himself, *The Containment of Urban England* (1973); Donald L. Foley, "British Town Planning: One Ideology or Three?" (1960) 11 Brit. J. Sociol. 211 and in Andreas Faludi (ed.), *A Reader in Planning Theory* (Oxford: Pergamon, 1973); M.J. Bruton (ed.), *The Spirit and Purpose of Planning* (London: Hutchinson, 1974); Simmonds, "The Conflicting Aims of Planning" in K.G. Willis (ed.), *Contemporary Issues in Town Planning* (Aldershot: Gower, 1986).

[50] Faludi (ed.), A *Reader in Planning Theory* (1973), p.291. The systems analysis approach of the 1960s viewed towns as complex systems where physical, economic and social environments were interrelated: see Alison Ravetz, *The Government of Space—Town Planning in Modern Society* (London: Faber, 1986).

[51] Gordon E. Cherry, Town Planning in its Social Context (London: Leonard Hill, 1970); Loughlin's social-needs model: Martin Loughlin, "Planning Gain: Law, Policy and Practice" (1980) 1 O.J.L.S. 61 at 74–75; Maurice Broady, *Planning for People: Essays on the Social Context of Planning* (London: National Council for Social Service, 1968).

[52] See generally, Thomas A. Broadbent, *Planning and Profit in the Urban Economy* (London: Methuen, 1977).

its value. The Thatcher Government of the 1980s emphasised this economic dimension, believing that the planning system could be used to encourage economic prosperity.[53]

Various influences act as a brake on the pursuit of wider social and economic objectives,[54] and limit the extent of planning powers. Planning is a professional activity and must be influenced by the opinions and theories of the planning profession.[55] More importantly, planning functions within a political and legal structure, and this structure acts as a limiting factor. Planning is a political function, both in the sense that it is a power vested in government, central and local, and also because it is a process of choice and must therefore have an inherently political nature.[56] Planning powers are vested in local government, subject to the guidance of central government, which initiates all planning legislation. At every stage of the planning process, politicians take the final decisions,[57] enabling the planners to claim political neutrality, although this claim is undermined by the reliance often placed on their advice by the politicians.[58] While the planner may argue that his advice is apolitical, it must be influenced by his own values and those of the planning profession.

The political influence on planning is demonstrated by the changes made to the planning system by the Thatcher Government. The political impetus was to promote economic growth by simplifying the planning system, and concepts such as the urban development area, enterprise zones and simplified planning zones represent political manipulation of the planning system to encourage industrial development.[59]

In general, the political will does not favour a truly comprehensive and broadly **1.18** based planning system, as this is too reminiscent of communist-planned economies. Writers may argue for planning to be given an explicit social and economic role, but this is resisted by the politicians. The political context of planning has limited it to a passive and negative character, responding to pressures for development rather than initiating development.[60] Local authorities have few positive planning powers enabling them to take active steps to achieve the policies promoted in development plans. Instead the development control function is emphasised and planning appears negative in character. Treating planning on this application-by-application basis provides no possibility for applying broad theories of social and

---

[53] Michael Heseltine, quoted in Cherry,*The Politics of Town Planning* (1982), Ch.4; Address by Mrs Roe MP, Parliamentary Under Secretary of State, Department of Environment [1988] J.P.L. 517.

[54] See generally, M.L. Harrison, "Development Control—Influence of Political, Legal and Ideological Factors" (1972) 48 T.P. Rev. 254; D.E. Regan, "Pathology of British Landuse Planning", 1978 4(2) *Local Government Studies* 3.

[55] For example, Patsy Healey, Glen McDougall and Michael J. Thomas (eds), *Planning Theory—Prospects for the 1980s* (Oxford: Pergamon, 1982).

[56] See generally, Andrew Blowers, *The Limits of Power: The Politics of Local Planning Policy* (Oxford: Pergamon, 1980); Cherry, *The Politics of Town Planning* (1982); Michael Goldsmith, *Politics, Planning and the City* (London: Hutchinson, 1980); Jack Hayward and Michael Watson (eds), *Planning Politics and Public Policy* (London: Cambridge University Press, 1975); Michael Keating, *The City that Refused to Die—Glasgow: The Politics of Urban Regeneration* (Aberdeen: Aberdeen University Press, 1988).

[57] Although the politicians often decide to delegate specified types of decision-making to the officers.

[58] See Stephen L. Elkin, *Politics and Land-use Planning: The London Experience* (London: Cambridge University Press, 1974), Ch.5; Patrick McAuslan, *Land, Law and Planning* (London: Weidenfeld and Nicolson, 1975), p.360, "The Role of Planning Officials" and p.401, "The Actual Determination by the Committee".

[59] Michael Redman, "Simplifying the System?" [1989] J.P.L. 563.

[60] Blowers, *The Limits of Power: The Politics of Local Planning Policy* (1980).

economic planning. Thus the political framework within which planning operates has placed considerable limitations on what it may achieve.

Planning is also a legal activity, with its powers derived from statute and subject to judicial control, which is a further limiting factor on the extent of planning powers,[61] as will be demonstrated in later chapters. One writer concluded that the judiciary appear sympathetic towards individual property rights at the expense of the public control of land use represented by planning powers.[62] This serves as a reminder that the law and its institutions are not wholly neutral, and that the personal planning theories or values of the judiciary must influence its decisions on the breadth of planning powers.

As a result of these diverse influences, only general comments can be made about the extent of planning powers. The objectives attributed to planning powers reflect the prevailing political, legal, social and economic influences. Planning is predominantly concerned with the use of land, but social and economic considerations have a varying influence. Planning powers are exercised to preserve and enhance the environment, but only to the extent permitted by such influences as the political framework within which planning operates. The question, "what is planning?" cannot be answered fully, because the activity of planning is not static and it changes or develops to reflect prevailing influences. This can be seen from the significant role of planning in promoting sustainable development (see Ch.5 below). It was only in 2009 that any mention of sustainable development was made in the Town and Country Planning (Scotland) Act 1997, and then only in relation to development planning (see Ch.3 below), although many of the material considerations used in the determination of planning applications (see Ch.5 below) promote aspects of sustainable development. Also, the Climate Change (Scotland) Act 2009 imposes general requirements on public bodies, including planning authorities, to achieve climate change targets (see Ch.3 below).

CONCLUSION

1.19   The evolution of planning law has not been a linear process, but a pattern of successive actions and reactions, with great leaps and small steps. Despite this fitful evolution, two trends have consistently influenced legislation. The preparation of town planning schemes and development plans has always been slow. The other problem has been the delays in the development control process.

A criticism frequently made of statutory planning is that it has consistently promised far more than it could hope to deliver. However, this is a result of inflated claims of what planning can achieve, made when the powers available have been insufficient to attain the desired aims. Immediately after major town planning legislation has been passed there have been periods of optimism and enthusiasm in planning, for example in 1909, 1947 and 1969. However, this has given way to disillusionment once it is realised that what could be achieved was much less than was expected. Since 1947, planners have sought an increased scope for town plan-

---

[61]   See generally, McAuslan, *Land, Law and Planning* (1975); McAuslan, "Planning Law's Contribution to Problems of an Urban Society" (1974) 37 M.L.R. 134; McAuslan, "The Plan, the Planners and the Lawyers" [1971] P.L. 247; McEwan, *Planning Law and Ideological Disorder* (Edinburgh: Edinburgh College of Art/Heriot-Watt University, Research Paper, 1982).

[62]   McAuslan, *The Ideologies of Planning Law* (Oxford: Pergamon, 1980), and article of same name (1979) 2 U.L. & P. 1. See also, J.A.G. Griffiths, *The Politics of the Judiciary*, 3rd edn (Manchester: Manchester University Press, 1985), Ch.9, in particular p.202.

ning, but central government has consistently taken the view that planning and the development plan is solely concerned with land use and the quality of the physical environment.

After a century of statutory town planning, and more than 60 years of the universal requirement to obtain planning permission, it is interesting to trace the evolution of development control. The first planning powers were permissive and geographically limited (1909 Act). After some compulsory planning (1919 Act), planning became voluntary once again, although planning control could be exercised over more areas of land. After the Second World War, planning became both compulsory and comprehensive, covering all land. Since 1947 this has remained the situation, although in the late 1980s some control was removed from local authorities. The universal requirement to obtain planning consent for development has been a feature of development control since the 1947 Act. This process is modelled on the voluntary process of interim development control which existed, in some form, since the 1919 Act. The tools of development control have been in existence since 1919, and only their function and importance have changed.

CHAPTER 2

THE PLANNING SYSTEM

Subsequent chapters examine in detail the important elements of the planning
system. However, to appreciate its full magnificence and complexity, one must
understand the basic "nuts and bolts" of the system, including the personnel who
operate the system, and the tools which they use.

2.01

TERRITORIAL LIMITS

Planning permission is required for development in, on, over or under land.[1]
"Land" includes land covered with water.[2] However, planning control extends only
to the mean low water mark around the coast.[3] From this point to the 12-mile limit
of British territorial waters, planning authorities have no control over development, except the operation of marine fish farms.[4]

2.02

By virtue of the principle of accession, a structure which is attached to land is
itself land. It is unclear whether a structure such as a bridge requires planning
permission, or if the parts of the structure which lie below the level of the sea at
low water mark, i.e. the lower parts of the piers and their foundations, lie beyond
planning control.[5]

Marine Scotland, a directorate of the Scottish Government, has the primary
responsibility for marine planning, conservation and licensing from mean high
water springs out to 200 nautical miles. In the intertidal zone, between low and high
water springs, there is an overlap in responsibility between the terrestrial planning
authority and Marine Scotland.[6]

PERSONNEL

(a) Parliament

Much of the basic structure of the planning system comes from legislation passed
by Parliament in the form of Acts of Parliament and statutory instruments (see
para.2.17 below).

2.03

Planning is within the legislative competence of the Scottish Parliament.

---

1   Town and Country Planning (Scotland) Act (TCPSA) 1997 s.26. See Ch.4 below.
2   See TCPSA 1997 s.277.
3   *Argyll and Bute DC v Secretary of State for Scotland*, 1976 S.C. 248; 1977 S.L.T. 33.
4   TCPSA 1997 ss.26(1), (6), (6AA)–(6J), 26AA. Planning Circular 1/2007, Planning Controls for
   Marine Fish Farming (Scottish Executive, 2007).
5   *Lerwick Port Authority v Scottish Ministers* [2007] CSOH 156 at [52]–[55].
6   Planning Circular 1/2015, The Relationship between the Statutory Land Use Planning System and
   Marine Planning and Licensing (Scottish Government, 2015).

However, the power of the Scottish Parliament to legislate is limited by the require-ment that its legislation be compatible with EU law and certain rights created by the European Convention on Human Rights. In addition, its jurisdiction does not extend to matters reserved to the Westminster Parliament, which include aspects of electricity, oil and gas, coal, nuclear energy, energy conservation, road transport, rail transport, marine transport and air transport.[7]

(b) European Union

2.04   It is an objective of EU policy to preserve, protect and improve the quality of the environment. EU law introduced environmental assessment (see Ch.5 below) and several statutory designations protecting areas of land (see Ch.9 below).

(c) Scottish Ministers/Scottish Government

2.05   The First Minister and the Scottish Ministers form the Scottish Government (previously known as the Scottish Executive) and have the executive responsibil-ity for the Scottish planning system.[8] The Secretary of State for Scotland remains associated with the Westminster Parliament.

The Scottish Ministers' responsibility for the planning system includes:

(i)   initiating new legislation governing the planning system and piloting it through Parliament;

(ii)   taking ministerial responsibility for the activities of the Directorate for Planning and Environmental Appeals (DPEA) (see para.2.06 below);

(iii)   drawing up national planning policies and issuing guidance on policy mat-ters in the form of Scottish Planning Policy (SPP), Planning Advice Notes (PANs) and circulars (see para.2.27 below);

(iv)   preparation of the National Planning Framework (NPF), which includes designation of national developments (see Ch.3 below);

(v)   approving strategic development plans and intervening if necessary in the preparation of proposed local development plans (see Ch.3 below);

(vi)   determining appeals against a range of planning decisions (see Ch.8 below), normally by delegating the decision to a reporter;

(vii)   calling-in applications for planning permission for decision (see Ch.5 below).

In determining appeals and called-in applications, the Scottish Ministers consider the planning merits of the matter and generally have the same powers, and are subject to the same legal restrictions, as the planning authority.

(d) Directorate for Planning and Environmental Appeals

2.06   The DPEA (often referred to as the Reporters' Unit) are responsible for administering planning appeals and the public inquiries system (both for planning and other statutory regimes).[9] Where the Planning Acts require an appeal against a planning decision to be submitted to the Scottish Ministers, the notice of appeal

---

[7]   Scotland Act 1998.

[8]   The functions of the Secretary of State in the TCPSA 1997 were transferred to the Scottish Ministers by the Scotland Act 1998 s.53.

[9]   See *http://www.dpea.scotland.gov.uk/* [Accessed 2 February 2016].

should be forwarded to the DPEA who will advise on further procedure and organise the administrative aspects of the appeal (see Ch.8 below).

The DPEA maintain a list of reporters to hear appeals, either by written submissions or at a hearing or public inquiry, and to chair hearings and public inquiries. There is a small core of full-time reporters supplemented by part-time reporters. All reporters are professionally qualified, and have experience in planning or a related discipline. The DPEA appoint a reporter to each appeal or inquiry, and the parties have no say in this process.

A wide range of planning appeals have been delegated by the Scottish Ministers to reporters for decision, to the extent that over 90 per cent of appeals are now decided by reporters. The Ministers retain the right to "claw-back" for their decision any appeal within these delegated classes. In a delegated appeal, the reporter hears the evidence at the hearing or inquiry, or considers the written submissions, and issues his/her decision letter. Where the decision is to be made by the Scottish Ministers, the reporter hears the case and reports to the Ministers, usually with a recommendation on its disposal. The decision on the appeal is made by the Scottish Ministers who can reject any recommendation made in the report.

The reporter is the master of procedure at a hearing or public local inquiry. He/she is entitled to adopt an interventionist role and to ask witnesses questions, rather than merely note the evidence brought out during examination by the parties. In reaching conclusions, the reporter is entitled to make use of his planning experience and expertise.[10] In common with the planning authority, the reporter is obliged to take account of all material considerations and not merely those raised by the parties at the inquiry or in their written submissions.[11] Where the reporter identifies a planning issue which he considers may be material to the decision, but which has not been addressed by either party, the reporter is not entitled to reach a conclusion on that issue and found upon it as a factor material to his decision without giving the parties an opportunity of commenting upon it.[12]

(e) Planning authorities

It is left to planning authorities to operate the grass-roots level of the planning system. They are responsible for implementing the policies of the Scottish Ministers/Scottish Government, preparing development plans, determining applications for planning permission, and enforcing planning controls.

2.07

Each of the local authorities has responsibility for determining planning applications and preparation of the local development plan for their area. The authorities in the four city regions have shared responsibility with other authorities in the region to prepare the strategic development plan (see Ch.3 below).

The national park authorities (NPAs) also have planning roles.[13] The Loch Lomond & The Trossachs NPA has full planning powers in its area, including

---

[10] *Narden Services Ltd v Secretary of State for Scotland*, 1993 S.L.T. 871.
[11] But see *Anwar v Secretary of State for Scotland*, 1992 S.C.L.R. 875.
[12] *Bancon Developments Ltd v Scottish Ministers* [2011] CSOH 137; *Anduff Holdings Ltd v Secretary of State for Scotland*, 1992 S.L.T. 696; cf. *Ladbroke Racing Ltd v Secretary of State for Scotland*, 1990 S.C.L.R. 705.
[13] The National Parks (Scotland) Act 2000 (asp 10) s.10; Cairngorms National Park Designation Transitional and Consequential Provisions (Scotland) Order 2003 (SSI 2003/1); Loch Lomond and The Trossachs National Park Designation, Transitional and Consequential Provisions (Scotland) Order 2002 (SSI 2002/201).

deciding planning applications, and preparing the local development plan. The Cairngorms NPA also prepares a local development plan, but planning applications within the Cairngorms National Park are submitted to the relevant local authority. There is an agreement between the four local authorities (Aberdeenshire, Angus, Highland and Moray Councils) whereby the Cairngorms NPA can call-in a planning application for its decision.[14]

Each NPA must ensure that the following statutory aims are collectively achieved in relation to the national park in a co-ordinated way. In the event of a conflict, greater weight must be given to the first aim[15]:

- to conserve and enhance the natural and cultural heritage;
- to promote the sustainable use of the natural resources of the area;
- to promote understanding and enjoyment (including enjoyment in the form of recreation) of the special qualities of the area by the public; and
- to promote sustainable social and economic development of the communities of the area.

(f) Councillors

2.08   The planning powers vested in the local authorities are exercised by the elected councillors, either in a full meeting of the council or a planning sub-committee. The councillors will typically take decisions involving adoption of planning policies and development plans (see para.2.26 below and Ch.3 below), determination of applications for planning permission (see Ch.5 below), and decisions on enforcement action (see Ch.7 below). Their power to decide planning applications is often delegated to planning officers (see Ch.5 below).

In making decisions on the exercise of these powers, the councillors are advised by the Director of Planning (or the holder of the equivalent position) and the officers in his department. However, they are not bound to follow the recommendation of the professional planners.

There is (and will always be) a continuing debate about the wisdom of conferring the final say on planning decisions to councillors.[16] Some argue that the decisions are best left to the professional planning officers, rather than councillors who may have little knowledge of the planning system. However, others would respond that these officers are too hidebound by their professional theories and that the councillors can be relied upon to bring common sense into decision-making, if necessary acting contrary to the advice given by the planning officers. Furthermore, our democratic ideals of government frown upon vesting power in unelected officials. However, the democratic pressures upon councillors, particularly from concerned local residents, may not always result in the best decision from a planning viewpoint. All that can be said with any confidence is that each side of the debate can be supported by examples of planning decisions proving the strength of

---

[14] Cairngorms Planning Advice Note, *Applying for Planning Permission in the Cairngorms National Park* (Cairngorms National Park Authority, June 2014).

[15] The National Parks (Scotland) Act 2000 ss.1, 9. *Cairngorms Campaign v Cairngorms National Park Authority* [2012] CSOH 153; *Dalfaber Action Group v Scottish Ministers* [2007] CSOH 180.

[16] The Nolan Committee upheld the current system of permitting councillors to make decisions contrary to officers' recommendations, but recommended good practice guidelines, training for councillors and effective external scrutiny where necessary—Jean McFadden, "The Nolan Committee on Planning", 1997 63 S.P.E.L. 96; and "Nolan on Planning: The Government's Preliminary Response", 1998 68 S.P.E.L. 73.

their argument. Most of those involved in the planning system are comfortable with the present decision-making process, if perhaps not entirely happy.

Where planning powers are conferred by statute upon the planning authority, the power must be exercised by the authority and no other person or body. However, the authority can competently delegate its powers to sub-committees (of councillors) or planning officers.[17] Where a discretionary power is conferred, the authority can (or is sometimes obliged to) take into account the views of other bodies and persons on how that power should be exercised, but cannot allow those views necessarily to dictate its decision.[18]

In 2009 a new procedure was introduced for certain planning permission appeals to be determined by a local review body (LRB) rather than the Scottish Ministers (see Ch.8 below). The LRB is a committee of the planning authority comprising at least three councillors. This procedure gives councillors the final say, subject only to legal challenge in the Court of Session.[19]

The Councillors' Code of Conduct sets out standards of conduct to be applied by councillors. It addresses specific issues such as lobbying and access to councillors, as well as decisions on planning matters.[20]

(g) Planning officers

Councillors are rarely professional planners and may have limited knowledge of **2.09** the planning system. They cannot be expected to attend to the administrative work required before decisions can be made. As a result, councillors require the advice and administrative assistance of the planning department (in some councils planning may form part of the responsibility of departments such as environment, regulatory services, community services or enforcement services).

Members of the planning department are responsible for administration of all planning functions up to the point at which a decision must be taken by the councillors, or appropriate delegates. In making the decision, the councillors must take into account the professional recommendation of the planning department, but may choose to reach a contrary decision. It is therefore vital to appreciate that any views or advice offered by a planning officer cannot dictate the eventual decision by the councillors and will not bind them.[21] However, officers normally have enough experience of the decisions reached by their councillors to be able to predict their decisions with a reasonable degree of accuracy, and their advice should be seriously considered. Planning officers and clerical members of the planning department have responsibility for:

(i)   maintenance of the statutory registers which must be available for public inspection (see below);
(ii)   drafting development plan proposals and organising publicity and consultation in relation to those proposals;

---

[17] TCPSA 1997 s.43A required planning authorities to prepare schemes of delegation for deciding planning applications; more general provisions relating to delegation are contained in the Local Government (Scotland) Act 1973 s.56, as amended.

[18] *Ynys Mon BC v Secretary of State for Wales* [1993] J.P.L. 225.

[19] See TCPSA ss.47(1A), 237(3A), 239(4).

[20] Standards Commission Scotland, *The Councillors' Code of Conduct* (Scottish Government, 2010). The NPAs have separate codes of conduct for their members.

[21] *Western Fish Products Ltd v Penwith DC* [1981] 2 All E.R. 204; *R. (on the application of Reprotech (Pebsham) Ltd) v East Sussex CC* [2002] J.P.L. 821; cf. *Camden LBC v Secretary of State for the Environment* [1993] J.P.L. 1049.

(iii) pre-application discussions with potential developers, which may include advising on relevant policies and possible alterations to proposals;

(iv) responding to communications or queries from members of the public (most authorities maintain a scheme whereby a duty planning officer is always available to speak to members of the public);

(v) preparing reports on applications for planning permission and, where appropriate, deciding these applications in terms of delegated powers (see below);

(vi) preparing cases for appeals and giving evidence on behalf of the authority at inquiries (the Royal Town Planning Institute (RTPI) advise their members not to give evidence where a decision has been made contrary to their recommendation and their professional opinion will not allow them to support that decision, not least because their true opinion is likely to be exposed during cross-examination and used to support the opposing side);

(vii) checking compliance with planning consents or the need for planning permission to be obtained for works, and recommending to the councillors when enforcement action should be taken (see Ch.9 below).

The extent of the duties of planning officers can be seen in the procedure leading up to determinations of applications for planning permission (see Ch.5 below). An application is submitted to the department. Compliance with the statutory requirements is checked, and the application registered. Responsibility for handling the application is given to a planning officer, who is a qualified planner. The officer will consult the appropriate bodies in connection with the application. He will prepare a report to the councillors, taking account of the development plan, consultation responses, representations received from the public and any other material considerations. This report will recommend to the councillors how they should determine the application. If the Director of Planning (the chief planning officer) does not have delegated powers to decide the application, the report is presented to the councillors who will make their decision.

In 2009 a specific power was added to the TCPSA for local authorities to delegate determination of planning applications to officers (see Ch.5 below).[22] These s.43A schemes of delegation only apply to planning applications for local developments. The amount of delegation varies between councils. For example, additional restrictions on delegation include applications either recommended for approval contrary to the provisions of the development plan, raising controversial or major planning issues, or where objections to the proposed development are received.

Membership of the RTPI is usually a prerequisite for employment as a planning officer. The RTPI has laid down professional standards of conduct to be met by its members and will investigate complaints concerning failure to comply with these standards.

(h) Developers

2.10   Developers are the life-blood of the planning system. For all the views of the planning authority expressed in the development plan, there are few opportunities

---

[22] Under pre-2009 schemes of delegation, generally about 83–85 per cent of applications each year were delegated to officers—regulatory impact assessment forming part of executive notice on the Town and Country Planning (Schemes of Delegation and Local Review Procedure) (Scotland) Regulations 2008 (SSI 2008/433).

to put these views into practice unless and until developers seek permission for proposed developments.

Although the requirement to obtain planning permission (see Ch.4 below) is an onerous burden placed upon landowners, the planning system protects them from over-restrictive control by providing rights to challenge planning decisions (see Ch.8 below) and requiring planning authorities to justify refusals of permission (see Ch.5 below). The inability to obtain permission in some circumstances undoubtedly leads to dissatisfaction. However, the development management system also provides landowners/developers with some guarantee that their amenity will not be adversely affected by development on surrounding land. This reflects the need to balance the rights granted by the European Convention on Human Rights: for example, a householder can use art.8 (right to respect for private and family life) and the First Protocol art.1 (protection of property) to support an argument that planning permission should be granted for a house extension, but his neighbours can also argue that their rights under the same provisions dictate that planning permission should be refused.

Although accepting the need for the planning system, developers complain that the process for obtaining permission is too slow, that planning officers and authorities have no sense of commercial reality, and that there is too much interference with matters of detail, such as design.

(i) Official bodies

Depending upon the nature of a development, various official bodies must be consulted and asked for their views, such as Scottish Natural Heritage, the Scottish Environment Protection Agency and community councils. These bodies also have a role to play in the formulation of development plan policies and proposals. However, their views cannot dictate the decision reached by the planning authority.[23]

2.11

(j) Public interest

The planning system is broadly intended to control development in the public interest. Without interest and input from members of the public, the system cannot maintain the public confidence which it requires to function efficiently.

2.12

Chapter 10 examines public participation in the planning system in more detail. Both the development plan and development management parts of the system contain many requirements for matters to be publicised, to alert members of the public to their opportunity to lodge representations and have their views taken into account as part of the decision-making process.

The weakness in the planning system perceived by members of the public is their lack of any right of appeal against a decision to grant planning permission.[24] This omission confines them to use of the judicial review procedure (described in Ch.8), which only allows the legality and not the merits of the decision to be challenged, and is therefore of limited value. As Ch.10 explains, this omission can be linked to the presumption in favour of development. Put simply, to require a landowner to obtain permission before developing his land is restrictive enough, but to allow

---

[23] *Ynys Mon BC v Secretary of State for Wales* [1993] J.P.L. 225.
[24] The Scottish Government rejected calls for the Planning etc. (Scotland) Bill to include a third party right of appeal—see Ch.1 above.

a member of the public to challenge any grant of permission would be going too far. However, this leaves the unsatisfactory position that members of the public have no means of reversing a decision which they consider to be wrong on planning merits, but which was made legally.

(k) New towns

2.13   The new town development corporations have been wound up. The corporations had no planning powers as such, but in terms of special development orders made for each new town, other than Glenrothes, they were entitled to authorise development within land which they owned or had previously owned which conformed with the proposals approved by the Secretary of State in those orders. This authorisation is equivalent to a grant of planning permission.

(l) Courts

2.14   According to British constitutional theory, Parliament makes laws and the courts apply those laws. The courts have been responsible for fleshing out many of the statutory planning provisions, through the process of statutory interpretation. For example, the seemingly wide discretionary power vested in planning authorities to impose "such conditions as they think fit" is now subject to a series of legal restrictions declared by the courts (see Ch.6 below). In addition, through the use of common law concepts such as natural justice and fairness, the courts seek to secure procedural fairness within the planning system. The introduction of the European Convention on Human Rights into the UK also potentially increases the role of the courts (see Ch.1 above). In addition, issues regarding the competence of legislation passed by the Scottish Parliament are raised in the courts.

The role of the courts must be contrasted with that of the Scottish Ministers/ reporter deciding an appeal. The jurisdiction of the courts is limited to reviewing the decision to ensure that all legal requirements have been met, and the judges are not entitled to intervene where they consider that the decision is wrong on its merits. Even where a decision is declared to be illegal, the court cannot change that decision but must quash it and return the matter to the decision-maker for a fresh decision to be made in a legal manner. In contrast, the Scottish Ministers/reporter determines the matter as if application had been made to him in the first instance, and is entitled to reach a decision on the merits of the matter.

The powers of the courts are examined in Ch.8.

(m) Ombudsman

2.15   Complaints relating to both decisions and actions of planning authorities can be made direct to the Scottish Public Services Ombudsman (SPSO), which replaced the Local Government Ombudsman (see Ch.8 below).[25] The SPSO can only consider a complaint if a member of the public has suffered hardship or injustice as a result of maladministration or service failure in the provision of a public service.

LAW AND POLICY

2.16   The planning system is a mixture of law and policy. Planning authorities and other participants must act according to the law, and compliance mechanisms, such

---

[25]   See *http://www.spso.org.uk* [Accessed 2 February 2016].

as judicial review and prosecution, exist to enforce the law. The skeletal legal framework is fleshed out by policy, which is necessary to ensure that the wide discretionary planning powers are exercised consistently, both within districts and throughout the country.

One of the keys to understanding the planning system is appreciating the difference between law, which must be observed at all times, and policies, which are not binding, with departures from policy being competent in individual cases.

Law

The Act and Treaty of Union (1707) guaranteed the preservation of Scots law and a separate Scots legal system. The distinct nature of Scots law is carried into planning law, with different Acts of Parliament and statutory instruments applying to Scotland (some apply to the whole of Britain). However, despite separate legal provisions, the law in Scotland is very similar to that applicable to England and Wales, with many of the differences relating to the separate Scottish local government and court structure. Where appropriate, subsequent chapters highlight the differences, to avoid any confusion. In consequence of the similarities between the two sets of planning law, reference is made to court decisions from England and Wales in the absence of any decision of the Scottish courts.

2.17

(a)   Acts of Parliament

The basic framework of the planning system in Scotland is laid down by the TCPSA 1997, and the Planning (Listed Buildings and Conservation Areas) (Scotland) Act 1997 (PLBCASA), the Planning (Hazardous Substances) (Scotland) Act 1997 and the Planning (Consequential Provisions) (Scotland) Act 1997. There are several other statutes which affect the planning system, such as the Local Government (Scotland) Act 1973 and the Nature Conservation (Scotland) Act 2004.[26]

2.18

The planning system was modernised by the Planning etc. (Scotland) Act 2006, which amended the TCPSA 1997.

Acts of Parliament are frequently amended by subsequent legislation. When referring to Acts, either in an official form or in a commercial publication, it is therefore necessary to check whether or not any subsequent amendments have been incorporated into the text.

(b)   Human rights

The Human Rights Act 1998 incorporates the European Convention on Human Rights into Scots law. It imposes an obligation on all public authorities to act in a manner which is compatible with Convention Rights. It also requires the courts to interpret all legislation (Acts of Parliament and statutory instruments) so as to be compatible with the Convention so far as it is possible to do so.

2.19

It is unlawful for a public authority to act in a way which is incompatible with Convention rights, unless the authority could not have acted differently, or was giving effect to legislation which could not be interpreted so as to be compatible with

---

[26]   Text of some Acts is available on the internet: see *http://www.opsi.gov.uk* [Accessed 2 February 2016]. Information on forthcoming legislation can also be obtained: see *http://www.parliament.uk* [Accessed 2 February 2016].

the Convention. The victim of such an unlawful act by a public authority has the right to raise a legal action against the authority and to seek damages.

The Scotland Act 1998 states that the Scottish Parliament may not legislate contrary to the Convention, and the Scottish Ministers must not act contrary to the Convention.

These Acts introduced a rights-based culture into British law. Convention rights apply to all persons, and are not divided into developer and third party/objector rights. In consequence, the Convention rights do not fit neatly or easily into the statutory framework for the planning system.[27] In many instances the decision reached will be the same as it would have been if the 1998 Acts did not apply, but different factors may have had to be taken into account.

As Convention rights are expressed very broadly, it is difficult to predict how the courts will apply them to individual planning cases. Prior to the 1998 Acts the British planning system had received little adverse attention from the European Court of Human Rights.[28] Commentators predicted significant changes to planning practice. Those predictions seemed to be borne out by the initial decision in the *County Properties* case, which held that the Scottish Ministers' decision to call-in for their determination County Properties' application for listed building consent, and the appointment of a reporter to hold an inquiry and report on the application, were incompatible with County Properties' rights under art.6(1) to a hearing by an independent and impartial tribunal.[29] However, the decision was overturned on appeal,[30] following the decision of the House of Lords in the *Alconbury* case that a statutory right of appeal to the courts, or potential for non-statutory judicial review, satisfies the art.6 requirement for an independent and impartial tribunal.[31] The Court of Session held that there had been a breach of art.6 in respect of delay, where the Scottish Ministers had received a recommendation from a reporter in April 1999 but had not issued a decision on the called-in planning application when the court issued its decision in October 2000.[32] It appears that the new LRBs are art.6 compliant (see Ch.8 below).[33]

The other Convention rights most relevant to planning are the art.8 right to respect for private and family life[34] and the First Protocol art.1 protection of property. These have received close attention from the courts in enforcement cases involving gypsies (see Ch.7 below). There have also been unsuccessful arguments that grant of planning permission for liquefied natural gas terminals breached the

---

[27] Convention rights are discussed throughout this book. See also Neil Collar, *Planning and Human Rights* (Edinburgh: W. Green, 2001).

[28] In *Buckley v UK* [1996] J.P.L. 1018 and *Bryan v UK* [1996] 1 P.L.R. 47 the planning enforcement system was held human rights compliant.

[29] *County Properties v Scottish Ministers*, 2000 S.L.T. 965.

[30] *County Properties v Scottish Ministers*, 2001 S.L.T. 1125.

[31] *R. v Secretary of State for the Environment, Transport and the Regions Ex p. Holdings & Barnes Plc* [2001] 2 W.L.R. 1389; [2001] 2 All E.R. 929; [2001] J.P.L. 920. But in *Tsfayo v UK* (2009) 48 E.H.R.R. 18 the European Court held that the Housing Benefit Review Board did not comply with art.6, notwithstanding the judicial review jurisdiction.

[32] *Lafarge Redland Aggregates Ltd v Scottish Ministers*, 2000 S.L.T. 1361.

[33] In *Sally Carroll v Scottish Borders Council* [2015] CSIH 73, none of the parties suggested that the statutory provisions relating to LRBs are incompatible with the Convention.

[34] *Lough v First Secretary of State* [2005] J.P.L 208; *R. (on the application of Gosbee) v First Secretary of State* [2003] J.P.L. 1467; *R. (on the application of Brennon) v Bromsgrove DC* [2003] J.P.L. 1444; *Matthews v Secretary of State for the Environment* [2002] J.P.L. 716; *R. (on the application of Vetterlein) v Hampshire CC* [2002] J.P.L. 289; *R. (on the application of Malster) v Ipswich BC* [2001] EWHC Admin 711.

right to life under art.2,[35] and that the right to freedom of expression under art.10 had been breached by criminal proceedings for displaying a banner without advertisement consent.[36]

(c) Statutory Instruments/Scottish Statutory Instruments

The TCPSA 1997 and other statutes confer power upon the Scottish Ministers to prepare regulations (also variously known as statutory instruments or delegated legislation). These are placed before Parliament/Scottish Parliament.[37] In many cases these regulations prescribe detailed procedural codes for various parts of the planning system.

2.20

The principal statutory instruments affecting the planning system in Scotland are the Use Classes Order, the General Permitted Development Order and the Development Management Procedure Regulations. Reference to these and other statutory instruments are made in subsequent chapters. As with Acts, care must be taken to ensure that account is taken of subsequent amendments. For example, the General Permitted Development Order has been amended by more than 10 subsequent statutory instruments since its publication in 1992.

(d) EU Directives

As noted above, the EU has a significant influence on planning. Directives, such as that on environmental assessment, oblige Member States to incorporate provisions into their national law within a specified period. If the provision has not been incorporated by the end of this period, an individual may be able to rely on the provisions of the Directive when bringing an action in the Scottish courts (see Ch.8 below). This is known as the direct effect of EU law.[38]

2.21

(e) International Treaties

International Treaties are not part of our domestic law until incorporated into domestic law by UK legislation. For example, the Aarhus Convention on Access to Information, Public Participation in Decision-making and Access to Justice in Environmental Matters was ratified by the UK in 2005 and is being brought into force through statutory instruments such as the Environmental Information (Scotland) Regulations 2004 (SSI 2004/520).

2.22

(f) Case law

Under our unwritten constitution, Parliament is responsible for making laws, and the courts are responsible for interpreting those laws and declaring how they should apply in particular circumstances. Court decisions can therefore be used as authoritative statements on the meaning of legal provisions and their application in practice. Within the legal system, court decisions form precedents which often bind judges hearing future cases to decide those cases in a particular way. Previous deci-

2.23

---

35   *Hardy v Pembrokeshire CCI* [2006] EWCA Civ 240.
36   *Butler v Derby City Council* [2006] J.P.L. 830.
37   Text of some statutory instruments is available on the internet: see *http://www.opsi.gov.uk* [Accessed 2 February 2016].
38   Information on EU legislation is available on the website *http://www.europa.eu* [Accessed 2 February 2016].

sions can therefore be used as an indication of how a future case might be decided. The weight to be given to a court decision depends upon various factors such as the position of the court in the hierarchy, the planning expertise of the judge(s), and the extent to which the decision is applicable only to the facts and circumstances of the particular case. Subsequent chapters refer to court decisions where these decisions explain or illustrate how a legal provision may be applied.[39] Despite Scotland having a different legal system from the rest of Britain, there are few differences between the planning laws and widespread use is made in Scotland of case law from the English courts. While a decision of an English court (other than the Supreme Court, previously the House of Lords) is not binding on a Scottish judge, it will be very persuasive. With the introduction of the European Convention on Human Rights (see above), the case law of the European Court on Human Rights is relevant.

(g) Comment

2.24   It is of concern that the planning system, which is supposedly open to public participation, is regulated by such a myriad of legal sources. For example, the landowner who wishes to know whether planning permission is required for a proposed development must consult the TCPSA 1997, the General Permitted Development Order and the Use Classes Order. Assuming the landowner can obtain copies, he then has to interpret these provisions. It is a common criticism that the drafting of Acts of Parliament renders them impossible to read and difficult to understand, and planning law is one of the prime examples of this criticism. It is little wonder that our landowner gives up in disgust, only to be threatened by the planning authority with enforcement action for failing to obtain planning permission. When one of the underlying principles of Scots law is that ignorance of the law is no excuse, it seems unacceptable that an activity such as planning, which touches on the activities of so many members of the public, is regulated by laws which are often inaccessible to those persons, even after their best efforts.

Policy

2.25   Contrary to popular belief, the law supports the use of policy, within certain confines. Policies promote consistent decision-making which, in turn, ensures that every person is treated equally and in the same manner. Policies also provide a degree of certainty. What the law seeks to discourage is the blind, unthinking application of policy, which can lead to injustice in some cases. In every case, the decision-maker should consider whether the circumstances of that case justify making an exception to the policy. As has already been observed, one of the keys to understanding the planning system is appreciating the difference between law, which must be observed at all times, and policies, which are not binding, with departures from policy being competent in individual cases.

Consistency does not mean immutability of policies or their interpretation. The decision-maker need not adhere slavishly to a policy or a previous interpretation of it, but must clearly explain the reasons for not doing so in a particular case. Fairness may require notice of the change to be given to affected parties (Ch.8 discusses the concept of legitimate expectations). For example, an appeal decision was

---

[39]   Court of Session judgments: see *http://www.scotcourts.gov.uk* [Accessed 2 February 2016]. Scottish and English court judgments: see *http://www.bailii.org* [Accessed 2 February 2016].

quashed on the ground of unfairness where, by reason of the decision-maker's inconsistency in the interpretation and application of his policy, a person dealing with him had been taken by surprise and had had no adequate opportunity to meet the new approach before the relevant decision was made.[40]

(a)   Development plans

The development plan contains the policies and proposals of the planning author-   **2.26**
ity with regard to use of the land in that area (see Ch.3 below).[41] When exercising planning powers, the authority is generally required to have regard to the provisions of the development plan, so far as material, and to any other material considerations, and to act in accordance with the provisions of the plan unless material considerations indicate otherwise (commonly referred to as "the plan-led system").[42] This does not amount to a requirement to always follow the policies and proposals contained in the plan. The House of Lords have indicated that the assessment of the facts and the weighing of the considerations is for the decision-maker, and the courts will only intervene where the assessment of the considerations is irrational or perverse.[43] However, the meaning of the development plan is a matter for the court, not for the judgment of the decision-maker.[44]

Draft development plans are a material consideration in the planning process, but do not carry the full weight of a development plan until approved/adopted (see Chs 3 and 5 below).

(b)   Scottish Government

The Scottish Government periodically issues policies.[45] These form one of the   **2.27**
material considerations to which the planning authority must have regard in exercising its planning powers, but the authority is not bound to comply with the policy. As the policy will be applied by the Scottish Ministers/reporter in determining any appeal against the exercise of power by the authority, the sanction underlying such statements of policy is that by failing to comply with the policy the authority risks losing such an appeal and having to pay the costs incurred by the appellant (see Ch.8 below).

With the exception of the NPF (see Ch.3 below), the TCPSA 1997 does not empower the Scottish Ministers to issue policy.[46] Indeed, the Act does not refer to policy, which therefore has no statutory role, other than its role as a material consideration.

The policies issued by the Government fall into the following categories:

- SPP—the statement of Scottish Government policy on nationally important land use matters[47];
- NPF—the Scottish Government's strategy for Scotland's long term spatial development (see Ch.3 below);

---

[40]   *Barnet Meeting Room Trust v Secretary of State for the Environment* [1993] J.P.L. 739.
[41]   Local authority websites generally include copies of the development plan for the area.
[42]   TCPSA 1997 ss.25, 37(2).
[43]   *Edinburgh City Council v Secretary of State for Scotland*, 1998 S.L.T. 120.
[44]   *Tesco Stores v Dundee City Council* [2012] UKSC 13 per Lord Reed at 18.
[45]   See *http://www.gov.scot/Topics/Built-Environment/planning* [Accessed 2 February 2016].
[46]   *West Berkshire DC v Department for Communities and Local Government* [2015] EWHC 2222 (Admin) discusses the legal restrictions on Ministers making planning policy.
[47]   The single SPP replaces the previous series of SPPs and National Planning Policy Guidelines.

- Circulars—Scottish Government policy on the implementation of legislation or procedures; and
- PANs—advice and information on technical planning matters.

(c) Non-statutory policies

2.28   An urgent policy response may be required to an issue which has come to prominence since adoption of the development plan. Alternatively, a policy may require to be stated in such detail as is not suitable for inclusion in the plan, such as development briefs for particular sites or design guides for certain types of development. As a result, policies other than those contained in the development plan may be applicable to an exercise of planning powers by the authority (such policies are commonly referred to as non-statutory policies). These policies form one of the material considerations to be taken into account by the authority.

As part of the modernisation of the planning system in 2009, some forms of supplementary planning guidance form part of the development plan (see Ch.3 below).

(d) Directions by Scottish Ministers

2.29   The Scottish Ministers have power to issue directions to planning authorities restricting the grant of planning permission for a particular development or type of development.[48] A variety of directions have been issued authorising authorities to grant permission for certain types of development only after specified procedures have been followed. These often include notification of the proposed decision to the Scottish Ministers to allow exercise of their call-in powers (see Ch.5 below). The directions are often attached to circulars issued by the Scottish Government.

DEVELOPMENT PLANS AND DEVELOPMENT MANAGEMENT

2.30   The planning system can be divided into two parts: development plans and development management.

The development plan and its significance for the planning system is discussed in the next chapter. The development plan is an expression of the views of the planning authority with regard to the future use of land within its district. In this sense it operates as authoritative guidance to developers on the views of the authority. However, the plan does not relieve developers of the need to obtain planning permission, even in circumstances where the proposed development is entirely in accordance with the provisions of the plan. The development management process provides the authority with the opportunity to prevent development which is not in accordance with its views as expressed in the plan.

What authorities lack are positive powers to achieve the objectives outlined in the plan other than compulsory purchase powers. At present the function of the development plan is to encourage developers by showing which developments are likely to be given permission. However, if these developments are not attractive to developers, no application for planning permission will be forthcoming. The complete vision of the planning authority will be replaced by piecemeal development.

Unlike the passive development planning, development management is a nega-

---

48   Town and Country Planning (Development Management Procedure) (Scotland) Regulations 2013 (SSI 2013/155) (the Development Management Procedure Regulations 2013) reg.32.

tive process. If work amounts to "development" and does not enjoy permitted development rights, planning permission must be obtained before that work can commence. The development management process determines when permission is required (see Ch.4 below), the procedure for obtaining that permission (see Ch.5 below), the restrictions which may be placed on any permission granted (see Ch.6 below), and the enforcement action which may be taken if work commences without permission or in breach of the terms and conditions of a permission (see Ch.7 below). Where an application for planning permission is lodged, the development management process involves determination of that application according to the law, policy and planning merits of the proposed development.

EFFECT OF PLANNING PERMISSION

The consequences flowing from a grant of planning permission are examined in Ch.5. Every grant of planning permission carries a time limit for the commencement of development. If no start is made within that time limit, the permission expires. Once a start has been made, the permission exists in perpetuity and there is no time limit for completing the development, unless there is an express condition attached to the permission specifying such a time limit or the planning authority serve a completion notice. As a result, it is only possible to take enforcement action where a negative condition, such as a restriction on use, is breached or where there is a failure to comply with a positive obligation which is subject to an express time limit.

2.31

PLANNING INFORMATION

For the planning system to operate efficiently and maintain the confidence of all involved in or affected by it, information must be freely available. Planning authorities are required to keep registers detailing such matters as the progress and decision of applications for planning permission, enforcement action, and the progress with alteration or repeal and replacement of development plans.[49] These registers must be kept up-to-date and available for public inspection, along with copies of the development plan. Copies of the agenda for the planning committee meeting and any reports to committee must be available to the public at least three days prior to any meeting.[50]

2.32

The Freedom of Information (Scotland) Act 2002 and the Environmental Information (Scotland) Regulations 2004 (SSI 2004/520) give rights to request information from public bodies.[51] The 2004 Regulations part implement the Aarhus Convention.

---

[49] e.g. TCPSA 1997 ss.36, 36A and the Development Management Procedure Regulations 2013 regs 21, 22.

[50] Local Government (Scotland) Act 1973 s.50B.

[51] The Scottish Information Commissioner's website explains further: see *http://www.itspublicknowledge.info* [Accessed 2 February 2016].

CHAPTER 3

DEVELOPMENT PLANS AND NATIONAL PLANNING FRAMEWORK

Since 1947 the development plan has been a central feature of the planning **3.01** system. This role was heightened by the introduction of the plan-led system in 1994. The plan is an expression of the views of the planning authority (possibly as modified by the Scottish Ministers) with regard to use of the land within its district, formulated after consultation with official bodies and the general public. It also provides the framework within which the authority exercises its day-to-day control of development. Rather than being a prescriptive rule book, the development plan provides authoritative guidance to those wishing to develop land.

The deficiency associated with development plans lies in the lack of any positive power conferred upon the planning authority to implement its views as expressed in the plan. Unless the authority has a legal interest in the land concerned, it cannot implement the proposals identified in the plan. These proposals therefore amount to no more than encouragement for developers to submit applications for planning permission for those proposed land uses. In this sense, planning authorities have few positive planning powers and are restricted to the negative role of approving or rejecting proposals made by developers, which inevitably leads to piecemeal implementation of the development plan proposals. However, a development plan allocation can assist in justifying the exercise of compulsory purchase powers.

Significant changes were introduced to the development plan system in 2009. The system of structure and local plans is being phased out and replaced by a local development plan (LDP) for every local authority area; and in the city regions a strategic development plan (SDP) in addition to the LDPs. Supplementary guidance associated with the LDP or SDP is part of the development plan. Changes were also made to the procedures for plan preparation. Statutory time limits are imposed for the preparation of development plans.

National Planning Framework 3 (NPF3) was published by the Scottish Ministers in 2014. NPF3 is not a development plan but must be taken into account in the preparation of the SDPs and LDPs.[1] It designates specified developments as national developments.

EQUALITY, SUSTAINABLE DEVELOPMENT, CLIMATE CHANGE AND NATURAL HERITAGE

In addition to the specific statutory provisions relating to development plans, **3.02** planning authorities preparing development plans must also fulfil the duties imposed

---

[1] Interaction between other planning policies issued by Ministers and development plans is discussed in *West Berkshire DC v Department for Communities and Local Government* [2015] EWHC 2222 (Admin) at [108]–[143].

by more general statutory provisions relating to equality, sustainable development, climate change and natural heritage.

The general public sector equality duty applies to preparation of development plans.[2] Due regard must be had to the need to eliminate discrimination, harassment, victimisation and any other conduct which is prohibited by or under the Equality Act 2010; to advance equality of opportunity between persons who share a relevant protected characteristic and persons who do not share it; and to foster good relations between persons who share a relevant protected characteristic and persons who do not share it. The relevant protected characteristics are: age, disability, gender reassignment, pregnancy and maternity, race, religion or belief, sex, and sexual orientation.

In preparing and revising the NPF, the Scottish Ministers must exercise their functions with the objective of contributing towards sustainable development. A similar duty applies to planning authorities preparing their development plans. Regard must be had to any guidance issued by the Ministers for this purpose.[3]

Fresh guidance was issued in June 2014,[4] introducing a presumption in favour of development that contributes to sustainable development. Policies and decisions are to be guided by the following principles:

- giving due weight to net economic benefit;
- responding to economic issues, challenges and opportunities, as outlined in local economic strategies;
- supporting good design and the six qualities of successful places;
- making efficient use of existing capacities of land, buildings and infrastructure including supporting town centre and regeneration priorities;
- supporting delivery of accessible housing, business, retailing and leisure development;
- supporting delivery of infrastructure, for example transport, education, energy, digital and water;
- supporting climate change mitigation and adaptation including taking account of flood risk;
- improving health and wellbeing by offering opportunities for social interaction and physical activity, including sport and recreation;
- having regard to the principles for sustainable land use set out in the Land Use Strategy[5];
- protecting, enhancing and promoting access to natural heritage, including green infrastructure, landscape and the wider environment;
- reducing waste, facilitating its management and promoting resource recovery; and
- avoiding over-development, protecting the amenity of new and existing development and considering the implications of development for water, air and soil quality.

---

[2] Equality Act 2010 s.149 and Equality Act 2010 (Specific Duties) (Scotland) Regulations 2012 (SSI 2012/162) reg.5. For discussion of this duty in relation to planning policies generally, see *West Berkshire DC v Department for Communities and Local Government* [2015] EWHC 2222 (Admin) at [174]–[200]. General guidance is available from the Equality and Human Rights Commission— *http://www.equalityhumanrights.com* [Accessed 2 February 2016].

[3] See Town and Country Planning (Scotland) Act 1997 (TCPSA) ss.3D, E.

[4] Scottish Planning Policy (SPP), Principal Policy on Sustainability, paras 24–35.

[5] Scottish Government, *Getting the Best from Our Land—A Land Use Strategy for Scotland* (Scottish Government, 2011). A consultation on a draft Land Use Strategy 2016–2021 was launched on 20 November 2015.

The Climate Change (Scotland) Act 2009 introduced a general requirement on public bodies to act in a way best calculated to contribute to delivery of the targets set in or under Pt 1 of the Act; in the way best calculated to help deliver any programme laid before the Scottish Parliament under s.53 of the Act; and in a way considered by the body to be most sustainable.[6] It also imposes a specific requirement that LDPs include policies requiring all developments to be designed so as to ensure that all new buildings avoid a specified and rising proportion of the projected greenhouse gas emissions from their use, calculated on the basis of the approved design and plans for the specific development, through the installation and operation of low and zero-carbon generating technologies.[7]

In the exercise of all statutory functions, including planning, the Scottish Ministers and planning authorities are required to have regard to the desirability of conserving the natural heritage of Scotland, and to further the conservation of biodiversity.[8] There is also a duty to protect the water environment.[9] Where proposals in a development plan are likely to have a significant effect on a European site, additional requirements must be met.[10]

STRATEGIC ENVIRONMENTAL ASSESSMENT

The requirement for strategic environmental assessment (SEA) was introduced by an EU Directive.[11] In Scotland, the SEA requirement has been extended to include a wider range of plans and programmes, including strategies.[12]

3.03

SEA is a process for the early identification and assessment of the likely significant environmental effects of certain programmes and plans developed by the public sector. It combines with the requirement for environmental impact assessment (EIA) of consent applications for certain projects (see Ch.5 below). When SEA is undertaken, the environmental effects can only be addressed in a broad manner. More information will become available as the details of the project emerge, and when consent applications are submitted, the EIA process will build on the SEA by addressing the environmental effects at a more detailed level.

SEA must be carried out before the plan or programme to which it relates is adopted or submitted to legislative procedures. As the requirement was initially introduced by the EU Directive, it is expressed in very broad terms and it is therefore difficult to identify the processes which will be subject to SEA. However, it is clear that all development plans and the NPF must go through SEA (although some supplementary guidance might be exempt because of lack of significant environmental effects). The Scottish Ministers expect SEA to be carried out as an integral part of the early stages of the plan and programme development and

---

6   Climate Change (Scotland) Act 2009 s.44— in force from 1 January 2011.
7   Climate Change (Scotland) Act 2009 s.72, adding s.3F to the TCPSA 1997 from 1 April 2010.
8   Countryside (Scotland) Act 1967 s.66 and Nature Conservation (Scotland) Act 2004 s.1. *Cairngorms Campaign v Cairngorms National Park Authority* [2012] CSOH 153.
9   Water Environment and Water Services (Scotland) Act 2003 s.2(5).
10   Conservation (Natural Habitats etc.) Regulations 1994 (SI 1994/2716), discussed in Ch.9.
11   Directive 2001/42/EC on the assessment of the effects of certain plans and programmes on the environment [2001] OJ L197/30.
12   The Environmental Assessment (Scotland) Act 2005, which replaced the Environmental Assessment of Plans and Programmes (Scotland) Regulations 2004 (SSI 2004/258) from 20 February 2006.

decision-making process.[13] A failure to undertake SEA, or to follow the correct procedures, could lead to the plan or programme being quashed by the courts.[14]

The requirement for SEA applies to plans and programmes, including strategies, prepared or adopted by a responsible authority at a national, regional or local level, or prepared by a responsible authority for adoption through a legislative procedure, which relate solely to the whole or any part of Scotland. It also applies to modifications of those plans and programmes. However, SEA only applies to the extent that the plan or programme relates to matters of a public character. The main category of plans or programmes which require SEA are those required by a legislative, regulatory or administrative provision, and which are prepared for agriculture, forestry, fisheries, energy, industry, transport, waste management, water management, telecommunications, tourism, town and country planning or land use, and which set the framework for future development consent of specified projects. A responsible authority is defined as any person, body or office holder exercising functions of a public character.

SEA procedure has similarities to EIA for individual projects. There is an initial screening procedure to determine whether SEA is required (only if there are likely to be significant environmental effects); scoping, to determine what environmental effects should be assessed and the level of detail; and production of an environmental report detailing the environmental impacts. Historic Environment Scotland, the Scottish Environment Protection Agency, and Scottish Natural Heritage are consulted as part of the screening and scoping. There are also publicity requirements. The opinions expressed in response to the consultations and publicity, and the environmental report, must be taken account of by the responsible authority in the preparation of the plan or programme. A post-adoption SEA statement must be prepared and publicised, indicating how the responses were taken into account.

HABITATS REGULATIONS APPRAISAL

3.04   Development plans require a Habitats Regulations Appraisal (HRA), to make an appropriate assessment of the implications for any European site.[15]

NATIONAL PLANNING FRAMEWORK

3.05   NPF3 was published by the Scottish Ministers in 2014. It is prepared under statutory powers.[16]

The legal status of NPF3 is unusual. It is excluded from the statutory definition of the "development plan".[17] However, it must be taken into account in preparing

---

13   Planning Advice Note 1/2010, Strategic Environmental Assessment of Development Plans (Scottish Government, 2010).
14   For example *St Albans City and DC v Secretary of State for Communities and Local Government* [2009] EWHC 1280 (Admin); [2010] J.P.L. 70. Argued unsuccessfully in *McGinty v Scottish Ministers* [2013] CSIH 78, *Walton v Scottish Ministers* [2012] UKSC 44.
15   The Conservation (Natural Habitats etc.) Regulations 1994, as amended, regs 85A–E. Planning Circular 6/2013, Development Planning (Scottish Government, 2013) paras 100–104. *Cairngorms Campaign v Cairngorms National Park Authority* [2012] CSOH 153.
16   TCPSA 1997 s.3A–D.
17   TCPSA 1997 s.24.

SDPs and LDPs.[18] Inconsistency with the NPF is one of the reasons why a planning authority can decline to make modifications to a proposed LDP as recommended by the appointed person.[19]

In the determination of planning applications, the NPF is a "material consideration". If the application is for a national development (see below), the designation of that development by the NPF is the mechanism for establishing the need for the development. That is because the statutory provisions state that, unless material considerations indicate otherwise, the application must be determined in accordance with any statement of need by the Scottish Ministers in the NPF which relates to that national development, is expressed as applying for the purposes of development management, and is to the effect that the development in question (or a development such as the development in question) could and should occur. In these circumstances, if there is any incompatibility between the NPF and the development plan, whichever of them is later in date is to prevail.[20]

The NPF is a spatial plan for Scotland. It sets out in broad terms how the Scottish Ministers consider that the development and use of land could and should occur. It must contain a strategy for Scotland's spatial development and a statement of what the Ministers consider to be priorities for that development. It may contain an account of such matters as the Ministers consider affect, or may come to affect, the development and use of land. In preparing and revising the NPF the Ministers must exercise their functions with the objective of contributing to sustainable development (see para.3.02 above). The Ministers are also required to have regard to the desirability of conserving Scotland's flora and fauna, geological and physiographical features, and its natural beauty and amenity; and to further the conservation of biodiversity (see para.3.02 above). The NPF may also designate national developments, either by designating individual developments or by designating each development within a class of development. If it designates national developments, the NPF must contain a statement of the Ministers' reasons for considering that there is a need for the national development in question.[21]

The Ministers prepare and publish the NPF. They have a duty to keep it under review. Within five years of publishing each NPF the Ministers are either to revise the NPF or publish an explanation of why they have decided not to revise it.

A participation statement is to be prepared and published by the Ministers, indicating when consultation on the preparation or review of the NPF is likely to take place and with whom, and of its likely form and of the steps to be taken to involve the public at large in the preparation or review.

There is a "period for Parliamentary consideration", which is 60 days from the day on which the proposed NPF is laid before the Scottish Parliament. The Ministers are to have regard to any resolution or report of the Scottish Parliament or any of its committees made during this period about the proposed NPF. The published NPF must be laid before the Scottish Parliament with a report on compliance with the participation statement, and a statement giving details of any resolu-

---

18 TCPSA 1997 ss.8, 16.
19 TCPSA 1997 s.19(10) and Town and Country Planning (Grounds for Declining to Follow Recommendations) (Scotland) Regulations 2009 (SSI 2009/53).
20 TCPSA 1997 s.25.
21 For an unsuccessful legal challenge to designation as a national development, see: *McGinty v Scottish Ministers* [2013] CSIH 78.

tion or report of the Parliament or its committees and the changes made in light of the resolution/report.

DEVELOPMENT PLAN AND DEVELOPMENT MANAGEMENT

3.06   Although the development plan expresses the views of the planning authority with regard to the use of the land within its district, it does not remove the need to seek planning permission for development (see Ch.4 below). Indeed, even a development which conforms to the provisions of the plan is not guaranteed to obtain planning permission. The development plan system can therefore be distinguished from the rigidity of the zoning systems used by many other countries, whereby proposals in accordance with the zoning either cannot be refused consent or enjoy deemed consent without the necessity for an application (as in the British system of enterprise zones and simplified planning zones, see Ch.9 below).

When determining an application for planning permission, the planning authority is directed to have regard to the provisions of the development plan, so far as material to the application, and to any other material considerations.[22] The authority must also determine the application in accordance with the provisions of the development plan unless material considerations indicate otherwise.[23] The definition of "the development plan" is discussed below.

Although these provisions impose a presumption in favour of the development plan, this does not amount to a requirement that the authority decide all applications according to the terms of the plan.[24] If there has been a material change in circumstances, that may justify a departure from the development plan.[25]

The authority has to decide in light of the whole plan whether the proposal accords with it, and then if there are material considerations of such weight as to indicate that the plan should not be accorded priority. The House of Lords have stated that the assessment of the facts and the weighing of considerations remains in the hands of the decision-maker. The assessment of the considerations can only be challenged on the ground that it is irrational or perverse.[26] The law does not require a material consideration to have any special weight to overcome the presumption in favour of the development plan.[27] These provisions are discussed further in Ch.5.

3.07   The House of Lords' decision indicates the following approach[28]:

- The decision-maker must consider the development plan, identify any provisions in it which are relevant to the question before him and make a proper interpretation of them. His decision will be open to challenge if he fails to have regard to a policy in the development plan which is relevant to the application or fails properly to interpret it.
- He will also have to consider whether the development proposed in the ap-

---

[22]   TCPSA 1997 s.37(2).

[23]   TCPSA 1997 s.25. This does not apply to applications under the Electricity Act 1989 s.36—*Wm Grant & Sons Distillers Ltd v Scottish Ministers* [2012] CSOH 98.

[24]   In *Tesco Stores Ltd v Dundee City Council* [2012] UKSC 13, the Supreme Court upheld a grant of planning permission which was not in accordance with the development plan.

[25]   *Tesco Stores Ltd v Aberdeen City Council* [2012] CSIH 81 at [27].

[26]   *Edinburgh City Council v Secretary of State for Scotland*, 1998 S.L.T. 120.

[27]   *St Albans DC v Secretary of State for the Environment* [1993] J.P.L. 374.

[28]   *Edinburgh City Council v Secretary of State for Scotland*, 1998 S.L.T. 120, per Lord Clyde at 127G–L.

plication before him does or does not accord with the development plan. There may be some points in the plan which support the proposal but there may be some considerations pointing in the opposite direction. He will require to assess all of these and then decide whether in light of the whole plan the proposal does or does not accord with it.

- He will also have to identify all the other material considerations which are relevant to the application and to which he should have regard. He will then have to note which of them support the application and which of them do not, and he will have to assess the weight to be given to all of these considerations. He will have to decide whether there are considerations of such weight as to indicate that the development plan should not be accorded the priority which the statute has given to it.
- Having weighed these considerations and determined these matters he will require to form his opinion on the disposal of the application.
- If he fails to take account of some material consideration or takes account of some consideration which is irrelevant to the application, his decision will be open to challenge. But the assessment of the considerations can only be challenged on the ground that it is irrational or perverse.
- It is undesirable to devise any universal prescription for the method to be adopted by the decision-maker. Different cases will invite different methods. It should be left to the good sense of the decision-maker, acting within his powers, to decide how to go about the task before him in the particular circumstances of each case.

Some importance thus now attaches to the decision whether the proposed development accords with the development plan. In some instances, this decision will rely on the interpretation of the policy. In a subsequent case, the Supreme Court rejected the proposition that the meaning of the development plan was a matter to be determined by the planning authority, unless the view taken by the planning authority was perverse or irrational. The correct approach is for development plans to be interpreted objectively in accordance with the language used, read in its proper context.[29]

Until the plan has been approved by the Scottish Ministers (SDPs) or adopted by the authority (LDPs and supplementary guidance), the policies and proposals in the plan are no more than a material consideration.[30]

The planning authority is not necessarily prevented from granting a planning permission which effectively prejudges a representation to a proposed SDP or LDP, provided the representation is taken into account in the determination of the planning application.[31] The relevant factors are: the stage reached in the plan process; the timescale for the determination of the plan process; the centrality or otherwise of the issue to be determined in the plan process to the decision whether or not to issue the planning permission under consideration; the assessment of the prospects of success of the representation in the plan process; and the consequences of the determination in the plan process for the validity of the planning permission.[32]

---

[29] *Tesco Stores v Dundee City Council* [2012] UKSC 13 per Lord Reed at 18.
[30] *Glasgow DC v Secretary of State for Scotland and William Hill (Scotland) Ltd*, 1992 S.C.L.R. 453; 1992 36 S.P.L.P. 56.
[31] *Watson v Renfrew DC*, 1995 S.C.L.R. 82; 1995 50 S.P.E.L. 68.
[32] *Land Securities Group Plc v North Lanarkshire Council*, 2005 S.L.T. 849.

DEVELOPMENT PLAN

3.08   Prior to the 2009 changes, "the development plan" was two separate plans: the structure plan and the local plan. The structure plan dealt with strategic matters and statements of broad policy, the details of which were fleshed out by the local plan. Following local government reorganisation in 1996, each unitary authority had responsibility for preparing a local plan; and there were 17 structure plan areas, with some authorities jointly carrying out structure plan functions.

Since 2009, structure and local plans are being replaced. In the city regions, there is a SDP and a LDP; elsewhere, there will only be a LDP.[33]

A further change introduced in 2009 is that any supplementary guidance issued in connection with either a SDP or a LDP is part of "the development plan".

From 2009, "the development plan" consists of[34]:

(a)   in a SDP area, the SDP, together with the Scottish Ministers' notice of approval of that plan, and any supplementary guidance issued in connection with that plan; and

(b)   the LDP, together with a copy of the resolution of adoption by the planning authority or the notice of approval by the Scottish Ministers, and any supplementary guidance issued in connection with that plan.

Note that the NPF is not part of the "development plan".

STRATEGIC DEVELOPMENT PLAN

3.09   In most of Scotland, the development plan will be the LDP, but in the four largest city regions there is also a SDP addressing land use issues that cross local authority boundaries and strategic infrastructure.[35] The SDP will provide a framework for LDPs in the city regions, as there is a statutory requirement for those LDPs to be consistent with the SDP.[36] The SDPs require to be submitted to the Scottish Ministers for approval before the plan can take effect, and the Ministers can impose modifications contrary to the wishes of the strategic development plan authority (SDPA). There is a statutory requirement for SDPs to be replaced within a specified time period.[37] The Ministers have default powers where the SDPA are not, within a reasonable period, doing what is required, or have not met a specified time limit.[38]

Strategic development plan areas

3.10   One SDP is prepared for each of the four city regions[39]:

(a)   Glasgow and Clyde Valley—East Dunbartonshire Council, East Renfrew-

---

33   Until new plans are approved/adopted, "the development plan" will be the approved structure plan and adopted local plan: TCPSA 1997 Sch.1, as amended by Planning etc. (Scotland) Act 2006 (PSA) s.53, Planning etc. (Scotland) Act 2006 (Development Planning) (Saving Provisions) Order 2008 (SSI 2008/165).

34   TCPSA 1997 s.24, substituted by PSA 2006 s.2.

35   Supplementary guidance associated with the SDP/LDP is also part of the development plan.

36   TCPSA 1997 s.16(6).

37   TCPSA 1997 s.10(8)—the proposed replacement SDP must be submitted to the Ministers within four years of the date of the approval of the current SDP.

38   TCPSA 1997 s.23B.

39   TCPSA 1997 ss.4, 5; Planning Circular 1/2013, Strategic Development Plan Areas (Scottish Govern-

shire Council, Glasgow City Council, Inverclyde Council, North Lanarkshire Council, Renfrewshire Council, South Lanarkshire Council and West
Dunbartonshire Council;

(b) Aberdeen City and Shire—Aberdeen City Council and Aberdeenshire
Council;

(c) Dundee, Perth, Angus and North Fife (Tayplan)—Angus Council, Dundee
City Council, Fife Council and Perth and Kinross Council; and

(d) Edinburgh and South East Scotland (SESPlan)—City of Edinburgh Council,
East Lothian Council, Fife Council, Midlothian Council, Scottish Borders
Council and West Lothian Council.

Form and content

The SDP sets out[40]:
3.11

(a) a vision statement, being a broad statement of the authority's views as to
how the development of the area could and should occur, and the matters
which might be expected to affect that development. The matters to be set
out in the vision statement include the principal physical, economic, social
and environmental characteristics of the area; the principal purposes for
which land is used in that area; the size, composition and distribution of the
population of the area; the infrastructure of the area, including communications, transport and drainage systems and systems for the supply of water
and energy; how that infrastructure is used; and any change which the
authority think may occur in relation to those matters[41];

(b) a spatial strategy, being a broadly based statement of proposals as to the
development and use of land within the area;

(c) an analysis of the relationship of the vision statement and spatial strategy
to general proposals for the development and other use of land in neighbouring areas.

The SDP must contain a map or diagram (or a combination thereof) describing the
spatial strategy set out in the SDP.[42] It can contain or be accompanied by other
maps, diagrams, illustrations and descriptive matter to explain or illustrate the
proposals in the plan. These form part of the plan.[43]

If there is an intention to use supplementary guidance, the matters to be dealt with
in that supplementary guidance must be expressly identified in a statement in the
SDP.[44]

Scottish Ministers expect SDPs to be concise visionary documents that set clear
parameters for subsequent LDPs and inform decisions about strategic infrastructure
investment. Vision statements should provide a realistic expression of what the plan
area could be like in 20 years' time. The spatial strategy should provide a locational
strategy for new development up to year 12 from plan approval and a broad indication of the scale and direction for growth up to year 20. The principal topics for

---

ment, 2013).

[40] TCPSA 1997 s.7(1).
[41] TCPSA 1997 s.7(4).
[42] Town and Country Planning (Development Planning) (Scotland) Regulations 2008 (SSI 2008/426)
(DPSR) reg.2.
[43] TCPSA 1997 s.7(3).
[44] DPSR 2008 (SSI 2008/426) reg.27(2).

SDPs are expected to be: land for housing, business, shopping and waste management development, strategic infrastructure (including transport, water supply and waste water) and strategic greenspace networks (including green belts). SDPs may be site specific especially where there are no realistic alternative sites.[45]

Information and considerations

3.12   In preparing a SDP the authority must take into account[46]:

(a)   the NPF;
(b)   the resources available or likely to be available for the carrying out of the policies and proposals set out in the SDP;
(c)   any SDP or proposed SDP for an adjoining area;
(d)   any adopted national marine plan or regional marine plan for an adjoining area[47];
(e)   any regional transport strategy for the area;
(f)   any approved flood risk management plan or finalised flood risk management plan relating to the area;
(g)   any river basin management plan relating to the area;
(h)   any local housing strategy relating to the area;
(i)   the national waste management plan;
(j)   issues arising out of the European Directive on the control of major accident hazards involving dangerous substances.[48]

In preparing the SDP, the authority must fulfil its statutory duties on equality, sustainable development, climate change and natural heritage (see para.3.02 above).

Procedure for preparation or alteration of strategic development plan

3.13   The TCPSA 1997 prescribes the procedure for the preparation and approval of SDPs.

---

[45] Planning Circular 6/2013, Development Planning, para.41.
[46] TCPSA 1997 s.8 and DPSR 2008 (SSI 2008/426) reg.3. (as amended).
[47] Planning Circular 1/2015, The Relationship between the Statutory Land Use Planning System and Marine Planning and Licensing (Scottish Government, 2015).
[48] Directive 2012/18/EU on the control of major-accident hazards involving dangerous substances [2012] OJ L197/1.

Fig.3.1 Preparation/alteration of SDP

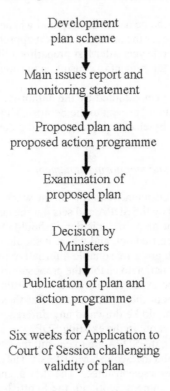

Development
plan scheme

Main issues report and
monitoring statement

Proposed plan and
proposed action programme

Examination of
proposed plan

Decision by
Ministers

Publication of plan and
action programme

Six weeks for Application to
Court of Session challenging
validity of plan

(a)   Development plan scheme

A development plan scheme is a document setting out the SDPA's programme **3.14**
for preparing and reviewing their SDP and/or LDP.[49]

The development plan scheme is to include proposed timetabling; details of what
is likely to be involved at each stage of preparation or review; and the participation statement.

The proposed timetabling must include the timetable (specifying the proposed
month) for publication of the main issues report; publication of the proposed SDP;
and the submission of the proposed SDP to the Ministers.[50]

The participation statement is an account of when consultation is likely to take
place and with whom and of its likely form and of the steps to be taken to involve
the public at large in the stages of preparation or review.[51] Where there is an
examination of the proposed SDP, the reporter first examines the extent to which
the consultation by the authority and its involvement of the public at large as

---

[49]   TCPSA 1997 s.20B, as inserted by PSA 2006 s.2.
[50]   DPSR 2008 (SSI 2008/426) reg.24.
[51]   TCPSA 1997 s.20B(4).

respects the proposed plan have conformed with the participation statement.[52] The reporter can recommend that the authority take further steps to consult or involve the public at large.[53]

A development plan scheme has to be prepared whenever required by the Scottish Ministers, and whenever the authority think it appropriate to do so. A scheme must be prepared within one year after last preparing a SDP.

There is no statutory requirement to consult on the content of development plan schemes.[54]

After the scheme has been adopted by the authority, as soon as is reasonably practicable two copies should be sent to the Scottish Ministers, the scheme should be published (including by electronic means), and a copy placed in each public library in the SDP area.

(b) Main issues report and monitoring statement

3.15   The main issues report is intended to inform the work of the SDPA in preparing the SDP.[55] It is compiled by the SDPA and sets out the authority's general proposals for development in the area. In particular, it should set out proposals for where development should be carried out, and where it should not. It should also set out general proposals which are a reasonable alternative to those proposals. There should be sufficient information to enable the proposals to be readily understood by any person who might be expected to want an opportunity to submit representations to the authority about the report, and so that those representations can be meaningful. Attention should be drawn to any differences between the proposals and the spatial strategy set out in the existing SDP.

In compiling the report, the SDPA are to consult the "key agencies", neighbouring planning authorities and the Scottish Ministers.[56] The authority is to have regard to the views expressed by these consultees. The "key agencies" are Scottish Natural Heritage, Historic Environment Scotland, the Scottish Environment Protection Agency, Scottish Water, Scottish Enterprise, Highlands and Islands Enterprise, a regional transport partnership, the Crofting Commission and a health board.[57] These agencies have a duty to cooperate with the SDPA in the compilation of the main issues report.

The main issues report is published and a copy made available for inspection at the office of each of the planning authorities comprising the SDPA and in every public library in the SDP area.[58] It is also published on the internet. A copy is sent to the Scottish Ministers. A notice is published in a local newspaper circulating in the area and on the internet. The notice contains a statement that the report has been prepared and where and at what times it may be inspected; a brief description of the content and purpose of the report; details of how further information may be obtained regarding the report, including that it is to be published on the internet; a statement that any person wishing to do so may make representations on the content

---

52   TCPSA 1997 s.12(2), as inserted by PSA 2006 s.2.
53   TCPSA 1997 s.12A(1), as inserted by PSA 2006 s.2
54   Planning Circular 6/2013, Development Planning, para.21.
55   TCPSA 1997 s.9, as inserted by PSA 2006 s.2.
56   TCPSA 1997 s.9(4) and DPSR 2008 (SSI 2008/426) reg.4.
57   TCPSA 1997 s.23D, as inserted by PSA 2006 s.2, and DPSR 2008 (SSI 2008/426) reg.28; reg.28(3) specifies limitations applicable to some key agencies.
58   TCPSA 1997 s.9(6), as inserted by PSA 2006 s.2 and DPSR 2008 (SSI 2008/426) reg.5.

of the report; and information as to how and to whom any representations should be made and the date by which they should be made. A notice containing this information should also be sent to the key agencies, the neighbouring planning authorities and any community council within the SDP area.

Any person whatsoever has the right to make representations to the authority about the main issues report.[59]

A monitoring statement must be published by the authority whenever they publish a main issues report.[60] This is a statement about the carrying out of their duty to keep the SDP under review. That duty requires them to monitor changes in the principal physical, economic, social and environmental characteristics of the area, and the impact of the policies and proposals contained within the SDP.[61]

(c) Proposed plan and proposed action programme

The proposed SDP is published in the same manner as the main issues report (see **3.16** para.3.15 above).[62] In preparing the proposed SDP, the authority must have regard to representations timeously received by them about the main issues report.

A copy of the proposed SDP is sent to each key agency (see para.3.15 above), and neighbouring planning authorities. Notification is sent to any person who made representations timeously about the main issues report, indicating where a copy of the proposed SDP is available for inspection and at what reasonable times.

The authority must consult on the proposed SDP with the key agencies and the Scottish Ministers.[63] The key agencies have a duty to co-operate with the authority in the preparation of the proposed SDP.[64]

Publication must include specification of a date, not less than six weeks after the date of publication, by which any representations about the proposed plan must be made to the authority.

After that date, the authority may modify the proposed plan to take account of any representations timeously received by them about the plan; any matter arising in consultation with key agencies and the Scottish Ministers; and any minor drafting or technical matters.

Where a proposed plan is modified, the modified plan is to be published in the same manner as the main issues report (see above). However, if the modifications would change the underlying aims or strategy of the proposed plan, a new proposed SDP must be prepared.

When a new proposed SDP is prepared in this manner, there is an additional requirement to consult all persons who made timeous representations to the original proposed plan.[65]

The proposed plan, whether or not modified, is submitted to the Scottish Ministers. It is accompanied by a note of representations timeously made to the authority and of whether those representations were taken account of in the plan (and if so to what extent); a report on compliance with the authority's participation statement (see above); and a copy of their proposed action programme for the

---

59 TCPSA 1997 s.9(7), as inserted by PSA 2006 s.2.
60 TCPSA 1997 s.4(10), as inserted by PSA 2006 s.2.
61 TCPSA 1997 s.4(9), as inserted by PSA 2006 s.2.
62 TCPSA 1997 s.10.
63 TCPSA 1997 s.10(1)(d) and DPSR 2008 (SSI 2008/426) reg.6.
64 TCPSA 1997 s.10(9).
65 DPSR 2008 (SSI 2008/426) reg.6.

plan. The authority must advertise that they have submitted the proposed plan to the Ministers, by publishing a notice in a local newspaper and on the internet, publishing the plan on the internet, and making a copy of the proposed plan available for inspection at the office of each of the planning authorities within the area and in every public library. A copy of the notice should be sent to the key agencies and all those persons who submitted representations to the proposed plan.[66]

The proposed SDP must be submitted to the Ministers within four years of the date of the approval of the current SDP.[67]

The proposed action programme must be published when the authority publish the proposed SDP.[68] This is a document setting out how the authority propose to implement the SDP. The action programme sets out a list of actions required to deliver each of the policies and proposals contained in the SDP; the name of the person who is to carry out each such action; and the timescale for conclusion of each such action. The actions might include the delivery of key infrastructure and the preparation of supplementary guidance.[69]

In preparing the action programme, the authority must consult the key agencies (para.3.15) and have regard to their views. The authority must also consult the Scottish Ministers, and any person the authority proposes to name in the action programme. The programme must be adopted and published within three months after the date on which the plan to which it relates is constituted. The authority must keep the action programme under review and update and republish it whenever required to do so by the Scottish Ministers and in any event within two years after last publishing it. When an action programme is published, two copies are to be sent to the Scottish Ministers, copies placed in local libraries, and published electronically.

(d) Examination of proposed plan

3.17   There will be an examination of the proposed SDP if representations timeously made have not been withdrawn and were not fully taken account of by any modifications.[70] There will also be an examination if the SDP includes alternative proposals because the individual planning authorities cannot agree. The Ministers can also direct that there will be an examination if they consider it appropriate. The cost of the examination is met equally by the authority and the Ministers, but parties' individual costs incurred preparing and presenting evidence should be met by that party.[71] The authority is not necessarily prevented from granting a planning permission which effectively prejudges a representation before it has been considered at examination, provided the representations are taken into account in the determination of the planning application.[72]

If the Ministers direct that there will be an examination, they must advertise the making of the direction in a local newspaper, and serve notice on the authority. If the examination is made because of unwithdrawn representations, notice must be

---

[66] DPSR 2008 (SSI 2008/426) reg.7.
[67] TCPSA 1997 s.10(8).
[68] TCPSA 1997 s.21 and DPSR 2008 (SSI 2008/426) regs 25, 26.
[69] Planning Circular 6/2013, Development Planning, para.131.
[70] TCPSA 1997, s.12 and DPSR 2008 (SSI 2008/426) regs 18–23.
[71] DPSR 2008 (SSI 2008/426) reg.23. Planning Circular 6/2013, Development Planning, para.125
[72] *Watson v Renfrew DC*, 1995 S.C.L.R. 82; 1995 50 S.P.E.L. 68; *Land Securities Group Plc v North Lanarkshire Council*, 2005 S.L.T. 849.

served on each of the persons who made the representations. On receiving notice from the Ministers, the authority must advertise the making of the direction in the public libraries in the area. When advertising or giving notice of the examination, the Ministers and the authority are to include a statement that the authority has/ will provide the appointed person with a summary of the issues it considers should be assessed at the examination and information about where the summary, and other information and documents provided by the authority in connection with the examination, can be inspected.[73]

Within 14 days of receiving notice, the authority must send to the appointed person a summary of the unresolved issues; copies of the unresolved representations; the environmental report prepared in connection with the proposed plan and copies of the opinions expressed; the proposed action programme; the most recently published monitoring statement; and a copy of the participation statement.[74] The summary of unresolved issues must include, in the form set out, a summary of the issues raised in the unresolved representations, and a statement of the authority's reasons for not modifying the plan in relation to each issue.[75] Those reasons should generally be expressed in less than 800 words per issue.[76] The authority should also submit any supporting productions at this stage, but these should be concise, proportionate and limited in number. There is no provision for any further material to be submitted, either by the authority or by those who have made representations, unless required to do so by the appointed person.[77]

The appointed person is first to examine the extent to which the consultation carried out by the authority and the involvement of the public at large have conformed with the participation statement (para.3.14). If the appointed person is not satisfied with the actings, he is to prepare a report setting out his reasons for not being satisfied and recommending that the authority take specified further steps with regard to consultation or involving the public at large.[78] The report is submitted to the Scottish Ministers and copied to the authority. There is a four week period for the authority to make representations to the Ministers as regards the report. After the four weeks have elapsed, the Ministers may direct the authority to take the further steps specified in the report, or direct the appointed person to proceed to an examination.

3.18

If the authority are directed to take further steps, after taking those steps the authority may modify the proposed SDP to take account of any further representations made to them. If the modifications would change the underlying aims or strategy of the proposed plan, the authority are to prepare and publish a new proposed SDP.

After taking the steps, the authority submit the proposed SDP, whether or not modified, to the Ministers. It is submitted with a note of any representations made and of whether those representations are taken account of in the plan, and, if so, to what extent. The note also reports on the extent to which the authority's consultation and involvement of the public at large have conformed with the specification of further steps. Submission of the proposed plan is to be advertised.

---

73 DPSR 2008 (SSI 2008/426) reg.20(3).
74 DPSR 2008 (SSI 2008/426) reg.20.
75 DPSR 2008 (SSI 2008/426) reg.20(2). Schedule 4 sets out the form. *Eadie Cairns Ltd v Fife Council* [2013] CSIH 109.
76 Planning Circular 6/2013, Development Planning, para.106.
77 *Eadie Cairns Ltd v Fife Council* [2013] CSIH 109. Planning Circular 6/2013, Development Planning, para.113.
78 TCPSA 1997 s.12A.

The procedure used for the examination is at the discretion of the appointed person, for example, whether it should be in public or whether persons who made representations are to be heard or are to present written submissions.[79] The Ministers expect the majority of issues to be dealt with without any need for further information to be submitted. Where further evidence is requested, this will normally be in written form. Where an oral session is required, this will normally follow the hearing format rather than formal inquiry sessions.[80] At any stage of the examination the appointed person may by notice request that a person make further representations or provide further information.[81]

The examination is to assess: issues raised in unresolved representations; any alternative proposals included in the proposed plan because the individual planning authorities cannot agree; and any matters specified in the Ministers' direction.[82] The Ministers intend the appointed person to, within the bounds of the issues raised in representations, primarily examine the appropriateness and sufficiency of the content of the proposed plan. The task is not to make the plan as good as it can be, but to modify the parts that are clearly inappropriate or insufficient.[83]

On completing the examination, the appointed person is to prepare a report. The report sets out the person's conclusions and recommendations, which may include recommendations for amendments to the proposed plan. Intelligible reasons must be given for the conclusions and recommendations.[84] The report includes the matters considered in relation to compliance with the participation statement. The report is submitted to the Ministers, copied to the authority, and published (including electronically). If the examination is made because of unwithdrawn representations, notice must be served on each of the persons who made the representations.

The Scottish Ministers expect the process from appointment to reporting normally to take around six months, and rarely to exceed nine months.[85]

(e)   Decision by Ministers

3.19   The Scottish Ministers may approve the proposed SDP, in whole or in part, and with or without modifications, or reject it.[86]

Where the proposed SDP has been subject to examination, the Ministers are to set out in the instrument by which approval is given the modifications and the reasons for making them.[87] There is no statutory requirement to provide an opportunity for representations to be submitted.

If there has been no examination, the Ministers are to publish in such manner as they think fit the modifications they intend to make and the reasons for making them. They must specify a date at least six weeks after publication of the modifications by which any representations with respect to the intended modifications must be made to the Ministers. The SDPA are to be notified of any representations received. The Ministers are also to consult the key agencies, the SDPA and such other persons (if any) as they consider appropriate. In approving the plan, the

---

79   TCPSA 1997 s.12(3).
80   Planning Circular 6/2013, Development Planning, para.115.
81   DPSR 2008 (SSI 2008/426) reg.22.
82   DPSR 2008 (SSI 2008/426) reg.21.
83   Planning Circular 6/2013, Development Planning, para.117.
84   *Eadie Cairns Ltd v Fife Council* [2013] CSIH 109.
85   Planning Circular 6/2013, Development Planning, para.105.
86   TCPSA 1997 s.13.
87   *Uprichard v Scottish Ministers* [2013] UKSC 21.

Ministers may make the intended modifications as published, or such modifications as they think fit, having regard to any representations timeously made and to any matters arising in consultation.

In making their decision, the Ministers must consider the relevant planning policy guidance which they have issued. If they decide not to follow that guidance, sufficient reasons must be provided.[88]

(f) Publication of plan and action programme

As soon as is reasonably practicable after the SDP has been approved, the authority are to send two copies of it to the Scottish Ministers, publish it (including electronically), and place a copy in each public library in the area.[89] The authority are also to notify each person who made representations on the proposed plan or modifications, and advertise in a local newspaper that the plan has been published.   **3.20**

The action programme must be adopted and published within three months after the date on which the SDP is approved. Two copies of the programme are to be sent to the Scottish Ministers, copies placed in local libraries, and published electronically.

(g) Six weeks for application to Court of Session challenging validity of plan

An action may be raised in the Court of Session challenging the validity of the SDP within six weeks from the date of publication of the first notice of its approval (see below).   **3.21**

(h) Replacement SDP

The proposed replacement SDP must be submitted to the Ministers within four years of the date of the approval of the current SDP.[90]   **3.22**

LOCAL DEVELOPMENT PLAN

In most of Scotland, the development plan will be the LDP, but in the four largest city regions there will also be a SDP addressing land use issues that cross local authority boundaries and strategic infrastructure.[91] The SDP will provide a framework for LDPs in the city regions, as there is a statutory requirement for those LDPs to be consistent with the SDP.[92]   **3.23**

The LDP is adopted by the planning authority, although the Scottish Ministers have the power to direct the authority to consider modifying it, and to direct that the LDP requires approval by the Ministers.[93] The two national park authorities (NPAs) are responsible for preparing the LDPs within their national parks (see Ch.2 above).

There is a statutory requirement for LDPs to be replaced at intervals of no more

---

[88] *Scottish Housebuilders Association v Secretary of State for Scotland*, 1995 S.C.L.R. 1039; 1995 52 S.P.E.L. 109.

[89] TCPSA 1997 s.14.

[90] TCPSA 1997 s.10(8).

[91] Supplementary guidance associated with the SDP/LDP is also part of the development plan.

[92] TCPSA 1997 s.16(6).

[93] TCPSA 1997 s.20(4)–(7).

than five years.[94] The Scottish Ministers expect LDPs in SDP areas to be adopted within two years of the approval of the SDP.[95]

The Ministers have default powers where the planning authority are not, within a reasonable period, doing what is required, or have not met a specified time limit.[96]

Form and content

3.24   An LDP sets out a spatial strategy, being a detailed statement of the planning authority's policies and proposals for the development and use of the land.[97] If the land is not within an SDP area, the LDP is also to set out a vision statement, which is a broad statement of the planning authority's views as to how the development of the land could and should occur, and the matters which might be expected to affect that development. Those matters include the principal physical, economic, social and environmental characteristics of the district; the principal purposes for which the land is used; the size, composition and distribution of the population of the district; the infrastructure of the district (including communications, transport and drainage systems and systems for the supply of water and energy); how that infrastructure is used; and any change which the planning authority think may occur in relation to any of these matters.

The LDP contains a map or maps, known as "the proposals map", describing the policies and proposals set out in the LDP, so far as practicable to illustrate such policies or proposals spatially.[98] The proposals map is to be sufficiently detailed so as to enable the location of proposals for the development and use of land to be identified. Other diagrams, illustrations and descriptive matter can be included to explain or illustrate the proposals in the plan.

If there is an intention to use supplementary guidance, the matters to be dealt with in that supplementary guidance must be expressly identified in a statement in the LDP.[99]

If the LDP contains policies or proposals for the occurrence of development on land owned by the planning authority, or views as to the occurrence of such development, the plan must include a schedule which identifies the land, states that it is so owned and refers to the policies, proposals or views in question.[100] The Scottish Ministers intend this provision to relate to policies, proposals or views relating to specific built developments on specific sites, and not to broad policy designations.[101] Where the LDP is prepared by a NPA, the schedule of land ownership is to include any land owned by a local authority within the park area.

The Scottish Ministers expect LDPs to be concise map-based documents that focus on their specific main proposals for the period up to year 10 from adoption.[102] Outside SDP areas, they should also provide a broad indication of the scale and location of growth up to year 20. Minor proposals and detailed policies may be

---

94   TCPSA 1997 s.16(1).
95   Planning Circular 6/2013, Development Planning, para.18.
96   TCPSA 1997 s.23B.
97   TCPSA 1997 s.15.
98   TCPSA 1997 s.15(4) and DPSR 2008 (SSI 2008/426) reg.8.
99   DPSR 2008 (SSI 2008/426) reg.27(2).
100   TCPSA 1997 s.15(3) and DPSR 2008 (SSI 2008/426) reg.9. The form of schedule is set out in Sch.1 to the 2008 Regulations.
101   Planning Circular 6/2013, Development Planning, Table 1.
102   Planning Circular 6/2013, Development Planning, para.79 and Table 1.

removed to supplementary guidance (see para.3.39 below). In SDP areas, the LDPs need not repeat policy material contained in the SDP.

Information and considerations

In preparing a LDP the authority must ensure that the LDP is consistent with the SDP.[103] They must also take into account[104]:

    3.25

(a) the NPF;

(b) the resources available or likely to be available for the carrying out of the policies and proposals set out in the LDP;

(c) any LDP prepared for a different purpose for the LDP area (different LDPs may be prepared for different purposes);

(d) any LDP or SDP for an adjoining area, or proposed LDP or SDP;

(e) any adopted national marine plan or regional marine plan for an adjoining area[105];

(f) any regional transport strategy for the area;

(g) any approved flood risk management plan or finalised flood risk management plan relating to the area;

(h) any local transport strategy for the area;

(i) any river basin management plan relating to the area;

(j) any local housing strategy relating to the area;

(k) the national waste management plan;

(l) where the area adjoins land in England, any regional spatial strategy or local development framework published in respect of that land;

(m) issues arising out of the European Directive on the control of major accident hazards involving dangerous substances.[106]

In preparing the LDP, the authority must fulfil its statutory duties on equality, sustainable development, climate change and natural heritage (see para.3.02 above).

Although the existence of a planning permission is relevant, it would be incorrect in principle for a site to be identified as suitable for development simply because there is existing planning permission.[107]

    3.26

---

[103] TCPSA 1997 s.16(6). *Bellway (Scotland) Ltd v Stirling Council*, 2008 G.W.D. 25–401.

[104] TCPSA 1997 s.16 and DPSR 2008 (SSI 2008/426) reg.10.

[105] Planning Circular 1/2015, The Relationship between the Statutory Land Use Planning System and Marine Planning and Licensing.

[106] Directive 2012/18/EU.

[107] *Cairngorms Campaign v Cairngorms National Park Authority* [2012] CSOH 153. Relevance of planning permission—*Eadie Cairns Ltd v Fife Council* [2013] CSIH 109.

Fig.3.2 Preparation/alteration of LDP

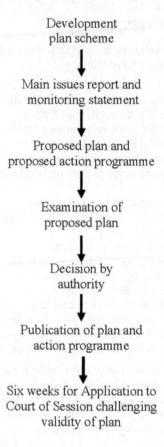

Development
plan scheme

↓

Main issues report and
monitoring statement

↓

Proposed plan and
proposed action programme

↓

Examination of
proposed plan

↓

Decision by
authority

↓

Publication of plan and
action programme

↓

Six weeks for Application to
Court of Session challenging
validity of plan

(a)   Development plan scheme

3.27   A development plan scheme is a document setting out the planning authority's programme for preparing and reviewing their SDP and/or LDP.[108] The development plan scheme is to include proposed timetabling; details of what is likely to be involved at each stage of preparation or review; and the participation statement.

The proposed timetabling must include the timetable (specifying the proposed month) for publication of the main issues report; publication of the proposed LDP; and the submission of the proposed LDP to the Ministers.[109]

The participation statement is an account of when consultation is likely to take place and with whom and of its likely form and of the steps to be taken to involve the public at large in the stages of preparation or review.[110] Where there is an examination of the proposed LDP, the reporter first examines the extent to which

---

[108] TCPSA 1997 s.20B, as inserted by PSA 2006 s.2.
[109] DPSR 2008 (SSI 2008/426) reg.24.
[110] TCPSA 1997 s.20B(4).

[52]

the consultation by the authority and its involvement of the public at large as respects the proposed plan have conformed with the participation statement.[111] The reporter can recommend that the authority take further steps to consult or involve the public at large.[112]

A development plan scheme has to be prepared whenever required by the Scottish Ministers, and whenever the authority think it appropriate to do so. A scheme must be prepared within one year after last preparing a LDP.

There is no statutory requirement to consult on the content of development plan schemes.[113]

After the scheme has been adopted by the authority, as soon as is reasonably practicable two copies should be sent to the Scottish Ministers, the scheme should be published (including by electronic means), and a copy placed in each public library in the LDP area.

(b)   Main issues report and monitoring statement

The main issues report is intended to inform the work of the local authority in preparing the LDP.[114] It is compiled by the local authority and sets out the authority's general proposals for development in the area. In particular, it should set out proposals for where development should be carried out, and where it should not. It should also set out general proposals which are a reasonable alternative to those proposals. There should be sufficient information to enable the proposals to be readily understood by any person who might be expected to want an opportunity to submit representations to the authority about the report, and so that those representations can be meaningful. Attention should be drawn to any differences between the proposals and the spatial strategy set out in the existing LDP.   **3.28**

In compiling the report, the authority are to consult the "key agencies", neighbouring planning authorities, the NPA if there is an adjoining national park, and the Scottish Ministers.[115] If any part of the district is within a strategic development plan area, the authority must consult with the other authorities which form part of the SDPA. The authority is to have regard to the views expressed by these consultees. The "key agencies" are Scottish Natural Heritage, Historic Environment Scotland, the Scottish Environment Protection Agency, Scottish Water, Scottish Enterprise, Highlands and Islands Enterprise, a regional transport partnership, the Crofting Commission and a health board.[116] These agencies have a duty to cooperate with the authority in the compilation of the main issues report.

The main issues report is published and a copy made available for inspection at an office of the authority and in every public library in the LDP area.[117] It is also published on the internet. A copy is sent to the Scottish Ministers. A notice is published in a local newspaper circulating in the area and on the internet. The notice contains a statement that the report has been prepared and where and at what times it may be inspected; a brief description of the content and purpose of the report;

---

[111] TCPSA 1997 s.19(4), as inserted by PSA 2006 s.2.
[112] TCPSA 1997 s.19A(1), as inserted by PSA 2006 s.2.
[113] Planning Circular 6/2013, Development Planning, para.7.
[114] TCPSA 1997 s.17, as inserted by PSA 2006 s.2.
[115] TCPSA 1997 s.17(4) and DPSR 2008 (SSI 2008/426) reg.11.
[116] TCPSA 1997 s.23D, as inserted by PSA 2006 s.2, and DPSR 2008 (SSI 2008/426) reg.28; reg.28(3) specifies limitations applicable to some key agencies.
[117] TCPSA 1997 s.17(6), as inserted by PSA 2006 s.2 and DPSR 2008 (SSI 2008/426) reg.12.

details of how further information may be obtained regarding the report, including that it is to be published on the internet; a statement that any person wishing to do so may make representations on the content of the report; and information as to how and to whom any representations should be made and the date by which they should be made. A notice containing this information should also be sent to the key agencies, the neighbouring planning authorities and any community council within the LDP area. Where any part of the area is within a strategic development plan area, a notice must also be sent to the other authorities comprising the SDPA.

Any person whatsoever has the right to make representations to the authority about the main issues report.[118]

A monitoring statement must be published by the authority whenever they publish a main issues report.[119] This is a statement about the carrying out of their duty to keep the LDP under review. That duty requires them to monitor changes in the principal physical, economic, social and environmental characteristics of the area, and the impact of the policies and proposals contained within the LDP.[120]

(c) Proposed plan and proposed action programme

3.29   The proposed LDP is published in the same manner as the main issues report (see para.3.28 above).[121] In preparing the proposed LDP, the authority must have regard to representations timeously received by them about the main issues report. The Scottish Ministers expect the proposed plan to represent the planning authority's settled view as to what the final adopted content of the plan should be, and not to be used to "test the water".[122]

A copy of the proposed LDP is sent to each key agency (see para.3.28 above). Notification is sent to any person who made representations timeously about the main issues report, indicating where a copy of the proposed LDP is available for inspection and at what reasonable times.

Where the proposed LDP includes a proposal for development relating to a specific site which, if implemented, would be likely to have a significant effect on the use or amenity of that site or of neighbouring land, the planning authority are to give notice to the owner, lessee or occupier of any premises situated on that site, or on the neighbouring land. The notice is to be in the prescribed form and be accompanied by a map showing the location of the site in question. It is to be sent to the premises situated on the site or neighbouring land, addressed to, "the Owner, Lessee or Occupier".[123] "Neighbouring land" is land which is conterminous with or within 20m of the boundary of the specific site.[124] The importance of fulfilling these requirements is highlighted by the examples of failure to comply with notification requirements in relation to planning applications resulting in the quashing of the subsequent grant of planning permission (see Ch.5 below).

---

118 TCPSA 1997 s.17(7), as inserted by PSA 2006 s.2.
119 TCPSA 1997 s.16(9), as inserted by PSA 2006 s.2.
120 TCPSA 1997 s.16(8), as inserted by PSA 2006 s.2.
121 TCPSA 1997 s.18.
122 Planning Circular 6/2013, Development Planning, paras 78 and 80.
123 DPSR 2008 (SSI 2008/426) reg.14. The form of notice is set out in Sch.2.
124 DPSR 2008 (SSI 2008/426) reg.1.

The authority must consult on the proposed LDP with the key agencies and the Scottish Ministers.[125] The key agencies have a duty to co-operate with the authority in the preparation of the proposed LDP.[126]

Publication must include specification of a date, not less than six weeks after the date of publication, by which any representations about the proposed plan must be made to the authority. Although there is no statutory limit, the Scottish Ministers state that representations by stakeholders and the general public should be concise—no more than 2,000 words plus any limited supporting productions. As there is no automatic opportunity for parties to expand on their representation later in the process, the Ministers advise that representations should fully explain the issues that people wish to be considered at the examination stage. Authorities might therefore wish to offer a longer period, of up to 12 weeks for complex plans, to give parties sufficient time to formulate the entirety of their case.[127]

Landowners who are uncertain of their long-term development proposals will seek the widest possible allocation for their land in the plan to avoid restricting the available development options. These are inevitable consequences of the introduction of the plan-led system, whereby it is important for development proposals to be in accordance with the provisions of the development plan.

After the expiry of the period for representations to be made, the authority may modify the proposed plan to take account of any representations timeously received by them about the plan; any matter arising in consultation with key agencies and the Scottish Ministers; and any minor drafting or technical matters.[128] If the modifications would change the underlying aims or strategy of the proposed plan, a new proposed LDP must be published.[129]

For certain types of modifications, further publicity and the opportunity to make representations must be given. This applies where the modifications would remove or significantly alter any policies or proposals set out in the proposed LDP, or introduce new policies or proposals into the proposed LDP. In such circumstances, the modified plan is to be published in the same manner as the main issues report (see above). There is an additional requirement to give notice to the owner, lessee or occupier of any premises situated on a relevant site or on neighbouring land. "Relevant site" means land in respect of which a modification removes, alters or introduces a specific proposal for the development of that land which if implemented would be likely to have a significant effect on the use or amenity of that land or neighbouring land. Publication must include specification of a date, not less than six weeks after the date of publication, by which any representations about the proposed plan must be made to the authority. After that date, the authority may further modify the proposed plan to take account of any representations timeously received by them about the plan; and any minor drafting or technical matters. If those further modifications would remove or significantly alter any policies or proposals, or introduce new policies or proposals, the publication and notification procedure will have to be undertaken again.[130]

3.30

Where no modifications are proposed, or if there is no requirement for publicity

---

[125] TCPSA 1997 s.18(1)(d) and DPSR 2008 (SSI 2008/426) reg.13.

[126] TCPSA 1997 s.18(10).

[127] Planning Circular 6/2013, Development Planning, para.84.

[128] TCPSA 1997 s.18(3).

[129] TCPSA 1997 s.18(8).

[130] TCPSA 1997, s.18 and DPSR 2008 (SSI 2008/426) reg.15. The form of notice is set out in Sch.3 of the 2008 Regulations; "neighbouring land" is defined by reg.1.

and notification of the proposed modifications, or once the publicity and notification requirements have been fulfilled, the proposed plan is submitted to the Scottish Ministers. It is accompanied by a report on compliance with the authority's participation statement (see above); and a copy of their proposed action programme for the plan. The authority must advertise that they have submitted the proposed plan to the Ministers, by publishing a notice in a local newspaper, publishing the plan on the internet, and making a copy of the proposed plan available for inspection at an office of the planning authority and in every public library in the LDP area. There is no requirement to send a copy of the notice to the key agencies and those persons who submitted representations to the proposed plan. If no request is made by the authority for an examination (see below), the authority in publishing the plan advertise their intention to adopt it.[131]

The proposed action programme must be published when the authority publish the proposed LDP.[132] This is a document setting out how the authority propose to implement the LDP. The action programme sets out a list of actions required to deliver each of the policies and proposals contained in the LDP; the name of the person who is to carry out each such action; and the timescale for conclusion of each such action. The actions might include the delivery of key infrastructure and the preparation of supplementary guidance, and are not limited to those by the planning authority.[133]

In preparing the action programme, the authority must consult the key agencies (para.3.15) and have regard to their views. The authority must also consult the Scottish Ministers, and any person the authority proposes to name in the action programme. The programme must be adopted and published within three months after the date on which the plan to which it relates is constituted. The authority must keep the action programme under review and update and republish it whenever required to do so by the Scottish Ministers and in any event within two years after last publishing it. When an action programme is published, two copies are to be sent to the Scottish Ministers, copies placed in local libraries, and published electronically.

(d) Examination of proposed plan

3.31   There will be an examination of the proposed LDP if representations timeously made have not been withdrawn and were not fully taken account of by any modifications.[134] In those circumstances, the authority when submitting the proposed LDP request the Ministers to appoint a person to examine the proposed plan. If no request is made the Ministers can appoint such a person if it appears to them that representations timeously made have not been withdrawn and were not fully taken account of by any modifications. Unlike SDPs, the Ministers do not have any general power to direct that there will be an examination.

The examination is an opportunity for a planning expert independent of the plan preparation process to examine the soundness of the representation. In contrast to the previous local plan inquiry procedure, the person who submitted the representation has no automatic right to submit further material in support of the representation or to appear before the appointed person to argue the case (see para.3.32

---

[131] DPSR 2008 (SSI 2008/426) reg.16
[132] TCPSA 1997 s.21 and DPSR 2008 (SSI 2008/426) regs 25, 26.
[133] Planning Circular 6/2013, Development Planning, para.131.
[134] TCPSA 1997 s.19 and DPSR 2008 (SSI 2008/426) regs 18–23.

below). However, the recommendations by the appointed person can only be rejected by the planning authority on very limited grounds, whereas the authority had discretion whether to accept the recommendations from a local plan inquiry.

The planning authority is not necessarily prevented from granting a planning permission which effectively prejudges the representation before it has been considered at the examination, provided the representations were taken into account in the determination of the planning application.[135] The relevant factors are: the stage reached in the plan process; the timescale for the determination of the plan process; the centrality or otherwise of the issue to be determined in the plan process to the decision whether or not to issue the planning permission under consideration; the assessment of the prospects of success of the representation in the plan process; and the consequences of the determination in the plan process for the validity of the planning permission.[136]

The practice of conjoining planning permission appeals and local plan inquiries was abandoned several years ago, and is unlikely to be revived for development plan examinations.

The cost of the examination is met by the authority, but parties' individual costs incurred preparing and presenting evidence should be met by that party.[137]

The authority must advertise the forthcoming examination of the proposed plan in a local newspaper, and in public libraries. They must also serve notice on each of the persons who made the representations which have not been withdrawn. When advertising or giving notice of the examination, the authority are to include a statement that the authority has/will provide the appointed person with a summary of the issues it considers should be assessed at the examination and information about where the summary, and other information and documents provided by the authority in connection with the examination, can be inspected.[138]

The Ministers notify the authority of the name of the appointed person as soon as practicable after the appointment.[139] Within 14 days the authority must send to the appointed person a summary of the unresolved issues; copies of the unresolved representations; the environmental report prepared in connection with the proposed plan and copies of the opinions expressed; the proposed action programme; the most recently published monitoring statement; and a copy of the participation statement.[140] The summary of unresolved issues must include, in the form set out, a summary of the issues raised in the unresolved representations, and a statement of the authority's reasons for not modifying the plan in relation to each issue.[141] Those reasons should generally be expressed in less than 800 words per issue.[142] The authority should also submit any supporting productions at this stage, but these should be concise, proportionate and limited in number. There is no provision for any further material to be submitted, either by the authority or by those who have made representations, unless required to do so by the appointed person.[143]

The appointed person is first to examine the extent to which the consultation car- **3.32**

---

[135] *Watson v Renfrew DC*, 1995 S.C.L.R. 82; 1995 50 S.P.E.L. 68.

[136] *Land Securities Group Plc v North Lanarkshire Council* [2005] CSOH 116.

[137] DPSR 2008 (SSI 2008/426) reg.23. Planning Circular 6/2013, Development Planning, para.125.

[138] TCPSA 1997 s.19(6) and DPSR 2008 (SSI 2008/426) reg.20(3).

[139] DPSR 2008 (SSI 2008/426) reg.19.

[140] DPSR 2008 (SSI 2008/426) reg.20.

[141] DPSR 2008 (SSI 2008/426) reg.20(2); Sch.4 sets out the form. *Eadie Cairns Ltd v Fife Council* [2013] CSIH 109.

[142] Planning Circular 6/2013, Development Planning, para.106.

[143] *Eadie Cairns Ltd v Fife Council* [2013] CSIH 109. Planning Circular 6/2013, Development Plan-

ried out by the authority and the involvement of the public at large have conformed with the participation statement (para.3.13). If the appointed person is not satisfied with the actings, he is to prepare a report setting out his reasons for not being satisfied and recommending that the authority take specified further steps with regard to consultation or involving the public at large.[144] The report is submitted to the Scottish Ministers and copied to the authority. There is a four week period for the authority to make representations to the Ministers as regards the report. After the four weeks have elapsed, the Ministers may direct the authority to take the further steps specified in the report, or direct the appointed person to proceed to an examination.

If the authority are directed to take further steps, after taking those steps the authority may modify the proposed LDP to take account of any further representations made to them. If the modifications would change the underlying aims or strategy of the proposed plan, the authority are to prepare and publish a new proposed LDP.

After taking the steps, the authority submit the proposed LDP, whether or not modified, to the Ministers. It is submitted with a note of any representations made and of whether those representations are taken account of in the plan, and, if so, to what extent. The note also reports on the extent to which the authority's consultation and involvement of the public at large have conformed with the specification of further steps. Submission of the proposed plan is to be advertised.

The procedure used for the examination is at the discretion of the appointed person, for example, whether it should be in public or whether persons who made representations are to be heard or are to present written submissions.[145] The Ministers expect the majority of issues to be dealt with without any need for further information to be submitted. Where further evidence is requested, this will normally be in written form. Where an oral session is required, this will normally follow the hearing format rather than formal inquiry sessions.[146] At any stage of the examination the appointed person may by notice request that a person make further representations or provide further information.[147]

The examination is only to assess issues raised in unresolved representations.[148] The Ministers intend the appointed person to, within the bounds of the issues raised in representations, primarily examine the appropriateness and sufficiency of the content of the proposed plan. The task is not to make the plan as good as it can be, but to modify the parts that are clearly inappropriate or insufficient.[149]

On completing the examination, the appointed person is to prepare a report. The report sets out the person's conclusions and recommendations, which may include recommendations for amendments to the proposed plan. Intelligible reasons must be given for the conclusions and recommendations.[150] The report includes the matters considered in relation to compliance with the participation statement. The report

---

ning, para.113, 115.
[144] TCPSA 1997 s.19A.
[145] TCPSA 1997 s.19(5).
[146] Planning Circular 6/2013, Development Planning, para.115.
[147] DPSR 2008 (SSI 2008/426) reg.22.
[148] DPSR 2008 (SSI 2008/426) reg.21(2).
[149] Planning Circular 6/2013, Development Planning, para.117.
[150] *Eadie Cairns Ltd v Fife Council* [2013] CSIH 109.

is submitted to the authority, and published (including electronically). Notice must be served on each of the persons who made the unresolved representations.[151]

The Scottish Ministers expect the process from appointment to reporting normally to take around six months, and rarely to exceed nine months.[152]

(e)   Decision by authority

The authority have three months from receipt of the report by the appointed person to decide how to proceed. They can make modifications recommended by the appointed person, and such other modifications as appear to them to be requisite having regard to the report.[153] The Ministers intend those other modifications to be wholly consequent on the appointed person's recommendations, e.g. to rectify any factual or terminological inconsistencies created by the recommended modifications, and not to introduce unconnected new material into the plan.[154]

3.33

The authority may carry out an environmental assessment of the proposed plan as so modified.[155]

The authority has very limited scope for declining to follow the recommendations by the appointed person. This is in contrast to the previous local plan preparation procedure in which the authority had discretion whether to accept the recommendations from the local plan inquiry. The authority can only decline to make modifications to the proposed LDP as recommended by the appointed person if[156]:

- the modification would make the proposed LDP inconsistent with either the NPF, any SDP for the land to which the proposed LDP relates, or any national park plan for such land;
- the adoption of the LDP as so modified would not be compatible with the requirements of Pt IVA of the Conservation (Natural Habitats etc.) Regulations 1994 (SI 1994/2716);
- the recommendation is based on conclusions that the appointed person could not reasonably have reached on the evidence considered in the examination.[157]

The Scottish Ministers explain that the reference to the Natural Habitats Regulations 1994 is primarily intended to allow the authority to carry out and take account of an appropriate assessment where they suspect a proposed modification may have a significant effect on a European site. The final criterion is intended to relate to the possibility of clear errors (including factual errors) by the appointed person, but not to occasions where the appointed person has reached a different planning judgment to the authority's.[158]

The authority publish the modifications, together with the proposed plan as modified (or, if no modifications are made, publish the proposed plan). They must publish

---

[151] TCPSA 1997 s.19(8).
[152] Planning Circular 6/2013, Development Planning, para.105.
[153] TCPSA 1997 s.19(10).
[154] Planning Circular 6/2013, Development Planning, para.95.
[155] TCPSA 1997 s.19(11).
[156] TCPSA 1997 s.19(10) and Town and Country Planning (Grounds for Declining to Follow Recommendations) (Scotland) Regulations 2009 (SSI 2009/53). *Retail Property Holdings Ltd v Renfrewshire Council* [2015] CSIH 69.
[157] The authority cannot take into account subsequent or new material—*Tesco Stores Ltd v Aberdeen City Council* [2012] CSIH 81.
[158] Planning Circular 6/2013, Development Planning, para.94.

a notice in a local newspaper containing a statement that the authority intend to adopt the proposed plan; information on whether or not the proposed plan has been modified following receipt of the report prepared following examination; and where and at what times the proposed plan and any modifications may be inspected. Copies of the proposed plan and any modifications must be made available for inspection at an office of the planning authority and in every public library in the area. The proposed plan and any modifications must be published on the internet. The authority also advertise their intention to adopt the plan, and notify each person who made representations.[159]

Within three months of receiving the report, the authority must send the Scottish Ministers a copy of: the modifications to the proposed LDP (if any); a statement explaining why any modification recommended by the appointed person has not been made; the proposed plan (whether or not modified); the report; any environmental assessment carried out in relation to the proposed plan as modified; and the advertisement of their intention to adopt the proposed plan.[160]

(f)   Intervention by Scottish Ministers

3.34   The Scottish Ministers have the power to[161]:

- delay the adoption of the LDP;
- direct the authority to consider modifying it in such respects as are indicated in the direction;
- direct that the proposed plan is to be constituted if and when approved by the Ministers.

A planning authority given a direction to consider modifying the proposed plan cannot adopt the plan unless they satisfy the Scottish Ministers that they have made the modifications necessary to conform with the direction, or the Ministers withdraw the direction.

(g)   Constitution and publication of plan and action programme

3.35   The planning authority cannot adopt the LDP until 28 days after advertisement of their intention to adopt it, or the expiry of any longer period specified in a direction issued by the Scottish Ministers.[162]

On being adopted by the planning authority the proposed LDP is constituted as the LDP. As soon as is reasonably practicable after the LDP has been constituted, the authority are to send two copies of it to the Scottish Ministers, publish it (including electronically), and place a copy in each public library in the area.[163] The authority are also to notify each person who made representations on the proposed plan or modifications, and advertise in a local newspaper that the plan has been published.

The action programme must be adopted and published within three months after the date on which the LDP is approved. Two copies of the programme are to be sent

---

159   TCPSA 1997 s.19(10) and DPSR 2008 (SSI 2008/426) reg.17.
160   TCPSA 1997 s.19(12).
161   TCPSA 1997 s.20(4)–(7).
162   TCPSA 1997 s.20(3), (4).
163   TCPSA 1997 s.20A.

to the Scottish Ministers, copies placed in local libraries, and published electronically.[164]

(h)   Six weeks for application to Court of Session challenging validity of plan

An action may be raised in the Court of Session challenging the validity of the LDP within six weeks from the date of publication of the first notice of its adoption (see para.3.38 below).   3.36

(i)   Replacement LDP

The Act states that replacement LDPs must be prepared whenever required by the Scottish Ministers or at intervals of no more than five years.[165] It is not clear whether "prepared" requires a replacement LDP to be adopted within five years of the adoption of the LDP.   3.37

APPLICATION TO COURT OF SESSION CHALLENGING VALIDITY OF PLAN

There is a statutory right of appeal against a SDP or LDP. In the absence of any statutory right of appeal against the NPF or supplementary guidance, challenges to the NPF or supplementary guidance will be by judicial review (see Ch.8 below).   3.38

An action may be raised in the Court of Session challenging the validity of a SDP or LDP within six weeks from the date of publication of the first notice of the approval or adoption of the plan or its alteration, repeal or replacement.[166] No challenge will be possible outside this time limit (see Ch.8 below).

The action may be raised by any "person aggrieved" by the SDP or LDP or any alteration, repeal or replacement of the plan. This includes a neighbouring planning authority,[167] but not the planning authority responsible for preparing the plan where it seeks to challenge modifications made by the Scottish Ministers.[168] The court has rejected the argument that "person aggrieved" has a different meaning for the purposes of challenging the validity of a development plan from other legal challenges (see Ch.8 below). A landowner who had a legitimate interest in the policies and proposals in the plan and the way in which the council dealt with their objections to those policies and proposals was a "person aggrieved".[169] A member of the public whose property was not directly affected by the policies and proposals in the plan and took no objection to them during the plan process was not a "person aggrieved".[170] It would also seem to include bodies consulted during the plan process.[171]

The grounds of challenge are that the plan is not within the powers conferred by the TCPSA 1997 in relation to development plans, or that any of the regulations made under the TCPSA 1997 have not been complied with in relation to the approval or adoption of the plan, alteration, repeal or replacement. These grounds of challenge are discussed in detail in Ch.8. A failure to comply with the regulations

---

[164] TCPSA 1997 s.21(8).
[165] TCPSA 1997 s.16(1).
[166] TCPSA 1997 s.238.
[167] *Central RC v Secretary of State for Scotland*, 1991 S.L.T. 702; 1991 33 S.P.L.P. 49.
[168] *Strathclyde RC v Secretary of State for Scotland*, 1989 S.L.T. 821.
[169] *Mackenzie's Trustees v Highland RC*, 1994 S.C.L.R. 1042; 1994 46 S.P.E.L. 93.
[170] *Lardner v Renfrewshire DC*, 1997 S.L.T. 1027; 1997 62 S.P.E.L. 81.
[171] *Glasgow for People v Secretary of State for Scotland*, 1991 S.C.L.R. 775.

only invalidates the plan if substantial prejudice results, and this may be difficult to show.[172]

The Court of Session has the power to suspend in the interim the plan, its alteration, repeal or replacement, either generally or only in so far as it affects the applicant's property. When considering an application for an interim order, the nature and degree of harm likely to be suffered by the parties to the appeal by the grant or refusal of the order is not the only issue. The public interest lies in the plan taking effect. The question whether the operation of the plan should be suspended is therefore dealt with by an assessment of the strength of the competing arguments, albeit on a prima facie basis.[173] Interim suspension of all the local plan policies relating to greenfield release sites was refused on the grounds that there was scope for a site to be added and it would lead to a disproportionate upheaval in the planning process.[174]

Following a successful challenge, the court has the discretion to quash wholly or partly the plan, alteration, repeal or replacement, either generally or in so far as it affects the applicant's property. There is no requirement for the court to order the whole process to start again.[175] The approval by the Secretary of State of the Strathclyde Structure Plan Update 1992 was quashed because of his failure to adjudicate in the dispute on the criteria to be used in calculating housing land supply.[176] The part of a local plan relating to a site was quashed where the reporters provided no intelligible reason for holding the principle of use to be reversible if the existing permission was not implemented.[177] A site was deleted from a local plan because the reasons given by the planning authority for not accepting the reporters' recommendations neither gave express reasons for disagreement nor any reasoned explanation for ignoring them.[178] Specific provisions of an LDP were held as delete, following a decision to quash the LDP in so far as it designated a town centre.[179] The court refused to quash where the failure to take into account certain housing forecasts would not have made any difference to the decision to approve the structure plan.[180]

SUPPLEMENTARY GUIDANCE

3.39   From 2009 any supplementary guidance issued in connection with either a SDP or a LDP is part of "the development plan".[181]

Supplementary guidance may only deal with the provision of further information or detail in respect of the policies or proposals set out in the SDP or LDP. These matters must be expressly identified in a statement contained in the SDP or LDP

---

[172] *SHBA Ltd v Aberdeen City Council* unreported 10 April 2002 OH; *Mackenzie's Trustees*, 1994 S.C.L.R. 1042; 1994 46 S.P.E.L. 93. But see *Eadie Cairns Ltd v Fife Council* [2013] CSIH 109 and *FSH Airport (Edinburgh) Services Ltd v Edinburgh City Council*, 2007 G.W.D. 39-687.

[173] *Mackenzie's Trustees*, 1994 S.C.L.R. 1042; 1994 46 S.P.E.L. 93.

[174] *John Dickie Homes Ltd v Glasgow City Council* unreported 31 October 2003 IH.

[175] *Hallam Land Management Ltd v City of Edinburgh Council* [2011] CSOH 75.

[176] *Scottish Housebuilders Association v Secretary of State for Scotland*, 1995 S.C.L.R. 1039; 1995 52 S.P.E.L. 109.

[177] *Eadie Cairns Ltd v Fife Council* [2013] CSIH 109.

[178] *FSH Airport (Edinburgh) Services Ltd v Edinburgh City Council*, 2007 G.W.D. 39-687. See also *Hallam Land Management Ltd v City of Edinburgh Council* [2011] CSOH 75.

[179] *Retail Property Holdings Ltd v Renfrewshire Council* [2015] CSIH 69.

[180] *SHBA Ltd* unreported 10 April 2002 OH.

[181] TCPSA 1997 ss.22 and 24, substituted by PSA 2006 s.2.

as matters to be dealt with in supplementary guidance.[182] Other matters may still be dealt with in guidance issued and adopted by the planning authority, but that guidance will not be part of "the development plan" and should not be termed supplementary guidance.[183]

Supplementary guidance may be prepared and adopted alongside the SDP or LDP, or subsequently. Guidance adopted in connection with a plan falls when that plan is replaced, but if it remains up-to-date, authorities may readopt it in connection with the replacement plan after limited reconsultation.[184]

The authority must take steps to secure that adequate publicity of the proposed supplementary guidance is given in their district or SDP area, including intimation of a date by which representations require to be received by the authority. Before adopting and issuing the supplementary guidance, the authority must consider any representations timeously made to them.

The supplementary guidance cannot be adopted and issued until a copy of the proposed guidance is submitted to the Scottish Ministers. The authority must also provide the Ministers with a statement describing the steps taken to secure adequate publicity of the proposal; any representations made to the authority; and the extent to which such representations were taken account of in the preparation of the proposed guidance. The Ministers have 28 days to decide whether to require the authority to make specified modifications, but can extend that period by direction to the authority.[185] Scrutiny by Scottish Ministers is likely to focus more on ensuring that the principles of good public involvement and a proper connection with the SDP or LDP have been achieved consistently, than on detailed policy content.[186]

The Ministers' intention is that much detailed material can be contained in supplementary guidance. Suitable topics include: detailed policies where the main principles are already established; local policy designations that do not impact on the spatial strategy of the wider plan area; development briefs and masterplans; exact levels of developer contributions or methodologies for their calculation; forestry and woodland strategies; and aquaculture framework documents. The Ministers consider that the LDP or SDP, not the supplementary guidance, should deal with: departures from national planning policy; development proposals of more than local impact; green belt boundaries; and items for which financial and other contributions, including affordable housing, will be sought, and the circumstances (locations, types of development) where they will be sought.[187]

READING DEVELOPMENT PLANS

Planning authorities are obliged to publish the proposed and approved/adopted SDP/LDP, including electronically, and place a copy in each public library in the area.

When consulting the provisions of the SDP/LDP, reference should be made

3.40

---

[182] DPSR 2008 (SSI 2008/426) reg.27(2). See letter from Chief Planner to all heads of planning dated 15 January 2015, *Development Plans—Supplementary Guidance* (Scottish Government, 2015).

[183] TCPSA 1997 s.22(9). Planning Circular 6/2013, Development Planning, para.148.

[184] Planning Circular 6/2013, Development Planning, para.145.

[185] TCPSA 1997 s.22.

[186] Planning Circular 6/2013, Development Planning, para.143. The letter from the Chief Planner, *Development Plans—Supplementary Guidance* (2015), sets out concerns about supplementary guidance.

[187] Planning Circular 6/2013, Development Planning, para.139.

initially to the map or diagram, which will allow the appropriate provisions to be found in the written statement without reading the entire text.

Attention should be paid to the term used to describe any particular provision, and to any glossary explaining the interpretation of that term. The weight to be given to the provision may depend upon which "label" is used.

OBJECTING TO PROPOSED PLANS

3.41   With the enhanced status of development plans resulting from the plan-led system, it is important for all persons, whether developers, landowners or members of the public, to monitor changes to development plans. For example, under the plan-led system allocation of a site for housing in effect indicates that the principle of housing development on the site is acceptable, subject to acceptable details being submitted in a planning application and approved by grant of planning permission. Monitoring of changes to development plans has several different objectives:

(a) landowners/developers should ensure that any proposals for development of their land, even if uncertain or long-term, will be consistent with the plan;

(b) landowners/occupiers will also be anxious to preserve land value and amenity by ensuring that the plan does not contain proposals which may have a negative effect on land value, such as allocating neighbouring land for a sewage works;

(c) members of the public should ensure that the plan makes provision for the proper planning of their neighbourhood, town or area, or any items or issues of special interest or concern to them.

It is important to note that publicity requirements attached to the plan process do not always include notification to individual landowners of proposals to change policies applicable to their land. There is no such notification for preparation of SDPs, and the notification requirements for LDPs may not be as extensive as landowners might expect.

Monitoring draft plans in this way will inevitably lead to submission of objections. This can be done by completing the form obtainable from the authority, or submitting an objection in writing. The objection itself should specify the provision(s) of the plan to which the objection relates, and explain the reasons for the objection.

There are no limits to the content of the objection. It may relate to a provision contained in the plan, or point to something omitted from the plan. It may concern a minor error or a complex policy issue. No particular expertise is required, and a strong argument can often be made on the basis of general local knowledge. The only essential element is that the objection identify the provision in the plan and the result sought by the objector in relation to that provision, i.e. removal, modification, etc. As there is no automatic opportunity for parties to expand on their objections later in the process, it is important for objections to fully explain the issues.

In pursuing the objection, one should be aware of the constraints on the authority. For instance, if the provision in the plan relates to a development which has already been granted planning permission, the authority cannot change that provision as it has no power to stop the development from proceeding, short of revoking the permission and exposing itself to a claim for compensation. Landowners or developers should also be realistic, and accept that authorities can rarely allocate sites for what amounts to any possible development idea which might arise during the next decade.

Campaigning against planning issues is examined in more detail in Ch.10.

CHAPTER 4

DEVELOPMENT MANAGEMENT I—THE NEED FOR PLANNING PERMISSION

The keystone of the planning system is the requirement to obtain planning **4.01** permission for any development of land. It provides a means for planning authorities to control unsuitable development either by refusing permission or granting permission subject to conditions (see Chs 5 and 6 below), and the other elements within the system flow from the requirement for planning permission. Development plans have little practical effect until their policies are applied in the determination of applications for planning permission. Unless there is a breach of planning control caused by the failure to obtain planning permission or to observe the terms and conditions attached to a grant of planning permission, planning authorities have few enforcement powers over land short of compulsory purchase.

To determine whether planning permission is required, the following questions must be asked of the proposed activity (see fig.4.1 below):

(a) Does it fall within the statutory definition of "development"?
(b) Is it an activity which is declared not to amount to "development", for example, in terms of the Use Classes Order (UCO, see para.4.35 below)?
(c) Is planning permission deemed to be granted for the proposed activity, for example, in terms of the Permitted Development Order (PDO, see para.4.18 below)?

Depending upon the answer to any of these questions, an application for planning permission must be submitted before the proposed activity can be commenced. In practice, these questions are asked in reverse, principally because of the ease of reference of the UCO and PDO as the main sources of exemptions. The thorny question of "development" is only considered if the UCO and PDO fail to exempt the proposed activity from the need for planning permission.

This may be expressed diagrammatically, thus:

Fig.4.1 The need for planning permission

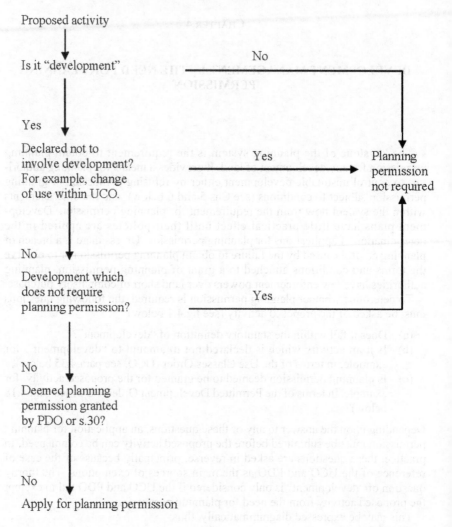

It is a question of the facts and circumstances of each individual case whether the proposal falls within the requirement for permission. There is a procedure for obtaining a formal answer from the planning authority on the need for planning permission, with a right of appeal to the Scottish Ministers.

REQUIREMENT FOR PLANNING PERMISSION

Planning permission is required for the carrying out of any development of land **4.02**
(including land covered with water) or buildings,[1] which is defined as the carrying
out of:[2]

(a) building operations;
(b) engineering operations;
(c) mining operations; or
(d) other operations in, on, over or under land; or
(e) the making of any material change in the use of any building or other land;
or
(f) the operation of a marine fish farm in certain circumstances.[3]

Building, engineering, mining or other operations are generally described as
operational development. This description highlights the difference in character
between these forms of development and material changes of use. It is possible for
an activity to involve both operational development and change of use.

The question of whether what is proposed amounts to "development" and,
therefore, requires planning permission is one of fact and circumstances for the
planning authority, or the Scottish Ministers on appeal, to decide. As a result, the
courts will be reluctant to interfere unless the decision is unreasonable.

The imprecise definition of terms such as "building operations", combined with
the residual term "other operations", gives ample scope for disputes with planning
authorities on this question. For example, prior to statutory intervention (see
para.4.03 below), the courts decided that demolition could be a building operation[4] or an engineering operation,[5] thereby requiring planning permission, or an
operation for which planning permission was not required.[6] In an appeal decision
the reporter held that provision of a limited number of unmarked and unfenced
private graves did not constitute a material change of use from grazing land, and
digging those graves by hand was not an engineering operation. Planning permission was therefore not required.[7]

Operational development

(a) Building operations

Planning permission is required for building operations, which include demoli- **4.03**
tion of buildings (discussed further below), rebuilding, structural alterations of or
additions to buildings, and other operations normally undertaken by a person carrying on business as a builder.[8]

A "building" is defined as including any structure or erection, and any part of a

---

1 Town and Country Planning (Scotland) Act 1997 (TCPSA) ss.28 and 277.
2 TCPSA 1997 s.26, as amended by Planning etc. (Scotland) Act 2006 (PSA).
3 See TCPSA 1997 s.26AA. *Friends of Loch Etive v Argyll and Bute Council* [2015] CSOH 61.
4 *Cambridge City Council v Secretary of State for the Environment* [1991] J.P.L. 428 (reversed on appeal); *Glasgow DC v Secretary of State for Scotland*, 1982 S.L.T. 28 per Lord Justice-Clerk
   Wheatley at 32.
5 *Coleshill v Minister of Housing and Local Government* [1969] 1 W.L.R. 746.
6 *Cambridge City Council v Secretary of State for the Environment* [1992] J.P.L. 644 CA.
7 *Scotsman*, 3 December 1992.
8 TCPSA 1997 s.26(4).

building.[9] Size, permanence and degree of attachment of the structure are factors to be considered.[10] Erection of a marquee was a building operation despite its periodic removal.[11]

As a result of the confusion caused by conflicting court decisions (see para.4.02 above), the Planning and Compensation Act 1991 added demolition to the list of building operations, thereby requiring planning permission for demolition of a building.[12] In addition, an amendment was made to the PDO requiring approval for demolition to be sought from the planning authority in certain circumstances.[13] Requirements for listed building consent or conservation area consent may apply (see Ch.9 below)

In consequence of these provisions, it may be important to determine whether works are demolition or another form of building operation. This is a question of fact in each case.[14]

4.04   The PDO class 70 grants deemed planning permission for demolition, unless the building has been rendered unsafe or uninhabitable by the action or inaction of any person having an interest in the land on which the building stands, and it is practicable to secure safety or health by repair works or works for affording temporary support. The PDO also does not apply to demolition of part of a building.

The PDO imposes a prior notification procedure for demolition of residential properties and some properties adjacent to residential properties. This procedure does not apply demolition of part of a building, or excluded demolition, which is demolition necessary to implement a planning permission for redevelopment of the site, or required or permitted to be carried out by statute or by any provision of a s.75 agreement.

The prior notification procedure involves the submission of an application to the planning authority for a determination as to whether their prior approval will be required for the method of the proposed demolition and any proposed restoration of the site. The application must contain a written description of the proposed development.

4.05   If, after 28 days from the date of receipt by the planning authority of the application, the authority have not made any determination as to whether the approval is required or notified the applicant of their determination, development can commence. Development can also start if the applicant receives written notice of their determination that their prior approval is not required. If the authority notify the applicant within the 28-day period that their prior approval is required, the development cannot start until that approval is given.

Where the prior approval of the authority is required for demolition, the development must be carried out in accordance with the details approved. If no prior approval is required, it must be carried out in accordance with the details submitted

---

9   TCPSA 1997 s.277.

10   *Barvis Ltd v Secretary of State for the Environment* (1971) 22 P. & C.R. 710. The concept of fixtures in property law may provide a useful parallel see, for example, William M. Gordon, *Scottish Land Law* (Edinburgh: SULI/W. Green, 2009).

11   *Skerritts of Nottingham Ltd v Secretary of State for the Environment (No.2)* [2000] J.P.L. 1025.

12   The Scottish Ministers revoked the Direction that demolition of certain types of building did not require planning permission—Town and Country Planning (Demolition which is not Development) (Scotland) Revocation Direction 2011, attached to Scottish Executive Development Department, Planning Circular 4/2011 (Scottish Executive, 2011).

13   Class 70 inserted by Town and Country Planning (General Permitted Development) (Scotland) Amendment (No.3) Order 1994 (SI 1994/3294), as amended.

14   *Shimizu (UK) Ltd v Westminster City Council* [1997] 1 All E.R. 481.

with the application. The development must be carried out within five years from the date of the approval, or, where no approval was required, from the date of receipt of the application.

Internal maintenance or improvement works or other alteration of a building (other than structural alterations) do not require planning permission unless the works materially affect the external appearance of the building,[15] or have the effect of increasing the gross floor space of the building by an amount or percentage specified by the Scottish Ministers.[16] The distinction between alteration, which does not require planning permission, and rebuilding works, which do need permission, may be difficult to draw.

In considering whether the works materially affect the external appearance of the building, what must be taken into account is the external appearance of the building, and not its exterior. The alteration must be one which affects the way in which the exterior of the building is or can be seen by an observer outside the building. The degree to which the alteration is capable of being seen by observers is also relevant, from any vantage point on the grounds or in or on any neighbouring building. Whether the external appearance is materially affected depends on part of the degree of visibility, and must take into account the nature of the particular building which it is proposed to alter, including whether it is listed (see Ch.9 below). The effect on the external appearance must be judged for its materiality in relation to the building as a whole, and not by reference to a part of the building taken in isolation.[17]   **4.06**

The statutory wording suggests that when assessing the effect of the proposed works on the external appearance of the building, no account should be taken of the appearance of the surrounding area. Canopies, grilles, roller shutters, stone cladding, and replacement windows are all works which may materially affect the external appearance of a building.

Planning permission is also required for works to provide additional space below ground, such as lowering the floor level or creating a basement.

The PDO grants deemed planning permission for many forms of building operations, including those within the curtilage of a dwellinghouse and agricultural buildings (see para.4.18 below). For example, planning permission is deemed to be granted for painting a building. This deemed permission does not extend to listed buildings and buildings situated in conservation areas. However, planning permission is only required if the painting of such a building amounts to development because it will materially affect the external appearance of the building.

(b)   Engineering operations

Engineering operations are defined as operations usually undertaken by or under the supervision of an engineer or which would require engineering skills, irrespective of whether an engineer is actually involved,[18] including the placing or assembly in inland waters or up to 12 nautical miles from the shore of any equip-   **4.07**

---

[15]   TCPSA 1997 s.26(2)(a). Listed building consent is required for internal works which affect the character of a listed building (see Ch.9 below).

[16]   TCPSA 1997 s.26(2AA). This is aimed principally at mezzanine floors in retail premises. The Scottish Ministers have yet to indicate when they will make an order specifying the amount or percentage.

[17]   *Burroughs Day v Bristol City Council* [1996] 1 P.L.R. 78.

[18]   *Fayrewood Fish Farms v Secretary of State for the Environment* [1984] J.P.L. 267.

ment for the purpose of fish farming,[19] and the formation or laying out of means of access to roads.[20] Drainage repair works may be engineering operations.[21]

Although not specifically identified as engineering operations, the carrying out of irrigation or drainage for agriculture or of any other water management project for that purpose, is "development".[21]

Planning permission is not required for the following works, which might be considered to be engineering operations: works carried out on land within the boundaries of a road by the roads authority for the maintenance or improvement of that road[22]; and works carried out by the local authority or statutory undertakers for inspecting, repairing or renewing any sewers, mains, pipes, cables or other apparatus, including the breaking open of any road or other land for that purpose.[23]

(c) Mining operations

4.08   Mining operations include the removal of material of any description from a mineral-working deposit, from a deposit of pulverised fuel ash or other furnace ash or clinker, or from a deposit of iron, steel or other metallic slags, and the extraction of minerals from a disused railway embankment.[24] For the purposes of the PDO, mining operations are defined as the winning and working of minerals in, on or under land, whether by surface or underground working.

Unlike building and engineering operations, mining is a continuous operation lasting for many years. Special controls apply to mining operations (see Ch.9 below). The removal of each shovelful constitutes a separate mining operation and it will therefore be rare for unauthorised mining operations to become lawful.[25]

(d) Other operations

4.09   There is no definition of what amounts to "other operations". It has been suggested that these are operations of a positive, constructive and identifiable character[26] which result in some physical alteration to land.[27] Arguably the definition of development is not intended to comprehend every operation on land. Clearly there are some operations on land which should not require planning permission, for example, mowing a lawn. The phrase "other operations", therefore, does not refer to all other operations.[28] Indeed, it has been suggested that this residual category may be restricted to operations similar to building, engineering or mining operations.[29]

For practical purposes, "other operations" will include any form of operational

---

[19]   TCPSA 1997 s.26(6), as amended by Planning etc. (Scotland) Act 2006 and Water Environment and Water Services (Scotland) Act 2003.

[20]   TCPSA 1997 s.277.

[21]   *Cartledge v Scottish Ministers* [2011] CSOH 53.

[22]   Planning permission is required for works which may have significant adverse effects on the environment and which are not exclusively for the maintenance of the road—TCPSA 1997 s.26(2)(b), as amended by Environmental Impact Assessment (Scotland) Regulations 1999 (SSI 1999/1) reg.47(1).

[23]   TCPSA 1997 s.26(2)(b), (c).

[24]   TCPSA 1997 s.26(5).

[25]   *Thomas David (Porthcawl) Ltd v Penybont Rural DC* [1972] 1 W.L.R. 1526.

[26]   *Coleshill v Minister of Housing and Local Government* [1969] 1 W.L.R. 746 per Lord Wilberforce at 765.

[27]   *Parkes v Secretary of State for the Environment* [1978] 1 W.L.R. 1308 per Lord Denning at 1311E.

[28]   *Cambridge City Council v Secretary of State for the Environment* [1992] J.P.L. 644.

[29]   cf. *Coleshill v Minister of Housing and Local Government* [1969] 1 W.L.R. 746 per Lords

development which does not fall within the other categories, but which the planning authority or the Scottish Ministers may reasonably consider requires planning permission—for example, any excavation and levelling works which cannot be considered engineering or mining operations.[30]

Although not specifically identified as "other operations", the carrying out of irrigation or drainage for agriculture or of any other water management project for that purpose, is "development".[31] That means that activities such as the operation of mobile water abstraction and mobile spray irrigation equipment are subject to planning control.

Material change of use

Following nationalisation of development rights in 1947, owners were left with their existing (1947) use rights and required to obtain planning permission from the State for any material change of use of land or buildings. **4.10**

Certain changes of use are declared to be material and therefore require planning permission[32]:

(a) Sub-division of a single dwellinghouse resulting in its use as two or more separate dwellinghouses. In contrast to the PDO, this provision extends to sub-division of flats.

(b) Deposit of refuse or waste materials on land, notwithstanding that the land is already used for that purpose, if either the superficial area of the deposit is thereby extended or the height of the deposit is extended to exceed the level of the land adjoining the site.

(c) Use of any external part of a building for the display of advertisements, if it is not normally used for that purpose. However, if the advertisement is displayed in accordance with the Town and Country Planning (Control of Advertisements) (Scotland) Regulations 1984 (see Ch.9 below), planning permission is deemed to have been granted.[33] Flags and lighting used by businesses may require advertisement consent.[34]

(d) Use of equipment in inland waters or up to 12 nautical miles from the shore for fish farming.[35]

Wilberforce and Guest.

[30] In *Forbes v Aberdeenshire Council* [2010] CSOH 01 at [27], the parties accepted planning permission was required for the planting of marram grass, preparatory earth works and chestnut pale fencing, but there is no discussion of whether this was a building operation, engineering operation or other operation.

[31] TCPSA 1997 s.26(2A), inserted by Environmental Impact Assessment (Water Management) (Scotland) Regulations 2003 (SSI 2003/341) reg.2(b). The Regulations also insert class 18A into the PDO, granting permitted development rights for the carrying out of irrigation or drainage for agriculture or of any other water management project for that purpose. A planning application will only be required for development which requires EIA.

[32] TCPSA 1997 s.26(3), (7).

[33] TCPSA 1997 s.184.

[34] *Taylor v Secretary of State for Scotland*, 1997 S.L.T. 535; *Great Yarmouth BC v Secretary of State for the Environment* [1997] J.P.L. 650.

[35] TCPSA 1997 ss.26(6AA) and 26AA, inserted by PSA 2006.

These changes of use should be distinguished from the changes of use which are declared not to involve development and, therefore, do not require planning permission[36]:

(a)   The use of any buildings or other land within the curtilage of a dwelling-house, as for any purpose incidental to the enjoyment of the dwellinghouse does not amount to a material change of use and, therefore, requires no planning permission. Where a granny flat was not intended to be used as a separate dwelling, its use was incidental to the main dwelling and no planning permission was required.[37] Keeping up to 44 dogs as a hobby was not an incidental use of the dwellinghouse.[38] Subject to the provisions of the PDO planning permission may be required for erection of the buildings.

(b)   The change of use to agricultural or forestry use (including afforestation) of land and any building occupied together with the land does not require planning permission (see Ch.9 below). However, planning permission might be required for the carrying out of irrigation or drainage for agriculture or of any other water management project for that purpose.[39]

(c)   A change of use within any class specified in the UCO (see para.4.35 below).

Whether any other change of use is "material" and therefore requires planning permission is a question of fact and degree for the planning authority, or the Scottish Ministers on appeal, to decide and the courts will only interfere with an unreasonable decision. There is no general guidance on when a change of use will be considered "material". Some assistance is provided by case law, but much of this area of planning law remains conceptual in nature.[40]

The first step in assessing whether a material change of use has occurred is the identification of the area of land or the building to be used as the reference point against which the change can be judged. This area of land or building is known as the "planning unit".

4.11   The correct identification of the planning unit may be of crucial importance to the planning authority or the owner. In general, the larger the planning unit, the less likely that a change of use will be material. For example, a lean-to building in a car-breakers yard had been used as the yard office and for retail sales of car parts salvaged from vehicles broken up on the site. New owners used the lean-to for the sale of new vehicle parts and camping equipment. They appealed against an enforcement notice on the ground that the planning unit was the whole yard and that looking at the site as a whole, the intensification of the retail sale use was insufficient to amount to a material change of use. The Secretary of State held that the planning unit was the lean-to and there had been a material change of use. The court

---

36   TCPSA 1997 s.26(2)(d), (e), (f).
37   *Glasgow DC v Secretary of State for Scotland*, 1997 S.C.L.R. 711.
38   *Wallington v Secretary of State for the Environment* (1991) J.P.L. 942.
39   TCPSA 1997 s.26(2A), inserted by Environmental Impact Assessment (Water Management) (Scotland) Regulations 2003 (SSI 2003/341) reg.2(b). The Regulations also insert class 18A into the PDO, granting permitted development rights for the carrying out of irrigation or drainage for agriculture or of any other water management project for that purpose. A planning application will only be required for development which requires EIA.
40   See Rowan Robinson, Young, Purdue and Farquharson-Black, *Scottish Planning Law and Procedure* (Edinburgh: SULI/W. Green, 2001) paras 5.71–5.86.

tended to agree with the Secretary of State, but found that he had applied the wrong test and returned the matter to him for re-decision.[41]

A court also found that the wrong test had been applied in reaching the conclusion that outbuildings were used as one unit for the purposes of holiday accommodation comprising 10 apartments rather than as 10 single dwellinghouses.[42] Identification of the planning unit is a question of the facts and circumstances of each case, but some broad criteria have been suggested.[43] If there is a single main use, perhaps with secondary activities which are incidental or ancillary to that use, the area of land occupied as a single holding (the unit of occupation) is the planning unit. Where the occupier carries on a variety of activities, the unit of occupation may still be the planning unit. However, if these activities occupy separate and distinct areas, each area which can be identified as being used for a different main purpose forms a separate planning unit (the unit of activity replaces the unit of occupation).

In general, the unit of occupation is the planning unit unless and until some smaller unit can be recognised as the site of activities which amount to a separate use both physically and functionally. Physical separation of plots of land within the same occupation may cause the individual plots to form separate planning units.

The planning unit may be larger than the unit of occupation, but only in exceptional circumstances.[44] This avoids the possibility of enforcement action directed against an occupier sharing a planning unit with others (except for joint occupiers) in respect of activities carried on by the other occupiers over which he has no control. Thus the Secretary of State on appeal rejected the argument that a whole group of lock-up garages previously used for a taxi business, but gradually let singly or in groups to different persons, formed a single planning unit. The appropriate planning unit was the unit of occupation and each garage individually occupied became a separate planning unit. Enforcement notices alleging a material change of use were validly directed against garages in separate occupation where vehicle repairing was being carried out.[45] Similarly, the individual units within the Metro Centre shopping centre are occupied in their own right, and each is therefore a separate planning unit.[46]

The Scottish Government indicate that where the occupants of bed-sitting rooms share some communal facilities such as a bathroom, the planning unit is likely to be the whole building, in use for the purpose of multiple residential occupancy, rather than each individual bed-sit room.[47]

After the planning unit has been identified, it is possible to consider whether there **4.12** has been a material change of use within it. Once again, this is a matter of fact and degree to be determined by the planning authority or the Scottish Ministers on appeal. Relevant factors in assessing the materiality of a change of use are the character and intensity of the various uses, the degree to which the uses are dependent on each other, the proportion of the planning unit devoted to each activity, and any planning effects on the locality. The scope of any planning permission may be an important issue (see "Interpretation" at para.5.96 below).

[41] *Burdle v Secretary of State for the Environment* [1972] 1 W.L.R. 1207.
[42] *Moore v Secretary of State for the Environment, The Times,* 18 February 1998.
[43] *Burdle v Secretary of State for the Environment* [1972] 1 W.L.R. 1207 per Bridge J.
[44] *Rawlins v Secretary of State for the Environment* [1989] J.P.L. 439; *Kwik Save v Secretary of State for Wales* (1979) 37 P. & C.R. 170.
[45] *Johnston v Secretary of State for the Environment* (1974) 28 P. & C.R. 424.
[46] *Church Commissioners for England v Secretary of State for the Environment* [1995] 2 P.L.R. 99.
[47] Planning Circular 10/2009, Planning Enforcement (Scottish Government, 2009), Annex A, para.8.

Determining whether a change of use is involved can raise difficult questions. For example, helicopters landing on or taking off from a vessel floating but not moored on the River Thames could constitute a change of use of the river bed.[48]

If the general character of the use remains the same, but there is a change from one particular purpose to another particular purpose, there may not be a material change of use. Where land was used as a railway storage depot, there was no material change of use when it came to be used for storage of motor vehicles mainly destined for rail transport instead of coal for transport by rail. What should be considered is the character of the use of the land, not the particular purpose of a particular occupier.[49] However, a change from one leisure activity to another is capable of constituting a material change of use if the particular nature of the type of leisure activity has changed.[50] The change of use of a caravan site from holiday purposes to permanent residential purposes can be a material change of use.[51] The courts have also held that a dwellinghouse does not necessarily cease to be used as such because it is managed for the commercial purposes of holiday or other temporary lets.[52] Intensification of use does not necessarily amount to a material change of use.[53]

4.13 The character of the use is determined by the primary or main use. A motor dealership that comprised the sale of vehicles and a workshop was a mixed use because the workshop was not ancillary to the sale of vehicles.[54]

Changes in ancillary or incidental uses do not involve a material change of use, provided the subordinate and dependent character of the ancillary use is preserved. Once an ancillary use is no longer subordinate and linked to the main use, or has become a main use in its own right, a material change of use may have occurred. Thus, in terms of a planning permission for a quarry operation, backfilling the quarry with waste material from the quarrying operation was ancillary to the main activity. When the quarry came to be used for dumping refuse from outside, the ancillary dumping use had become a main use. The character of the use had altered and a material change of use had occurred.[55] Similarly, keeping up to 44 dogs in a dwellinghouse as a hobby amounted to a material change of use because it was not incidental to the enjoyment of the dwellinghouse.[56] Intensification of use can be problematic.[57]

It is relevant to consider the size and scale of the development and its physical layout. The distinctive characteristic is not the building's actual or intended use, but the ability to use it.[58]

The size of the area devoted to a use is not conclusive. The use of cubicles for viewing films in a sex shop was held not to be ancillary to the main retail use.[59] Although residential use of a caretaker's flat in an office building may be ancillary

48   *Thames Heliport Plc v Tower Hamlets LBC* [1997] J.P.L. 448.
49   *East Barnet Urban DC v British Transport Commission* [1962] 2 Q.B. 484.
50   *Shepherd and Love v Secretary of State for the Environment* [1992] J.P.L. 827.
51   *Forest of Dean DC v Secretary of State for the Environment* [1994] E.G. 138 (C.S.).
52   *Moore v Secretary of State* [2012] EWCA Civ 1202.
53   *R. (on the application of Reed) v Secretary of State for Communities & Local Government* [2014] EWCA Civ 241.
54   *Cocktails Ltd v Secretary of State* [2008] EWCA (Civ) 1523.
55   *Alexandra Transport Co Ltd v Secretary of State for Scotland*, 1974 S.L.T. 81.
56   *Wallington v Secretary of State for the Environment* [1991] J.P.L. 942.
57   *Bass Taverns v Secretary of State for Scotland* unreported 20 August 1999 IH.
58   *Eagles v Minister for the Environment* [2009] EWHC 1028 (Admin).
59   *Lydcare v Secretary of State for the Environment* [1984] J.P.L. 39.

to the principal office use, it is often considered that these are two physically separate and distinct primary uses, and the flat and the office therefore form separate planning units.

It may also be relevant to consider whether the change of use will have material or relevant planning considerations, such as adverse effects on the locality. The limited environmental health effects of the sale of heated food from a shop was a factor in the decision that there had been no material change of use.[60]

Creation of a new planning unit is not conclusive evidence of a material change of use. As the general rule is that the planning unit is the unit of occupation, a new planning unit is therefore formed when part of a site is sold or leased to another person. However, the primary use may remain as before,[61] in which case there is no material change of use (with the exception of a sub-division of a dwellinghouse into two or more dwellinghouses which is always a material change of use). In contrast, a material change of use caused by an ancillary use becoming a main use in its own right will not necessarily result in the creation of a new planning unit unless it occupies a separately identifiable part of the site.

If existing use rights are lost, the planning unit has a nil use and planning permission will be required for any new use or resumption of the previous use. Confusingly, this is often referred to as the creation of a new planning unit, when what is meant is that there has been a fresh start or new chapter in the planning history.

Demolition of a building results in the right to continue its use being extinguished. Resumption of that use thereafter requires planning permission.[62] Rebuilding operations would probably require planning permission in any case, but there may be circumstances in which permission would not be forthcoming for a resumption of the use, for example, a disco in a residential area.

Loss of existing use rights may also occur when a planning permission is implemented. Where planning permission was granted for construction of retail units, but a unit was used as an air terminal in terms of a separate permission, resumption of the retail use required fresh planning permission.[63] If the existing use is supplanted or superseded by another use, the right to resume the existing use is lost and planning permission will be required for its resumption, even if the change to the supplanting use did not require planning permission.[64] The erection of a building will not of itself result in the loss of existing use rights.[65] **4.14**

A temporary discontinuance of use does not lead to loss of existing use rights.[66] As a result, no planning permission is required to resume the discontinued use, unless the land has been used for some different purpose in the meantime. In contrast, where a use has been abandoned, the land has a nil use and planning permission will be required for any use, including resumption of the former use.[67] In distinguishing between a temporary cessation of use and abandonment, at least four factors should be considered: the physical condition of the land or building; the length of

---

60 *Glasgow DC v Secretary of State for Scotland*, 1985 S.L.T. 19.
61 *R. v Kensington and Chelsea RLBC Ex p. Europa Foods Ltd* [1996] E.G. 5 (C.S.).
62 *Iddenden v Secretary of State for the Environment* [1972] 1 W.L.R. 1433 per Buckley L.J. at 1440; see also App./6/90/p.4225/1 [1992] J.P.L. 579.
63 *Regent Lion Properties v Westminster City Council* [1991] J.P.L. 569.
64 *JL Engineering v Secretary of State for the Environment* [1993] E.G. 24 (C.S.).
65 *Jennings Motors Ltd v Secretary of State for the Environment* [1982] 1 Q.B. 541.
66 *Paul v Ayrshire CC*, 1964 S.C. 116; 1964 S.L.T. 207.
67 Planning permission for operational development can never be abandoned, but may be incapable of implementation (see Ch.5 below).

the period of non-use; whether there has been any other use; and evidence of the owner's intentions.[68] Any action inconsistent with retention of the right to resume the use, such as removal of petrol tanks and pumps at a filling station, will also be relevant. Cessation of a car sales use for four years was sufficient grounds to find that the use had been abandoned.[69] The test is objective, and the wishes and intentions of the site owner are not decisive.[70] Neither the stated intention of the owner to resume the use in question, even where the existence of that intention was clearly proved, nor the state of the site, were determinative.[71]

Use can fluctuate—where pavement furniture was used by a restaurant, the use of the pavement fluctuated, but was subject to the overriding requirement that the use could only be taken advantage of whilst the restaurant was open for business.[72]

It is important to determine when a change of use occurs. Although land is converted to allow a new use, there is no change until the land is actually put to the new use.[73] If the change of use has occurred gradually over a period, it will be necessary to identify the point at which the change became material. At that point any failure to obtain planning permission results in a breach of planning control which may be the subject of enforcement action (see Ch.7 below).

OPERATIONS AND USES DECLARED NOT TO INVOLVE DEVELOPMENT

4.15   The following operations and uses are declared not to involve development and therefore will not require planning permission[74]:

(a)   internal maintenance or improvement works or other alteration of a building (other than structural alterations), unless the works materially affect the external appearance of the building, or have the effect of increasing the gross floor space of the building by an amount or percentage specified by the Scottish Ministers (see "Building operations", above);

(b)   works required for the maintenance or improvement of a road which are carried out by a roads authority on land within the boundaries of the road[75];

(c)   works carried out by a local authority or statutory undertaker for the purpose of inspecting, repairing or renewing any sewers, mains, pipes, cables or other apparatus, including the breaking open of any road or other land for that purpose;

(d)   use of any buildings or other land within the curtilage of a dwellinghouse for a purpose incidental to the enjoyment of the dwellinghouse as such (see "Material Change of Use", above);

(e)   use of any land for the purposes of agriculture or forestry (including afforestation) and the use for any of those purposes of any building occupied together with land so used (see Ch.9 below). However, planning permis-

---

[68]   *Trustees of Castel-y-Mynach Estate v Secretary of State for Wales* [1985] J.P.L. 40.
[69]   *Hartley v Minister of Housing and Local Government* [1970] 1 Q.B. 413.
[70]   *Hughes v Secretary of State for the Environment, Transport and the Regions* [2000] J.P.L. 826.
[71]   *William Tracey Ltd v Scottish Ministers*, 2005 G.W.D. 4-56.
[72]   *Westminster CC v Secretary of State* [2013] EWHC 23 (Admin).
[73]   *Caledonian Terminal Investments Ltd v Edinburgh Corp*, 1970 S.C. 271; 1970 S.L.T. 362.
[74]   TCPSA 1997 s.26(2).
[75]   Planning permission is required for works which may have significant adverse effects on the environment and which are not exclusively for the maintenance of the road—TCPSA 1997 s.26(2)(b), as amended by Environmental Impact Assessment (Scotland) Regulations 1999 (SSI 1999/1) reg.47(1).

sion might be required for the carrying out of irrigation or drainage for agriculture or of any other water management project for that purpose[76];

(f) a change of use within the terms of the UCO (see para.4.35 below).

Development Which Does Not Require Planning Permission

Notwithstanding the definition of "development", planning permission is not required in certain restricted circumstances.[77] In consequence of the substitution of the 10–year immunity period for changes of use without planning permission, for the previous rule that only changes prior to 1965 were immune (see Ch.7 below), the only important categories are:

4.16

(a) if on 1 July 1948 land was used on occasions for a purpose other than its normal use, whether or not at regular intervals, permission will not be required for use of the land for that other purpose on similar occasions on or after 8 December 1969 if the land has been used for that other purpose on at least one similar occasion between 1 July 1948 and before the beginning of 1969;

(b) planning permission is not required for resumption of the normal use of the land on the expiry of a temporary planning permission (see Ch.5 below), provided that use was not in breach of planning control (see Ch.7 below);

(c) where planning permission has been granted by a development order, such as the PDO (see below), planning permission is not required for resumption of the normal use of the land, provided that use was not in breach of planning control; and

(d) where an enforcement notice has been served in respect of any development of land, planning permission is not required to change the use of the land to any use which would have been lawful if that development had not been carried out. Uses which are immune from enforcement action are deemed to be lawful (see Ch.7 below).

In 2006, Crown immunity from planning control was removed, with the result that planning permission is now required for development on Crown land or any other land which is undertaken by the Crown (see Ch.9 below).

Deemed Planning Permission (Permitted Development Rights)

In certain circumstances planning permission is deemed to have been granted and no application for permission is therefore necessary. The main source of deemed planning permission (sometimes referred to as permitted development rights) is the PDO (see below).

4.17

Deemed planning permission for the display of an advertisement in accordance with the Town and Country Planning (Control of Advertisements) (Scotland) Regulations 1984, development in enterprise zones and simplified planning zones and development by a planning authority is discussed in Ch.9.

---

[76] TCPSA 1997 s.26(2A), inserted by Environmental Impact Assessment (Water Management) (Scotland) Regulations 2003 (SSI 2003/341) reg.2(b). The Regulations also insert class 18A into the PDO, granting permitted development rights for the carrying out of irrigation or drainage for agriculture or of any other water management project for that purpose. A planning application will only be required for development which requires EIA.

[77] TCPSA 1997 s.28 and Sch.2.

Permitted Development Order

4.18   The PDO is the main source of deemed planning permission/permitted development rights.[78] Changes to householder permitted development rights were made in 2011, with changes to other parts of the Order in 2014. There are extensive differences from the equivalent rights in England.

Planning permission is deemed to be granted for developments within the descriptions printed in bold type in Sch.1 to the PDO. The sub-paragraphs below each description specify the circumstances in which there is no deemed planning permission granted (although planning permission will only be required if the proposed work falls within the definition of development). Important terms are defined in art.2(1) or the appropriate part of Sch.1.

For example, class 9 is in the following form:

(1) *The stone cleaning or painting of the exterior of any building or works.*
(2) Development is not permitted by this class—
    (a) for the purposes of advertisement, announcement or direction;
    (b) where the building or works are in a conservation area;
    (c) where the building is a listed building;
    (d) it would be development described in class 2B(1).[79]

The effect of class 9 is that planning permission is deemed to be granted for stone cleaning or painting of the exterior of a building. If the circumstances fall within one of the exceptions, an application for planning permission will be required only if the stone cleaning or painting falls within the definition of development. For example, there is no deemed planning permission for stone cleaning a building in a conservation area, but planning permission will only be required if the cleaning will materially affect the exterior of the building (see "Building operations", above).

The 1992 PDO introduced a prior notification and approval procedure for certain categories of permitted development, including agricultural and forestry buildings and operations (see Ch.9 below), demolition (see above), and some public utility developments. It is a condition of permitted development for these classes that prior notification is made to the planning authority, which then has the opportunity to control aspects of the development in the interests of amenity.

The prior notification procedure involves submission of an application to the planning authority to determine whether their prior approval is required. Work cannot proceed until notification is received from the planning authority that its prior approval is not required, or its approval is received, or 28 days have elapsed since the application was lodged and the authority has reached no decision. The prior approval requirement is restricted to the siting, design and external appearance of the building.

There is a right of review by the local review body or appeal to the Scottish Ministers against the refusal of prior approval, the grant of approval subject to conditions, or, having decided that the prior approval is required, the failure of the planning authority to determine the prior notification application within two months of its receipt. Any appeal must be lodged within three months of the decision or

---

[78] TCPSA 1997 s.30; Town and Country Planning (General Permitted Development) (Scotland) Order 1992 (SI 1992/223), as amended.
[79] Any improvement, addition or other alteration to the external appearance of a dwellinghouse that is not an enlargement.

within three months of the expiry of the two-month period. This is discussed further in Ch.8.

The work must be carried out in accordance with the approved details, or, if no approval is required, in line with the details submitted with the application. It must also be carried out within five years of the date on which approval was given, or if no approval was given, the date of the application.

The PDO cannot permit development[80]:   **4.19**

(a) in breach of any condition attached to a grant of planning permission or deemed permission granted in terms of another order;

(b) in connection with a building, if the building operations involved in the constructions of that building are unlawful (see Ch.7 below);

(c) in connection with an existing use, if that use is unlawful;

(d) involving the formation, laying out or material widening of a means of access to a trunk or classified road, or which creates an obstruction to the view of persons using any road used by vehicular traffic, so as to be likely to cause danger to such persons (with some exceptions);

(e) entailing the laying or construction of a notifiable pipeline other than by a public gas supplier;

(f) any development which requires or involves the demolition of a building (but not part of a building), other than as permitted by class 70; and

(g) any development which, if it were the subject of an application for planning permission, would require environmental assessment, other than the categories of developments specified in art.3(10)—the effect of this provision is to remove permitted development rights for any development which, but for those permitted development rights, would require environmental assessment (see Ch.5 below).

Any deemed planning permission granted by the PDO for development which is likely to have a significant effect on a European site in Great Britain (either alone or in combination with other plans or projects), and is not directly connected with or necessary to the management of the site, is subject to a requirement to obtain the approval of the planning authority before commencing development.[81] European sites are important nature conservation sites protected by the Habitats Directive,[82] including special areas of conservation (see Ch.9 below). This requirement applies to any development which has not yet started. In addition, any development begun and not completed should not be continued until approval from the planning authority has been obtained. The authority can only approve a development after having ascertained that it will not adversely affect the integrity of the site.

Permitted development rights conferred by the PDO may be removed for any particular development or class of development within a specified geographical area (frequently a conservation area), by an art.4 direction.[83] If an art.4 direction removes permitted development rights for work and a subsequent application for planning permission for that work made within 12 months of the direction is refused, a claim

---

[80] See art.3, as amended.
[81] See art.3(1), as amended; Conservation (Natural Habitats etc.) Regulations 1994 (SI 1994/2716) regs 60–63.
[82] Council Directive 92/43/EEC on the conservation of natural habitats and of wild fauna and flora.
[83] See art.4.

for compensation may arise.[84] It is also competent to restrict future exercise of permitted development rights by imposing a condition upon a grant of planning permission (see Ch.6 below).

The PDO specifies classes of permitted development listed in Sch.1 Pts 1–32, ranging from development within the curtilage of a dwellinghouse to development at amusement parks. As many of the classes are of specialised interest only, the following discussion concentrates on the provisions which are likely to have a wider effect.

Part 1 Development Within the Curtilage of a Dwellinghouse

4.20   It is important to note that the definition of "dwellinghouse" for the purposes of the PDO does not include a building containing one or more flats, or a flat contained within such a building. However, the amendments introduced in 2011 added specific permitted development rights for flats.[85]

Neither the PDO nor the TCPSA 1997 defines "curtilage". Broadly, the curtilage of a building includes any land or building used for its comfortable enjoyment or serving the purpose of the building in some necessary or reasonably useful way, although not marked off or enclosed in any way.[86] The curtilage of a typical dwellinghouse is its garden.

The extent of the curtilage is a question of fact and circumstances. The geographical relationship and the use made of the land and buildings will be important. Curtilage is generally constrained to a small area about a building; an intimate association with land which is undoubtedly within the curtilage is required in order to make the land under consideration part and parcel of that undoubted curtilage land; and although it is not necessary for there to have been physical enclosure of the land which was within the curtilage, the land in question at least needs to be regarded in law as part of one enclosure with the house. The appropriate time for consideration of the curtilage boundary is the time the development took place, but historical associations can be used in looking for identification of the curtilage at the time of the development.[87] Current ownership may be irrelevant, for example, the large grounds which often form the curtilage of listed buildings can be in the hands of several different owners.

Changes to householder permitted development rights were made in 2011.[88] The classes of development are now:

Class 1A:

Single storey ground floor extensions.

Class 1B:

Other ground floor extensions.

---

[84]   TCPSA 1997 s.77.

[85]   Class 4A.

[86]   *Sinclair-Lockhart's Trustees v Central Land Board*, 1951 S.L.T. 121 per Lord Mackintosh at 123. See Paul Q. Watchman and Eric Young, "The Meaning of 'Curtilage'", 1990 (News) S.L.T. 77; Charles Mynors, "The Extent of Listing" [1993] J.P.L. 99. See also discussion in relation to listed buildings at para.9.02 below.

[87]   *McAlpine v Secretary of State for the Environment, The Times,* 6 December 1994.

[88]   Planning Circular 1/2012, Guidance on Householder Permitted Development Rights (Scottish Government, 2012).

Class 1C:

Porches.

Class 1D:

Roof extensions.

Class 2A:

Access ramps.

Class 2B:

Other development on the roof or external walls.

Class 3A:

Ancillary buildings within the curtilage.

Class 3B:

Other development required for a purpose incidental to the enjoyment of the dwellinghouse.

Class 3C:

Hard surfaces.

Class 3D:

Decks or other raised platforms.

Class 3E:

Gates, fences, walls and other means of enclosure.

Class 4A:

Alterations to the external appearance of a dwelling within a building containing flats..

Part 1A Installation of Domestic Microgeneration Equipment

This enables more microgeneration equipment to be installed on existing domestic buildings without the need to apply for planning permission—biomass, ground source heat pump, water source heat pump, combined heat and power, wind turbine, and air source heat pump.[89]   **4.21**

Classes 2B and 4A:

Permit installation of solar photovoltaic (PV) and solar thermal equipment that would be attached to a wall or roof of a dwellinghouse or a flat.

---

[89] Added by the Town and Country Planning (General Permitted Development) (Domestic Microgeneration) (Scotland) Amendment Order 2009 (SSI 2009/34), as amended by the Town and Country Planning (General Permitted Development) (Domestic Microgeneration) (Scotland) Amendment Order 2010 (SSI 2010/27).

Class 3B:

Permits the installation of free-standing solar PV and solar thermal equipment for a dwellinghouse.[90]

Pt 1B Installation of Non Domestic Microgeneration Equipment

Classes 6I–6M:

4.22   For non-domestic buildings, classes 6I–6M permit installation of underground pipes for ground/water source heat pumps, solar PV or solar thermal equipment, and biomass.[91]

Part 2 Sundry Minor Operations

Class 7: The erection, construction, maintenance, improvement or alteration of a gate, fence, wall or other means of enclosure

4.23   The height of any new enclosure must not exceed 2m above ground level, or 1m if within 20m of a road. The height of an existing enclosure cannot be increased beyond these limits. Development is not permitted by this class if it would involve an enclosure surrounding a listed building or development within its curtilage or is development authorised by class 3E(1) (above). Permitted development rights under this class are not restricted to development within the curtilage of a dwellinghouse.

Class 9: The stone cleaning or painting of the exterior of any building or works

This permitted development right does not include stone cleaning or painting for purposes of advertisement, announcement or direction, to which the Town and Country Planning (Control of Advertisements) (Scotland) Regulations 1984 will apply (see Ch.9 below). Although the stone cleaning or painting of a listed building or building within a conservation area is also excluded, planning permission for these activities is required only if the external appearance of the building will be materially affected.[92] Painting includes the application of colour. Class 9 does not include works authorised by class 2B(1) (above).

Part 2A Shops or Catering, Financial or Professional Services Establishments

Class 9A:

4.24   Permits extension or alteration of shops or financial or professional services establishments.

---

90   Planning Circular 1/2012, Guidance on Householder Permitted Development Rights, para 6.3. Previous classes 6A and 6B re solar PV and solar thermal were removed by the Town and Country Planning (General Permitted Development) (Domestic Microgeneration) (Scotland) Amendment Order 2011 (SSI 2011/357).
91   Inserted by Town and Country Planning (Non-Domestic Microgeneration) (Scotland) Amendment Order 2011 (SSI 2011/136).
92   TCPSA 1997 s.26(2)(a).

Class 9B:

Permits erection or construction of a trolley store for a shop.[93]

Part 2B Schools, Colleges, Universities and Hospital Buildings

Class 9C:

Permits extension or alteration of schools, colleges, universities and hospital buildings, including nursing homes.[94]   **4.25**

Part 2C Office Buildings

Class 9D:

Permits extension or alteration of office buildings.[95]   **4.26**

Part 2D Recharging Electrical Outlets

Classes 9E and 9F:

Permit installation, alteration or replacement of recharging electrical outlets.[96]   **4.27**

Part 2E Access Ramps

Class 9G:

Permits erection, construction or alteration of an access ramp outside the external door of a non domestic building.[97]   **4.28**

Part 3 Changes of Use

The UCO provides that changes of use within defined classes do not require planning permission (see para.4.35 below). A material change of use from one class to another will require permission. Part 3 of the PDO permits certain changes of use between classes without permission (see fig.4.2 below).   **4.29**

Class 10:

Permits a change of use from a use within class 2 (financial, professional and other services), or class 3 (food and drink), from use for the sale of hot food for consumption off the premises, or for the sale or display for sale of motor vehicles to a use within class 1 (shops). From 2 February 1998, the change of use from sale or display for sale of motor vehicles to class 1 use is only permitted by the PDO if the total floor area of the building does not exceed 235sq m.

---

93 Classes 9A and 9B inserted by Town and Country Planning (General Permitted Development) (Scotland) Amendment Order 2014 (SSI 2014/142).

94 Inserted by Town and Country Planning (General Permitted Development) (Scotland) Amendment Order 2014 (SSI 2014/142).

95 Inserted by Town and Country Planning (General Permitted Development) (Scotland) Amendment Order 2014 (SSI 2014/142).

96 Inserted by Town and Country Planning (General Permitted Development) (Scotland) Amendment Order 2014 (SSI 2014/142).

97 Inserted by Town and Country Planning (General Permitted Development) (Scotland) Amendment Order 2014 (SSI 2014/142).

Class 11:

Permits a change of use from class 3 (food and drink) or for the sale of hot food for consumption off the premises to class 2 (financial, professional and other services).

Class 12:

Permits a change of use from class 5 (general industrial) or class 6 (storage or distribution) to class 4 (business).

Class 13:

Permits a change of use from class 4 (business) or class 5 (general industrial) to class 6 (storage or distribution), provided the change of use relates to no more than 235sq m of the floor area in the building.

Part 4 Temporary Buildings and Uses

Class 14: The provision on land of buildings, moveable structures, works, plant or machinery required temporarily in connection with and for the duration of operations being or to be carried out on, in, under or over that land or on land adjoining that land

4.30   Any planning permission required for the operations must have been obtained. When the operations have been carried out, all buildings, structures, works, plant and machinery must be removed and the land on which these items were situated reinstated to its previous condition as soon as is reasonably practicable. Development is not permitted by this class in connection with mining operations.

Class 15: The use of land (other than a building or land within the curtilage of a building) for any purpose, except as a caravan site, on not more than 28 days in total in any calendar year, and the erection or placing of moveable structures on the land for the purposes of that use

This class permits temporary uses such as rock concerts and open air markets,[98] and the erection of moveable structures such as tents in connection with these uses. The use of any site for such purposes must not exceed 28 days in a calendar year. The calendar year basis applies even where an enforcement notice does not take effect until later in the year.[99]

Part 6 Agricultural Buildings and Operations and Pt 7 Forestry Buildings and Operations

4.31   Planning controls over agricultural and forestry development are examined in Ch.9.

---

[98]   The exclusion of open air markets was removed by Town and Country Planning (General Permitted Development) (Scotland) Amendment Order 2014 (SSI 2014/142).

[99]   *Attorney General's Reference (No.1 of 1996)* [1997] J.P.L. 749; [1996] E.G. 164 (C.S.).

Fig.4.2 Changes of use without planning permission

From class	To class
2 (Financial, professional and other services)	1 (shops)
3 (Food and Drink)	1 (shops) or 2 (Financial, professional and other services)
4 (Business)	6 (Storage or Distribution), unless the floor area involved exceeds 235sqm
5 (General Industrial)	4 (Business) or 6 (Storage or Distribution), subject to 235sqm limit
6 (Storage or Distribution)	4 (Business)
Sale or display for sale of motor vehicles subject to 235sqm limit	1 (shops)
Hot food takeaway	1 (shops) or 2 (Financial, professional and other services)

Part 8 Industrial and Warehouse Development

Class 23: The extension or alteration of an industrial building or a warehouse

4.32 The building as extended or altered must be used for the purposes of the undertaking concerned, and in the case of an industrial building, may only be used for the carrying out of an industrial process or the provision of employee facilities, or in the case of a warehouse, for storage or distribution or the provision of employee facilities. There are also restrictions on the size of the building as extended or altered, including a restriction on the increase in floor area to a maximum of 25 per cent, or 1,000sq m, whichever is the greater. The planning authority can require an application for planning permission to be submitted if the external appearance of the premises would be materially affected by the extension or alteration.

Class 24: Development carried out on industrial land for the purposes of an industrial process consisting of:

(a)   the installation of additional or replacement plant or machinery;
(b)   the provision, rearrangement or replacement of a sewer, main, pipe, cable or other apparatus; or
(c)   the provision, rearrangement or replacement of a private way, private railway, siding or conveyor.

Development is not permitted if it would materially affect the external appearance of the premises or any plant or machinery would be higher than 15m above ground level or the height of anything replaced, whichever is the greater.

Part 12 Development by Local Authorities

Class 30: The erection or construction and the maintenance, improvement or other alteration by a local authority of:

4.33 (a)   any building, works or equipment not exceeding 4m in height or 200 cubic m in capacity on land belonging to or maintained by them, being building works or equipment required for the purposes of any function exercised by them on that land otherwise than as statutory undertakers;
(b)   street furniture required in connection with the operation of any public service administered by them.[100]

Class 31:

The carrying out by a roads authority on land outwith but adjoining the boundary of an existing road of works required for or incidental to the maintenance or improvement of the road.

Part 23 Demolition of Buildings

4.34 See para.4.04 above.

---

[100] Amended by Town and Country Planning (General Permitted Development) (Scotland) Amendment Order 2014 (SSI 2014/142).

USE CLASSES ORDER

The UCO specifies 11 classes of use. There are extensive differences from the **4.35** equivalent rights in England. Within each class are listed uses of a broadly similar character. Provided both uses are in the same class, a change from one use to another does not involve development and, therefore, no planning permission is required for the change.[101] For example, any change from use as a post office to use for the sale of tickets will not amount to development because both uses are within class 1 (see below). Primary use is the determining factor for the provisions of the UCO and planning permission is not required where ancillary or incidental uses fall within a different class from the primary use.[102] A newsagent's shop selling hot pies at lunchtime involves shop use (class 1) and hot food takeaway use (sui generis, below). If the sale of hot pies cannot be described as ancillary or incidental to the shop use, a material change of use may have occurred and planning permission be required.[103]

It should not be assumed that any change of use from one class to another automatically requires permission. There may be deemed planning permission for the change under the PDO (see fig.4.2 above). In the absence of deemed permission, an application for planning permission is only necessary if the change of use is material.

The TCPSA 1997 declares that certain changes of use will always be material and, therefore, require planning permission (see "Material Change of Use" above), such as sub-division of a dwellinghouse into two or more dwellinghouses,[104] which would otherwise be a change of use within class 9 (houses). In addition, a condition imposed upon a grant of planning permission can restrict changes of use notwithstanding that the change of use does not constitute development in terms of the UCO (see Ch.6 below).

The following uses, often described as sui generis, are excluded from the provi- **4.36** sions of the UCO and planning permission will, therefore, be required for any change to or from these uses (the character of these uses is such that the change is likely to be material):

(a)   as a theatre;
(b)   as an amusement arcade or centre, or funfair;
(c)   for the sale of fuel for motor vehicles;
(d)   for the sale or display for sale of motor vehicles[105];
(e)   for a taxi business or for the hire of motor vehicles;
(f)   as a scrap-yard or a yard for the breaking of motor vehicles;
(g)   for the storage or distribution of minerals;

---

[101] TCPSA 1997 s.26(2)(f), as amended; Town and Country Planning (Use Classes) (Scotland) Order 1997 (SI 1997/3061), as amended by the Town and Country Planning (Use Classes) (Scotland) Amendment Order 1998 (SI 1998/1196) art.2. Planning Circular 1/1998, The Town and Country Planning (Use Classes) (Scotland) Order 1997 (Scottish Executive, 1998) explained the changes from the 1989 UCO.
[102] See art.3(3).
[103] *Glasgow DC v Secretary of State for Scotland*, 1985 S.L.T. 19.
[104] TCPSA 1997 s.26(3)(a).
[105] A change of use of a building with a floor area of 235sq m or less from sale and display for sale of motor vehicles to class 1 (shops) does not require planning permission—PDO class 10.

(h)   as a public house[106];

(i)   for any works registrable under the Alkali, etc. Works Regulation Act 1906; or

(j)   for the sale of hot food for consumption off the premises.[107]

Where a single undertaking occupies land on a single site or on adjacent sites which are used for purposes within classes 4 and 5 (business and general industrial), those uses may be treated as if they were in a single class in considering the use of that land, provided this will not result in a substantial increase in the area used for a purpose falling within class 5 (general industrial).[108]

The 11 use classes are:

Class 1: Shops

4.37

(a)   *The retail sale of goods other than hot food;*

(b)   *as a post office;*

(c)   *for the sale of tickets;*

(d)   *as a travel agency;*

(e)   *for the sale of cold food for consumption off the premises;*

(f)   *for hairdressing;*

(g)   *for the direction of funerals;*

(h)   *for the display of goods for sale;*

(i)   *for the hiring out of domestic or personal goods or articles;*

(j)   *as a launderette or dry cleaners; or*

(k)   *for the reception of goods to be washed, cleaned or repaired;*

where the sale, display or service is principally to visiting members of the public.

The retail sale of goods within class 1 includes supermarkets, pharmacies[109] and auction houses,[110] but not bureaux de change.[111] The Scottish Government guidance states that a sandwich bar does not cease to be within class 1 merely because it sells hot drinks, or if a few customers eat on the premises.

The PDO permits change of use of some motor vehicle showrooms and premises falling within class 2 (financial, professional and other services) or class 3 (food and drink) and food takeaways to a class 1 use without planning permission.

Class 2: Financial, professional and other services

Use for the provision of:

4.38

(a)   *financial services;*

(b)   *professional services; or*

(c)   *any other services (including use as a betting office);*

which it is appropriate to provide in a shopping area and where the services are provided principally to visiting members of the public.

---

[106]   Class A4 in England.

[107]   Class A5 in England.

[108]   UCO art.3(4).

[109]   *R. v Maldon DC Ex p. Pattani* [1998] E.G. 135 (C.S.).

[110]   *R. v Kensington and Chelsea RLBC Ex p. Europa Foods Ltd* [1996] E.G. 5 (C.S.).

[111]   *Palisade Investments Ltd v Secretary of State for the Environment* [1994] 3 P.L.R. 49.

Thus a change of use from an estate agency to a betting office will not require planning permission, as both uses fall within class 2. Office uses which do not serve the public directly fall within class 4 (business), to avoid loss of shopfront property. Bureaux de change fall within class 2.[112] A solicitor's office will fall within class 2 where it provides services principally to visiting members of the public, whether or not by prior appointment.[113] Where a solicitor's practice is largely undertaken by telephone and written communication, it may fall within class 4 (see below).

Class 2 only includes uses which are appropriate to provide in a shopping area (the equivalent English use class does not impose this requirement on financial and professional services).

In terms of the PDO, where the established use of a property falls within class 2, no planning permission is required for a change to a use within class 1 (shops). However, in consequence of the perceived desirability of preserving shop units, planning permission will be required for a change of use from class 1 to class 2. The PDO also provides that no permission is required for a change of use from class 3 (food and drink) or hot food takeaway to class 2.

Class 3: Food and drink

Use for the sale of food and drink for consumption on the premises.

___

This class includes restaurants, cafes and snack bars. Previously class 3 also included hot food takeaways. The 1997 UCO now excludes these from class 3 and the other use classes, with the result that a change of use from a restaurant to a hot food takeaway, or vice versa, will require planning permission. However, a restaurant whose trade is primarily in-house dining can operate a minor takeaway without requiring planning permission. Planning permission is required if a cafe is to become a public house.[114] **4.39**

In terms of the PDO, a change of use from class 3 to either class 1 (shops) or class 2 (financial, professional and other services) does not require planning permission. The potential to change from a hot food takeaway to class 1 or class 2 is also preserved by the PDO, notwithstanding that a hot food takeaway no longer falls within class 3.

Class 4: Business

(a) *As an office, other than a use within class 2 (financial, professional and other services);* **4.40**

(b) *for research and development of products or processes;*

(c) *for any industrial process;*

being a use which can be carried on in any residential area without detriment to the amenity of that area by reason of noise, vibration, smell, fumes, smoke, soot, ash, dust or grit.

___

This combines non-class 2 office use and non-class 5 industrial use, often described as light industry.

___

[112] *Palisade Investments Ltd v Secretary of State for the Environment* [1994] 3 P.L.R. 49.

[113] *Kalra v Secretary of State for the Environment* [1996] 1 P.L.R. 37.

[114] See UCO art.3(5).

The Scottish Government guidance indicates that there is neither a requirement for a class 4 building to be located in a residential area, nor for it to be physically capable of accommodating all the uses within the class. An application for a use within class 4 should not be refused permission on the grounds that the land is allocated for class 4 as a whole, or for a different use within the class, unless such a refusal would accord with development plan policy. The presumption against the use of planning conditions or agreements to limit future changes of use permitted by the UCO or PDO applies with particular force to class 4.

Even if the building satisfies the residential amenity test in class 4, planning permission can still be refused on the grounds of traffic generation, design, density, loss of mature trees, and so on. If the intensification of the use leads to the development no longer satisfying the residential amenity test, the use is no longer a class 4 use, with the result that there has been a material change of use requiring planning permission.

The flexibility of this class is increased by the permitted changes of use under the PDO from classes 5 (general industrial) and 6 (storage or distribution) to class 4. In addition, no permission is required for a change of use from class 4 to class 6 (storage or distribution) provided the floor area involved does not exceed 235sq m.

Class 5: General industrial

Use for the carrying on of an industrial process other than one falling within class 4 (business).

4.41   Class 5 includes the processes falling within the special industrial use classes, classes 7–10 of the previous UCO. The other legislation applying to these processes is considered sufficiently comprehensive to control potential pollution.

The PDO permits a change of use from class 5 to class 4 (business). A change to class 6 (storage and distribution) is also competent without permission provided the floor area involved does not exceed 235sq m.

Class 6: Storage or distribution (previously class 11)

Use for storage or as a distribution centre.

4.42   An established class 6 use holds the potential of a change without permission to the flexible class 4 (business).

Class 7: Hotels and hostels (previously class 12)

Use as a hotel, boarding house, guest house, or hostel where no significant element of care is provided, other than premises licensed for the sale of alcoholic liquor to persons other than residents or to persons other than persons consuming meals on the premises and other than a use within class 9 (houses).

4.43   No planning permission is required to change a nurses' home to a hotel use, despite such planning consequences as increased traffic, especially buses and taxis, with resultant parking difficulties, and increased cooking smells. The reference to the sale of alcoholic liquor excludes public house uses from class 7 (public houses are completely excluded from the UCO).

Class 8: Residential institutions (previously class 13)

Use:

(a) *for the provision of residential accommodation and care to people in need of care other than a use within class 9 (houses);*   **4.44**

(b) *as a hospital or nursing home;*

(c) *as a residential school, college or training centre.*

____

The Scottish Government guidance directs planning authorities to concentrate on land-use planning considerations when considering a planning application for a change of use to a use within class 8. It explains that private and voluntary residential care homes have to register with the local authority where they provide a substantial amount of care or support. Planning authorities should therefore concern themselves mainly with the impact of a proposed institution on amenity and the environment.

Class 8A: Secure residential institutions

Use for the provision of secure residential accommodation, including use as a prison, young offenders institution, detention centre, secure training centre, custody centre, short-term holding centre, secure hospital, secure local authority accommodation or use as military barracks.   **4.44A**

Class 9: Houses (previously class 14)[115]

Use:

(a) *as a house, other than as a flat, whether or not as a sole or main residence, by:*   **4.45**

    (i)   *a single person or by people living together as a family; or*

    (ii) *not more than five residents living together including a household where care is provided for residents;*

(b) *as a bed and breakfast establishment or guesthouse (not in either case being carried out in a flat), where at any one time not more than two bedrooms are, or in the case of premises having less than four bedrooms one bedroom is, used for that purpose.*

____

Working at home may involve a change of use of part of the dwellinghouse to use for business purposes. However, planning permission will not be required if the overall character of the use as a residence is unchanged. Factors such as increased visitors and deliveries will be relevant. A change of use to multiple occupancy involving more than five residents who are not members of a family will require

---

[115] The English Class C3 does not exclude flats, and refers to "not more than six residents…". The English Class C4 deals with houses in multiple occupation.

planning permission.[116] The courts have also held that a dwellinghouse does not necessarily cease to be used as such because it is managed for the commercial purposes of holiday or other temporary lets.[117]

The Scottish Government guidance explains that the single household concept provides more certainty over the planning position of small group homes, which play a major role in the Government's community care policy. Any resident care staff should be included in the calculation of the number of people accommodated. The class also includes groups of people such as students who live on a communal basis as a single household.

The 1997 UCO extends this class to include limited use as a bed and breakfast or guest house.

Class 10: Non-residential institutions (previously class 15)

Use, not including residential use:

4.46
    (a) *as a crèche, day nursery or day centre;*
    (b) *for the provision of education;*
    (c) *for the display of works of art (otherwise than for sale or hire);*
    (d) *as a museum;*
    (e) *as a public library or public reading room;*
    (f) *as a public hall or exhibition hall;*
    (g) *for, or in connection with, public worship or religious instructions, or the social or recreational activities of a religious body; or*
    (h) *as a law court.*

Class 11: Assembly and leisure (previously class 16)

Use as a:

4.47
    (a) *cinema;*
    (b) *concert hall;*
    (c) *bingo hall or casino;*
    (d) *dance hall or discotheque; or*
    (e) *swimming bath, skating rink, gymnasium or area for other indoor or outdoor sports or recreation, not involving motorised vehicles or firearms.*

DETERMINATION WHETHER PLANNING PERMISSION REQUIRED: CERTIFICATES OF LAWFULNESS OF USE OR DEVELOPMENT

4.48
With the lack of a precise definition of "development", it is often unclear whether planning permission is necessary for an operation or change of use. Such difficulties can be resolved by obtaining a formal determination from the planning authority, either in advance of the development or following its completion.

Determinations are given in the form of certificates of lawfulness of use or development.[118] The applicant for a certificate must provide the planning authority with the information to reach its decision. The procedure cannot be used as a "fish-

---

[116] Planning Circular 2/2012, Houses in Multiple Occupation: Guidance on Planning Control and Licensing (Scottish Government, 2012).
[117] *Moore v Secretary of State* [2012] EWCA Civ 1202.
[118] TCPSA ss.150–155 and Town and Country Planning (Development Management Procedure)

ing expedition" to obtain information from the planning authority on existing lawful uses or development, or an indication of what classes of use or development
would be lawful.

This procedure would seem to remove the possibility of arguing that a written
statement by an officer is a formal determination even although no formal application had been made for such a determination. It is a well-established principle that
statements by planning officers cannot bind the planning authority. Notwithstanding a statement by a planning officer that planning permission is not required for
proposed work, the planning authority may take enforcement action against the
work on the grounds that permission was required (see Ch.7 below). Under the
certificate procedure the only way to prevent such enforcement action is to apply
for a certificate.

A certificate of lawfulness of proposed use or development (CLOPUD) will be
issued if the planning authority is satisfied that the use or operations would be lawful (presumably by reference to statute, the PDO or UCO, and case law) if begun
at the time of the application. There is an irrefutable presumption that the use or
operations specified in the certificate are lawful, unless the law changes before the
use or operations are begun.

4.49

The certificate of lawfulness of existing use or development (CLEUD) is a
determination of the lawfulness of either any existing use of land or building, or any
operations which have been carried out, or any failure to comply with a condition
or limitation attached to a grant of planning permission. The lawfulness of any use
or development specified in the certificate is conclusively presumed. For the first
time this enables a statutory document to be obtained certifying the lawfulness of
existing operational development or use as a single dwellinghouse.

A use or operation is lawful if it is immune from enforcement action (see Ch.7
below) and is not in contravention of the requirements of any enforcement notice
or breach of condition notice which is in force (this removes the concept of
established or immune development). Once the lawfulness of a use or operation has
been certified, that use or operation enjoys the permitted development rights
conferred by the PDO.[119]

Any person (not just the owner of the land) may apply to the planning authority
for a certificate of lawfulness of proposed/existing use or development. There is no
requirement to give notice to persons with an interest in the land which is the subject
of the application, or neighbours. The planning authority is not obliged to publicise
the application. Owners/tenants/neighbours/other interested parties will therefore
not be alerted to the application unless they routinely inspect the planning register
in which details of the application will be entered. Although the planning authority is not required to consult interested parties, it may choose to do so.

The application must be in writing and specify:

(a) the land and describe the use, operations or other matter in question;
(b) the paragraph of ss.150(1) or 151(1) under which the application is made;
(c) depending on which of those paragraphs applies, the date on which the use,
     operations or other matter began or, in the case of operations carried out

---

(Scotland) Regulations 2013 (SSI 2013/155) regs 42–46. Guidance is given in Planning Circular 10/
2009, Planning Enforcement, Annex F. Section 51 determinations and established use certificates
granted prior to 25 September 1992 remain valid.

[119] Following revocation of art.2(3) of the PDO by the Town and Country Planning (General Permitted Development) (Scotland) Amendment No.2 Order (SI 1992/2084).

without planning permission, the date on which the operations were substantially completed; the name of any use class which the applicant considers applicable to the existing use (see para.4.35 above); sufficient details of the relevant planning permission to enable it to be identified; the use of the land at the date of the application (or, when the land is not in use at that date, the purpose for which it was last used) and the name of any use class which the applicant considers applicable to the proposed use;

(d) the applicant's reasons, if any, for regarding the use, operations or other matter described in the application as lawful; and

(e) such other information as the applicant considers to be relevant to the application.

The application must also be accompanied by a plan identifying the land to which the application relates, and such evidence verifying the information included in the application as the applicant can provide. There must also be a statement setting out the applicant's interest in the land, the name and address of any other person known to the applicant to have an interest in the land and whether any such other person has been notified of the application.

4.50   On receipt of the application and any fee payable, the planning authority must send the applicant an acknowledgment of the application as soon as reasonably practicable. The authority must give the applicant written notice of their decision on the application within two months beginning with the date of receipt of the application and fee. If no decision is issued within that time period, the applicant may appeal to the Scottish Ministers against a deemed refusal (see below).

If, after sending the acknowledgement, the planning authority consider that the application is invalid by reason of the failure to comply with any statutory requirement, they must notify the applicant that the application is invalid as soon as practicable (not "reasonably practicable").

The planning authority may by notice in writing require the applicant to provide such further information as may be specified to enable them to deal with the application.

The onus is on the applicant to provide sufficient information of the lawfulness to satisfy the planning authority, but not to prove the lawfulness beyond reasonable doubt. Corroboration of the applicant's evidence does not appear to be required. If there is no evidence to contradict or cast doubt upon the applicant's evidence, the Scottish Government advises that the application should not be refused, provided the evidence is sufficiently precise and unambiguous to justify the grant of a certificate on the balance of probability.[120] This leaves open the question of whether it is ever competent for the planning authority to adopt an active role to seek out information to rebut the applicant's evidence.

It is an offence either knowingly or recklessly to make a statement which is false or misleading in a material particular or, with intent to deceive, to use any document which is false or misleading in a material particular, or to withhold material information. The planning authority may revoke a certificate without compensation if a statement was made or a document used which was false in a material particular or any material information was withheld. The possibility of revocation without compensation will limit the value of a certificate to any subsequent owner of the land. However, before revoking a certificate, the authority must give notice

---

[120] Planning Circular 10/2009, Planning Enforcement, Annex F, para.21.

of the proposed revocation to the owner of the land affected, the occupier, and any other person who will in their opinion be affected by the revocation. If the certificate was issued by the Scottish Ministers, notice must be served on them. The notice invites the recipient to make representations on the proposal to the authority within 14 days of service of the notice.

The origin and identity of the applicant, and the planning merits of the use or development have no relevance to the legal issues involved in the determination of the application. As a result, it may be appropriate for determination of such applications to be delegated to planning officers rather than left in the hands of the councillors sitting on the planning committee.

If sufficient information is provided, the authority will issue a certificate which **4.51** shall conclusively presume the lawfulness of any use, operations or other matters specified in the certificate. For the purposes of certain statutes, the certificate will have effect as if it were a grant of permission. A refusal is not conclusive evidence that the use or development is unlawful and will not preclude a further application based on new evidence.

There is a prescribed form for a certificate.[121] As the effect of a certificate is similar to a grant of planning permission, the authority will require to specify precisely the description of the use or development and the boundaries of the site, to avoid giving permission for more than is intended. The authority may modify the description of the use, operation or other matter specified in the application, presumably to avoid refusing the application. An aggrieved person could seek judicial review of the decision to issue a certificate, on the grounds that its terms are wider than the existing use.[122]

Where an application is refused in whole or in part (including a case in which the authority modify the description of the use, operations or other matter in the application, or substitute an alternative description for that description), the notice of decision must be in writing and state the reasons for the decision, and include a statement that the applicant can appeal to the Scottish Ministers.

The applicant has a right of appeal to the Scottish Ministers against a refusal or part refusal to issue a certificate. There is also a right of appeal against a failure to determine an application within the two-month time limit.[123] The notice of appeal must be submitted within three months from the date of the decision, or in a deemed refusal appeal, three months from the expiry of the two-month time limit for making the decision.[124] The normal appeal procedures apply (see Ch.8 below). The appeal is decided by a reporter.[125]

The decision of the Scottish Ministers on appeal may be challenged in the Court of Session (see Ch.8 below).[126] However, such a challenge is limited to allegations that they acted illegally and their decision on the facts is final.

---

[121] Town and Country Planning (Development Management Procedure) (Scotland) Regulations 2013 (SSI 2013/155) reg.44 and Sch.8.

[122] *R. v Sheffield City Council Ex p. Power* [1994] E.G. 101 (C.S.).

[123] TCPSA 1997 s.154(1)(b) and Town and Country Planning (Development Management Procedure) (Scotland) Regulations 2013 (SSI 2013/155) reg.44(4).

[124] Town and Country Planning (Appeals) (Scotland) Regulations 2013 (SSI 2013/156) reg.23.

[125] Town and Country Planning (Determination of Appeals by Appointed Persons) (Prescribed Classes) (Scotland) Regulations 2010 (SSI 2010/467) reg.3(h).

[126] For example, *East Dunbartonshire Council v Secretary of State for Scotland*, 1998 G.W.D. 40-2079; 1999 71 S.P.E.L. 16; *William Tracey Ltd v Scottish Ministers*, 2005 S.L.T. 191; *Cartledge v Scottish Ministers* [2011] CSIH 23.

CHAPTER 5

DEVELOPMENT MANAGEMENT II—APPLYING FOR PLANNING PERMISSION

If planning permission is required for a proposed development, an application for **5.01** that permission must be made to the planning authority for the district in which the development site is located. When applying for planning permission it is easy to fall into the trap of treating the planning authority as the "enemy" to whom information should only be given as a last resort. In reality they fulfil a valuable consultative role. All but the simplest of applications for planning permission should be discussed in advance with the planning officer responsible for the area in which the development site lies. Although any indications given by the officer cannot dictate the decision eventually reached by the planning committee on the application, careful consideration should be given to his comments regarding relevant policies and possible alterations to the proposals to make the application more likely to be awarded permission. No fee can be charged for this service.[1]

The general rules governing the procedure for applying for planning permission are contained in the Development Management Procedure Regulations (DMPR).[2] In addition to these rules, each planning authority has its own internal procedures for handling planning applications.

Significant changes to development management procedures were introduced in 2009. The creation of a hierarchy of development provides a means for adopting a more proportionate approach to handling applications, responsive to different types of development proposal. National and major developments require pre-application consultation with the community and may be subject to further enhanced scrutiny before being determined. Local developments can be delegated to officers for decision.

---

[1] *R. v Richmond upon Thames LBC Ex p. McCarthy & Stone (Developments) Ltd* [1991] 3 W.L.R. 941; 1992 35 S.P.L.P. 22.

[2] Town and Country Planning (Development Management Procedure) (Scotland) Regulations 2013 (SSI 2013/155) (DMPR). Regulation 2 indicates when the Regulations apply to applications for planning permission for the operation of marine fish farms.

Fig.5.1 Deemed refusals

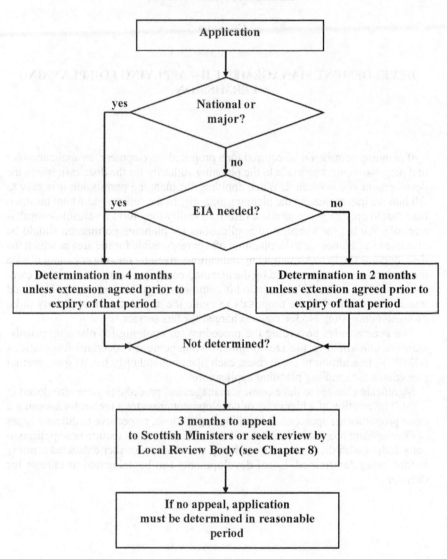

Reproduced by permission of Brodies LLP.

TIME LIMITS FOR DETERMINING APPLICATION FOR PLANNING PERMISSION

5.02 Although the statutory provisions impose a time limit for planning applications to be decided, applications can remain undetermined for many months or even years after the expiry of the time limit. That is because the application does not automatically expire at the end of the specified time period. Instead the applicant is given the opportunity to submit an appeal/application for review against a deemed refusal of permission. If there are still issues requiring resolution, often an applicant will decide not to submit such an appeal/review but instead continue to work with the planning authority towards resolving those issues, rather than pursue an appeal/ review which might have poor prospects of success unless and until the unresolved issues are addressed.

The planning authority must give notice to the applicant of their decision on the planning application within a specified time: for national and major developments, and for developments which require environmental impact assessment[3]— four months; for other developments—two months (fig.5.1).[4]

If the planning authority fail to determine the application within the specified time limit, the remedy for the applicant is to appeal/seek review against a deemed refusal (see Ch.8 below). If the applicant does not appeal/seek review, the planning authority can continue to process and ultimately decide the application. However, the timing of the decision on the planning application is in the hands of the planning authority. If the authority are reluctant to decide the application, e.g. if there is disagreement over the amount of information required to resolve a matter, a deemed refusal/review might be the only way of bringing the matter to a head. If the time limit for a deemed refusal/review has expired, the applicant might have to pursue court action to have the application decided.[5]

The applicant and planning authority can agree in writing to an extension of the period for determining the planning application, provided the extension is agreed prior to the expiry of the initial two or four month period.[6] This may form part of the processing agreement (see para.5.13 below). There is no right of deemed refusal appeal until the expiry of that extended period.

TYPES OF APPLICATION

Before applying for planning permission, a decision has to be made on the type of permission to be sought, as this must be indicated on the application form. This decision will be influenced by the nature of the proposed development, the planning history of the site and, to some extent, the attitude of the planning authority as indicated in pre-application consultations (see above).

5.03

(a) Full or detailed planning permission

The terms "full" or "detailed" planning permission do not appear in the Town and Country Planning (Scotland) Act 1997 (TCPSA), but are used interchangeably in practice to highlight the difference between what the Act refers to as "planning permission" and "planning permission in principle" (previously "outline planning permission"). An application for full or detailed planning permission is appropriate where the applicant has decided all or most of the details of the proposed development and these details can be submitted to the planning author-

5.04

---

[3] Town and Country Planning (Environmental Impact Assessment) (Scotland) Regulations 2011 (SSI 2011/139) reg. 44, as amended by Town and Country Planning (Miscellaneous Amendments) (Scotland) Regulations 2015 (SSI 2015/249).

[4] DMPR 2013 (SSI 2013/155) reg.26.

[5] For example, *Lafarge Aggregates Ltd v Scottish Ministers*, 2004 S.C. 524.

[6] TCPSA 1997 s.47(2). The judgment in *Vattenfall Wind Power Ltd v Scottish Ministers*, 2009 S.L.T. 516 is poorly drafted, but appears to require the extension to be agreed prior to the expiry of the specified time period. Since 2013 there is power to extend the time limit for an application to be determined by a planning officer in terms of the s.43A scheme of delegation—DMPR 2013 (SSI 2013/155) reg.26(3).

ity for its approval. If that approval is given, the development can proceed and be completed without further applications to the authority, unless permission is needed to change some of the details of the development or the permission is subject to a condition requiring the approval of the authority for some further matter. It is competent for permission to be granted in detail for part of the development and in principle for the remainder, for example where details of roadworks have been approved but the only information submitted relating to the proposed foodstore is the footprint within which it is to be built.[7]

(b) Planning permission in principle

5.05 Since 2009, applications are made for planning permission in principle, which replaces the former concept of outline planning permissions.[8] It is competent for planning permission in principle to be granted for the carrying out of any development except a material change of use (see Ch.4 above).

Planning permission in principle is sought when the applicant wishes to obtain consent to the outlines or principle of the development before drawing up a detailed scheme, thereby saving the expense of that work if permission is not granted. Following a grant of planning permission in principle, a further application(s) must be made to the authority for its approval of the detailed scheme, in compliance with the condition imposed upon every grant of planning permission in principle requiring subsequent approval to be obtained from the planning authority for specified areas of detail (previously known as reserved matters).

Where it is intended to sell land with the benefit of permission (the grant of permission will normally increase the value of the land and therefore its sale price), it is often advisable to obtain planning permission in principle rather than detailed planning permission. A grant of planning permission in principle provides a guarantee that the broad outlines of the development have been approved, leaving the purchaser free to draw up detailed proposals to his own requirements and obtain approval by submitting a further application.

An application for planning permission in principle necessarily contains less detail than an application for detailed permission. It does not require plans and drawings, other than a location plan; does not require a design or design and access statement; but requires to describe the location of the access points to the development from a road.[9] No design statement is required (see para.5.22 below). Further details and information can be requested from the applicant.[10] The existence of uncertainties regarding matters such as noise do not necessarily prevent a grant of planning permission in principle.[11]

In a pre-2009 case, an outline application which specified the floor area committed those concerned to a development on that scale, subject to minimal adjustments for siting, design and external appearance.[12] Accordingly, matters such as traffic generation could not be reassessed during the determination of the applica-

---

[7] *Lothian Borders and Angus Co-operative Society Ltd v Scottish Borders Council*, 1999 G.W.D. 6–316.

[8] TCPSA 1997 s.59.

[9] DMPR 2013 (SSI 2013/155) reg.10; Planning Circular 3/2013, Development Management Procedures (Scottish Government, 2013).

[10] DMPR 2013 (SSI 2013/155) reg.24.

[11] *R. v Northampton BC Ex p. Rice & Co* [1998] E.G. 84 (C.S.).

[12] *R. v Newbury DC Ex p. Chieveley Parish Council* [1998] E.G. 131 (C.S.); *The Times,* 10 September 1998.

tion for approval of reserved matters. A similar approach is likely to be taken post-2009.

The application(s)[13] for further approval must be submitted within three years from the date the planning permission in principle was granted, or six months from the date any earlier application for approval was refused, or six months from the date of the dismissal of an appeal against such a refusal,[14] whichever is the latest. However, the planning authority may attach a direction to the planning permission in principle substituting longer or shorter periods, or specify separate periods for separate parts or phases of the development.[15]

(c) Approval of matters specified in conditions

There is a separate procedure for applying to the planning authority for approval, consent or agreement required by a condition imposed on a grant of planning permission in principle.[16]   **5.06**

Prior to 2009 these specified matters were known as "reserved matters", which could be any matters concerning the siting, design or external appearance of a building, or its means of access, or the landscaping of the application site, in respect of which details were not given in the application for outline planning permission.[17] Since 2009, there is no restriction on which matters can be reserved for further approval.

The application must be in writing and identify the planning permission to which it relates. It must also contain a description of the matter in respect of which the application is made, and state the name and address of the applicant and any agent. Where it relates to the alteration or construction of buildings, other structures or roads or to landscaping, plans and drawings must be submitted describing the matter in respect of which the application is made.[18]

Pre-2009, the details submitted, and the reserved matters approval granted, could not depart from the ambit of the outline planning permission. For example, a reserved matters application could not be refused on the grounds that the design provided more office floor space than was needed to make the class 4 development viable.[19] Where an office building had been erected on part of a site for which outline planning permission had been granted for five houses, the subsequent application for approval of reserved matters was held not to be in accordance with the outline permission, as the entire development authorised by the outline permission could not be constructed with the generous plots envisaged in that permission.[20] Since 2009 the statutory provisions do not contain a similar prohibition on depart-

---

[13]   The Scottish Government guidance advises that the time limits only apply to conditions which require approval to be obtained before development can begin—Planning Circular 3/2013, Development Management Procedures, para.4.109.

[14]   Including an application for review of a refusal (see Ch.8 below)—TCPSA s.59(2)(a), amended by Planning Etc (Scotland) Act 2006 (Supplementary and Consequential Provisions) Order 2013 (SSI 2013/26) art.2(5).

[15]   TCPSA 1997 s.59(2)–(5). See guidance in Planning Circular 3/2013, Development Management Procedures, Annex H.

[16]   TCPSA 1997 s.59(1)(b) and DMPR 2013 (SSI 2013/155) reg.12.

[17]   Court decisions on the scope of "reserved matters" include *R. v Newbury DC Ex p. Chieveley Parish Council* [1998] E.G. 131 (C.S.); *Inverclyde DC v Inverkip Building Co*, 1983 S.L.T. 563; *Tesco Stores Ltd v North Norfolk DC* [1999] J.P.L. 920.

[18]   DMPR 2013 (SSI 2013/155) reg.12.

[19]   *Camden LBC v Secretary of State for the Environment* [1993] J.P.L. 466.

[20]   *Orbit Development v Secretary of State for the Environment* [1996] E.G. 91 (C.S.).

ing from the ambit of the planning permission in principle, but the concept of the planning permission in principle is sufficiently similar to outline permissions that it is likely that a similar approach will be taken.

The application[21] must be submitted (but need not be granted) within three years from the date permission was granted, or six months from the date any earlier application for approval was refused, or six months from the date of the dismissal of an appeal against such a refusal,[22] whichever is the latest, unless the planning permission in principle specifies a different period.[23] Moreover, in relation to any matter, only one application may be made after three years from the date permission was granted. However, submission of an application in respect of some, but not all, of the matters specified by the condition, or for part only of the site, within the time limit does not enable further applications to be submitted after the time limit has expired.[24]

An application for approval does not require to comply with all the procedural requirements which apply to applications for full planning permission or planning permission in principle.[25] The following requirements do not appear to apply: notification of owners and agricultural tenants; pre-application consultation; design and access statements; and holding of pre-determination hearings. Applications for approval are regulated by s.43A schemes of delegation (see para.5.37 below). In the absence of any specific reference to applications for approval of matters specified in conditions, it appears there is no requirement for planning authorities to notify the Scottish Ministers of their intention to grant such applications (see "Notification" below).

(d) Variation of planning permission

5.07   An applicant may request the planning authority to vary the grant of planning permission. Such variation is competent provided it appears to the authority that the change sought is not material.[26] This allows minor changes to be made to the details of a development without the submission of a fresh application for planning permission. As the change is not material, the normal requirements for an application, such as notification of parties, do not apply.

If the variation is material, a fresh application for planning permission has to be submitted. Although the description of development may refer to the variation, if the application is granted, there are two permissions: the original permission and the varied permission.

(e) Retrospective planning permission

5.08   As a result of the complex rules governing when planning permission is required (see Ch.4 above), as well as public ignorance, it is inevitable that development is

---

21 The Scottish Government guidance advises that the time limits only apply to conditions which require approval to be obtained before development can begin—Planning Circular 3/2013, Development Management Procedures, para.4.109.

22 Including an application for review of a refusal (see Ch.8 below)—TCPSA s.59(2)(a), amended by Planning Etc (Scotland) Act 2006 (Supplementary and Consequential Provisions) Order 2013 (SSI 2013/26) art.2(5).

23 TCPSA 1997 s.59(2)–(5). See guidance in Planning Circular 3/2013, Development Management Procedures, Annex H.

24 *Hunterston Development Co Ltd v Secretary of State for Scotland*, 1992 S.L.T. 1097.

25 Planning Circular 3/2013, Development Management Procedures, para.3.13.

26 TCPSA 1997 s.64.

sometimes carried out without planning permission. Often the omission only comes to light during the sale of land or buildings, or when the planning authority takes enforcement action (see Ch.7 below). In these circumstances an application may be made for permission for development already carried out, more commonly known as retrospective planning permission.[27] The procedure for submitting such an application is similar to that for an application for full planning permission. If permission is granted, it will have retrospective effect from the date on which the work or use began, unless an enforcement notice was issued before the date of the application. This procedure may also be used where development has been carried out in breach of a condition attached to a planning permission, or has not ceased on the expiry of a temporary planning permission (see para.5.82 below).

(f) Renewal of permission

The permission is implemented by commencing the development prior to the expiry of the time limit (see "Duration" at para.5.97 below).

5.09

If commencement of development is not possible or desirable, an application can be submitted for renewal of the permission. This application, referred to in TCPSA 1997 as a "further application",[28] must be submitted prior to the expiry of the time limit for the commencement of development and, for a planning permission in principle, also the time limit for submission of matters for approval. It appears that the application is determined as if it were a fresh planning application. The Scottish Government guidance on the previous statutory provisions advises that as a general rule such applications should be refused only where there has been some material change in planning circumstances since the original permission was granted, or there is likely to be continued failure to begin the development and this will contribute unacceptably to uncertainty about the future pattern of development in the area, or the application is premature because the permission still has a reasonable time to run.[29]

For the renewal application, the main requirements are that the application be made in writing and identify the previous grant of permission, and that owners and agricultural tenants of the application site be notified.

Previously, the other option was to apply for variation of the time limit condition.[30] However, since 2009 time limits are no longer imposed by condition, so this option will only apply to earlier permissions.

(g) Duplicate applications: twin tracking

Where problems in obtaining permission are anticipated, the applicant can submit two applications in exactly the same terms. The submission of duplicate applications allows an appeal/review to be lodged against the deemed refusal (see para.5.78 below) of one application while negotiations continue with the planning authority with a view to permission being granted for the other application.

5.10

A similar practice involves the submission of a fresh application for the same

---

[27] TCPSA 1997 s.33. The planning authority has power to issue a notice under s.33A requiring a retrospective application to be made.

[28] DMPR 2013 (SSI 2013/155) reg.11.

[29] Planning Circular 4/1998, The Use of Conditions in Planning Permission (Scottish Office, 1998), Annex, para.52.

[30] TCPSA 1997 s.42; DMPR 2013 (SSI 2013/155) reg.11.

development when an appeal/review is lodged in respect of the original application. In most such cases, no fee is payable in respect of the duplicate application provided it is submitted within 12 months. The appeal/review decision may be a material consideration which the authority must take into account when deciding the application (see below). One option available to the planning authority is to refuse the application as premature until the appeal/review has been decided.

(h) Permission to develop land without compliance with condition

5.11   An application can be made to the planning authority for permission to develop the site without complying with the conditions subject to which the permission was granted.[31] In effect, this is an application to vary a planning condition(s).

Hierarchy of Developments

5.12   An important change introduced in 2009 is the hierarchy of developments, which classifies developments into three categories: national, major and local.[32] This enables different procedural requirements to be specified depending on the scale and significance of the development. For example:

- processing agreements are encouraged for national and major developments;
- planning applications for national and major developments have to be determined within four months, and two months for local developments (unless environmental impact assessment (EIA) is required);
- pre-application consultation is required for national and major developments;
- design and access statements are required for national and major developments (with exceptions—see para.5.22 below);
- pre-determination hearings are required for national developments, and major developments which are significantly contrary to the development plan;
- the full council, and not a committee, must decide applications for national developments, and major developments which are significantly contrary to the development plan;
- site notices must be displayed during national and major developments (and also bad neighbour developments);
- the right of appeal to the Scottish Ministers has been removed for planning applications for local developments determined by officers under s.43A delegated powers, and replaced by the right to apply to the local review body for review of the officer's decision (see Ch.8 below).

National developments:

Are developments designated as national developments in the National Planning Framework (NPF) (see Ch.3 above).[33]

---

[31] TCPSA 1997 s.42; DMPR 2013 (SSI 2013/155) reg.11. Planning Circular 3/2013, Development Management Procedures, Annex I. See Ch.6 below.
[32] TCPSA 1997 s.26A.
[33] TCPSA 1997 s.3A(4)(b).

Major developments:

Are identified using the table in the regulations.[34] Column 1 describes classes of development, and col.2 indicates the threshold or criterion beyond which the development is major. For example, housing is major development where the development comprises 50 or more dwellings, or the area of the site is or exceeds 2 hectares. The thresholds and criteria are the same for all parts of Scotland, despite larger developments being of more significance outside of the cities. There are no anti-avoidance provisions, so the size of developments specified in planning applications can be increased or lowered depending on whether or not the applicant wants it to be a major development, for example, the development can be split into phases, with each phase being the subject of a separate application.

Local developments:

Are all developments which are not national or major developments.[35]

PROCESSING AGREEMENTS

Although there are no statutory provisions relating to processing agreements, the Government encourages the use of these agreements with planning applications for national and major developments, to provide greater clarity about the timescales and processes that will take place before a determination is made on these proposals.[36]   **5.13**

A processing agreement is essentially a framework for project managing a complex planning application. The key objective is to establish a realistic timetable for processing which takes account of the information which needs to be considered and the process to determine the application. The Government have indicated that the pre-application stage will be the most appropriate point to conclude the terms of a processing agreement.

In the absence of statutory provisions, use of processing agreements is a matter for the parties involved to decide. However, where there is a processing agreement in place there will be no right to appeal against non-determination until the expiry of the period in the agreement (see Ch.8 below).

PRE-APPLICATION CONSULTATION

In 2009 a requirement was introduced for pre-application consultation with the local community to be carried out by applicants for national and major developments (para.5.12).[37] The importance of this new procedure is emphasised by the requirement that the planning authority decline to determine the application if, in their opinion, there has not been compliance with the pre-application consultation requirements.[38] The statutory right of appeal does not appear to extend to such a   **5.14**

---

[34]   Town and Country Planning (Hierarchy of Developments) (Scotland) Regulations 2009 (SSI 2009/51) reg.2(1), Schedule.

[35]   Town and Country Planning (Hierarchy of Developments) (Scotland) Regulations 2009 (SSI 2009/51) reg.2(2).

[36]   Planning Circular 3/2013, Development Management Procedures, paras 2.3–2.5 and 6.1–6.11.

[37]   TCPSA 1997 ss.35A–C; DMPR 2013 (SSI 2013/155) regs 4–7. Planning Advice Note (PAN) 3/2010, Community Engagement (Scottish Government, 2010).

[38]   TCPSA 1997 s.39(1A).

decision to decline to determine the application,[39] so the only means of challenge may be judicial review (see Ch.8 below).

There is no requirement for pre-application consultation for s.42 applications (permission to develop land without compliance with condition).[40]

The purposes of this consultation is to improve the quality of planning applications, mitigate negative impacts where possible, address misunderstandings, and air and deal with any community issues that can be tackled. However, the applicant is not required to take onboard community views or directly reflect them in any subsequent application. Moreover, this consultation process does not remove the right to object to the planning application or submit representations on it.[41]

If there is uncertainty whether the requirement applies, the applicant can submit a screening notice to the planning authority, requiring the authority to state whether or not in their opinion the development falls within these classes of development. The screening notice must contain a description in general terms of the development; the postal address of the site (if any); a plan showing the outline of the site sufficient to identify that site; and details as to how the applicant may be contacted and corresponded with. It must also contain a statement as to whether or not the planning authority have adopted a screening opinion relating to EIA of the development or the Scottish Ministers have made a screening direction.

If the planning authority respond by stating that pre-application consultation is not required, any application for planning permission submitted within 12 months after the notice was given does not require pre-application consultation, provided the development does not differ materially from the information contained in the notice. The underlying purpose of the screening notice is to obtain certainty whether or not the 12 week pre-application period applies to the proposed development. The planning authority must provide the requisite statement within 21 days, unless the authority require further information from the applicant.

If the development requires pre-application consultation, the applicant must give a proposal of application notice to the planning authority at least 12 weeks before submitting the planning application. The applicant must also give a copy of the notice to every community council whose area includes or adjoins the application site. The planning authority can also require copies to be given to other persons.

The proposal of application notice must contain a description in general terms of the development; the postal address of the site (if any); a plan showing the outline of the site sufficient to identify that site; and details as to how the applicant may be contacted and corresponded with. It must also contain an account of what consultation the applicant intends to undertake, when such consultation is to take place, with whom and what form it will take. There is a requirement to consult every community council whose area includes or adjoins the application site. The applicant must also hold at least one public event where members of the public may make comments to the applicant as regards the proposed development. The applicant must also publish in a local newspaper a notice containing a description of and the location of the proposed development; details of where further information may be obtained concerning the proposed development; the date and place of the public event; and a statement explaining how, and by when, persons can make comments

---

[39] TCPSA 1997 s.47(1) does not mention an exercise of the s.39 power. Subsection (2) provides that a deemed refusal appeal can be submitted if the s.39 power has not been exercised.

[40] TCPSA 1997 s.35A(1A), added by Public Services Reform (Planning) (Pre-application consultation) (Scotland) Order 2013 (SSI 2013/25).

[41] Planning Circular 3/2013, Development Management Procedures, para.2.7.

to the applicant. The notice also has to state that comments made to the applicant are not representations to the planning authority and if a planning application is submitted there will be an opportunity to make representations to the planning authority.

While the Government acknowledge that there is scope for proposals to alter between pre-application consultation and the application being submitted, the application needs to be recognisably linked to what was described in the proposal of application notice. Both applicants and planning authorities need to be aware of potentially creating a situation where a very detailed or narrow descriptive content in the proposal of application notice means that relatively minor changes could trigger the need to repeat pre-application consultation.[42]

In response to the proposal of application notice, the planning authority may within 21 days notify the applicant that additional consultation must be undertaken, specifying what form that consultation is to take. In considering whether to require additional consultation, the authority are to have regard to the nature, extent and location of the proposed development and to the likely effects, at and in the vicinity of that location, of its being carried out. The Government state that additional consultation requirements should be proportionate, specific and reasonable in the circumstances.[43] There is no specific appeal mechanism to challenge any requirement for additional consultation, so the only means of challenge may be to petition the Court of Session for judicial review (see Ch.8 below).[44]

If pre-application consultation is required, the applicant must submit a pre-application consultation report, indicating what has been done to effect compliance with the requirements.[45] Although the statutory provisions state that a pre-application consultation report is to be in such form as may be prescribed, no form has been prescribed. The applicant is under no obligation to take on board community views, or directly reflect them in the application.[46]

The Scottish Government suggest that as a minimum the pre-application consultation report should specify who has been consulted; set out what steps were taken to comply with the statutory requirements and those of the planning authority; set out how the applicant has responded to the comments made, including whether and the extent to which the proposals have changed as a result of the consultation; provide appropriate evidence that the various prescribed steps have been undertaken, e.g. copies of advertisements of the public events and reference to material made available at such events; and demonstrate that steps were taken to explain the nature of pre-application consultation, i.e. that it does not replace the application process whereby representations can be made to the planning authority.[47]

---

[42] Planning Circular 3/2013, Development Management Procedures, para.2.13.
[43] Planning Circular 3/2013, Development Management Procedures, para.2.22.
[44] An application for planning permission could be submitted, but if the planning authority declined to determine it under s.39(1A), there would be no right of appeal.
[45] DMPR 2013 (SSI 2013/155) regs 9(3)(e) and 10(3)(e).
[46] Planning Circular 3/2013, Development Management Procedures, para.2.7.
[47] Planning Circular 3/2013, Development Management Procedures, para.2.36.

ENVIRONMENTAL IMPACT ASSESSMENT

5.15   Certain types of development cannot be granted planning permission until EIA has been carried out.[48] EIA is the term used to describe the process of gathering information and reporting on the environmental effects of the proposed development: the direct and indirect effects of the proposed development on human beings, fauna and flora; soil, water, air, climate and the landscape; and material assets and cultural heritage; and the interaction between those factors. The result of the process is the submission of an environmental statement (ES) which reports on the environmental impact of the proposed development. Public authorities and the public are given the opportunity to comment on the ES. The ES and those comments must be taken into account by the planning authority when it determines the planning application.[49]

EIA is a different process from strategic environmental assessment (SEA), which applies to certain plans and programmes, including all development plans (see Ch.3 above), rather than to planning applications.

The need for EIA also triggers other provisions. The planning authority have four months to determine the planning application rather than the usual two months. Schedule 1 development (see below) is a major development (see para.5.12 above). However, there is no longer a requirement to notify the Scottish Ministers before granting planning permission for a development subject to EIA (para.5.89). Also, there is no prohibition on s.43A schemes of delegation delegating decisions on EIA development to planning officers (see para.5.37 below).

Even if EIA is not required, the environmental impact of the proposed development is likely to be a material consideration (see para.5.48 below) and planning authorities have general powers to require further information from the applicant.[50] For non-EIA development, planning applications are often submitted with accompanying environmental information, in reports carefully titled "environmental report" or similar, to avoid any suggestion that the EIA requirements apply.

5.16   Screening is the process of determining whether EIA is required. The first question is whether the application falls within Sch.1 or Sch.2 of the Regulations.

Environmental impact assessment is required for every Sch.1 development, which includes crude oil refineries, major chemical and steel works, aerodromes with runway lengths over 2,100m, and the permanent storage or final disposal of radioactive and other toxic waste.

If the application does not fall within Sch.1, the next step is to consider Sch.2. EIA is required for a development which falls within the descriptions of development mentioned in col.1 of the table in Sch.2, provided:

- the development is likely to have significant effects on the environment by virtue of factors such as its nature, size or location; and

---

[48]   Town and Country Planning (Environmental Impact Assessment) (Scotland) Regulations 2011 (EIA 2011) (SSI 2011/139). In particular, reg.47 indicates that EIA may be required for development which would otherwise have permitted development rights (see Ch.4). Guidance on EIA is contained in Planning Circular 3/2011, The Town and Country Planning (Environmental Impact Assessment) (Scotland) Regulations 2011 (Scottish Government, 2011) and PAN 1/2013, Environmental Impact Assessment (Scottish Government, 2013). Legislation will be required to implement Directive 2014/52/EU on the assessment of the effects of certain public and private projects on the environment (amending Directive 2011/92/EU) OJ L124/1 by 16 May 2017.

[49]   EIA 2011 (SSI 2011/139) reg.3A, substituted by Town and Country Planning (Miscellaneous Amendments) (Scotland) Regulations 2015 (SSI 2015/249) reg.5(3) (14 September 2015).

[50]   DMPR 2013 (SSI 2013/155) reg.24.

- any part of the development is to be carried out in a "sensitive area",[51] or any of the thresholds or criteria in the corresponding part of col.2 of the table is respectively exceeded or met in relation to that development.

In deciding whether Sch.2 development requires EIA, the authority must take into account the selection criteria in Sch.3, which are grouped under the headings of characteristics of development, location of development, and characteristics of the potential impact.[52] Although remediation measures might offset significant adverse effects, it may be safer to require EIA so that those measures can be subject to scrutiny.[53]

Where development might be Sch.2 development, the planning authority must make a screening opinion, which is a decision whether or not EIA is required. The applicant can request the opinion before the planning application has been submitted, or the authority can make the opinion after receipt of the application. The screening opinion must be adopted within three weeks of receiving a request.[54] An opinion which concludes EIA is required must include full reasons for that conclusion; if it concludes EIA is not required, reasons must be provided if requested.[55] The Scottish Ministers also have powers to make screening directions.[56]

Difficulties have arisen from the potential in the planning system to seek planning permission in principle, in advance of supplying details of the development for approval. It is now clear that EIA requirements must be satisfied in full, even if the application is for planning permission in principle. However, a further EIA may be required for the subsequent application for approval of matters specified by condition.[57] That will depend on the extent to which the environmental effects had been identified at the earlier stage.[58] An application for planning permission in principle can satisfy EIA requirements provided that it includes specific parameters and stringent conditions are imposed to ensure that the project remains within the anticipated boundaries of the original application.[59] There may be no need for further EIA where the planning permission in principle is fenced with conditions to ensure that, from an environmental impact point of view, the final development stays within the bounds of what is foreseen and has been the subject of an EIA at the planning permission in principle stage.[60]

Difficulties have also arisen from planning permission being sought for different parts of a development in separate planning applications. The development should not be considered in isolation if in reality it was properly to be regarded as an integral part of an inevitably more substantial development.[61] A link road and residential development were not a single project, where there was a strong plan-

5.17

---

[51] EIA 2011 (SSI 2011/139) reg.2 defines "sensitive areas" as Sites of Special Scientific Interest, sites subject to a nature conservation order, European sites, World Heritage Sites, scheduled ancient monuments, National Scenic Areas and national parks (see Ch.9 below).

[52] EIA 2011 (SSI 2011/139) reg.5(6). For an example of an unsuccessful argument that environmental assessment was required, see *Uprichard v Fife Council*, 2000 S.C.L.R. 949.

[53] *R. (on the application of Champion) v North Norfolk DC* [2015] UKSC 52.

[54] See EIA 2011 (SSI 2011/139) reg.6(4).

[55] EIA 2011 (SSI 2011/139) reg.5(7) and (8).

[56] EIA 2011 (SSI 2011/139) reg.5(10).

[57] Applications for multi-stage consent—see EIA 2011 (SSI 2011/139) regs 4 and 27–31.

[58] *R. (on the application of Barker) v Bromley LBC* [2007] J.P.L. 744.

[59] *R. v Rochdale MBC Ex p. Milne (No.2)* [2001] J.P.L. 470, which considered the earlier and related case of *R. v Rochdale MBC Ex p. Tew* [1999] 3 P.L.R. 74.

[60] *Forbes v Aberdeenshire Council* [2010] CSOH 01 at [45].

[61] *R. v Swale BC Ex p. RSPB* [1991] J.P.L. 39; *BAA Plc v Secretary of State for Transport, Local*

ning need for the link road to complete a by-pass, whether or not the residential site was developed.[62] Although borrow pits formed an integral part of a wind farm development, it was not illegal to separate the borrow pits from the assessment of the wind farm where the assessments did not identify any significant environmental effects of the borrow pits whether considered alone or cumulatively with the wind farm.[63] EIA was not required for an application for full planning permission which was not a separate stand alone application but was part of a development for which outline planning permission had been granted after the required EIA was provided.[64]

Schedule 2 includes changes or extensions to existing developments. If there is a change or extension to a project, it is necessary to assess the cumulative effect, not just the effect of the change or extension.[65] A change to an existing installation, such as a proposal to burn waste tyres as a partial substitute for use of conventional fuel, may not require EIA.[66]

If the planning authority adopt a screening opinion that EIA is required after receiving a planning application, or fail to issue a screening opinion within the three week period, the applicant can request the Scottish Ministers for a screening direction.[67]

After adopting a screening opinion that EIA is required, the planning authority should suspend consideration of the planning application. The four month period after which the applicant can appeal against a deemed refusal of the planning application does not begin until an ES has been submitted.

5.18 There is no prescribed form of ES, but it must include specified information such as a description of the proposed development, comprising information about the physical characteristics of the whole development and the land-use requirements during the construction and operational phases; a description of the main characteristics of the production processes; and an estimate, by type and quantity, of expected residues and emissions resulting from the operation of the development. There must be an outline of the main alternatives studied and indication of the main reasons for the choice made, taking into account the environmental effects.[68] It should describe the likely significant environmental effects of the proposed development on population, fauna, flora, soil, water, air, climate, material assets including architectural and archaeological heritage, landscape, and the interaction between these effects. It should cover the direct effects and any indirect, secondary, cumulative, short, medium and long term, permanent and temporary, positive and negative effects of the development, resulting from the existence of the development, the use of natural resources, and the emission of pollutants, the creation of nuisances and the elimination of waste. Where significant adverse effects are identified, a

Government and the Regions [2003] J.P.L. 610.
[62] *R. (on the application of Larkfleet Ltd) v South Kesteven District Council* [2014] EWHC 3760 (Admin).
[63] *Skye Windfarm Action Group Ltd, Petitioners* [2008] CSOH 19 at [76].
[64] *Forbes v Aberdeenshire Council* [2010] CSOH 01.
[65] *R. (on the application of Baker) v Bath and North East Somerset DC* [2009] J.P.L. 1498.
[66] *R. (on the application of Edwards) v Environment Agency (No.2)* [2008] UKHL 22; [2008] J.P.L. 1278.
[67] EIA 2011 (SSI 2011/139) reg.6(6).
[68] There is no general requirement to study alternatives, but comment is required if alternatives have been studied; a requirement to study alternatives might arise from the circumstances of the development—*Skye Windfarm Action Group Ltd, Petitioners* [2008] CSOH 19 at [56] and [62].

description must be given of the measures envisaged in order to prevent, reduce or offset those effects. A non-technical summary must be given.[69]

There is no legal requirement that all the environmental information be in one document. It is sufficient that the documents comprising the ES are available for inspection by the public, and are presented in a way which allows the public not only to ascertain without much difficulty the conclusions reached on the various environmental effects but also to study in more detail the methods used to reach those conclusions.[70] However, the legal requirements were not met where the environmental information was contained in documents such as the applicant's statement of case for a public inquiry, letters from interested environmental bodies, and proofs of evidence made available at the inquiry.[71]

The applicant can seek a scoping opinion from the planning authority on what should be included in the ES. The authority must adopt the scoping opinion within five weeks of receiving the request; if they fail to do so, the applicant may seek a scoping direction from the Scottish Ministers.

Certain public bodies must, if requested, make information in their possession available to the applicant for the purposes of preparing an ES.

Where an application includes an ES, there are additional publicity requirements. **5.19** The planning authority must serve notice on all notifiable neighbours. In addition, the planning authority must advertise submission of the ES in a local newspaper and the *Edinburgh Gazette*, at the expense of the applicant. Both the advertisement and the notice served upon neighbours must state that a copy of the ES is available for public inspection and purchase at a specified address in the locality, specifying the charge (if any), and that there is a four-week period for making representations to the authority in connection with the statement.

Copies of the ES must be submitted to the authority, who must place one copy on the planning register. The planning authority is given four months to determine the application, rather than the usual two months. It is obliged to consult various bodies including Scottish Natural Heritage, the Health and Safety Executive, the Scottish Environment Protection Agency, and Historic Environment Scotland, allowing them four weeks to lodge representations. It is always open to the authority to request further information from the applicant. The decision on the application must be intimated to the applicant, the Scottish Ministers, all consultees, and the notifiable neighbours, and a notice published in the local newspaper.

As the EIA process is carried out by the applicant, many objectors to proposed developments cast doubt on the reliability of the information contained in the ES. Planning authorities in appropriate cases may choose to employ an environmental consultant to comment on the ES lodged with the application. The planning authority has the power to require further information to be submitted.[72] Whether or not information is to be regarded as sufficient or adequate is a matter of judgment for the planning authority.[73]

---

[69] EIA 2011 (SSI 2011/139) Sch.4.
[70] *Skye Windfarm Action Group Ltd, Petitioners* [2008] CSOH 19 at [52].
[71] *Berkeley v Secretary of State for the Environment, Transport and the Regions* [2001] 2 A.C. 603; [2001] J.P.L. 58.
[72] EIA 2011 (SSI 2011/139 reg.23.
[73] *Petition of The John Muir Trust* [2015] CSOH 163 per Lord Jones at [97].

If additional information is provided, similar publicity and consultation procedures must be undertaken.[74]

Any failure to comply with the environmental assessment procedures might form grounds for a petition for judicial review seeking the quashing of a grant of planning permission. For example, a consent was quashed because of failure to comply with publicity requirements for additional information.[75] The failure to require environmental assessment may be illegal,[76] even if it could be shown that the outcome of the planning application would not have been affected.[77] Where a planning permission condition required surveys to be undertaken to obtain information on the likely effects on protected species, the court quashed the permission on the grounds that the outcome of the surveys and any necessary mitigation measures should have been included in the ES.[78] However, mitigation of non-significant effects can be addressed through planning conditions.[79]

SUBMISSION OF APPLICATION

5.20   An application for planning permission is submitted to the planning authority for the area in which development is proposed.[80]

The application is made by completing and submitting an application form, obtained from the planning authority. The application must contain a written description of the development; the postal address of the site (if it has no postal address, a description of its location); and the name and address of the applicant and any agent. The application must be accompanied by a plan sufficient to identify the location of the site of the proposed development, and showing the situation of the land in relation to the locality and in particular in relation to neighbouring land. The application should also include such other plans and drawings as are necessary to describe the proposed development.[81] The application form usually specifies the number of copies of the form and associated plans and drawings required by the planning authority. Copies are requested to enable at least one copy of the application and supporting plans to be made available for public inspection. The planning authority may require the applicant to provide further information or evidence in respect of information accompanying the application, including plans or drawings.[82]

If it is unclear whether the planning authority will grant permission, and an appeal/review might be necessary, it is important to submit full supporting information with the application, as there is a general prohibition on raising a matter which

---

[74] EIA 2011 (SSI 2011/139) reg.24. In practice, this is referred to as Supplementary Environmental Information (SEI) or Further Environmental Information (FEI).

[75] *Petition of The John Muir Trust* [2015] CSOH 163 per Lord Jones at [59]-[106]. That case concerned the Electricity Works (Environmental Impact Assessment) (Scotland) Regulations 2000 (SSI 2000/320), which specify different procedural requirements from the 2011 Regulations.

[76] *Swan v Secretary of State for Scotland*, 1998 S.C.L.R. 763; 1998 69 S.P.E.L. 102; *R. v North Yorkshire CC Ex p. Brown, The Times*, 12 February 1999.

[77] *Berkeley v Secretary of State for the Environment, Transport and the Regions* [2001] 2 A.C. 603; [2001] J.P.L. 58.

[78] e.g. *R. v Cornwall CC Ex p. Hardy* [2001] J.P.L. 786; contrast *Feeny v Secretary of State for Transport* [2013] EWHC 1238 (Admin).

[79] *Skye Windfarm Action Group Ltd, Petitioners* [2008] CSOH 19 at [69].

[80] DMPR 2013 (SSI 2013/155) reg.8.

[81] DMPR 2013 (SSI 2013/155) reg.9.

[82] DMPR 2013 (SSI 2013/155) reg.24.

was not before the authority at the time the application was decided.[83] The planning application cannot be varied after an appeal has been made.[84]

In addition to lodging the completed application form and supporting plans, the applicant must also submit signed certificates relating to notification of owners and agricultural tenants, and enclose any fee payable for the application. There may also be a requirement to submit a pre-application consultation report and/or a design and access statement.

Description of proposed development

The description of the proposed development given on the application form is important because it governs the extent of the permission sought. Ancillary documents such as plans cannot extend the description. The description is also significant because it is used in both the notices served by the applicant upon notifiable persons and newspaper advertisements, which alert parties to their opportunity to inspect the application and lodge representations.

5.21

The description must be accurate, convey the substance of what is applied for and give full and fair notice to possible objectors. A grant of planning permission for petrol stations, restaurants, car parks and a 40-bed lodge was challenged successfully by a third party on the grounds that the application, neighbour notification notices and newspaper advertisements had merely described the proposed development as a roadside petrol station, notwithstanding that the full extent of the development had been shown in the accompanying plans.[85]

Where pre-application consultation is required (see para.5.14 above), the Government acknowledge that there is scope for proposals to alter between pre-application consultation and the application being submitted, but state that the application needs to be recognisably linked to what was described in the proposal of application notice. Both applicants and planning authorities need to be aware of potentially creating a situation where a very detailed or narrow descriptive content in the proposal of application notice means that relatively minor changes could trigger the need to repeat pre-application consultation.[86]

Design and access statements, and design statements

Since 2009 design and access statements must be submitted with planning applications for national developments or major developments (see "Hierarchy of Developments" above). Design statements must be submitted in relation to local developments where the application site is in a World Heritage Site, a conservation area, a historic garden or designed landscape, a national scenic area, the site of a scheduled monument, or the curtilage of a category A listed building (see Ch.9 below).[87]

5.22

Certain applications are exempt from the requirement for a design and access statement or design statement: applications to vary conditions (see Ch.6 below); for engineering or mining operations; for development of an existing dwellinghouse, or development within the curtilage of such a dwellinghouse for any purpose

---

83 TCPSA 1997 s.47A for appeals and s.43B for reviews.
84 TCPSA 1997 s.32A(3). There is no equivalent provision for review procedure.
85 *Cumming v Secretary of State for Scotland*, 1993 S.L.T. 228.
86 Planning Circular 3/2013, Development Management Procedures, para.2.13.
87 DMPR 2013 (SSI 2013/155) reg.13. PAN 68, Design Statements (Scottish Executive, 2003).

incidental to the enjoyment of the dwellinghouse as such, or any material change in the use of land or buildings, or an application for planning permission in principle.[88] Also, a design statement is not required for the alteration or extension of an existing building. However, planning authorities have general powers to require submission of additional information, which could be exercised to obtain information on design and/or access for developments not requiring a design and access statement or design statement.

A design statement is a written statement about the design principles and concepts that have been applied to the development. It explains the policy or approach adopted as to design and how any policies relating to design in the development plan have been taken into account. It also describes the steps taken to appraise the context of the development and demonstrates how the design of the development takes that context into account in relation to its proposed use. It states what, if any, consultation has been undertaken on issues relating to the design principles and concepts, and what account has been taken of the outcome of the consultation.

A design and access statement is a document containing both a design statement and written statement about how issues relating to access to the development for disabled people have been dealt with. It explains the policy or approach adopted to such access; how policies relating to such access in the development plan have been taken into account; how any specific issues which might affect access to the development for disabled people have been addressed; describes how features which ensure access to the development for disabled people will be maintained; and states what, if any, consultation has been undertaken on issues relating to access to the development for disabled people and what account has been taken of the outcome of any such consultation.

Where a design or design and access statement is required, the information within the statement may be material and in such cases must be taken into account by the planning authority when considering the proposed development.[89]

Notification of owners and agricultural tenants

5.23   Although the applicant seeking permission is not required to own or control the site of the proposed development nor obtain the consent of the owner of the land to the application, the benefit of any grant of planning permission attaches to the land rather than to the applicant, who will be unable to commence the development without obtaining the necessary property law rights from the landowner.

The applicant must notify the owner that an application for planning permission is being submitted for a proposed development on his land.[90] This avoids the possibility of an owner selling land without knowing its true value following a grant of planning permission. The applicant must also notify any tenant of agricultural land on the site, whose security of tenure may be affected by a grant of permission. Special rules apply for developments consisting of the working and winning of minerals (see Ch.9 below).

For these purposes the expression "owner" refers to any person who owned the land 21 days before the date of the application, and includes a tenant with a lease

---

[88]   DMPR 2013 (SSI 2013/155) reg.13(3).
[89]   Planning Circular 3/2013, Development Management Procedures, para.3.36.
[90]   TCPSA 1997 s.35; DMPR 2013 (SSI 2013/155) reg.15.

which still has more than seven years to run.[91] The identity of the owner or tenant may be ascertained from the valuation roll kept by the council, or from a search of the Register of Sasines or the Land Register.[92] The applicant must utilise all steps reasonably open to him for tracing the owner, but there is provision for advertisement of applications if the owner cannot be traced (see below).

Agricultural land means land comprised in a lease constituting a 1991 Act tenancy within the meaning of the Agricultural Holdings (Scotland) Act 2003 or comprised in a lease constituting a short limited duration tenancy or limited duration tenancy within the meaning of that Act. There is no conclusive method for identifying agricultural tenants, other than requesting this information from the landowner or making inquiries in the locality.

Notice is given in the prescribed form. The notice is intended to alert these parties to the submission of the application and their opportunity to obtain information on the application from the planning authority or to make representations about the application. The notice also states that the grant of permission does not affect owners' rights to retain or dispose of their property unless there is an agreement to the contrary, but that it may affect the security of tenure of a tenant of an agricultural holding.

The applicant completes the notice by filling in details of the application, including the description of the proposed development (see above). The notice is normally sent by recorded delivery post or delivered by hand (methods of serving notices are examined in Ch.7).

Together with the completed application form, the applicant must submit a signed certificate stating, as appropriate: **5.24**

(a) whether or not any part of the application site is agricultural land;
(b) that at the date 21 days before the date of the application no person other than the applicant was the owner of the site or an agricultural tenant;
(c) that he has served notice on every person who at the date 21 days before the date of the application was the owner or an agricultural tenant of the site, setting out the name of every such person, and the address at which and the date on which each notice was served;
(d) that he has been unable to serve notice on some or all of these persons, and has taken reasonable steps (which must be specified) to ascertain the names and addresses of the others but has been unable to do so. In such circumstances, the planning authority will publish a newspaper notice (see below).

The planning authority cannot entertain a planning application unless these requirements relating to notification have been satisfied.[93] In most cases the authority will simply check that the appropriate certificates have been completed correctly. It seems unlikely that this statutory duty extends to checking the accuracy of the notification process, but this point is uncertain. Errors in the notification process, particularly those pointed out to the planning authority prior to its decision, but not remedied, may leave a grant of permission open to challenge in the courts by a person with a notifiable interest who received no notification of the application.[94]

In addition, it is an offence to issue knowingly or recklessly a certificate which

---

91 TCPSA 1997 s.35(7). The general definition of "owner" is contained in s.277.
92 Members of the public can carry out searches in person at the Registers of Scotland in Edinburgh or a professional searcher can be instructed.
93 TCPSA 1997 s.35(4).
94 *R. (on the application of Pridmore) v Salisbury DC* [2005] J.P.L. 655. See also cases re neighbour

contains a statement which is false or misleading in a material particular, with liability on summary conviction to a fine not exceeding level 5 on the standard scale (see Appendix 1 below). Proceedings for such an offence may be brought within two years of commission of the offence rather than the normal six-month period.

Application fees

5.25   A fee is payable for submission of most applications for planning permission.[95] This is intended to cover the administrative costs incurred by the planning authority in processing and determining applications, although fees are charged on a general scale rather than by reference to the time spent on individual applications. Most authorities provide a list of fees when dispensing application forms; not every application requires payment of a fee. A telephone call to the authority prior to submission of the application should confirm the correct fee. Failure to pay the correct fee will delay validation of the application (see para.5.27 below).

PROCESSING OF APPLICATION

notification (see para.5.29 below).

[95] Town and Country Planning (Fees for Applications and Deemed Applications) (Scotland) Regulations 2004 (SI 2004/219).

Fig.5.2 Processing planning application

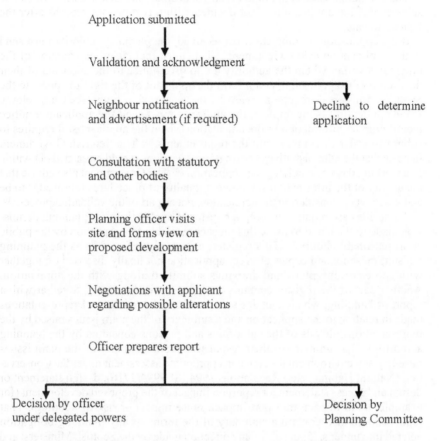

Application submitted

Validation and acknowledgment

Neighbour notification
and advertisement (if required)

Decline to determine
application

Consultation with statutory
and other bodies

Planning officer visits
site and forms view on
proposed development

Negotiations with applicant
regarding possible alterations

Officer prepares report

Decision by officer
under delegated powers

Decision by
Planning Committee

In the majority of cases the planning authority will decide straightforward ap- **5.26**
plications in two to three months. Some authorities have a better record than others and much will depend on the development pressures in the district at the time.
In complex cases a decision may not be received for many months or even years.
The applicant has the opportunity to appeal/seek review against a deemed refusal
after two or four months depending on the nature of the development, but if the
details of the proposed development are still being negotiated with the authority
such an appeal/review is unlikely to succeed and is not an option worth pursuing,
leaving the applicant with no alternative but to persevere with the application.

Each authority has its own internal procedures for processing applications, but
the general outline of the procedure is similar, as illustrated in fig.5.2.

(a) Validation and acknowledgement of applications

The validation date is the date on which the application is received by the plan- **5.27**
ning authority accompanied by the prescribed information and documents, and any
fee payable. If the application is incomplete, the validation date is the date when

the last of the items or information is received by the planning authority.[96] For EIA development, the ES must be submitted before the application can be validated.[97]

The validation date is important because a deemed refusal appeal/review can be submitted if the application is not decided within two or four months after the validation date.[98]

If the application is complete when received, the planning authority must send to the applicant an acknowledgment.[99] This must include an explanation of the timescales within which the authority are to give notice to the applicant of their decision on the application, and inform the applicant of the right to appeal to the Scottish Ministers or require a review by the local review body (see Ch.8 below). If the application is incomplete, the authority must send the applicant a notice identifying the information or documentation which the applicant still requires to submit in order to comply with the requirements.[100] The Scottish Government indicate that the administrative checking of applications should be carried out within five working days of receiving the application.[101] The Government also advise that the quality of the information submitted or quality of procedures followed is to be addressed when considering the application, not as part of the validation process.[102]

Authorities are required to keep a register of applications for planning permission made to them and to make this register available for inspection by the public at all reasonable hours.[103] This register, commonly referred to as the planning register, must contain copies of every application not finally disposed of, together with copies of any plans and drawings submitted along with the application. Another part of the register contains copies of decision notices, together with a report of handling, which contains a statement on the number of representations made in relation to the application and a summary of the main issues raised by the representations; details of the authorities and persons consulted by the planning authority and a summary of their responses; and a summary of the main issues raised by any environmental statement, appropriate assessment under the Conservation (Natural Habitats etc.) Regulations 1994 (SI 1994/2716), design statement or design and access statement, or report on impact of the proposed development (for example, retail impact, transport impact, noise impact or risk of flooding). That report should also contain a summary of the terms of any planning obligation entered into under s.75; details of any direction made by the Scottish Ministers; and details of the provisions of the development plan and any other material considerations to which the planning authority had regard in determining the application.

There is a separate requirement for the authority to keep a list of applications, to be revised weekly.[104] This list must include proposal of application notices received under the pre-application consultation procedures (see para.5.14 above).

96 DMPR 2013 (SSI 2013/155) reg.14.
97 Town and Country Planning (Appeals) (Scotland) Regulations 2013 (SSI 2013/156) regs 2 and 3(2), as amended by Town and Country Planning (Miscellaneous Amendments) (Scotland) Regulations 2015 (SSI 2015/249); Town and Country Planning (Schemes of Delegation and Local Review Procedure) (Scotland) Regulations 2013 (SSI 2013/157) regs 2 and 8(2), also as amended by SSI 2015/249.
98 DMPR 2013 (SSI 2013/155) reg.26(2).
99 DMPR 2013 (SSI 2013/155) reg.17.
100 DMPR 2013 (SSI 2013/155) reg.17(3).
101 Planning Circular 3/2013, Development Management Procedures, para.4.4.
102 Planning Circular 3/2013, Development Management Procedures, paras 4.5–4.7.
103 TCPSA 1997 s.36; DMPR 2013 (SSI 2013/155) reg.16 and Sch.2.
104 TCPSA 1997 s.36A; DMPR 2013 (SSI 2013/155) reg.21.

The authority must publish the list on their website and make it available for inspection at their principal office and at public libraries in their district.[105]

The planning authority must also send every community council in their district at weekly intervals a list of all applications made to the authority during the previous week, and make this list available for inspection at their principal office and at public libraries.[106] There is no requirement for the list to include proposal of application notices, presumably because applicants are required to copy those to community councils (see para.5.14 above).

Following validation, the application is allotted to a planning officer who is often named in the acknowledgment letter.

(b) Power to decline to determine application

The planning authority has power to decline to determine an application prior to **5.28** considering its merits in two situations: failure to comply with the pre-application consultation requirements; and repeat applications for the same or similar development.[107] The categories of repeat applications was extended in 2009.

If, in the opinion of the planning authority, there has been a failure to comply with the pre-application consultation requirements (see para.5.14 above), the authority must decline to determine the application. However, the authority may first request the applicant to provide specified additional information.

The planning authority also has power to decline to determine repeat applications for the same or similar development, but the exercise of this power is discretionary, not mandatory. This is a two-stage process: first, the authority has to decide whether as a matter of fact the application is "similar", and, secondly, whether as a matter of discretion to decline to consider it on its own merits.[108] The authority must also assess whether there has been any significant change in the development plan or in any other material considerations since the previous decision.

Applications are considered "similar" if the proposed development and the site to which the applications relate are the same or substantially the same.[109]

The power to decline to determine arises if, within the two years prior to submission of the applications:

- the Scottish Ministers had refused a similar application either on appeal or under a reference to them;
- the planning authority have refused more than one similar application, i.e. there have been two or more refusals. It is irrelevant for this purpose whether there has been an appeal to the Ministers against either/any of the refusals, provided the appeal(s) have yet to be determined;
- deemed refusal appeals have been submitted for more than one similar application but these appeals have yet to be determined;

[105] DMPR 2013 (SSI 2013/155) reg.22.
[106] DMPR 2013 (SSI 2013/155) reg.23.
[107] TCPSA 1997 s.39.
[108] *Noble Organisation Ltd v Falkirk DC*, 1994 S.L.T. 100.
[109] TCPSA 1997 s.39(2). Guidance was provided in Planning Circular 22/1991, Planning and Compensation Act 1991 (1991) Annex 2, now repealed. That guidance stated that if the application has been revised in what appears to be a genuine attempt to take account of objections to an earlier proposal, it should not be regarded as similar, and the power should be used only where the authority believes the applicant is intending to exert pressure by submitting repeated similar applications. In doubtful cases the authority should proceed to determine the application.

- the planning authority have refused one application and a deemed refusal appeal has yet to be determined in relation to a similar application.

In 2013, the references to appeals to the Scottish Ministers were extended to include applications for review to local review bodies.[110]

There is no right of appeal to the Scottish Ministers against the decision of the planning authority to decline to determine the application in this way. Judicial review of the decision of the authority will be competent, but requires the applicant to show that the exercise of this discretionary power was illegal rather than merely wrong (see Ch.8 below). Provided all relevant considerations are taken into account, the courts will be unwilling to interfere with the decision made by the authority on what is essentially a factual matter. For example, where a first application concerned an, "amusement centre and ancillary retail sales", and the second a reduced area for an, "amusement centre/snack bar (with exclusive retail area)", the authority were entitled to have regard to the fact that the second application raised substantially the same planning considerations as the first, including being contrary to the development plan, and to refuse the second application as similar.[111]

(c) Neighbour notification

5.29   Prior to 2009, the applicant for planning permission was required to serve notice of submission of the application upon the owners and occupiers of land neighbouring the site of the proposed development. In 2009 the responsibility for neighbour notification was transferred to the planning authority; the definition of "neighbouring land" was simplified, and the rules for service of notices were also simplified. The period for neighbours to submit representations was increased from 14 to 21 days.

The purpose of neighbour notification is to alert those who will be most affected by the proposed development of their opportunity to make representations to the planning authority regarding the application. The Scottish Government indicate that planning authorities should carry out neighbour notification as soon as possible after the application has been validated.[112]

Neighbour notification is one of the most problematic parts of the procedure for submission of planning applications. It generates many (unjustified) complaints from members of the public mainly because of widespread public overestimation of the extent of notification required. Broadly, only those neighbours within 20m of the site must be notified. In urban tenement property areas this may result in identification of over 100 notifiable neighbours, but in the majority of cases only 10–20 persons will require to be notified.

While notification of owners and agricultural tenants is required for "any application for planning permission", the requirement for neighbour notification extends to "any application for planning permission" and an application for consent, agreement or approval required by a condition imposed on a grant of planning permission in principle.[113]

The starting point is the definition of "neighbouring land", which means an area

---

[110] s.39(2A), inserted by Planning Etc. (Scotland) Act 2006 (Supplementary and Consequential Provisions) Order 2013 (SSI 2013/26).

[111] *Noble Organisation Ltd v Falkirk DC*, 1994 S.L.T. 100.

[112] Planning Circular 3/2013, Development Management Procedures, para.4.18.

[113] DMPR 2013 (SSI 2013/155) reg.18. Planning Circular 3/2013, Development Management Procedures, para 4.15.

or plot of land (other than land forming part of a road) which, or part of which, is conterminous with or within 20m of the boundary of the application site.[114] The statutory provisions do not regulate where the boundaries of a site can be drawn (and there have been instances of boundaries being redrawn to avoid notifying neighbours). The boundaries of the planning unit may be a useful guide (see Ch.4 above). The Scottish Government guidance acknowledges that the boundary need not be the property boundary, referring to the example of a farm or estate where a building is being erected in one part of the farm or estate, and it is not the whole farm or estate being developed, so it would not make sense to use the farm/estate boundary.[115]

Once neighbouring land has been identified, the next step is to identify if there **5.30** are premises on that land to which the notice can be sent. If there are such premises, a single notice is sent to the premises addressed to "the Owner, Lessee or Occupier".[116] If there are no premises on the neighbouring land, a newspaper notice must be published (see below).

The notice must state the date on which the notice is sent; the name of the applicant and any agent; the reference number given to the application by the planning authority; a description of the development to which the application relates; and the postal address of the application site, or if there is no postal address, a description of its location. The notice must also state how the application, plans or drawings relating to it and other documents submitted in connection with it may be inspected; and that representations may be made to the planning authority and include information as to how any representation may be made and by which date they must be made (not less than 21 days after the date on which the notice is sent). The notice must be accompanied by a plan showing the situation of the application site in relation to neighbouring land. There must also be a statement as to how information explaining the manner in which applications for planning permission are handled and the procedures which are followed in relation to such applications can be obtained. If the application required pre-application consultation (see para.5.14 above), the notice must state that, even if comments have been made to the applicant, persons wishing to make representations in respect of the application should do so to the planning authority in the manner indicated in the notice.

The Scottish Government advise that notices should be hand delivered or sent by first class post, since the use of second class mail could result in recipients having a significantly reduced period within which to make representations.[117]

The planning authority must not determine the application until the expiry of the **5.31** period allowed for the making of representations in the notice sent to the premises or published in the newspaper.[118]

Failure to notify a neighbour may leave a subsequent grant of permission open to challenge in judicial review proceedings (see below). Once possible deficiencies in the notification process are drawn to its attention, the planning authority should investigate and correct any errors. The objective of notification is to alert those persons whom the law perceives to have a special interest to the submission

---

114 DMPR 2013 (SSI 2013/155) reg.3. The previous definition was land conterminous with or within 4m of the boundary, but disregarding the width of any road up to 20m, and also excluding any land more than 90m from any part of the proposed development.

115 Planning Circular 3/2013, Development Management Procedures, para.4.16.

116 DMPR 2013 (SSI 2013/432) reg.18.

117 Planning Circular 3/2013, Development Management Procedures, para.4.32.

118 DMPR 2013 (SSI 2013/155) reg.26.

of the application and their opportunity to object to the application. The practice of most planning authorities is to suspend consideration of the application while serving notification on overlooked persons. At the end of the further period which must be allowed for representations to be received from those persons, the application is then considered in the normal way. This practice fulfils the objective of the notification requirements and therefore seems acceptable.

Errors in the notification process, particularly those pointed out to the planning authority prior to its decision, but not remedied, may leave a grant of permission open to challenge in the courts by a person with a notifiable interest who received no notification of the application.[119] A grant of permission was quashed where a failure to notify prejudiced a neighbour, as he was prevented from presenting his case and his standpoint was different from other objectors and might have had a material effect on the outcome of the planning application.[120] The extent of the error required before the permission may be challenged successfully is not clear. A factual error in a certificate could be regarded as a mere irregularity which would not justify the court in striking down the planning decision. The exercise of the court's discretion may be influenced by the length of time since the grant of permission and the knowledge or otherwise of the application for permission of the person seeking to challenge that permission.[121]

(d)   Advertisement

5.32   An application must be advertised in a local newspaper by the planning authority where[122]:

(i)   there are no premises situated on neighbouring land to which neighbour notification can be sent (see para.5.30 above). An advertisement is not required for applications for planning permission for householder development, or where the neighbouring land is owned by the planning authority or the applicant;

(ii)   the applicant certifies that he has been unable to serve notice on some or all of the owners or agricultural tenants of the site of the proposed development (see para.5.23 above);

(iii)   the applicant seeks permission for one of the specified classes of development known as "bad neighbour development", which are considered to have such a potentially adverse effect on amenity that applications for those developments must be advertised; bad neighbour developments include public conveniences, sewage works, theatres, fun fairs, licensed premises, hot food shops and other specified leisure-related premises[123];

(iv)   the proposed development does not accord with the provisions of the development plan.

Advertisement is also required where an ES is submitted in connection with a planning application (see para.5.15 above). If, in the opinion of the planning authority, the proposed development would affect the character or appearance of a conserva-

---

[119] *Forrester v Kirkcaldy DC*, 1996 G.W.D. 21–1244; 1996 56 S.P.E.L. 74; *Bonnes v West Lothian DC*, 1994 G.W.D. 31–1888.

[120] *Macpherson v Edinburgh City Council*, 2003 S.L.T. 1112.

[121] *Forrester v Kirkcaldy DC*, 1996 G.W.D. 21–1244; *Main v Swansea City Council* [1985] J.P.L. 558.

[122] TCPSA 1997 s.34; DMPR 2013 (SSI 2013/155) reg.20. The prescribed form for the advertisement DMPR 2013 (SSI 2013/155) Sch.4 as amended by reg.20A.

[123] DMPR 2013 (SSI 2013/155) Sch.3—see full list in Appendix 2 of this book.

tion area, or affect the setting of a listed building (see Ch.9 below), the application must be advertised by the planning authority and a site notice displayed for at least seven days.[124] Advertisements are also required for some applications for dangerous or hazardous substances.[125]

A single advertisement is sufficient to satisfy the requirements of all or any of the above provisions, other than submission of an ES.[126] The planning authority can recover the cost of the advertisement from the applicant.[127]

The planning authority cannot decide the application until the expiry of the appropriate period for representations to be made as specified in the advertisement.[128] Where a site notice is displayed because the development affects a conservation area or setting of a listed building, the application cannot be determined until 21 days after the first date of display.[129] The Scottish Government advise that advertisements should be published within 14 days of the validation date.[130]

(e) Consultation

Before making its decision on the application, the planning authority is required to consult various bodies requesting their views on the proposed development.[131] In addition to these statutory consultees, it is open to the planning authority to consult with any body regarding the application, and many authorities have informal consultation processes involving civic amenity groups. Such informal practices may give rise to a legitimate expectation of future consultation (see Ch.8 below).

5.33

The bodies to be consulted vary depending upon the circumstances of each development. A typical development would require consultation with the roads department on access and traffic issues, the environmental health department on issues such as smells or dust, and the water authority on drainage and sewerage provision. Developments in rural areas may require consultation with Scottish Natural Heritage (see Ch.9 below). The Scottish Environment Protection Agency are consulted on issues such as flood risk, mining operations, sewage treatment and disposal, works to river banks or beds, and waste disposal projects.

The community council within whose area the development is to take place must be consulted if:

(i) it informs the planning authority that it wishes to be consulted on an application for a development within its area, provided it informs the authority within seven business days from the date of dispatch by the authority to all community councils of the weekly list of applications; or

(ii) the development is likely to affect the amenity in the area of the community council.

---

[124] Planning (Listed Buildings and Conservation Areas) (Scotland) Act 1997 (PLBCASA) ss.60 and 65.
[125] DMPR 2013 (SSI 2013/155) reg.20(2)(e), inserted by Town and Country Planning (Hazardous Substances) (Scotland) Regulations 2015 (SSI 2015/181).
[126] DMPR 2013 (SSI 2013/155) reg.20(4)–(6).
[127] Town and Country Planning (Charges for Publication of Notices) (Scotland) Regulations 2009 (SSI 2009/257).
[128] DMPR 2013 (SSI 2013/155) reg.26(4).
[129] PLBCASA 1997 ss.60 and 65.
[130] Planning Circular 3/2013, Development Management Procedures, para.4.28.
[131] DMPR 2013 (SSI 2013/155) reg.25 and Sch.5. Regulation 37 contains specific requirements for consulting the Cairngorms National Park Authority.

Statutory consultees must be given at least 14 days' notice that the application is to be taken into consideration and the application cannot be determined until the expiry of that period. There is an opt-out provision whereby bodies that require to be consulted can inform the planning authority in writing that consultation will not be required in respect of any case or class of case or in respect of development within a specified area.

(f) Further information

5.34   The planning authority have a general power to require from the applicant further particulars, documents, materials or evidence which they consider that they require to enable them to deal with the application.[132] If the applicant considers the further information is not necessary, the remedy is to appeal/seek review against a deemed refusal, or to refuse to provide the information and request the planning authority to refuse permission, enabling an appeal/review to be submitted against that refusal.

(g) Variation of application

5.35   Applications can be varied after submission with the agreement of the planning authority.[133] The statutory provisions prohibit the authority from agreeing to the variation if they consider the variation involves a substantial change in the description of the proposed development.[134] When an application is varied, the planning authority may give such notice of the variation as they consider appropriate.

DECIDING THE APPLICATION

5.36   The decision-making process depends on the scheme of delegation adopted by each individual planning authority. Planning officers have delegated power to decide classes of application, with all other applications being decided by the councillors who sit on the planning committee of the authority.

It is important to identify which body within the authority will actually determine the application. If the application will be decided by the councillors, it must be considered whether the development proposals are presented in a clear and attractive fashion. The applicant may wish to brief in advance the councillors who will make the decision (not all councillors are receptive to lobbying). If a planning officer will make the decision, less care need be taken to avoid the use of technical terms.

The issue of who makes the decision also dictates the procedure available to challenge the decision: if the decision is made by an officer under a s.43A scheme of delegation, the decision is challenged by application to the local review body for review; but if the decision is made by the councillors (or by officers under other delegated powers), there is a right of appeal to the Scottish Ministers (see Ch.8 below).

---

[132] DMPR 2013 (SSI 2013/155) reg.24.

[133] TCPSA 1997 s.32A; s.32B gives the Scottish Ministers similar power.

[134] Court decisions pre-dating this statutory power might provide guidance: *Walker v Aberdeen City Council*, 1998 S.L.T. 427; 1997 61 S.P.E.L. 59; *Kent CC v Secretary of State for the Environment* (1977) 33 P. & C.R. 70; *Lothian Borders and Angus Co-operative Society Ltd v Scottish Borders Council* [1999] 2 P.L.R. 19; 1999 G.W.D. 6–316; *Bernard Wheatcroft Ltd v Secretary of State for the Environment* [1982] J.P.L. 37; *Breckland DC v Secretary of State for the Environment* [1992] 3 P.L.R. 89. See "Grant of Planning Permission for Revised Development", at para.5.87 below.

What are the factors behind the decision on the application? In making a decision on the application, the authority must not fetter its discretion and each application must be individually decided on its merits. The application must be determined in accordance with the provisions of the development plan unless material considerations indicate otherwise (commonly referred to as the "plan-led" system). The authority may refuse planning permission, or grant permission unconditionally or subject to conditions. It may also grant permission for a development in different terms to that proposed by the application.

The decision on the application is an exercise in balancing the competing considerations. The planning authority must take into account all considerations which are both material and relevant to the application and ignore any other matters. A failure to fulfil this duty may result in an illegal decision, unless the same decision would have been reached on other valid reasons.[135] The consideration challenged need not have been the dominant reason for reaching the decision, and provided it was not insubstantial or insignificant there is no requirement to prove that a different conclusion would have been reached had it not been taken into account.[136] The courts will not interfere with the decision of the planning authority on the weight to be given to each consideration.[137]

Where there is a material change in circumstances in the course of the determination of the application, the authority must take that change into account. This highlights the risk of so-called "minded to grant" decisions, which involve the authority resolving to grant permission once certain outstanding matters, normally execution of a s.75 agreement (see Ch.6 below), have been resolved. Such a decision gives the applicant no guarantee that permission will be granted. For example, where an authority resolved to grant permission once a s.75 agreement was concluded, it was open to that authority to refuse to enter into the agreement and not grant permission if there was a change of circumstances in the intervening period.[138]

Schemes of delegation

The Local Government (Scotland) Act 1973 gives local authorities the power to delegate decision-making to officers instead of being considered by elected members of the authority at committee.[139] This avoids committee time being spent deciding routine applications which raise no controversial issues or have attracted low numbers of objections.

5.37

In 2009 a specific power was introduced for local authorities to delegate determination of planning applications to officers.[140] These are referred to here as s.43A schemes of delegation, because it is important to be clear which scheme of delegation applies to the decision made, as decisions made by officers under s.43A schemes of delegation are challengeable by application to the local review body, whereas decisions made under other delegated powers are challenged by appeal to

135 *R. v Broadcasting Complaints Commission Ex p. Owen* [1985] Q.B. 1153.
136 *Simplex GE (Holdings) Ltd v Secretary of State for the Environment* [1988] 3 P.L.R. 25.
137 *Seddon Properties Ltd v Secretary of State for the Environment* [1978] J.P.L. 835.
138 *John G Russell (Transport) Ltd v Strathkelvin DC*, 1992 S.L.T. 1001.
139 Local Government (Scotland) Act 1973 s.56.
140 TCPSA 1997 s.43A; Town and Country Planning (Schemes of Delegation and Local Review Procedure) (Scotland) Regulations 2013 (SSI 2013/157); Planning Circular 5/2013, Schemes of Delegation and Local Reviews (Scottish Government, 2013).

the Scottish Ministers (see Ch.8 below). The Scottish Government note the potential for there to be two separate routes for challenging decisions on the same development, for example if it requires planning permission and listed building consent, and advise that the planning authority must consider which is the most effective route to determine the related applications.[141]

Section 43A schemes of delegation only apply to planning applications for local developments, and any application for consent, agreement or approval required by a condition imposed on a grant of planning permission for a local development. Local developments are all developments which are not classed as national or major (see "Hierarchy of Development", above).[142]

Even if the s.43A scheme of delegation results in an application being determinable by an officer, the councillors may, if they think fit, decide to determine the application themselves. A statement of their reasons for removing the decision-making power from the officer must be served on the applicant.

Each planning authority was required to prepare a s.43A scheme of delegation, and then has a duty to keep the scheme under review, and prepare fresh schemes at intervals of no greater than every five years, or whenever required to do so by the Scottish Ministers. The only procedural requirement is that the scheme cannot be adopted by the planning authority until it has been approved by the Scottish Ministers. There is no requirement for consultation with stakeholders. Once adopted, the s.43A scheme must be published on the internet and a copy available for inspection at an office of the planning authority and in all its public libraries.

Report to committee/report of handling

5.38   For applications which are to be determined by a committee of councillors, the planning officer normally prepares a report on the application. The report gives details of the proposed development and its site. It also summarises the representations received, the consultation responses, the relevant provisions of the development plans, and any relevant Scottish Government advice. The report ends with a recommendation of how the application should be decided. Copies of this report must be made available to members of the public, generally three clear days before the relevant committee meeting takes place.[143] The function of the report is to brief the person or persons determining the application and ensure that they are in possession of all the relevant considerations before making a decision. While the report recommends a decision, the decision-maker is not bound to follow the recommendation.

Any significant error in the report can result in the decision by the committee being invalid.[144] The courts are not prepared to submit a report to detailed textual analysis as if it were a statute or conveyancing deed, but rather view it in its overall context as a report to a committee generally versed in planning issues and having

---

[141] Planning Circular 5/2013, Schemes of Delegation and Local Reviews (Scottish Government, 2013) para.17.

[142] There is no longer a prohibition on delegating determination of an application for planning permission made by the planning authority or by a member of the planning authority, or an application relating to land in the ownership of the planning authority or to land in which the planning authority have a financial interest.

[143] Local Government (Scotland) Act 1973 ss.50B and 50E.

[144] *Campbell v Edinburgh City Council*, 1999 S.L.T. 1009. But see *Lothian Borders and Angus Co-operative Society Ltd v Scottish Borders Council*, 1999 G.W.D. 6-316; and *Freeport Leisure Plc v West Lothian Council*, 1999 S.L.T. 452.

a considerable degree of local knowledge in relation to the generality of the issues raised in the report. The overall context of the report must be examined to determine whether applicable tests are applied rather than merely rely on the presence or absence of a reference to specific statutory provisions.[145]

Since 2009 there is a requirement for the planning register to contain a copy of a report on the handling of the application (see "Validation and acknowledgement", above).[146] The Scottish Government advise that the format and structure of the report on handling is a matter for the planning authority, but it should be similar to the reports prepared for planning committees, and be proportionate to the nature, scale and complexity of the proposal.[147]

Pre-determination hearings

For applications for specified classes of development, the application cannot be determined until an opportunity has been given for a pre-determination hearing.[148] The relevant classes of development are national developments, and major developments which are significantly contrary to the development plan (for definitions of national and major developments, see "Hierarchy of Development", above). The Scottish Ministers' general expectation is that a development would be significantly contrary to the development plan where approval would be contrary to the vision or wider spatial strategy of the plan.[149] **5.39**

For those classes of development, the planning authority must give the applicant and any person who submitted representations to the authority in respect of the application an opportunity of appearing before and being heard by a committee of the authority. The authority is given the power to decide the procedures for arranging and conducting the hearing, and any other procedures consequent upon the hearing. It is also for the authority to decide which persons have the right to attend the hearing, other than for the purpose of appearing before and being heard by the committee.

The authority can also elect to hold a pre-determination hearing for any other application. The Scottish Government suggest that such voluntary hearings could be held for applications in which the authority has a financial interest, or applications that have attracted a given number and type of objections or applications relating to development in sensitive areas protected by statutory designations.[150]

The Scottish Government has provided advice on pre-determination hearings procedures.[151] The hearing should be held by the relevant committee. It should take place after the expiry of the period for making representations on the application but before the authority decides the application. The committee must decide whether it wishes to have hearings on the same day as the related planning applications are determined by the full council (see below), or make alternative arrangements. Procedural issues include: the order of proceedings—e.g. the applicant and those who made representations to address the committee in turn; the maximum number of individuals to speak on either side—it may be necessary to

---

145 *Uprichard v Fife Council* [2009] CSOH 170.
146 TCPSA 1997 s.36; DMPR 2013 (SSI 2013/155) reg.16 and Sch.2.
147 Planning Circular 3/2013, Development Management Procedures, para.4.54.
148 TCPSA 1997 s.38A; DMPR 2013 (SSI 2013/155) reg.27.
149 Planning Circular 3/2103, Development Management Procedures, para.4.73.
150 Planning Circular 3/2013, Development Management Procedures, Annex F, para.3.
151 Planning Circular 4/2009, Development Management Procedures, Annex F.

ask one objector to speak on behalf of a group of objectors; the maximum time available for applicants; responding to each other's statements; the opportunity for committee members to ask questions; and the opportunity for committee members to ask for additional advice and information from planning officers.

Referral of applications to full council for decision

5.40   The full council, and not a committee, must decide applications for national developments, and major developments which are significantly contrary to the development plan (for definitions of national and major developments, see "Hierarchy of Development", above).[152] The Scottish Ministers' general expectation is that a development would be significantly contrary to the development plan where approval would be contrary to the vision or wider spatial strategy of the plan.[153]

Presumption in favour of development?

5.41   When the requirement for planning permission was introduced nationally in 1947, it removed the rights of landowners to do as they pleased on their land and forced them to apply to the State for permission to develop their land. It would have been draconian to require them further to demonstrate why they should be allowed to develop their land in a particular way. As a result, it has been government policy that the State's control over development should only be exercised to prevent development where it can show good planning reasons for refusing permission. The previous Scottish Executive guidance required clear and intelligible reasons to be given for a refusal of planning permission, and stated that it was not enough to indicate that the proposal was contrary to the development plan[154]; earlier Scottish Office guidance stated that permission should only be refused where there were sound and clearcut reasons for such a refusal even if the proposal was contrary to the development plan.[155] The applicant therefore was not required to prove the case for the proposed development, and the onus was on the planning authority to demonstrate clearly why the development cannot be permitted.

To some extent this presumption has been modified by the introduction of the plan-led system (see "Development Plan", below), becoming a presumption in favour of development which accords with the provisions of the development plan. The current Scottish Government guidance states that there is a presumption in favour of development that contributes to sustainable development (see Sustainable development and climate change, below).[156]

The European Convention on Human Rights is neither pro-nor anti-development. Article 8 and the First Protocol art.1 confer the same general rights on the applicant for permission and neighbours. Both require the planning authority to show that a refusal of planning permission is necessary, for example to protect the rights and freedoms of others. This might be seen to support development. However, if a

---

[152] Local Government (Scotland) Act 1973 s.56(6A), inserted by Planning Etc. (Scotland) Act 2006 (PSA) s.14(2).

[153] Planning Circular 3/2013, Development Management Procedures, para.4.73.

[154] Scottish Executive Development Department, National Planning Policy Guideline (NPPG) 1: *The Planning System* (revised, 2000) para.47.

[155] Planning Circular 17/1985, Development Control—Priorities and Procedures (Scottish Office, 1985) para.3; NPPG 1: *The Planning System* (2000) para.44.

[156] Scottish Planning Policy (SPP) (Scottish Government, 2014) p.9.

grant of permission interferes with others' rights under art.8 or the First Protocol art.1, the planning authority has to justify granting the permission.

Development plan

When determining a planning application the planning authority are required to make the determination in accordance with the provisions of the development plan unless material considerations indicate otherwise.[157] This creates a presumption in favour of development proposals which are in accordance with the provisions of the development plan.

5.42

Although these provisions impose a presumption in favour of the development plan, this does not amount to a requirement that the authority decide all applications according to the terms of the plan.[158] If there has been a material change in circumstances, that may justify a departure from the development plan.[159]

The authority has to decide in light of the whole plan whether the proposal accords with it, and then if there are material considerations of such weight as to indicate that the plan should not be accorded priority. The House of Lords have stated that the assessment of the facts and the weighing of the considerations remains in the hands of the decision-maker. The assessment of the considerations can only be challenged on the ground that it is irrational or perverse.[160] The law does not require a material consideration to have any special weight to overcome the presumption in favour of the development plan.[161] The material consideration must however be identified in the decision.[162] The material consideration must normally be external to the factors within the development plan policy.[163]

The House of Lords' decision indicates the following approach[164]:

- The decision-maker must consider the development plan, identify any provisions in it which are relevant to the question before him and make a proper interpretation of them. His decision will be open to challenge if he fails to have regard to a policy in the development plan which is relevant to the application or fails properly to interpret it.[165]
- He will also have to consider whether the development proposed in the application before him does or does not accord with the development plan. There may be some points in the plan which support the proposal but there may be some considerations pointing in the opposite direction. He will require to assess all of these and then decide whether in light of the whole plan the proposal does or does not accord with it.
- He will also have to identify all the other material considerations which are relevant to the application and to which he should have regard. He will then have to note which of them support the application and which of them do

---

[157] TCPSA 1997 ss.25 and 37. This does not apply to applications under the Electricity Act 1989 s.36—*Wm Grant & Sons Distillers Ltd v Scottish Ministers* [2012] CSOH 98.
[158] In *Tesco Stores Ltd v Dundee City Council* [2012] UKSC 13, the Supreme Court upheld a grant of planning permission which was not in accordance with the development plan.
[159] *Tesco Stores Ltd v Aberdeen City Council* [2012] CSIH 81 at [27].
[160] *Edinburgh City Council v Secretary of State for Scotland*, 1998 S.L.T. 120.
[161] *St Albans DC v Secretary of State for the Environment* [1993] J.P.L. 374.
[162] *Perth and Kinross Council v Secretary of State for Scotland*, 1999 S.C. 144.
[163] *Aberdeenshire Council v Scottish Ministers*, 2008 S.C. 485 at [40].
[164] *Edinburgh City Council v Secretary of State for Scotland*, 1998 S.L.T. 120, per Lord Clyde at 127G–L.
[165] e.g. *Edinburgh City Council v Scottish Ministers*, 2002 S.L.T. 85.

not, and he will have to assess the weight to be given to all of these considerations. He will have to decide whether there are considerations of such weight as to indicate that the development plan should not be accorded the priority which the statute has given to it.

- Having weighed these considerations and determined these matters he will require to form his opinion on the disposal of the application.
- If he fails to take account of some material consideration or takes account of some consideration which is irrelevant to the application, his decision will be open to challenge. But the assessment of the considerations can only be challenged on the ground that it is irrational or perverse.
- It is undesirable to devise any universal prescription for the method to be adopted by the decision-maker. Different cases will invite different methods. It should be left to the good sense of the decision-maker, acting within his powers, to decide how to go about the task before him in the particular circumstances of each case.

Some importance thus now attaches to the decision whether the proposed development accords with the development plan. In a subsequent case, the Supreme Court rejected the proposition that the meaning of the development plan was a matter to be determined by the planning authority, unless the view taken by the planning authority was perverse or irrational. The correct approach is for development plans to be interpreted objectively in accordance with the language used, read in its proper context.[166]

5.43   The Scottish Government advise that the presumption in favour of sustainable development (see para.5.45 below) does not change the statutory status of the development plan as the starting point for decision-making. Proposals that accord with up-to-date plans should be considered acceptable in principle and consideration should focus on the detailed matters arising. For proposals that do not accord with up-to-date development plans, the primacy of the plan is maintained and the presumption in favour of development that contributes to sustainable development is a material consideration. Where relevant policies in a development plan are out-of-date or the plan does not contain policies relevant to the proposal, then the presumption in favour of development that contributes to sustainable development will be a significant material consideration. The same principle should be applied where a development plan is more than five years old. Where a plan is under review, it may be appropriate in some circumstances to consider whether granting planning permission would prejudice the emerging plan. Such circumstances are only likely to apply where the development proposed is so substantial, or its cumulative effect would be so significant, that to grant permission would undermine the plan-making process by predetermining decisions about the scale, location or phasing of new developments that are central to the emerging plan. Prematurity will be more relevant as a consideration the closer the plan is to adoption or approval.[167]

The person challenging the decision has the onus of proving that TCPSA s.25 has not been followed.[168] The courts have been unwilling to require decision-makers to follow the rigid pre-set formalistic order of approach taken by s.25.[169] It is not essential for the report to committee or reporter's decision letter to mention

---

[166] *Tesco Stores v Dundee City Council* [2012] UKSC 13 per Lord Reed at 18.
[167] SPP, paras 32–34.
[168] *McDonald v Moray Council*, 1998 G.W.D. 16-819; 69 S.P.E.L. 101.
[169] Lord Clyde in *Edinburgh City Council v Secretary of State for Scotland*, 1998 S.L.T. 120; *Budgens*

s.25 if examination of the report/letter shows that the conclusion was reached in a manner consistent with the provisions of that section.[170] Defects of presentation in the report to committee will not result in the decision on the application being quashed unless the overall effect of the report is significantly misleading.[171] If the report appears to give an incorrect view on the legal provisions, such that there is a real risk of the committee being misled as to the correct approach, their decision may be invalid.[172]

The presumption in favour of the development plan highlights the importance of making representations during the process of replacement or renewal of development plans (see Ch.3 above) in an attempt to ensure that the new or revised plan contains provisions favourable to envisaged development proposals or does not promote development detrimental to the interest of a landowner or developer. Once a provision is enshrined in an adopted development plan it will be difficult to overcome.

The importance of development plans to the determination of planning applications is underlined by various procedural requirements mentioned above. The planning authority require to publish a newspaper advertisement for applications for developments which do not accord with the provisions of the development plan. Pre-determination hearings must be held for major developments which are significantly contrary to the development plan (as well as all national developments), and applications for such developments must be decided by the full council, not a committee. Where the planning authority have an interest in a proposed development which would be significantly contrary to the development plan, the authority cannot grant planning permission for the development until they have notified the Scottish Ministers. However, there is no longer a requirement to notify the Scottish Ministers of intent to grant planning permission for any development which is a significant departure from a structure plan (see "Role of Scottish Ministers", below).

Other material considerations

In addition to the terms of the development plan, the planning authority must also take into account all other material considerations when determining an application. These considerations provide the grounds for the reasons both for granting/ refusing to grant planning permission and for objecting to planning applications. It is, therefore, not surprising that what amounts to a material consideration is one of the most debated topics in planning law.

5.44

No definition of "material considerations" is provided by the legislation.[173] As the power to determine an application for planning permission is vested in the planning authority by the TCPSA 1997, to be material a consideration must be a planning consideration. There are many theories of planning (see Ch.1 above) and therefore many different answers to the question: what is "planning"? Case law is

---

Stores Ltd v Secretary of State for the Environment [1998] E.G. 28 (C.S.); North Yorkshire CC v Secretary of State for the Environment [1996] J.P.L. 32.
[170] Newham LBC v Secretary of State for the Environment (1995) 70 P. & C.R. 288.
[171] Lothian Borders and Angus Co-operative Society Ltd v Scottish Borders Council, 1999 G.W.D. 6-316; Freeport Leisure Plc v West Lothian Council, 1999 S.L.T. 452; R. v Selby DC Ex p. Oxton Farms [1997] E.G. 60 (C.S.).
[172] Campbell v Edinburgh City Council, 1998 G.W.D. 17–877; 1998 69 S.P.E.L. 99.
[173] Concise guidance is given in Planning Circular 3/2013, Development Management Procedures, Annex A.

continually identifying new examples of planning considerations. Although this leads to uncertainty, it gives planning authorities a necessary degree of flexibility in the matters which they may take into account when deciding an application.

Broadly, any consideration which relates to the use and development of land is capable of being a material planning consideration.[174] The courts have provided more specific guidance, but only on a case-by-case basis. Court decisions make it possible to state whether or not certain matters are planning considerations, but do not give a general indication of what may amount to a material planning consideration.

As outlined in Ch.2, planning authorities are prohibited from acting in a way which is incompatible with Convention rights under the European Convention on Human Rights. In consequence, in addition to the recognised material considerations discussed below, planning authorities must also have regard to Convention rights when determining a planning application. In effect, the Convention rights have become material considerations—although the material considerations below and Convention rights are often the same or similar. Relevant Convention rights in any particular case might include: art.8—right to respect for private and family life, home and correspondence; art.9—freedom of thought, conscience and religion, for example, where a religious group seek planning permission for a place of worship; art.10—freedom of expression, a landowner who wants to erect a fibreglass shark on his terraced house for artistic reasons might argue that a refusal of planning permission amounts to a restriction on his freedom of expression; First Protocol art.1—peaceful enjoyment of possessions. Convention rights are not absolute, and individual cases require the rights of different parties with conflicting interests (for example, the applicant and objectors) to be balanced. The introduction of Convention rights might therefore be a relatively insignificant change. For example, art.8 and First Protocol art.1 may require the planning authority to take into account the loss of an individual's view in consequence of the proposed development, but the authority can conclude that the loss of the view is not important enough that refusal of permission is necessary. The European Court has held that there was no violation of art.8 where planning permission had been refused on the grounds that the siting of gypsy caravans was inappropriate in the green belt.[175]

Planning authorities must also comply with the public sector equality duty.[176] Due regard must be had to the need to eliminate discrimination, harassment, victimisation and any other conduct which is prohibited by or under the Equality Act 2010; to advance equality of opportunity between persons who share a relevant protected characteristic and persons who do not share it; and to foster good relations between persons who share a relevant protected characteristic and persons who do not share it. The relevant protected characteristics are: age, disability, gender reassignment, pregnancy and maternity, race, religion or belief, sex, and sexual orientation. The planning authority is not precluded from deciding that equality implications are outweighed by countervailing considerations: it has to decide what weight to accord to equality considerations and how to balance them against other factors.[177] The Secretary of State's decision to recover jurisdiction for planning appeals which

---

[174] *Stringer v Minister for Housing and Local Government* [1971] All E.R. 65 per Cooke J.
[175] *Chapman v UK*, The Times, 30 January 2001.
[176] Equality Act 2010 s.149. General guidance is available from the Equality and Human Rights Commission—*http://www.equalityhumanrights.com* [Accessed 2 February 2016].
[177] *R. (on the application of Core Issues Trust) v Transport for London* [2014] EWCA Civ 34 per Lord

related to the provision of travellers' pitches within the green belt constituted a breach of the public sector equality duty.[178] A grant of planning permission for redevelopment of a site was quashed because there was neither specific reference to a predecessor duty nor the substance of that duty.[179]

Specific examples of material considerations are now considered. The list is not exhaustive.

(a)   Sustainable development and climate change

Many of the material considerations discussed below contribute directly towards the general objective of sustainable development, which has been defined as "development that meets the needs of the present without compromising the ability of future generations to meet their own needs".[180] There is a statutory requirement for planning authorities to exercise their development plan functions with the objective of contributing to sustainable development (see Ch.3 above). Sustainable development objectives will therefore flow through into the determination of planning applications through the key role of development plans in those determinations (see para.5.42 above).

5.45

Fresh guidance was issued in June 2014,[181] introducing a presumption in favour of development that contributes to sustainable development. Policies and decisions are to be guided by the following principles:

- giving due weight to net economic benefit;
- responding to economic issues, challenges and opportunities, as outlined in local economic strategies;
- supporting good design and the six qualities of successful places;
- making efficient use of existing capacities of land, buildings and infrastructure including supporting town centre and regeneration priorities;
- supporting delivery of accessible housing, business, retailing and leisure development;
- supporting delivery of infrastructure, for example, transport, education, energy, digital and water;
- supporting climate change mitigation and adaptation including taking account of flood risk;
- improving health and well-being by offering opportunities for social interaction and physical activity, including sport and recreation;
- having regard to the principles for sustainable land use set out in the land use strategy;
- protecting, enhancing and promoting access to natural heritage, including green infrastructure, landscape and the wider environment;
- reducing waste, facilitating its management and promoting resource recovery;
- avoiding over-development, protecting the amenity of new and existing

---

Dyson at [71]–[76]. For example, the court upheld a grant of planning permission for development of a school on land regularly used by the disabled and elderly—*R. (on the application of Coleman) v Barnet LBC* [2012] EWHC 3725 (Admin).

[178]   *Moore v Secretary of State* [2015] EWHC 44 (Admin).

[179]   *R. (on the application of Harris) v Haringey LBC* [2010] EWCA Civ 703.

[180]   World Commission on Environment and Development (Brundtland Commission), *Our Common Future* (New York: World Commission on Environment and Development, 1987).

[181]   SPP, "Principal Policy on Sustainability", paras 24–35.

development and considering the implications of development for water, air and soil quality.

Many of these objectives will assist planning authorities in fulfilling their duties under the Climate Change (Scotland) Act 2009 (see Ch.3 above).

Given the overarching nature of the concept of sustainable development, it is inevitable that the following examination of specific examples of material considerations overlaps with many of the objectives mentioned in relation to sustainable development.

(b) Suitability of site

5.46   The suitability of the site for the proposed development is one of the main material considerations. Instability as a result of mine workings (the Coal Authority is a statutory consultee in areas of coal working), tipping, or liability to flooding,[182] may make sites unsuitable for certain types of development. Any potential contamination of the site is relevant and authorities will require investigation of likely contaminated sites prior to development.[183]

(c) Appearance of the proposed development and its relationship to its surroundings

5.47   The decision on the application necessarily involves consideration of the appearance of the proposed development and its relationship to its surroundings. Relevant matters include the materials to be used; the height, scale, massing, layout and density, in comparison to buildings in the surrounding area; landscaping; privacy, both for surrounding properties and the occupiers or users of the proposed development; overshadowing; lack of natural light; noise, smell and fumes; and glare from floodlights or headlights of vehicles.

The Scottish Government guidance states that planning should take every opportunity to create high quality places by taking a design-led approach.[184] Planning permission may be refused solely on design grounds.[185] Where a design or design and access statement is required (see para.5.22 above), the information within the statement may be material and in such cases must be taken into account by the planning authority when considering the proposed development.[186]

(d) Impact

5.48   The impact of the proposed development upon the surrounding area must be evaluated. Regard must be had to the desirability of preserving the setting of a listed building, and of preserving or enhancing the character and appearance of a conservation area or national scenic area (see Ch.9 below). Any general loss of amenity or privacy, increases in noise level[187] and volume of traffic, questions of

---

182   SPP, "Managing Flood Risk and Drainage", paras 254–268.
183   PAN 33, Development of Contaminated Land (Scottish Executive, revised 2000).
184   SPP, para.38
185   SPP, para.56.
186   Planning Circular 3/2013, Development Management Procedures, para.3.36.
187   PAN 1/2011, Planning and Noise (Scottish Government, 2011).

safety and other potential social costs must be considered.[188] The impact of the development on private individuals must also be considered. For example, there may be a resultant loss of privacy, sunlight or amenity suffered by neighbouring proprietors, whether or not these proprietors are notifiable neighbours. Thus material considerations may be either the public or private interests of both the applicant and objectors.[189] This reflects the rights both the applicant and objectors have under the European Convention on Human Rights (para.5.41).

In dismissing an appeal for a major toxic waste plant in England, the Secretary of State took into account the deleterious effect on local employment, investment and industry, and public fears of long-term effects on health, although the major determining factor was potential pollution of the underground acquifer.[190]

The development may result in pollution or contamination (see para.5.60 below). Local flooding likely to be caused by the development is relevant.[191]

Justified public concern in the locality about emanations from the land as a result of its proposed development can be a material consideration. The fear and concern felt by occupants of neighbouring land was as real in relation to a proposed extension to a bail hostel as in a case involving polluting discharges, and as relevant to the reasonable use of the land.[192] In considering a claim for expenses as a part of an appeal, it was an error of law to approach the question of whether the planning authority had behaved unreasonably on the basis that genuine fears on the part of the public, unless objectively justified, could never amount to a valid ground for refusal.[193] It therefore appears that public concerns, even if not justified on scientific or other grounds, can still be a material consideration which could be used as a reason for refusing planning permission.[194] The weight to be given to the concern is a matter for the judgment of the decision-maker.[195] There must be evidence to establish real concern.[196]

Even if planning permission is granted, this does not give immunity from a claim of nuisance brought by persons affected by the development.[197]

(e) Compatibility with existing uses

In addition to its general impact on the surrounding area, the compatibility of the proposed development with existing uses is a material consideration.[198] In one case, the effect of dust created by a proposed concrete plant on neighbouring factories

5.49

---

[188] *Esdell Caravan Parks Ltd v Hemel Hempstead Rural DC* [1965] 3 All E.R. 737 per Lord Denning at 743F.

[189] *Glasgow DC v Secretary of State for Scotland*, 1993 S.L.T. 1332; 1993 38 S.P.L.P. 21.

[190] APP/F4410/A/89/126733 (Doncaster Incinerator Appeal).

[191] SPP, "Managing Flood Risking and Drainage", paras 254–268; *WE Black v Secretary of State for the Environment* [1997] Env. L.R. 1.

[192] *West Midlands Probation Committee v Secretary of State for the Environment* [1998] J.P.L. 388.

[193] *Newport BC v Secretary of State for Wales* [1998] J.P.L. 377.

[194] Planning Circular 3/2013, Development Management Procedures, Annex A, para.5 gives examples of potential material considerations, including "legitimate public concern or support expressed on relevant planning matters".

[195] *Trevett v Secretary of State for Transport, Local Government and the Regions* [2002] EWHC 2696.

[196] *Smith v First Secretary of State* [2006] J.P.L. 386.

[197] *Wheeler v JJ Saunders Ltd* [1995] 2 All E.R. 697; also *Watson v Croft Promo-Sport Ltd* [2009] J.P.L. 1178.

[198] *Collis Radio Ltd v Secretary of State for the Environment* (1975) 29 P. & C.R. 390.

manufacturing precision products and requiring clean air was a relevant factor.[199] Alternatively, existing uses may be incompatible with proposed developments such as a proposed housing development on land neighbouring an explosives factory. However, it may be proper for a planning authority to wish to encourage residential development in an area of existing industrial users.[200] While planning powers should not be used to protect commercial interests, it may be relevant to consider the degree to which the opening of a shopping centre might lead to the decay of existing centres.[201] When determining an application for a hot food takeaway, the proximity of a school was a material consideration.[202] The desirability of preserving a balance of uses may also be a material consideration.

It will be important to assess the degree of incompatibility. A proposed waste transfer facility was refused on the grounds that any malodorous emissions could prejudice the operation of an adjacent factory manufacturing cocoa products. This decision was quashed by the court on the grounds that no effort had been made to estimate the likely frequency of the worst case scenario, and there was no evidence that a tainting incident would sooner or later be likely to occur.[203]

A grant of planning permission for an incompatible development will not give the developer immunity from a claim of nuisance. A grant of planning permission for intensification of pig farming did not give immunity from liability in nuisance to neighbouring landowners in respect of smells inevitably caused by implementation of the permission.[204]

(f) Desirability of retaining the existing use

5.50   The existing use of the site is a material consideration, such as the continuation of industrial uses which are important to the character and functioning of a city.[205] It may be desirable to continue an existing residential use in an area where there is a shortage of housing.[206] This ground would require evidence of a reasonable probability that a refusal of permission would result in the continuance of the existing use. Alternative permitted uses of the site must also be considered. The planning authority is not bound to apply a competing needs test of desirability of preserving the existing use versus the merits of the proposed new use.[207]

(g) Competing developments and existence of a better alternative site

5.51   Where several developers have each applied for planning permission for similar developments but on different sites, each will often allege that their site is the better/best. There is no general rule that alternative sites must always be considered.[208] The existence of a better site for the proposed development may be a material considera-

---

[199] *RMC Management Services v Secretary of State for the Environment* (1972) 222 E.G. 1593.
[200] *R. v Exeter City Council Ex p. Thomas* [1990] J.P.L. 129.
[201] *R. v Doncaster MDC Ex p. British Railways Board* [1987] J.P.L. 444; SPP, "Promoting Town Centres", paras 58–73.
[202] *R. (on the application of Copeland) v Tower Hamlets LBC* [2010] EWHC 1845 (Admin).
[203] *Envirocor Waste Holdings Ltd v Secretary of State for the Environment* [1996] J.P.L. 489.
[204] *Wheeler v JJ Saunders Ltd* [1995] 2 All E.R. 697.
[205] *Westminster City Council v Great Portland Estates* [1985] A.C. 661.
[206] *Clyde & Co v Secretary of State for the Environment* [1977] 1 W.L.R. 926.
[207] *London Residuary Body v Lambeth LBC* [1990] 2 All E.R. 309.
[208] *Derbyshire Dales DC v Secretary of State for Communities* [2009] EWHC 1729; *South Cambridgeshire DC v Secretary of State for Communities and Local Government* [2009] J.P.L. 467.

tion as a result of characteristics of either the proposed development or its site, including whether the adverse effects of the proposed development might have a reduced impact on a specified alternative site.[209] The criteria for the materiality of the relative merits of the application site and other sites have been expressed as: the presence of a clear public convenience or advantage in the proposal under consideration; the existence of inevitable and adverse effects or disadvantages to the public, or to some section of the public, in the proposal; the existence of an alternative site for the same project which would not have those effects, or would not have them to the same extent; and a situation in which there could only be one permission granted for such a development, or at least only a very limited number of permissions. These criteria were satisfied where there were several applications for service areas along a stretch of trunk road.[210]

If the existence of alternative sites is relevant, the planning authority is not required to determine which site is better, but only to consider the other site as an alternative.[211] Where the development on the proposed site is acceptable, planning permission should not be refused on the grounds that it would be more acceptable on an alternative site, with the possible exception of competing applications for the same development, but on different sites, in circumstances where permission can be granted for one development only.[212] If the site of the proposed development is unsuitable, the applicant may be required to demonstrate the need for the proposed development on that site. A decision that there was a strong possibility that another site would be available that would cause less harm than the current proposal was quashed where there was no evidence regarding any alternative sites.[213]

Where there are competing planning applications, and one is appealed to the Scottish Ministers or called-in by them for their decision, there is no requirement for the rival applications to be called-in for conjoined determination.[214] The planning authority can grant planning permission for a development notwithstanding a pending appeal on a rival development.[215]

(h) Financial viability

The cost of the proposed development is not a material consideration in itself.[216] **5.52** Assessment of the financial viability of the proposed development is best carried out by the developer and most planning authorities do not have the expertise to make such an assessment. However, the planning consequences of the financial viability of the proposal can be considered.[217] Lack of financial viability results in some developments being abandoned before completion, sterilising the site against

---

[209] *Ynystawe, Ynforgan & Glair Gipsy Site Action Group v Secretary of State for Wales* [1981] J.P.L. 874.

[210] *Secretary of State for the Environment v Edwards* [1994] 1 P.L.R. 62.

[211] *R. v Royal County of Berkshire Ex p. Mangnall* [1985] J.P.L. 258.

[212] *Trusthouse Forte Hotels Ltd v Secretary of State for the Environment* (1987) 53 P. & C.R. 293; [1986] 2 E.G.L.R. 185; *Greater London Council v Secretary of State for the Environment* [1986] J.P.L. 193.

[213] *Beech v Secretary of State for the Environment* [1993] E.G. 214 (C.S.).

[214] *ASDA Stores Ltd v Secretary of State for Scotland*, 1999 S.L.T. 503; *R. v Secretary of State for the Environment, Transport and the Regions Ex p. Carter Commercial Developments Ltd* [1999] 1 P.L.R. 1.

[215] *Bett Properties Ltd v Scottish Ministers*, 2001 S.C. 238.

[216] *J Murphy & Sons v Secretary of State for the Environment* [1973] 1 W.L.R. 560; [1973] 2 All E.R. 26.

[217] *Sosmo Trust v Secretary of State for the Environment* [1983] J.P.L. 806 per Woolf J.

future development and leaving the authority with the problem of how the site should be managed.

There may be assertions by the applicant that no other form of development is financially viable on the site and that as a result, permission should be granted for the proposed development. Securing the retention and use of existing buildings, especially listed buildings (see Ch.9 below), may require the authority to permit economically viable development notwithstanding that the proposed development is not wholly appropriate—this is generally known as enabling development.

(i) Planning benefits

5.53   Planning benefits are used by applicants to "sweeten the pill" by offsetting the planning disadvantages of the proposed development. Such benefits may arise from the terms of the application or provisions of a planning obligation entered into between the applicant and the authority (see Ch.6 below). If the benefits do not amount to material considerations, the authority must ignore them when determining the application.

The law regarding the extent to which planning benefits are permissible, and therefore become material considerations, has been settled by the decision of the House of Lords in the *Tesco* case.[218] Their Lordships held that a benefit which has nothing to do with the development will plainly not be a material consideration. If the benefit has some connection, then regard must be had to it. The extent to which it should affect the decision is a matter entirely within the discretion of the decision-maker. In exercising that discretion, he is entitled to have regard to his established policy.[219] This decision draws a clear distinction between the question of whether something is a material consideration and the weight which it should be given: the former is a question of law, and the latter is a question of planning judgment which is entirely a matter for the planning authority.

The House of Lords also upheld the decision in the *Plymouth* case[220] that the legal validity of taking into account an offer of a planning benefit did not depend on the benefit being necessary to overcome what would otherwise be planning objections to the proposed development, although such a test could be applied as a matter of policy. Lord Hoffmann also rejected the proposition that a planning agreement must have the effect of making acceptable what would otherwise have been unacceptable. In his view, this was indistinguishable from the test of necessity rejected in the *Plymouth* case.

The consequence of the *Tesco* decision is that the courts cannot intervene in cases where there is sufficient connection between the development and the planning benefit to make it a material consideration, but the benefit appears disproportionate to the external costs of the development.

5.54   To form a material consideration, the benefit must have a planning purpose and fairly and reasonably relate to the proposed development. It is not necessary for the benefit to be required to overcome, remedy or alleviate planning objections to the proposed development. There must be a clear and direct nexus or a recognised and real relationship between the benefit and the proposed development. This nexus or

---

[218] *Tesco Stores Ltd v Secretary of State for the Environment* [1995] 2 All E.R. 636.
[219] *R. v South Northamptonshire DC Ex p. Crest Homes* [1994] 3 P.L.R. 47. The Scottish Government policy is discussed in Ch.6.
[220] *R. v Plymouth City Council Ex p. Plymouth and South Devon Co-operative Society Ltd* [1993] 2 P.L.R. 75.

relationship may be geographic, functional or financial.[221] A reasonable prospect of the benefit arising is sufficient and there is no requirement that the benefit be guaranteed, for example, through a planning agreement.[222] The benefit does not necessarily have to be quantified.[223]

In determining an application for a sports facility at one site, it was a material consideration that the grant of permission would enable redevelopment of another site. The consequent benefits to the conservation area of this redevelopment outweighed the harm to important conservation interests at the site of the new sports facility.[224] In contrast, traffic management measures to be financed by the applicant were not a material consideration because there was no direct nexus between the proposed superstore and the improvements where these measures were aimed at problems already in existence.[225] Offers of community benefits such as provision of a tourist information centre, a bird-watching hide and a static art feature were upheld as a material consideration in the determination of an application for a superstore development.[226]

In the *Tesco* case, as part of its superstore application Tesco had offered to pay for a new link road required to resolve traffic problems in the town centre. The Secretary of State did not consider that the road was needed to enable the store proposal to go ahead, or was otherwise so directly related to the proposed development that the store ought to be permitted without it. The offer of funding therefore failed to comply with the provisions of the government guidance. The extent to which he would take it into account would be of such a limited nature that it would not tip the balance of the arguments. Tesco appealed on the ground that by discounting the funding offer the Secretary of State had failed to take into account a material consideration. This was rejected by the House of Lords, who held that, far from dismissing Tesco's offer as immaterial, the Secretary of State had carefully weighed up its significance. His decision was not therefore open to challenge.

There was a tenuous connection between a proposed development and some of the proposals from the applicant for making the town centre more attractive and accessible. However, the court held that there was no rational basis for believing that the payment of £100,000 could significantly redress the harm envisaged by the proposed development, let alone outweigh it.[227]

Policies contained in development plans seeking community benefits from applicants do not automatically render the offer (or lack of an offer) of such benefits material considerations.[228] Benefits sought by the authority in planning conditions or agreements must be imposed for a planning purpose, be fairly and reasonably related to the proposed development, and not so unreasonable that no reasonable authority could have imposed them (see Ch.6 below).

5.55

It has been held that where residential development made additional infrastructure necessary or desirable, there was nothing wrong in the planning authority having a policy requiring major developers to contribute to the cost of infrastructure

---

[221] *Northumberland CC v Secretary of State for the Environment* [1989] J.P.L. 700.

[222] *Crawley BC v Secretary of State for the Environment* [1993] J.P.L. 148.

[223] *R. (on the application of Tesco Stores Ltd) v Forest of Dean DC* [2015] EWCA Civ 800.

[224] *Wansdyke DC v Secretary of State for the Environment* [1992] J.P.L. 1168.

[225] *Safeway Properties Ltd v Secretary of State for the Environment* [1990] J.P.L. 759, but see *Tesco Stores Ltd v Secretary of State for the Environment* [1995] 2 All E.R. 636.

[226] *R. v Plymouth City Council Ex p. Plymouth and South Devon Co-operative Society Ltd* [1993] 2 P.L.R. 75.

[227] *R. (on the application of Lincoln Co-operative Society Ltd) v South Holland DC* [2001] J.P.L. 675.

[228] e.g. *Scottish Borders Council v Scottish Ministers* [2009] CSOH 70.

related to their development. The formula adopted by the authority, which was based on the enhanced value of the land, was not bad in law as insufficiently connecting the individual development with its associated infrastructure, as there was no suggestion that it would raise an amount disproportionate to what the developments required.[229]

The proposed development may be presented as enabling other more worthy development to proceed. The profits of the substantial office development included in the scheme for the redevelopment of the Royal Opera House, London, were to be applied to improve the opera house and it was competent for the planning authority to take this consideration into account when granting permission contrary to the provisions of the development plan.[230] This concept of enabling development is still evolving and it is uncertain what degree, if any, of functional, geographical or physical relationship is required.

Applications for housing or other highly profitable development frequently include proposals attractive to planning authorities such as renovation of listed buildings or relocation of football grounds to modern purpose-built stadia, with the applicant stating that the more attractive element of the proposed development cannot proceed without the funds generated from the housing development.[231] If this economic or planning benefit is a material consideration, the authority must consider whether the benefit is sufficient to justify granting permission. In most cases, the applicant will require to demonstrate that there is no source for securing these benefits other than the enabling development.

(j) Economic benefits

5.56 Economic benefits arising from the proposed development can be a material consideration.[232] It is common for applicants to point to the number of jobs which will be created if the development goes ahead. It was a material consideration that a proposed retail development would finance the relocation of a factory, safeguarding jobs which might otherwise be threatened.[233]

The Scottish Government state that planning decisions should give due weight to net economic benefit.[234]

(k) Social considerations

5.57 There is a social dimension to planning (see Ch.1 above) and some of the material considerations identified above have social elements. In so far as social considerations can be subsumed into planning considerations, these considerations will be material. In one case, the need for a period of social stability and consolidation was a good reason for refusing permission.[235] Many development plans contain policies on low-cost or affordable housing. The need for housing in a particular area is a material consideration. No sensible distinction can be drawn

---

[229] *R. v South Northamptonshire DC Ex p. Crest Homes Plc* [1994] 3 P.L.R. 47.

[230] *R. v Westminster City Council Ex p. Monahan* [1989] J.P.L. 107.

[231] *Brighton BC v Secretary of State for the Environment* [1979] J.P.L. 173; *South Oxfordshire DC v Secretary of State for the Environment* (1994) 68 P. & C.R. 551; *Worsted Investments Ltd v Secretary of State for the Environment* [1994] E.G. 66 (C.S.).

[232] *Northumberland CC v Secretary of State for the Environment* [1989] J.P.L. 700.

[233] *R. v Kingston upon Hull City Council Ex p. Kingswood Development Co Ltd* [1996] E.G. 200 (C.S.).

[234] SPP, para.29.

[235] *Severn Trent Water Authority v Secretary of State for the Environment* [1989] J.P.L. 21.

between a need for housing generally and a need for particular types of housing, whether or not the latter could be defined in terms of cost, tenure or otherwise. In each case the question is whether, as a matter of planning for the area under consideration, there is a need for housing which the grant or refusal of the application will affect.[236] Planning conditions requiring proportions of housing developments to be allocated to meet local authority housing needs were held to be illegal.[237]

(l) Provision of suitable access and transportation

The transportation aspects of the proposed development must be taken into account.[238] If the development involves forming or altering an access to a road, or is likely to cause a material increase in the volume of traffic entering or leaving the road, the planning officers generally consult their roads colleagues about the proposed development and take their comments into account when the application is determined. The Scottish Ministers must be consulted in specific circumstances where the development might affect a trunk road.[239] The roads authority may advise that the access from the development to the road is unsatisfactory or unsuitable, perhaps due to the dangers of turning traffic, or insufficient visibility and no possibility of visibility splays being provided to preserve visibility for vehicles using the access, or the unsuitability of the road for the traffic generated by the development, or insufficient parking provision.

5.58

The planning authority is not bound to follow the advice offered by the roads department.[240] In many cases, the roads department response is dictated by adopted policies and the planning authority may consider that the policy is not appropriate in the circumstances of the particular development.

(m) Sewerage, drainage and water

There must be provision for proper disposal of surface water and sewerage, and an adequate supply of water for the development.[241] Permission can be refused because of inadequacies of the existing public sewers.[242] Overcapacity in the drainage system is sometimes cited as a reason for refusing planning permission. The planning authority cannot allow a policy of the sewerage authority, imposing a total embargo on further sea discharges, to dictate its decision on a planning application, although this would be a relevant factor to be taken into account when determining the application.[243]

5.59

(n) Pollution and contamination

The likelihood of pollution as a result of the proposed development appears to be a material consideration, irrespective of the existence of other statutory powers

5.60

---

[236] *Mitchell v Secretary of State for the Environment* [1994] 2 P.L.R. 23.
[237] *R. v Hillingdon London BC Ex p. Royco Homes* [1974] 2 All E.R. 643; *David Lowe & Sons v Musselburgh Town Council*, 1973 S.C. 130.
[238] SPP, para.271.
[239] DMPR 2013 (SSI 2013/155) Sch.5.
[240] *Castle Rock Housing Association v Secretary of State for Scotland*, 1995 S.C.L.R. 850.
[241] PAN 79, Water and Drainage (Scottish Executive, 2006).
[242] *George Wimpey & Co Ltd v Secretary of State for the Environment* [1978] J.P.L. 773.
[243] *Ynys Mon BC v Secretary of State for Wales* [1993] J.P.L. 225.

such as integrated pollution control (IPC) under the Environmental Protection Act 1990 (EPA).[244] Public concerns, even if not justified on scientific or other grounds, may be a material consideration (see para.5.48 above).

Noise and odour have always been important planning issues, but it seems that planning authorities should now be taking into account pollution of any type. The environmental impact of emissions to the atmosphere is a material consideration, as is the existence of the statutory pollution control regime. There will come a point when the authority is entitled to be satisfied that, having had regard to the existence of EPA 1990 controls, residual concerns over pollution matters should not constitute a reason for refusal of planning permission.[245]

Contamination, or the potential for it, is a material consideration.[246] Contamination may give rise to hazards, for example putting at risk people working on, or in the immediate vicinity of, the site, or affecting structural durability. It may be possible to use the planning benefit of cleaning up contaminated land to justify the grant of permission for development which would not otherwise be permitted (see "Planning benefit", above).

The contents of any ES submitted in association with the application must be taken into account (see para.5.15 above).

A planning application cannot be determined on the basis of the worst case scenario without first conducting a risk assessment exercise to determine the likelihood of that situation occurring. An appeal decision was quashed because there was no evidence that a tainting incident would sooner or later be likely to occur. The inspector who determined the appeal was held to have made no effort to estimate the likely frequency of the worst case scenario.[247]

Scottish Government policy provides guidance on how planning authorities should deal with the overlap between planning, pollution control and waste management powers. In general the planning system should focus on whether the development itself is an acceptable use of the land, rather than control the process or substances involved; it should consider only the aspects of operations enforceable under planning control to minimise impacts on the environment, transport network and local communities; and secure decommissioning or restoration to agreed standards.[248]

Planning decisions will also have to have regard to the air quality objectives to be achieved by local authorities within their area.[249] The designation of an air quality management area (AQMA) may have implications for planning decisions. For example, development of a site allocated in the local plan for housing which subsequently falls within an AQMA might have to be reconsidered. In contrast, a superstore development in Bath was granted permission on the grounds that air quality would not suffer because traffic would be cut elsewhere.[250]

---

[244] Neil Collar, "Planning, Pollution Control and Waste Management", 1996 56 S.P.E.L. 67.
[245] *Gateshead MBC v Secretary of State for the Environment* [1994] 1 P.L.R. 85; *R. v Bolton MBC Ex p. Kirkham* (1998) J.P.L. 787; *R. (on the application of An Taisce) v Secretary of State* [2013] EWHC 4161 (Admin); *R. (on the application of Frack Free Balcombe Residents Assoc) v West Sussex CC* [2014] EWHC 4108 (Admin).
[246] PAN 33, Development of Contaminated Land (revised October 2000).
[247] *Envirocor Waste Holdings Ltd v Secretary of State for the Environment* [1996] J.P.L. 489.
[248] PAN 51, Planning, Environmental Protection and Regulation (Scottish Executive, revised 2006); *Online Planning and Waste Management Advice* (Scottish Executive, updated 8 July 2015).
[249] PAN 51, Planning, Environmental Protection and Regulation, para.61.
[250] Peter Weatherhead, "A breath of fresh air", 1997 E.G. 79.

(o) Archaeology

The effects of the proposed development on archaeological remains and their set-   **5.61**
ting is a material consideration. Where the physical preservation in situ of the
remains is not justified in the circumstances, and the development will result in the
destruction of the remains, the planning authority should satisfy itself before granting permission that the developer has made appropriate and satisfactory provision
for the excavation and recording of the remains.[251]

(p) Nature conservation

In determining an application for planning permission, the authority must have   **5.62**
regard to the desirability of conserving Scotland's flora and fauna, geological and
physiographical features, and its natural beauty and amenity. The authority also has
a duty to further the conservation of biodiversity, and must ensure that adequate
provision is made for the preservation or planting of trees. Nature conservation
(natural heritage) is discussed further in Ch.9.

(q) Need

To require the landowner to show the need for a proposed development is exces-   **5.63**
sive interference with rights of ownership. The need for the development only
requires to be demonstrated if its detrimental effects are such that an overriding need
must be shown. Thus an overriding need may require to be demonstrated for
particular types of development or development in particular locations, such as in
the green belt (see Ch.9 below), or where there is a better alternative site (see
above).

In the same way, lack of need is not a valid reason in itself for refusing permission, unless the lack of need is relevant because of the detrimental effects of the
development.[252]

(r) Creation of an undesirable precedent

Planning authorities are not obliged to follow their previous decisions on similar   **5.64**
applications. However, consistency in decision-making is desirable and it is a material consideration that granting permission for the proposed development might set
a precedent making it difficult for similar applications to be refused in the future.[253]
A generalised concern is insufficient and there must be some evidence for this
view.[254] However, it has been held that this principle should not be applied too nar-
rowly, and that unless an inspector's reliance on the existence of an outstanding appeal in the area was in some way perverse, his finding that the present proposal
would trigger similar proposals and seriously weaken the council's ability to enforce
the local plan policy, was not capable of successful challenge.[255]

[251] PAN 2/2011, Planning and Archaeology (Scottish Government, 2011).
[252] R. v Hambleton DC Ex p. Somerfield Stores Ltd [1998] E.G. 155 (C.S).
[253] Collis Radio Ltd v Secretary of State for the Environment (1975) 29 P. & C.R. 390.
[254] Poundstretcher v Secretary of State for the Environment [1988] 3 P.L.R. 69.
[255] Woolwich Building Society v Secretary of State for the Environment [1995] E.G. 114 (C.S.).

(s) Planning history of the site

5.65   It is relevant to consider what development can be carried out on the site in terms of existing permissions or by exercising permitted development rights under the Permitted Development Order or Use Classes Order (see Ch.4 above). Grants of planning permission for similar developments on the same site may be used to show that the authority have conceded the principle of development of the site.

Where an existing permission is cited as a fall back position, it is a material consideration, and there is no general rule requiring it to be shown that it is more likely than not that the development authorised by that permission will ever proceed.[256]

Previous planning decisions in respect of the site cannot be followed slavishly[257] and each application must be decided upon its merits. As a result, there may be several grants of permission for one site which are mutually inconsistent and conflicting.[258] Multiple implementation of permissions in such circumstances may be problematic (see para.5.106 below).

Where there are two different decisions on identical applications, the second decision is not necessarily irrational. Provided the planning authority act rationally and take into account all material considerations, they are not bound by their previous decisions.[259]

(t) Duplicate applications

5.66   The outcome of an appeal may be a material consideration for the planning authority in determining a duplicate application for the same or a similar development on the same site. Depending upon the stage reached in the appeal proceedings, the authority may be obliged either to delay deciding the application until the appeal decision has been received and can be taken into account, or to reject the application as premature. For example, where a public local inquiry had been held and the reporter's decision was awaited, it was unreasonable for the planning authority to grant permission for a duplicate application as the outcome of the appeal had become a material consideration to which the authority had to have regard when it considered the application.[260] The stage reached in the appeal proceedings is not conclusive.[261]

It may be competent for the planning authority to decide that the second application is materially different from the first, and that the outcome of the appeal is not a material consideration which they ought to await.[262]

(u) Decisions on similar proposals in respect of other sites

5.67   There is no concept of binding precedents in the planning system whereby an authority might be obliged to follow the same approach taken in a previous decision.

---

[256] *New Forest DC v Secretary of State for the Environment* [1996] J.P.L. 935.

[257] *North Wiltshire DC v Secretary of State for the Environment* [1992] J.P.L. 955; *Standard Securities Estates v Secretary of State for the Environment* [1992] E.G. 129 (C.S.); *Palm Developments Ltd v Secretary of State for the Environment* [1997] E.G. 173 (C.S.).

[258] *Pilkington v Secretary of State for the Environment* [1973] 1 W.L.R. 1527, per Widgery C.J. at 1531.

[259] *Moore v East Renfrewshire Council* , 2005 G.W.D. 30-584; *R. v Aylesbury Vale DC Ex p. Chaplin* [1996] E.G. 126 (C.S.).

[260] *Trusthouse Forte (UK) Ltd v Perth and Kinross DC*, 1990 S.L.T. 737.

[261] *Pickering v Kyle and Carrick DC*, 1991 G.W.D. 7–361.

[262] *Henderson v Argyll and Bute Council*, 1998 S.C.L.R. 1; 1997 64 S.P.E.L. 126.

Each application must be decided upon its individual merits. However, previous decisions by the same authority relating to other sites might be used to show a consistent pattern in the application of its policies. Decisions by other authorities are unlikely to be of assistance in this manner. A decision was quashed on the grounds of failure to take into account the decision of a reporter for similar facilities at another site in the same retail and leisure park.[263]

Appeal decisions are not binding precedents, but show how the policy of the Scottish Ministers has been applied. If appeal decisions showing that planning permission is likely to be granted on appeal can be exhibited to the planning authority, this can be a factor in its determination of the application. The desirability of avoiding losing an appeal should not be a material consideration in itself, but is an important administrative consideration for all authorities.

(v)   Statements of policy

Statements of the policy of the Scottish Ministers contained in the SPP and other **5.68** policy instruments are a material consideration,[264] although a decision of the Court of Session cast a doubt on whether the planning authority are bound to have regard to comments and observations by a civil servant in a circular.[265] The use of Scottish Government policy in final and draft form in the determination of planning appeals appears to be accepted by the Court of Session.[266] A failure to apply an SPP policy led to a grant of planning permission being quashed.[267] The interpretation of the policy is a matter for the judgment of the decision-maker, and the decision can only be quashed if no reasonable decision-maker could have interpreted the policy in the way in which it was interpreted, or that no reasonable planning authority could have regarded an assessment as rigorous and meeting policy guidance.[268]

Although the advice in the SPP has no binding or legal force, in practice there is pressure on planning authorities to follow the provisions of the SPP as these represent the policy which will be applied by the Scottish Ministers or their reporter when deciding an appeal. Thus ignoring the advice within the SPP carries with it a considerable risk of losing any subsequent appeal.

(w)   Draft development plan

The provisions of draft development plans can be a material consideration.[269] **5.69** However, taking into account the policies of a draft plan which have not been adopted by the planning authority may pre-empt the outcome of the plan-making process. An application may properly be refused on the ground that the development will be likely to prejudice the outcome of the draft development plan, but all that is required is that the effect of the proposed development on the policies and

---

263 *Carlton Clubs v Highland Council* , 2004 G.W.D. 12-279.
264 *Scottish Housebuilders Association v Secretary of State for Scotland*, 1995 S.C.L.R. 1039 at 1043E–F; *JA Pye (Oxford) Estates Ltd v Wychavon DC* [1982] J.P.L. 575; *EC Gransden & Co Ltd v Secretary of State for the Environment* [1987] J.P.L. 365; [1986] J.P.L. 519.
265 *Noble Organisation Ltd v Falkirk DC*, 1994 S.L.T. 100.
266 e.g. *Bondway Properties Ltd v Edinburgh City Council*, 1998 S.C.L.R. 225; 1998 66 S.P.E.L. 31; *M-I Great Britain Ltd v Secretary of State for Scotland*, 1996 G.W.D. 22-1303; 57 S.P.E.L. 93; *Dobbie v Secretary of State for Scotland*, 1996 G.W.D. 22–1302; 1996 57 S.P.E.L. 92.
267 *Carlton Clubs v Highland Council*, 2004 G.W.D. 12-279.
268 *Co-operative Group (CWS) Ltd v Highland Council*, 2008 G.W.D. 11-200.
269 *R. v City of London Corporation Ex p. Allan* (1980) 79 L.G.R. 223.

proposals of the draft plan should be considered before the application is decided. Provided the planning authority take into account all material considerations, it is not incompetent to grant a planning permission which pre-empts objections to the draft local plan which are due to be heard at the local plan inquiry.[270] The relevant factors are: the stage reached in the plan process; the timescale for the determination of the plan process; the centrality or otherwise of the issue to be determined in the plan process to the decision whether or not to issue the planning permission under consideration; the assessment of the prospects of success of the representation in the plan process; and the consequences of the determination in the plan process for the validity of the planning permission.[271]

(x) Applicant's personal circumstances

5.70   Planning relates to the use of land rather than to the user.[272] The general rule is that the personal circumstances or attributes of the applicant should be ignored by the authority. For example, it is not relevant that the applicant has lived in the area for many years. However, personal circumstances may be taken into account in exceptional cases where refusal of permission would cause an applicant great hardship.[273] Human rights and the public sector equality duty (see Ch.2 above) may make personal circumstances relevant.[274]

A more unusual instance of personal circumstances being relevant is where outline planning permission had been granted for a retail development following a retail impact assessment which adopted a notional turnover based on floor space reflecting the average of a number of selected UK companies operating superstores. The Northern Ireland Court of Appeal held that in determining a fresh planning application by Sainsbury, it was a material consideration that the business skills and experience of Sainsbury would cause a greater retail impact. A fresh retail impact assessment should therefore have been required.[275]

The private interests of the applicant are a material consideration and it was, therefore, held to be relevant to take into account improvements in efficiency, service and staff accommodation which would result from the proposed development.[276]

(y) Prematurity

5.71   Planning permission may be refused on grounds of prematurity where the development plan is in preparation or under review (see "Draft development plan", above). This would be competent only in respect of development proposals which are individually so substantial or likely to be so significant cumulatively, as to predetermine decisions about the scale, location or phasing of new development

---

270 *Watson v Renfrew DC*, 1995 S.C.L.R. 82; 1995 50 S.P.E.L. 68. See also *Blue Circle v Scottish Ministers*, 2002 S.L.T. 894 .
271 *Land Securities Group Plc v North Lanarkshire Council*, 2005 S.L.T 849.
272 *East Barnet Urban DC v British Transport Commission* [1962] 2 Q.B. 484 per Parker C.J. at 498; *David Lowe & Sons Ltd v Musselburgh Town Council*, 1973 S.C. 130 per Lord President Emslie at 142.
273 *Westminster City Council v Great Portland Estates Plc* [1985] A.C. 661 per Lord Scarman.
274 e.g. see discussion at para.7.46 below of English court decisions on the use of injunction powers for removal of unauthorised caravans.
275 *Re FA Wellworth; Re Boots* [1996] N.I. 509, CA (NI).
276 *City of Glasgow DC v Secretary of State for Scotland*, 1993 S.L.T. 1332; 1993 38 S.P.L.P. 21.

which ought properly to be taken in the development plan context.[277] An application may also be premature where an appeal decision for the same proposed development is awaited (see "Duplicate applications", above).

Non-material considerations

In general, the following considerations are not material and should be ignored:　**5.72**

(a) the personal circumstances of the applicant (but not always, see above);

(b) the identity of the occupier, user or developer[278];

(c) private interests[279] such as a landowner losing a desirable view from his property; however, it is relevant for the planning authority to take into account any loss of visual amenity (which in some respects includes loss of a view), daylight or privacy which will be caused to properties neighbouring the site of the proposed development[280];

(d) moral considerations arising from developments such as sex shops, or religious objections to Sunday working;

(e) political considerations or ideological dislike of projects such as private hospitals;

(f) the cost of the development (contrast financial viability, see above);

(g) title restrictions which may prevent the development from going ahead as the restrictions may be varied or discharged by the Lands Tribunal for Scotland[281];

(h) the applicant's lack of ownership of part of the application site.[282] The planning authority's function is to decide whether or not the proposed development is desirable in the public interest. The answer to that question should not be affected by the consideration that the landowner is determined not to allow the development. However, where there are competing sites for a desirable development, difficulties of bringing about implementation on one site which are not present in relation to the other might affect the choice of site to receive permission. All other things being equal it is possible that an assembled site package would be preferable to one with unresolved ownership problems;

(i) any other factor which indicates that there is a lack of any reasonable prospect of the development proceeding. The mere fact that a desirable condition, worded in a negative form, appears to have no reasonable prospects of fulfilment does not mean that planning permission need necessarily be refused as a matter of law.[283]

---

[277] *Arlington Securities Ltd v Secretary of State for the Environment* [1989] J.P.L. 166.

[278] But see *Re FA Wellworth; Re Boots* [1996] N.I. 509, CA (NI).

[279] *Willis v Argyll and Bute Council* [2010] CSOH 122.

[280] See Planning Circular 3/2013, Development Management Procedures, Annex A, para.6.

[281] See Roddy Paisley, "Feudal Conditions and Statutory Planning Powers", 1990 31 S.P.L.P. 74.

[282] *British Railways Board v Secretary of State for the Environment* [1994] J.P.L. 32. *Willis v Argyll and Bute Council* [2010] CSOH 122.

[283] Planning Circular 4/1998, Use of Conditions in Planning Permission (Scottish Office, 1998), para.38. For a different approach, see *Guidance on Dealing with Aviation and Associated Negative Conditions in Wind Turbine Consents* (Scottish Government, 2012).

Overlap with other statutory powers

5.73   It may be thought that planning powers should not be used to regulate matters more properly dealt with under other specific statutory powers. Indeed, Scottish Government policy strongly favours this view.[284] However, as a matter of law, it is competent for planning powers to be exercised in such circumstances provided a planning purpose is being served.

For example, the likely creation of litter as a result of a proposed development may be a relevant planning consideration because it could affect residential amenity.[285] The planning authority cannot disregard the effect on residential amenity of late night opening of licensed premises, on the basis that the issue will be dealt with under licensing legislation.[286] A refusal of permission on the ground that the land would be required for future road widening was held to be valid despite the result that the authority avoided paying the compensation which would have been due if other statutory powers had been exercised.[287] Planning powers can be used to restrict opening hours notwithstanding that the same power is available under the gaming legislation.[288] The overlap between planning and IPC powers conferred by the EPA 1990 may also cause difficulties. There will come a point when the existence of EPA 1990 controls results in residual concerns over pollution matters not forming a valid reason for refusing planning permission (see "Pollution and contamination", above).

If other statutory consents are required, there is no general rule requiring a decision on the planning application to be delayed until the outcome of the other statutory consent process(es).[289]

Representations received and consultation responses

5.74   When deciding an application for planning permission, the authority must also take into consideration representations received timeously under the provisions regarding notification of owners, agricultural tenants and neighbours, bad neighbour development, and the advertisement and display of notice under the provisions applicable to development within conservation areas (see above).[290]

Although the wording of the statute fails to qualify this requirement by limiting the relevance of such representations to planning considerations, this qualification is implicit in the general legal requirement that the planning authority ignores all irrelevant considerations. As a result, the authority should only take into account representations which raise planning considerations. Objections from neighbouring proprietors on the grounds that the proposed development will reduce the value of their property should therefore be ignored. However, some of the factors giving rise to the reduction in value may be relevant planning considerations.

It must also take into account responses timeously received from the bodies which it was required to consult. Although there is no requirement to consider representations by other interested parties, such representations may raise material considerations which the authority is obliged to consider.

---

[284] Planning Circular 4/1998, Use of Conditions in Planning Permission, paras 19–22.
[285] *Aberdeen DC v Secretary of State for Scotland*, 1993 S.L.T. 1325; [1992] 1 P.L.R. 1.
[286] *di Ciacca v Scottish Ministers*, 2003 S.L.T. 1031.
[287] *Westminster Bank Ltd v Minister of Housing and Local Government* [1971] A.C. 508.
[288] *Ladbroke (Rentals) v Secretary of State for the Environment* [1981] J.P.L. 427.
[289] *Lerwick Port Authority v Scottish Ministers* [2007] CSOH 156 at [90].
[290] TCPSA 1997 s.38; PLBCASA 1997 ss.60 and 65.

The authority would be acting illegally if it ignored material considerations on the grounds that these considerations were submitted late.

Environmental statement

The authority must also take into account the contents of any ES submitted with the application (see above), but these contents can only influence its decision in so far as they amount to planning considerations.

5.75

Fettering of discretion

The power to grant planning permission is discretionary. Improper exercise of this discretion may render the decision illegal (see Ch.8 below). The planning authority must always exercise its discretion freely and each case must be considered on its merits.

5.76

Proper exercise of the discretionary power requires the decision to be made by the planning authority. Unless authorised by statute, it is not competent for the authority to delegate this power. Planning authorities are permitted by statute to delegate the power to determine a planning application to a committee or sub-committee of the authority, an officer of the authority such as the Director of Planning, or another local authority in Scotland.[291] The authority remains responsible for the decision made under delegated powers and retains the power to revoke the delegation of power.

The views of other bodies on the application may be taken into account, but the authority cannot allow these views to dictate the decision on the application as the authority would be effectively delegating its power to that body. A decision to refuse permission on the grounds of a policy of another statutory body placing an embargo on future development was therefore held to be illegal.[292]

Each application must be decided on its merits. This principle does not prevent the authority from formulating policies applicable to certain types of development (indeed, policies encourage consistent decision-making). However, the policy cannot dictate the decision, otherwise the policy has fettered the exercise of discretion.[293] The authority can apply its policy in deciding the application but the possibility of making an exception to that policy must be considered in each case.

THE DECISION

The planning authority must give the applicant written notice of the decision, accompanied by a form notifying the applicant of his rights of appeal/review.[294] For the purposes of time limits for lodging an appeal/ review, the date of the decision by the authority is the date on which the notice bears to have been signed on behalf of the authority.[295]

5.77

---

[291] Local Government (Scotland) Act 1973 s.56, as amended; TCPSA 1997 s.43A—see "Schemes of Delegation" above.

[292] *Ynys Mon BC v Secretary of State for Wales* [1993] J.P.L. 225.

[293] *H Lavender & Son Ltd v Minister of Housing and Local Government* [1970] 3 All E.R. 871; *Stringer v Minister of Housing and Local Government* [1970] 1 W.L.R. 1281 per Cooke J. at 1298.

[294] TCPSA 1997 s.43(1A); DMPR 2013 (SSI 2013/155) reg.28.

[295] TCPSA 1997 s.37(4).

Once issued, the decision is treated as valid unless and until reduced or otherwise declared invalid by order of a competent court.[296]

Details of the decision must be entered into the planning register. The authority must also inform every person who made written representations in respect of the application of their decision and where a copy of the decision notice is available for inspection. Where representations are made by three or more persons in the same document, the planning authority can notify the person who sent the document to the planning authority, or if it is not possible to identify that person, the first named person in the document for whom an address is provided.

The decision notice must include a statement of the terms of the planning authority's decision, any conditions to which that decision is subject, and the reasons on which the authority based that decision. It must also include a description of the proposed development, including identification of the plans and drawings showing the proposed development; the postal address of the site or a description of its location; the reference number of the application; a description of any variation made to the application in accordance with s.32A; a statement of the effect of the statutory provisions on the duration of planning permission (see para.5.97 below); and identify where any s.75 obligation or summary thereof may be inspected.

The authority may refuse the application, or grant it unconditionally, or subject to such conditions as it thinks fit.[297] If the application is not determined within two months (four months in some circumstances—see para.5.78 below), the applicant may choose to lodge an appeal/review on the grounds that the authority is deemed to have refused planning permission. In addition, there is some scope for its decision to change the terms of the application. The various types of decision will now be explored.

(a) Deemed refusal

5.78   If the authority fails to determine the application within two months of the validation, the applicant has the option of lodging an appeal/review on the grounds that the authority is deemed to have refused the application. Such an appeal/review must be lodged within three months of the expiry of the two-month period. Where the authority obtains the written agreement of the applicant to an extension of the two-month period, no appeal/ review against a deemed refusal can be lodged until the agreed extension has expired (see para.5.02).

For national and major developments, and developments which require EIA, the planning authority has four months to determine the application, after which a deemed refusal appeal/review can be submitted.

The decision to appeal/review will be influenced by the costs involved in pursuing the appeal/review, the prospects of further delay when the authority may be close to a favourable decision, and the chances of the appeal/review being successful. It will be important to consider whether significant unresolved issues exist in connection with the application to render an appeal/review worthless. Deemed refusal appeals/reviews were used as a tactical device to pressurise authorities into granting permission on a duplicate application (see para.5.10 above).

---

[296] *Archid v Dundee City Council* [2013] CSOH 137.
[297] TCPSA 1997 s.37(1).

(b) Refusal

If the planning authority decides to refuse the application, the notice of its deci-   **5.79**
sion must specify its reasons for that decision. The application can only be refused
on planning grounds and these reasons will be drawn from the material considerations relevant to the application. The applicant has three months from the date of
the notice to appeal to the Scottish Ministers or apply for review by the local review
body, whichever is appropriate (see Ch.8 below).

(c) Resolution to grant permission

In the case of complex developments, it is not unusual for the planning author-   **5.80**
ity to resolve to grant permission once certain matters have been resolved, most
typically the execution of a s.75 obligation. The resolution, normally followed up
with a "minded to grant" letter which states that the authority is minded to grant
permission, does not amount to a grant of planning permission. Nor does it oblige
the authority to grant permission, as any change in circumstances must be taken into
account and could lead to a refusal of permission.[298] However, it may provide sufficient comfort to the applicant that permission will be granted to persuade him to
resolve the outstanding matters.

(d) Conditional grant of permission

The planning authority has a wide discretionary power to grant planning permis-   **5.81**
sion, "subject to such conditions as it thinks fit" (see Ch.6 below). Permissions for
large or complex developments may be subject to over 50 conditions. The reasons
for imposing each condition must be specified in the decision letter. There are various means by which the applicant can attempt to challenge the imposition of conditions (see Ch.6 below). Implementation of a permission (see below) implies acceptance of the conditions. The lack of any right of appeal against a breach of condition
notice (see Ch.7 below) emphasises the importance of ensuring that conditions are
acceptable prior to implementation.

It is not unlawful for permission to be granted in detail for roadworks and in
principle for development of a foodstore, where the store building is to be erected
within the footprint shown on the application plan.[299]

(e) Temporary and personal permissions

The planning authority may grant permission subject to a condition requiring the   **5.82**
removal of any buildings or works or discontinuance of any use of land authorised
by the permission at the end of a specified period.[300] Such a temporary permission
may be justified where a trial period is necessary to assess the effect of the development on the area. On expiry of the specified period, planning permission is not

---

[298] *John G Russell (Transport) Ltd v Strathkelvin DC*, 1992 S.L.T. 1001.
[299] *Lothian Borders and Angus Co-operative Society Ltd v Scottish Borders Council* [1999] 2 P.L.R.
    19.
[300] TCPSA 1997 s.41(1)(b).

required for resumption of the previous use provided that use is lawful (see "Lawful development", Ch.7 below).[301]

Planning permission normally enures for the benefit of the land rather than the applicant (see para.5.94 below). Personal permissions are grants of permission subject to conditions restricting the benefit of the permission to specified persons, often the applicant alone. It is seldom desirable to grant a personal permission but there may be exceptional circumstances where it is proposed to grant permission for use of a building for some purpose which would not normally be allowed, for some compassionate or other personal grounds.[302]

(f) Planning permission in principle

5.83   Planning permission in principle is granted subject to a condition requiring subsequent approval to be obtained from the planning authority for specified areas of detail.[303] It is competent for planning permission in principle to be granted for the carrying out of any development except a material change of use (see Ch.4 above).

Prior to 2009 these specified matters were known as "reserved matters", which could be any matters concerning the siting, design or external appearance of a building, or its means of access, or the landscaping of the application site, in respect of which details were not given in the application for outline planning permission.[304] Since 2009, there is no restriction on which matters can be reserved for further approval.

Rather than leaving an issue to be dealt with during the subsequent approval process, the authority have the power to require further details and information from the applicant.[305] However, the existence of uncertainties regarding matters such as noise do not necessarily prevent a grant of planning permission in principle.[306]

In a pre-2009 case, an outline application which specified the floor area committed those concerned to a development on that scale, subject to minimal adjustments for siting, design and external appearance.[307] Accordingly, matters such as traffic generation could not be reassessed during the determination of the application for approval of reserved matters. A similar approach is likely to be taken post-2009.

The application(s)[308] for further approval must be submitted within three years from the date the planning permission in principle was granted, or six months from the date any earlier application for approval was refused, or six months from the

---

[301] TCPSA 1997 s.28(2).

[302] Planning Circular 4/1998, Use of Conditions in Planning Permission, para.92.

[303] TCPSA 1997 s.59. This replaces the previous system of outline planning permissions and reserved matters applications.

[304] Court decisions on the scope of "reserved matters" include: *R. v Newbury DC Ex p. Chieveley Parish Council* [1998] E.G. 131 (C.S.); *The Times,* 10 September, 1998;; *Inverclyde DC v Inverkip Building Co Ltd*, 1983 S.L.T. 563; *Tesco Stores Ltd v North Norfolk DC* [1999] J.P.L. 920.

[305] DMPR 2013 (SSI 2013/155) reg.24.

[306] *R. v Northampton BC Ex p. Rice & Co* [1998] E.G .84 (C.S.).

[307] *R. v Newbury DC Ex p. Chieveley Parish Council* [1998] E.G. 131 (C.S.); *The Times,* 10 September 1998.

[308] The Scottish Government guidance advises that the time limits only apply to conditions which require approval to be obtained before development can begin—Planning Circular 3/2013, Development Management Procedures, para.4.109.

date of the dismissal of an appeal against such a refusal,[309] whichever is the latest. However, the planning authority may attach a direction to the planning permission in principle substituting longer or shorter periods, or specify separate periods for separate parts or phases of the development.[310]

(g) Approval of matters specified in conditions

There is a separate procedure for applying to the planning authority for approval, consent or agreement required by a condition imposed on a grant of planning permission in principle.[311] Pre-2009, the details submitted, and the reserved matters approval granted, could not depart from the ambit of the outline planning permission. For example, a reserved matters application could not be refused on the grounds that the design provided more office floor space than was needed to make the class 4 development viable.[312] Where an office building had been erected on part of a site for which outline planning permission had been granted for five houses, the subsequent application for approval of reserved matters was held not to be in accordance with the outline permission, as the entire development authorised by the outline permission could not be constructed with the generous plots envisaged in that permission.[313] The 2009 statutory provisions do not contain a similar prohibition on departing from the ambit of the planning permission in principle, but the concept of the planning permission in principle is sufficiently similar to outline permissions that it is likely that a similar approach will be taken.

5.84

(h) Variation of planning permission

An applicant may request the planning authority to vary the grant of planning permission. Such variation is competent provided it appears to the authority that the change sought is not material.[314] This allows minor changes to be made to the details of a development without the submission of a fresh application for planning permission.

5.85

(i) Permission to develop land without compliance with condition

The Scottish Government note the following in relation to TCPSA s.42 applications[315]:

5.86

- The effect of granting permission is such that a new and separate permission exists for the development with different (or no) conditions attached. The previous planning permission remains unaltered by, and is not varied by, the decision on the s.42 application.
- The duration of the new permission is specified in the TCPSA. Alternatively, authorities may direct that a longer or shorter period applies.

---

[309] Including an application for review of a refusal (see Ch.8 below)—s.59(2)(a), amended by Planning Etc (Scotland) Act 2006 (Supplementary and Consequential Provisions) Order 2013 (SSI 2013/26) art.2(5).
[310] TCPSA 1997 s.59(2)–(5). See guidance in Planning Circular 3/2013, Development Management Procedures, Annex H.
[311] TCPSA 1997 s.59(1)(b); DMPR 2013 (SSI 2013/155) reg.12.
[312] *Camden LBC v Secretary of State for the Environment* [1993] J.P.L. 466.
[313] *Orbit Development v Secretary of State for the Environment* [1996] E.G. 91 (C.S.).
[314] TCPSA 1997 s.64.
[315] Planning Circular 3/2013, Development Management Procedures, Annex I, para.2.

- The need to attach to the new permission any of the conditions from the previous permission which it is intended should apply to the new planning permission.
- The need to secure any s.75 legal obligation (or other agreement) to the new permission, where it is intended this should still apply.

(j) Grant of planning permission for revised development

5.87   In the negotiations prior to determination of the application for planning permission, it is common for the applicant to make changes to the proposals, often following suggestions by the planning officer dealing with the application. Applications can be varied after submission with the agreement of the planning authority.[316] The statutory provisions prohibit the authority from agreeing to the variation if they consider the variation involves a substantial change in the description of the proposed development. When an application is varied, the planning authority may give such notice of the variation as they consider appropriate.

Unless these changes are material, most authorities will not suggest that the application be re-notified/re-advertised. However, this may deprive those persons whose views must be taken into account by the authority of an opportunity to give their views on what would be a different proposal, with the possible result that the permission is illegal. If there is any doubt, the safest course must always be to re-notify all parties and give fresh notice by advertisement.

These statutory provisions were introduced in 2009, but appear to be based on previous caselaw, which provides guidance on how the provisions might be applied. The courts held that it is competent for the authority to grant planning permission for a development different from that proposed in the application.[317] The test identified by the courts was whether the amended proposal is different in substance. Where an original application sought permission for buildings of 85,000sq m, the planning authority did not act unreasonably in treating a revisal to 15,000sq m as not altering the substance of the application and in not re-notifying a party.[318] The planning authority were entitled to hold that an amendment did not change the substance of the application where the plans had been amended in detail but the physical appearance of the proposed building essentially remained the same.[319] A grant of planning permission which reduced the size of the proposed development from 35 acres and 420 dwellings to 25 acres and 250 dwellings was upheld on the basis that the result did not differ substantially from the development proposed in the original application.[320] This suggests a test of character: does the permitted development have a substantially different character from the development proposed in the original application? For example, an amendment was material where it increased the site area by 50 per cent, brought the proposed gypsy camp significantly closer to three nearby residences and increased the number of pitches which might be accommodated.[321]

The authority may also regulate matters ancillary or incidental to the proposed

---

[316] TCPSA 1997 s.32A; s.32B gives the Scottish Ministers similar power.
[317] *Kent CC v Secretary of State for the Environment* (1977) 33 P. & C.R. 70.
[318] *Walker v Aberdeen City Council*, 1998 S.L.T. 427; 1997 61 S.P.E.L. 59.
[319] *Burgon v Highland Council* [2007] CSOH 70.
[320] *Bernard Wheatcroft Ltd v Secretary of State for the Environment* [1982] J.P.L. 37. Discussed by Lord Jones in *Petition of The John Muir Trust* [2015] CSOH 163 at [103].
[321] *Breckland DC v Secretary of State for the Environment* [1992] 3 P.L.R. 89.

development, but which do not form part of the application, such as the provision of children's play areas and public open spaces for a large housing development.[322]

(k) Development contrary to the development plan

Provided that the authority have regard to the provisions of the development plan, **5.88** it is competent for planning permission to be granted for a development which is contrary to the terms of the plan. However, notice must have been given by advertisement in a local newspaper.[323] Pre-determination hearings must be held for major developments which are significantly contrary to the development plan (as well as all national developments), and applications for such developments must be decided by the full council, not a committee. There is no longer a requirement to notify the Scottish Ministers of intent to grant planning permission for a development which is a significant departure from a structure plan, and where the planning authority have an interest in the development notification is only required if the proposed development would be significantly contrary to the development plan (see para.5.90 below).

Role of Scottish Ministers

All planning applications, even for national developments, are dealt with by the **5.89** relevant local authority. However, the Scottish Ministers have powers to scrutinise the decisions made by planning authorities, and to call-in applications so that the decision is made by the Ministers rather than the planning authority.

(a) Notification

If the planning authority proposes to grant planning permission for certain types **5.90** of development, they must first notify the Scottish Ministers.[324] A failure to comply with this notification requirement could result in a grant of planning permission being invalid.[325] In the absence of any specific reference to applications for approval of matters specified in conditions, it appears there is no requirement for notification of intention to grant such applications.[326]

This notification procedure alerts the Ministers to applications which it may be appropriate for them to call in for determination. A more proportionate approach to notification was introduced in 2009, because around 90 per cent of applications notified to Ministers were not subsequently called-in. Some categories of development no longer require notification: for example, development contrary to development plans; major retail development; development subject to EIA; and changes have been made to the circumstances in which other categories of development require notification.

Since 2009, the types of development requiring notification are:

Development in which Planning Authorities have an Interest: either the plan-

---

[322] *Britannia (Cheltenham) Ltd v Secretary of State for the Environment* (1979) J.P.L. 534.
[323] DMPR 2013 (SSI 2013/155) reg.20.
[324] Town and Country Planning (Notification of Applications) (Scotland) Direction 2009, attached to Planning Circular 3/2009, Notification of Planning Applications (Scottish Government, 2009). Also Town and Country Planning (Neighbouring Planning Authorities and Historic Environment) (Scotland) Direction 2015 (Scottish Government, 2015).
[325] *Jermon Ltd v West Dunbartonshire Council*, 2008 G.W.D. 21-343.
[326] DMPR 2013 (SSI 2013/155) reg.31 refers to "applications for planning permission".

ning authority is the applicant/developer, or it has a financial or other (e.g. partnership) interest, or where the development is located on land wholly or partly in their ownership or in which they have an interest. The notification requirement only applies if the proposed development would be significantly contrary to the development plan.[327]

Development Affecting Trunk and Special Roads: where the Scottish Ministers, acting through Transport Scotland, have been consulted and have advised against the grant of permission or have recommended conditions which the planning authority do not propose to attach to the permission.

Development in the Vicinity of Major Hazards: where there has been consultation with the Health and Safety Executive and they have advised against the grant of planning permission or recommended conditions which the planning authority do not propose to attach to the permission.

Nature Conservation: where the development has the potential to affect a Site of Special Scientific Interest, a European site, a site which has been announced by the Scottish Ministers as a proposed Special Protection Area or proposed Special Area of Conservation, or an area designated as a Wetland of International Importance (these categories are discussed further in Ch.9), and Scottish Natural Heritage on being consulted by the planning authority has indicated that development may adversely affect such a site and has advised against granting planning permission or has recommended conditions which the planning authority do not propose to attach to the permission.

Historic Battlefields, World Heritage Sites, Scheduled Monuments and Category A Listed Buildings: where Historic Environment Scotland has been consulted and advised against the granting of planning permission or recommended conditions which the planning authority do not propose to attach to the permission.

Flooding: where the Scottish Environment Protection Agency has been consulted, and has advised against the granting of planning permission or has recommended conditions which the planning authority do not propose to attach to the permission.

Playing Fields: development which is likely to result in the loss of outdoor playing fields extending to not less than 0.2 hectares used for any sport played on a pitch, outdoor athletic tracks, golf courses, outdoor tennis courts, other than those within a private dwelling, hotel or other tourist accommodation, and outdoor bowling greens; prejudice the existing use of any of those outdoor sports facilities for that purpose; or prevent the use of land, which was last used as any of those outdoor sports facilities, from being used again for that purpose, to which the Scottish Sports Council (sportscotland) has objected or has recommended conditions which the planning authority does not intend to attach to the permission.

Marine Fish Farming: development which may affect a site designated as a controlled site under the Protection of Military Remains Act 1986 where the Secretary of State has advised against the granting of planning permission or recommended conditions which the planning authority does not propose to attach to the planning permission, or where the planning authority proposes to attach conditions which the Secretary of State has advised against.

---

[327] Previously notification was required where the proposed development did not accord with the adopted or approved local plan for the area, or had been the subject of a substantial body of objections.

Opencast Coal: development consisting of works connected with the extraction of coal by opencast methods, and other minerals extracted in association with works to extract opencast coal, where the site boundary falls within 500m from the edge of an existing community or sensitive establishment.

Neighbouring Planning Authorities: development which has been the subject of consultation with an adjoining planning authority where that authority have advised against the granting of planning permission or have recommended conditions which the planning authority does not propose to attach to the planning permission.

Together with the notification, copies must be sent of the application and plans, any ES, any appropriate assessment under the Conservation (Natural Habitats, etc.) Regulations 1994 (SI 1994/2716), observations by consultees and representations received, with the authority's comments on those observations and representations and the authority's reasons for proposing to grant permission. The Scottish Ministers confirm the date of receipt of notification and the planning authority cannot decide the application until 28 days after that date. If no response is forthcoming within the 28-day period, the authority may grant permission. The response within this period can direct that the application be referred to the Scottish Ministers, or further restrict the grant of planning permission for a further specified period or indefinitely, or require consideration of a condition (see below).

There are separate requirements to notify the Scottish Ministers for certain forms of development within National Scenic Areas where Scottish Natural Heritage advise against granting permission or recommend conditions other than those proposed by the planning authority (see Ch.9 below).

(b) Scottish Ministers' powers

The Scottish Ministers have power to make directions which must be complied with by planning authorities[328]: **5.91**

- requiring the planning authority to give the Ministers information on planning applications;
- restricting the grant of planning permission by a planning authority, either indefinitely or during a specified period;
- requiring the authority to consider imposing a condition specified in, or of a nature indicated in, the direction; and preventing the grant of planning permission without first satisfying the Ministers that a condition will either be imposed or need not be imposed.

The Scottish Ministers also have the power to direct that an application be referred to them for decision, instead of being determined by the planning authority.[329] This process is commonly known as calling in an application. Exercise of this call-in power is not restricted to applications notified to the Ministers by the planning authority. The Ministers can call in an application being reviewed by the Local Review Body (see Ch.8 below).[330] **5.92**

The Ministers have stated that this power will be exercised very sparingly, but

---

[328] DMPR 2013 (SSI 2013/155) regs 31–34.
[329] TCPSA 1997 s.46.
[330] TCPSA 1997 s.46(2)(ab), added by Planning etc (Scotland) Act 2006 (Supplementary and Consequential Provisions) Order 2013/26 art.2(4).

that there can be circumstances where a proposed development raises issues of such national importance that it is reasonable for the Ministers to call-in the application. Simply because a particular development proposal may be complex or controversial does not make it of strategic importance or of national interest. The existence of a substantial number of objections is not in itself sufficient ground to merit call-in. To protect the integrity of the planning system, Ministers may sometimes feel the need to become involved where a planning authority seeks to make a decision on a development in which it has an interest, where that proposed development would involve a significant departure from the authority's own development plan and in which the authority has not provided a reasonable or convincing argument to substantiate its decision.[331]

The Ministers' call-in power is exercised by giving a direction to a particular planning authority or authorities generally that any application or type of application be referred to the Ministers for decision.[332] Following such a direction, the planning authority serve on the applicant notice of the terms of the direction, any reasons given by the Ministers for requiring the application to be referred to them, and that the decision of the Ministers on the application will be final.[333]

The decision of the Scottish Ministers on the called-in application is final, but may be challenged by application to the Court of Session on legal grounds only within six weeks (see Ch.8 below).[334]

Where an application has been called-in for decision by the Scottish Ministers, other than the points mentioned above, the procedure for determining that application is the same as that applicable to determinations by planning authorities. The applicant and planning authority no longer have the right to require a hearing before a reporter.[335]

The exercise, or not, of the call-in power is significant for certain forms of development such as retailing and housing where issues of capacity may mean that only a limited number of permissions can be granted. If there are two applications in circumstances where only a single consent can be granted, and the Scottish Ministers call in only one of those applications, the planning authority can competently determine the remaining application. If the authority decides to grant that application, the called-in application will have to be refused on grounds of lack of capacity. A similar situation arises where one applicant appeals, and the Scottish Ministers refuse to call in the other application.

The courts have examined the legal issues arising in these situations. It was held that the Secretary of State did not act illegally in not calling in a rival application when he recalled an appeal for his determination on the grounds of its implication for a structure plan policy that was before him for decision. The Secretary of State is carrying out different statutory functions in dealing with an appeal and deciding whether to call in an application, and the same considerations do not necessarily apply. The reason given for recalling the appeal explained why that procedure had been adopted for the appeal, and did not justify a review of all relevant applications. Any prejudice caused to the appellant was inherent in the planning process because of the absence of a right of appeal against the grant of permission to a rival applicant. This decision overturned the judgment of the Outer House judge, who

---

[331] Planning Circular 3/2009, Notification of Planning Applications, paras 5–7.
[332] TCPSA 1997 s.46.
[333] TCPSA 1997 s.46(7); DMPR 2013 (SSI 2013/155) reg.35.
[334] TCPSA 1997 ss.46(7), 237 and 239.
[335] Following repeal of TCPSA s.46(5).

had held that procedural fairness required the Secretary of State to take account of the need to protect the interests of the appellant, because his decision not to call in the application was capable of resulting in substantial prejudice to the appellant and even to the pre-empting of their appeal.[336]

The Secretary of State's decision in a previous case was unlawful because in deciding not to call in the rival application he had considered the merits of the two sites and had therefore prejudged the issue and pre-empted the appeal.[337] This decision would probably have been valid if he had ignored the existence of alternative sites completely, even although this would still have effectively prejudged the outcome of the appeal.

EFFECT OF PLANNING PERMISSION

Many consequences arise from the grant of planning permission. The important legal consequences are examined below. An important practical consequence is that the permission generally increases the value of the land over which it has been granted. Once planning permission has been granted, other statutory consents, such as building warrants, may still be required before development can commence. A grant of planning permission by the Scottish Ministers or their reporter may prevent the local authority from refusing to grant other statutory consents or enter into necessary agreements on grounds which were determined as part of the appeal decision, such as road safety,[338] unless circumstances have changed since that decision.[339] Planning permission does not give immunity from liability in nuisance to neighbouring landowners.[340]

5.93

(a) Enures for the benefit of the land

With the exception of personal permissions (see para.5.82 above), the grant of planning permission is not personal to the applicant or the owner of the application site, but enures for the benefit of the land on which development is permitted and is transferred with the ownership of the land.[341]

5.94

Where the impact of the proposed development may depend upon the identity of the operator, the benefit of the permission may be limited to a particular class of person, notwithstanding the lack of any condition to this effect. Where outline planning permission had been granted for a retail development following a retail impact assessment which adopted a notional turnover based on floor space reflecting the average of a number of selected UK companies operating superstores, the Northern Ireland Court of Appeal held that in determining fresh planning applications by Sainsbury, it was a material consideration that the business skills and

---

[336] *ASDA Stores Ltd v Secretary of State for Scotland*, 1998 S.C.L.R. 246; 1998 66 S.P.E.L. 33; 1997 S.L.T. 1286 OH; 1997 61 S.P.E.L. 61; *R. v Secretary of State for the Environment, Transport and the Regions Ex p. Carter Commercial Developments Ltd* [1998] E.G. 130 (C.S.).

[337] *Lakin v Secretary of State for Scotland*, 1988 S.L.T. 780; *Bett Properties Ltd v Scottish Ministers*, 2001 S.C. 238.

[338] *R. v Warwickshire CC Ex p. Powergen Plc* [1998] J.P.L. 131.

[339] *R. v Cardiff City Council Ex p. Sears Group Properties Ltd* [1998] P.L.C.R. 262.

[340] *Wheeler v JJ Saunders Ltd* [1995] 2 All E.R. 697.

[341] TCPSA 1997 s.44(1).

experience of Sainsbury would cause a greater retail impact and a fresh retail impact assessment should therefore have been required.[342]

(b) Does not prevent future applications

5.95   There is no obligation to commence the development permitted by a grant of planning permission. While the grant of planning permission remains unimplemented it is competent for any person including the original applicant to make further applications for planning permission in respect of the same site. A further application may seek a more favourable grant of permission for a similar development, or propose an entirely different development. The planning authority is required to consider each application on its merits, ignoring any previous grants of permission and pending applications for the same site.[343] There is no limit on the number of grants of planning permission in respect of an individual site, and the owner can select which permitted development should proceed. This can lead to problems with multiple implementation of permissions (see para.5.106 below).

If planning permission is refused, either by the planning authority or on appeal, the planning authority has power in specified circumstances to decline to determine a further application for the same or similar development prior to considering its merits (see para.5.28 above).

(c) Interpretation

5.96   The wording of the decision letter granting planning permission will be given its ordinary and natural meaning.[344] It will not be construed against the interests of the authority in favour of the applicant (contra proferentem).[345] In general, only the document granting planning permission, and any reasons stated thereon, can be considered.[346] Other documents, such as the application form or plans, cannot be used to help interpret the permission, unless the permission refers to those documents. In determining whether a development which increased the floor space by some 45 per cent was within the terms of the outline planning permission, the court held that regard must be had to the permission. The inclusion of the application reference number in the permission was not sufficient to incorporate the application into the permission, for which words such as, "in accordance with the plans and application" would be necessary.[347] Where the permission was not ambiguous, regard should not have been had to the plan attached to it and the application.[348] Similarly, it will not be competent to refer to the resolution of the authority to grant permission, except where the issue is whether planning permission was granted.

---

[342] *Re FA Wellworth; Re Boots* [1996] N.I. 509, CA (NI).
[343] *Pilkington v Secretary of State for the Environment* [1973] 1 W.L.R. 1527.
[344] *Wyre Forest DC v Secretary of State for the Environment* [1989] J.P.L. 362.
[345] *Crisp from the Fens v Rutland CC* (1950) 48 L.G.R. 210.
[346] *Miller-Mead v Minister of Housing and Local Government* [1963] 2 Q.B. 196; but see *Wivenhoe Port v Colchester BC* [1985] J.P.L. 396.
[347] *R. v Secretary of State for the Environment Ex p. Slough BC* [1995] J.P.L. 1128; *Cartledge v Scottish Ministers* [2011] CSIH 23.
[348] *Springfield Minerals Ltd v Secretary of State for Wales* [1995] E.G. 174 (C.S.).

(d) Duration

Every grant of planning permission and planning permission in principle lapses **5.97**
if the development to which the permission relates is not begun within a specified
period.[349] Planning permissions in principle also lapse if the application for approval is not made within a specified period. There are separate provisions applicable to the limit of duration of planning permission for winning and working
minerals (see Ch.9 below).

The development must begin within three years of the date of the grant of
permission. The authority in granting a planning permission may direct that a longer
or shorter period shall apply, if the authority consider that longer or shorter period
appropriate having regard to the provisions of the development plan and to any
other material considerations. There is a right of appeal/review against the making
of such a direction, or failure to do so.

Planning permission in principle lapses if development has not begun within two
years from the requisite approval being obtained (if there are approvals for different matters on different dates, the two year period runs from the date of the approval for the last matter). The application for approval of specified matters must
be made within three years from the date of the grant of the permission, or six
months of refusal of an earlier application for approval, or six months from
dismissal of an appeal[350] against such a refusal, whichever is latest. If three years
from the grant of permission have elapsed, only one application for approval may
be made. This gives the applicant a last chance to submit an acceptable application.
Submission of an application for approval in respect of some but not all of the matters, or for part only of the development site, within the time limit will not preserve
the remainder of the permission from expiry.[351]

When granting permission in principle, the authority may substitute longer or
shorter time limits, having regard to the provisions of the development plan and to
any other material considerations. When a development is split into distinct parts
or phases, it is competent for the authority to specify separate periods for the
submission of applications for approval for each part or phase. The requirement for
commencement of development should be framed correspondingly by reference to
those parts rather than to the development as a whole. There is a right of appeal/
review against the making of such a direction, or failure to do so.

For these purposes, development begins on the earliest date on which any of the **5.98**
following material operations begin to be carried out[352]:

(i)   construction work in connection with the erection of a building;

(ii)   any work of demolition of a building;

(iii) digging of a trench for the foundations of a building, even although the
trenches are immediately back-filled[353];

(iv) laying any underground main or pipe to the foundations of a building or
to a trench for the foundations;

---

[349] TCPSA 1997 ss.58, 59, as amended by the PSA 2006, which changed the time limit for full planning permissions to be implemented from five to three years; it also simplified the time limits applicable to planning permissions in principle; and removed the reference to every planning permission being granted subject to a deemed condition imposing the time limit for commencement of
development.

[350] The statutory provisions do not refer to an unsuccessful application for review.

[351] *Hunterston Development Co Ltd v Secretary of State for Scotland*, 1992 S.L.T. 1097.

[352] TCPSA 1997 s.27.

[353] *High Peak BC v Secretary of State for the Environment* [1981] J.P.L. 366.

(v)   any placing or assembly of fish farming equipment in specified waters;
(vi)   any operation in the course of laying out or constructing part of a road, including marking out the route of a road with pegs[354];
(vii)   specified changes of use which constitute material development.

Any of these operations in respect of part of a development scheme will be sufficient for implementation of the entire scheme.[355]

Any development begun after the grant of permission has expired will be treated as not authorised by the permission and, therefore, as a breach of planning control (see Ch.7 below). To avoid expiry of the permission, an application for renewal of the permission may be made before its expiry (see para.5.09 above).

In general, operations which are in breach of a condition cannot amount to a commencement of development for the purposes of complying with these time limits. For example, where a condition requires works to take place in accordance with a scheme to be agreed with the planning authority, works which proceed where no scheme has been agreed do not commence the development in implementation of the permission.[356] Where the drainage information included within an application for approval of reserved matters was insufficient to constitute the full drainage details required by the condition to be approved before work commenced on site, and the planning authority were not alerted to the fact that approval of the drainage matters was sought, no application under the relevant condition had been submitted and the works on site were therefore in breach of the condition.[357] If the condition has in substance been complied with and work has been carried out with the full knowledge and co-operation of the planning and highways authorities, this general principle should be applied with common sense.[358]

If there are several planning permissions for development of the site, and work has commenced, it will be necessary to determine which permission has been implemented by the commencement of development. The erection of two houses in terms of a detailed planning permission did not constitute the commencement of development in terms of earlier outline planning permissions, which had therefore expired.[359]

For development to have commenced, it is not necessary for the works to have been undertaken with the intention of carrying out the development.[360] This has been described as "colourability". It is not necessary that there is an intention to proceed with the development immediately or at a definite date.[361]

---

354 *Malvern Hills DC v Secretary of State for the Environment* (1983) 46 P. & C.R. 58.
355 *Glasgow DC v Secretary of State for Scotland*, 1993 S.L.T. 268.
356 *FG Whitley & Sons Co Ltd v Secretary of State for Wales* [1992] 3 P.L.R. 72. But see *Doonin Plant v Scottish Ministers* [2011] CSOH 3, in which the condition did not prevent the commencement of development.
357 *Tesco Stores Ltd v North Norfolk DC* [1999] J.P.L. 920.
358 *R. v Flintshire CC Ex p. Somerfield Stores Ltd* [1998] E.G. 53 (C.S.).
359 *Campbell v Argyll and Bute DC*, 1997 S.C.L.R. 197; 1997 59 S.P.E.L. 15.
360 *East Dunbartonshire Council v Secretary of State for Scotland*, 1998 G.W.D. 40-2079; 1999 71 S.P.E.L. 16; cf. *Malvern Hills DC v Secretary of State for the Environment* (1983) 46 P. & C.R. 58.
361 *Tesco Stores Ltd v North Norfolk DC* [1999] J.P.L. 920; *Agecrest Ltd v Gwynedd CC* [1998] J.P.L. 325; cf. *R. v Arfon BC Ex p. Walton Commercial Group Ltd* [1997] J.P.L. 237.

(e) Abandonment

It cannot be implied that a valid planning permission capable of being **5.99** implemented has been abandoned or lost through the actions of the holder of the benefit of the permission.[362]

(f) Revocation or modification

The planning authority has power to revoke or modify any grant of permission **5.100** to such extent as it considers expedient at any time before the change of use has taken place or prior to completion of building or other operations.[363] However, instances of the exercise of this power are limited in consequence of the liability to pay compensation as a result.[364]

Once the revocation/modification order has been confirmed by the Scottish Ministers, only those building or other operations carried out prior to the date of confirmation are authorised by the permission. The only procedure for challenging the validity of a confirmed order is an application to the Court of Session (see Ch.8 below).[365]

(g) Variation

The planning authority may vary any permission granted by them at the request **5.101** of the applicant if it appears to them that the variation sought is not material.[366] This obviates the need for a fresh application and renotification/re-advertisement, but will necessarily be limited to minor variations.

CONSEQUENCES OF IMPLEMENTATION OF PLANNING PERMISSION

The grant of planning permission is implemented on commencement of any of **5.102** the specified operations (see "Duration", above). Implementation prevents expiry of the permission which then endures in perpetuity, with important implications for the completion of the development and the competence of implementing other permissions for the same site.

(a) Initiation of development

Before development is commenced, notice must be given to the planning author- **5.103** ity of the date on which development is to be initiated.[367] Failure to give this notice is a breach of planning control, entitling the planning authority to take enforcement action (see Ch.7 below).[368] The notice gives the planning authority the opportunity to check on compliance with any suspensive conditions imposed on the planning permission which prevent the commencement of development until specified approvals are obtained or other matters addressed.

---

[362] *Pioneer Aggregates (UK) Ltd v Secretary of State for the Environment* [1985] A.C. 132. Contrast with existing use rights (see Ch.4 above).

[363] TCPSA 1997 s.65; *Caledonian Terminal Investments Ltd v Edinburgh Corp*, 1970 S.C. 271.

[364] TCPSA 1997 s.76.

[365] TCPSA 1997 s.237.

[366] TCPSA 1997 s.64.

[367] TCPSA 1997 s.27A. The contents of the notice are prescribed by DMPR 2013 (SSI 2013/155) reg.40.

[368] TCPSA 1997 s.123(1)(c).

(b) Display of notice while development is carried out

5.104 For national and major developments (see "Hierarchy of Developments", above), and bad neighbour developments (para.5.32 above), a notice containing prescribed information must be displayed by a person carrying out the development until the development is completed. The notice must be displayed in a prominent place at or in the vicinity of the site of the development; readily visible to the public; and printed on durable material.[369] Failure to give this notice is a breach of planning control, entitling the planning authority to take enforcement action (see Ch.7 below).[370]

(c) Completion of development: notification of completion and completion notice

5.105 As soon as practicable after the development has been completed, notice of completion must be given to the planning authority.[371] If development is to be carried out in phases, a condition can be imposed on the planning permission requiring notice of completion to be given at the end of each phase.

There is no duty or obligation to complete a development which has been commenced. As a result, sites may be sterilised from future development. The possibility that the remainder of the permission may be implemented in due course would seem to be a material consideration in the determination of any fresh application. The planning authority should consider imposing a condition or suggesting a planning agreement to prevent further implementation of the permission, prior to granting a fresh permission.

The planning authority may serve a completion notice where the development has been begun but not completed by the date on which the permission would have lapsed had the development not been begun, and the authority are of the opinion that the development will not be completed within a reasonable time.[372] The notice will only take effect if confirmed by the Scottish Ministers.[373] On the expiry of the period specified in the notice no further development in terms of the permission will be competent and only the development carried out by that date will be authorised by the planning permission. The effectiveness of completion notices is therefore limited to situations in which the developer has some intention of proceeding with the development. Use of completion notices is unusual.

(d) Multiple implementation of permissions

5.106 Difficult questions arise where a permission has been partially or fully implemented and work commences in implementation of another permission applicable to the same site.[374] The central question is whether it is possible to carry out the development authorised by the permission, having regard to what was done

---

369 TCPSA 1997 s.27C; DMPR 2013 (SSI 2013/155) reg.41 and Sch.7.
370 TCPSA 1997 s.123(1)(d).
371 TCPSA 1997 s.27B. The statutory provisions do not specify any sanctions for failure to serve this notice.
372 TCPSA 1997 s.61.
373 TCPSA 1997 s.62.
374 Neil Collar, "Multiple Implementation of Planning Permissions" [1993] J.P.L. 627.

or authorised to be done under the permission which has been implemented.[375] If the position is uncertain, an application could be made to the planning authority for a certificate of lawfulness of proposed use or development (see Ch.4 above).

This test is one of physical possibility, not just of construction but also provision of the curtilage (see Ch.4 above) for the building identified in the application. Where two permissions authorised erection of a farmhouse, but in different locations within the same 50-acre site, their effect was that the landowner was entitled to build a farmhouse in either location for use as a farmhouse in connection with farming the 50 acres. Having built one, he could not build on the other so long as there was a farmhouse standing and used for farming the 50 acres.[376] Mere incompatibility with the other permission already implemented is insufficient.[377] The intention of the planning authority in granting permission may be thought relevant, but in interpreting planning permissions reference may only be had to the decision letter (see para.5.96 above).

A permission which is mutually inconsistent with an implemented permission remains in suspense (subject to time limits for implementation), until its implementation becomes physically possible.

(e)   Challenge of conditions

By implementing the permission, it might be thought that the developer impliedly **5.107** accepts the conditions attached to the permission and should not be able to challenge those conditions thereafter. However, there is no statutory bar to lodging an appeal/review against conditions in these circumstances. In addition, it is competent to apply for permission to develop the land without compliance with the conditions (see Ch.6 below).

Failure to Comply with Permission

If development proceeds contrary to the conditions imposed on the planning **5.108** permission, there is a breach of planning control, and the planning authority may take enforcement action (see Ch.7 below). Work in breach of planning conditions will not constitute a commencement of development for the purposes of preventing the expiry of the planning permission (see para.5.98 above).

Development which is not in accordance with the permission is also a breach of planning control, as it amounts to development without planning permission, and is therefore subject to potential enforcement action. Importantly, restrictions imposed on the development by conditions attached to the permission will not apply. A bungalow which was about 90ft west of the permitted location was not subject to the occupancy restriction imposed by the condition attached to the planning permission.[378] As a period for enforcement of development without planning permission is only four years in contrast to 10 years from a breach of planning condition, this is an important issue.

---

[375] *Pilkington v Secretary of State for the Environment* [1973] 1 W.L.R. 1527.
[376] *Ellis v Worcestershire CC* (1961) 12 P. & C.R. 178. Also *Orbit Development v Secretary of State for the Environment* [1996] E.G. 191 (C.S.).
[377] *Prestige Homes (Southern) Ltd v Secretary of State for the Environment* [1992] J.P.L. 842.
[378] *Handoll v Warner Goodman and Steat* [1995] J.P.L. 930.

CONSEQUENCES OF REFUSAL OF APPLICATION

(a) Challenging the refusal

5.109   Chapter 8 examines the procedures for challenging decisions on planning applications.

(b) Purchase notice

5.110   Following a refusal of planning permission, or a grant subject to conditions, the owner or lessee of land which is incapable of reasonably beneficial use may serve a purchase notice on the planning authority.[379] There is no requirement to demonstrate a causal connection between the decision on the planning application and the fact that the land is incapable of reasonably beneficial use.[380] The purchase notice must relate to the whole of the site refused planning permission.[381] If the planning authority is willing to comply with the notice, it is deemed to acquire the land compulsorily. Compensation is assessed as for compulsory purchase. If the authority refuses to comply, the notice is referred to the Scottish Ministers for decision. They may either confirm the notice, grant planning permission, revoke or amend conditions, or direct that planning permission be granted for an alternative development if the appropriate application is made.

---

[379] TCPSA 1997 s.88.
[380] *Purbeck DC v Secretary of State for the Environment* (1982) 80 L.G.R. 545.
[381] *Cook v Winchester City Council* (1995) 69 P. & C.R. 99.

CHAPTER 6

DEVELOPMENT MANAGEMENT III—PLANNING CONDITIONS, PLANNING AGREEMENTS AND GOOD NEIGHBOUR AGREEMENTS

Planning permission is a crude device for controlling development: either the **6.01** proposed development is acceptable or it is not. The power to impose conditions upon the grant of permission enables the planning authority to go beyond the adjudicative "yes/no" role by using conditions to control the detailed aspects of developments. Therefore, the imposition of conditions can be identified as a powerful tool for promoting flexibility within development management. However, the use of conditions is limited by legal restrictions.

As if to emphasise the weakness of the requirement to obtain planning permission as a development management tool, planning authorities have further statutory powers enabling them to enter into agreements with applicants. Controversially, these powers are often used to achieve "planning gain". Use of these powers has increased in the past decade, partly as a result of the restrictions placed on the use of conditions by the requirements for legal validity.

The Planning etc. (Scotland) Act 2006 created a new power for persons to enter into good neighbour agreements with community bodies.

PLANNING CONDITIONS

Planning conditions may be used to provide greater control and flexibility within **6.02** the development management process by virtue of their dual role:

(a) making an otherwise unacceptable development acceptable, thereby furthering the presumption in favour of development,[1] always subject to the limits to which conditions can modify the proposed development (see below); or

(b) controlling the details of an otherwise acceptable application, allowing the development to be "fine-tuned", making it more satisfactory. In this way, a development which is generally acceptable can be tailored to meet the needs of the surrounding locality and details such as landscaping and design settled.

There is no duty upon the planning authority to draw up and use a condition to make an otherwise unacceptable development acceptable, but if the application is acceptable it has a duty to consider whether conditions can be imposed to make it more acceptable.[2] Standard lists of conditions may be used to achieve parity of treatment between applications and to promote consistency of decisions, although the decision to impose conditions must be considered for each application on its merits.

---

[1] Planning Circular 4/1998, The Use of Conditions in Planning Permissions (Scottish Office, 1998) para.2.

[2] *Mason v Secretary of State for the Environment* [1984] J.P.L. 332; *Garbutt v Secretary of State for*

Conditions can also be used to control changes of use, as the description of the development in the planning permission does not necessarily prevent changes.[3]

The power to serve breach of condition notices (see Ch.7 below) highlights the importance of drafting precise conditions.[4]

Conditions attached to planning permissions should be scrutinised and their effect considered before the permission is implemented (see Ch.5 above), although there is no statutory bar to an appeal against the conditions imposed once the development has commenced.

If development does not proceed in accordance with the planning permission, such as a bungalow built about 90ft west of the permitted location, restrictions imposed on the development by conditions attached to the permission will not apply.[5] In such circumstances, there is a breach of planning control consisting of development without planning permission, and not a breach of condition. The significance is that the period for enforcement action is four years in contrast to 10 years for a breach of planning condition.

Conditions cannot infer a grant of anything which goes beyond the terms of the planning permission.[6] A planning permission for clay extraction granted subject to a condition requiring the excavations to be filled in was held to be capable of granting planning permission by implication for depositing waste on the site, as the necessary importation of material from outside the site was clearly contemplated by the condition.[7] Where the planning application for a waste plant stated that it would treat waste from the Highland area, it was invalid for a condition to be imposed which referred to potential for the development to deal with waste from other areas.[8]

Care has to be taken with the use of "tail pieces"—for example, "unless otherwise agreed in writing"—to avoid permitting development to take place which could be very different in scale and impact from that applied for, assessed or permitted and enable it to be created by means wholly outside any statutory process.[9]

Human rights

6.03   Conditions have a potentially important role in complying with Convention rights under the European Convention on Human Rights. They can be used to avoid the refusal of planning permission, thereby furthering the applicant's Convention rights, such as art.8 (respect for private and family life) and the First Protocol art.1 (protection of property). The ability to use conditions to regulate the development also provides an opportunity to ensure compliance with the Convention rights of third parties. For example, where a retail development is adjacent to residential properties, a condition could be imposed preventing deliveries outside specified hours, to prevent unacceptable noise during the night.

---

the Environment (1989) 57 P. & C.R. 284.

[3]   I'm Your Man v Secretary of State for the Environment (1999) 77 P.&C.R. 251; but see Winchester CC v Secretary of State [2015] EWCA Civ 563.

[4]   e.g. Rees v Secretary of State for the Environment [1994] E.G. 157 (C.S.); R. v Ealing BC Ex p. Zainuddin [1994] 3 P.L.R. 1.

[5]   Handoll v Warner Goodman and Streat [1995] J.P.L. 930.

[6]   Paisley Mills Development Co Ltd v Renfrewshire Council , 1997 G.W.D. 25-1279.

[7]   R. v Secretary of State for the Environment Ex p. Walsall MBC [1997] E.G. 23 (C.S.).

[8]   The Highland Council v Scottish Ministers [2014] CSIH 74.

[9]   Hubert v Carmarthenshire CC [2015] EWHC 2327 (Admin); R. (Midcounties Co-operative Ltd) v Wyre Forest DC [2009] EWHC 964 (Admin). Discussed in Trump International Golf Club v The Scottish Ministers [2015] UKSC 74 per Lord Hodge at [39].

Planning conditions can also interfere with the applicant's Convention rights. The superstore operator could argue that restricting the hours of deliveries interferes with the operator's rights under the First Protocol art.1. There is already a requirement for the planning authority to provide reasons for its decision.[10] However, if a condition interferes with the applicant's Convention rights, the planning authority will have to be able to justify imposing the condition. The planning authority might have to consider whether the normal reason given for imposing a condition might have to be expanded in order to justify interference with a Convention right.

In addition to reviewing whether the planning authority has complied with Convention rights, the courts are also bound to comply with these rights. This could have implications for the interpretation of conditions.

Power to impose conditions

In determining an application for planning permission, planning authorities "may grant planning permission, either unconditionally, or subject to such conditions as they think fit".[11] This power only extends to the imposition of conditions upon land which forms part of the site of the proposed development as identified in the application.

6.04

Without prejudice to this general power to impose conditions, there is an additional power to attach conditions regulating the development or use of any land under the control of the applicant (whether or not it forms part of the application site), or requiring the carrying out of any works on any such land, so far as appears expedient for the purposes of or in connection with the authorised development.[12] The consequence of this additional power is that only land which is neither within the terms of the application for planning permission nor under the control of the applicant is not potentially subject to a planning condition.[13] It is a question of fact and degree whether the applicant has sufficient control to ensure compliance with the conditions.[14]

There are also statutory powers to impose specific types of conditions.[15] A condition may be attached to a grant of temporary permission requiring removal of buildings or works authorised by the permission, or discontinuance of any authorised use of land, and reinstatement of the land on the expiry of that permission.[16] Conditions may also limit the benefit of a planning permission to a named person (a personal permission), or specify the use of a proposed building.[17] The planning authority has a duty to ensure that, where appropriate, conditions are imposed upon a grant of planning permission to secure adequate provision for the preservation and planting of trees.[18]

---

[10] Town and Country Planning (Scotland) Act 1997 (TCPSA) s.43(1A).
[11] TCPSA 1997 s.37(1).
[12] TCPSA 1997 s.41(1).
[13] *Birnie v Banff CC*, 1954 S.L.T. (Sh. Ct) 90.
[14] *George Wimpey & Co Ltd v New Forest DC* [1979] J.P.L. 314.
[15] Previously TCPSA s.58 stated that every permission was subject to an express or implied condition providing for the expiry of the permission if the development authorised by the permission is not commenced within a specified period of time. The Planning Etc. (Scotland) Act 2006 amended s.58 to achieve the same result without the use of an express or implied condition (see Ch.5 above).
[16] TCPSA 1997 s.41(1)(b).
[17] TCPSA 1997 s.44.
[18] TCPSA 1997 s.159.

Validity of planning conditions: legal

6.05   Planning authorities have the power to impose such conditions as they think fit. The width of this discretionary power is limited by the requirements for the legal validity of a planning condition which have been formulated by the courts through a process of statutory interpretation. A planning condition must have a planning purpose, fairly and reasonably relate to the permitted development, and not be so unreasonable that no reasonable planning authority could have imposed it.[19]

(a)   Planning purpose

6.06   The power to impose conditions is conferred by the planning legislation and must therefore be used to achieve a planning purpose and not an ulterior object.[20] As a result of the vagueness of the objectives of planning (see Ch.1 above), it is difficult to draw the line between a "planning" and an "ulterior" object. The TCPSA 1997 provides no guidance on the objects of planning powers, and the courts can only provide assistance on a case-by-case basis. As a result, there can be no precise guidelines on the requirement for a planning purpose. However, as the examination of material considerations has shown (see Ch.5 above), the scope of potential planning matters is wide-ranging and the need for a planning purpose should not be an onerous requirement.

Planning has been held to relate to the use of land rather than to the user.[21] However, if the purpose of the condition relates to the use of the land, it is valid notwithstanding that it limits categories of users.[22] Thus, a condition limiting occupation of a dwellinghouse to agricultural workers was valid because it was imposed to further the policy of protecting the green belt.[23] Other decisions on "planning purpose" also involve conditions imposed to further planning policies. Inclusion of a policy within the development plan may give it the badge of "planning purpose", although this will not always be the case.[24]

It was held that a condition restricting the extension or connection of water and sewerage service pipes to serve any other residential development had the valid planning purpose of prohibiting an arrangement between landowners which would lead to excessive provision of housing.[25] An agreement requiring the developer to provide an access road to an adjacent development site had a proper planning purpose.[26] In contrast, a condition amounting to a requirement that a road be constructed and dedicated to the public was invalid because it had the ulterior purpose of requiring the developer to take on the duty of the highway authority.[27] Similarly, conditions imposed on a housing development requiring that the houses should first be occupied by persons on the local authority's housing waiting list were invalid because they required the developer to assume the duty of the local author-

---

19   *Newbury DC v Secretary of State for the Environment* [1981] A.C. 578 at 607; [1980] J.P.L. 325.
20   *Pyx Granite Co Ltd v Ministry of Housing and Local Government* [1958] Q.B. 554 per Lord Denning at 572.
21   *Westminster City Council v Great Portland Estates Plc* [1985] A.C. 661.
22   cf. *David Lowe & Sons Co Ltd v Musselburgh Town Council*, 1973 S.C. 130.
23   *Fawcett Properties Ltd v Buckingham CC* [1961] A.C. 636.
24   *Westminster Renslade Ltd v Secretary of State for the Environment* [1983] J.P.L. 454. For example, development plans stating that the area has been declared a "nuclear-free zone".
25   *North-East Fife DC v Secretary of State for Scotland*, 1992 S.L.T. 373.
26   *McIntosh v Aberdeenshire Council*, 1998 G.W.D. 6–255; 1998 67 S.P.E.L. 56.
27   *Hall & Co Ltd v Shoreham-By-Sea Urban DC* [1964] 1 W.L.R. 240.

ity as a housing authority at his own expense.[28] However, the need for housing in a particular area is a material consideration, and no sensible distinction can be drawn between a need for housing generally and a need for particular types of housing, whether or not the latter could be defined in terms of cost, tenure or otherwise. In each case the question is whether, as a matter of planning for the area under consideration, there is a need for housing which the grant or refusal of the application will affect.[29]

A reporter did not make an error of law in deleting a condition preventing the erection of a gate until a public right of passage had been removed, as any infringement of a legal right of passage is dealt with by other statutory and common law provisions, and accordingly this was not a relevant issue for the planning decision.[30]

Other guidance on possible planning purposes may be found in the court decisions interpreting the scope of "material considerations" (see Ch.5 above).

The authority may have many purposes in mind when imposing a condition. A condition might have other purposes, but must not be imposed solely to serve some other purpose or purposes.[31] This suggests that the mere presence of a planning purpose is enough. There must, however, come a point at which the planning purpose becomes subordinated to the other purposes to such an extent that it has negligible influence on the decision. Another view suggests that the purpose must be solely or primarily to achieve a planning objective.[32] Once the planning purpose becomes secondary to the other purposes then the condition is invalid. This seems the preferable view. In practice, however, planning authorities are unlikely to mention any non-planning purposes in their written reasons for imposing the condition, in an attempt to avoid any appeal against their decisions.

(b) Fairly and reasonably relates to permitted development

The condition must fairly and reasonably relate to the development authorised by the permission.[33] This is the result of the wording of the statutory power to impose conditions which links inextricably, and subordinates, this power to the decision to grant permission. Since permission is given for a specified development, any condition must also relate to that development. **6.07**

This test should assist compliance with the applicant's Convention rights, either by preventing undue interference with those rights, or ensuring that any interference can be justified in terms of the particular Convention right. It should also assist the planning authority to comply with the principle of proportionality.

What is the meaning of "fairly and reasonably relates"? It has been suggested that a "recognised and real relationship" is required, which is a question of fact and judgment, rather than requiring the condition to be imposed to remedy some direct adverse consequence ("mischief") caused by the development. It would be enough

---

[28] *R. v Hillingdon LBC Ex p. Royco Homes Ltd* [1974] 2 All E.R. 643.
[29] *Mitchell v Secretary of State for the Environment* [1994] 2 P.L.R. 23. See PAN 2/2010, Affordable Housing and Housing Land Audits (Scottish Government, 2010).
[30] *South Lanarkshire Council v Secretary of State for Scotland*, 1997 S.L.T. 961; 1997 60 S.P.E.L. 34. The right of passage might now be considered to be protected under art.8 and/or First Protocol art.1, in which case the determination of the planning application would have to comply with the right of passage unless interference could be justified under art.8(2) and/or First Protocol art.1.
[31] *Newbury DC v Secretary of State for the Environment* [1981] A.C. 578 per Lord Fraser at 618.
[32] Malcolm Grant, *Urban Planning Law* (London: Sweet & Maxwell, 1981) p.337.
[33] *Pyx Granite Co Ltd v Ministry of Housing and Local Government* [1958] 1 Q.B. 554 per Lord Denning at 572.

that the condition was imposed because of matters "merely consequential" to the development. Any test is open to subjective application, and while the test of directness is capable of narrow application, the "merely consequential" test may achieve the same result as a test of directness applied broadly. Each case is determined on its facts and it is difficult to identify a consistent approach in the court decisions.

By including land within the application, the developer may be taken to admit the connection between that land and the proposed development. A more contentious issue arises where conditions are imposed on land under the control of the applicant which is not contained within the terms of the application. The statutory power to impose such conditions (see para.6.04 above) requires the conditions to be "expedient for the purposes of or in connection with the development authorised by the permission". This wording would appear to achieve a similar result to the "fairly and reasonably relates" test. Court decisions relating to this statutory power may therefore be used to help interpret the "fairly and reasonably relates" requirement.

Doubt has been expressed whether conditions attached to land under the control of the applicant a mile away rather than immediately adjacent to the development would be valid.[34] Geographical separation cannot be conclusive, but the directness of the relationship between condition and development must deteriorate with physical distance.[35]

Cases have affirmed conditions relating to land or buildings on the same site as the development, to the purpose of the development, and to its possible effects. Where machinery was used to process quarried stone, there was a direct relationship between the use of the machinery and the quarry development, with the result that a condition relating to the use of that machinery sufficiently related to the development.[36] As a factory extension allowed an existing building to be used more effectively, conditions controlling the use of machinery in the existing factory were valid as connected to the purpose of the permitted development.[37] A condition designed to control noise caused by air traffic fairly and reasonably related to the construction of a new terminal building required because of increased air traffic.[38]

Conditions have been struck down for failing to fairly and reasonably relate to the proposed development. A condition intended to restrict residential development elsewhere was held invalid because it did not reasonably relate to the proposed residential development.[39] A condition requiring demolition of buildings had nothing to do with the change of use for which planning permission was sought.[40] However, there was arguably an indirect connection because the continued use of the building affected the amenity of the neighbourhood. A condition regulating the killing of foxes could have been validly imposed on a grant of permission for construction of fox pens, but a condition preventing the slaughter of any animals on the premises was too remotely connected to the permitted development to be

---

[34] *Pyx Granite Co Ltd v Ministry of Housing and Local Government* [1958] 1 Q.B. 554 per Lord Denning at 572.

[35] *Peak Park Joint Planning Board v Secretary of State for the Environment* [1980] J.P.L. 114.

[36] *Pyx Granite Co Ltd v Ministry of Housing and Local Government* [1958] 1 Q.B. 554.

[37] *Penwith DC v Secretary of State for the Environment* (1977) 34 P. & C.R. 269.

[38] *British Airports Authority v Secretary of State for Scotland*, 1979 S.C. 200.

[39] *North-East Fife DC v Secretary of State for Scotland*, 1992 S.L.T. 373.

[40] *Newbury DC v Secretary of State for the Environment* [1981] A.C. 578; also *Delta Design and Engineering Ltd v Secretary of State for the Environment, Transport and the Regions* [2000] 4 P.L.R. 1.

valid.[41] Similarly, a condition requiring installation of frosted glass in windows imposed when an occupancy condition was altered to allow a change of occupier was held to be unrelated to the development and therefore invalid, since the requirement for the glass was not brought about by the proposed occupation, but dated back to the first occupation of the building.[42] However, it could be argued that the change of use did not cause the need for the condition, but continued that need.

A condition preventing the erection of a gate until a public right of passage had been removed was held not to reasonably relate to the proposed development as any infringement of a legal right of passage is dealt with by other statutory and common law provisions.[43]

(c) Reasonableness

The imposition of a condition must be reasonable, but in the special legal sense (referred to as *Wednesbury* reasonableness).[44] A condition will be invalid on the ground of unreasonableness only if it is so unreasonable that no reasonable planning authority would have imposed that condition. **6.08**

Unfortunately the term "reasonableness" has come to be used as an umbrella term for other legal requirements which have developed, such as certainty and necessity (see paras 6.11 and 6.13 below). It should be used as a residual category, for use only where a condition meets all other requirements, but demonstrates such a perverse or irrational exercise of the statutory discretion that it is illegal. The danger is that the concept of reasonableness may be stretched to the stage that it is used to interfere with the merits of the decision, enabling the court to reject a condition of which it disapproves without having to show that the condition is defective in any more specific way.

This problem may be resolved by adopting the formulation of the grounds for judicial review (see Ch.8 below) to restate the requirements for the legal validity of a condition as follows:

(i)   it must have a planning purpose;
(ii)   it must fairly and reasonably relate to the permitted development;
(iii)   it must be otherwise legal; and
(iv)   it must be otherwise rational, and not "so outrageous in its defiance of logic or of accepted moral standards that no sensible person who had applied his mind to the question to be decided could have arrived at it".[45]

Matters often discussed under the heading of reasonableness, which could be relocated under the heading of legality, include contributions from the applicant, derogation from the benefit of permission, certainty, enforceability and necessity.

Where a condition required the removal of all waste from the site within 12 months of the date of the permission, but another condition required a technical assessment to examine the environmental benefits and disbenefits of the wastes

---

[41] *Gill v Secretary of State for the Environment* [1985] J.P.L. 710.
[42] *Elmsbridge BC v Secretary of State for the Environment* [1989] J.P.L. 277.
[43] *South Lanarkshire Council v Secretary of State for Scotland*, 1997 S.L.T. 961; 1997 60 S.P.E.L. 34.
[44] *Associated Provincial Picture Houses Ltd v Wednesbury Corp* [1948] 1 K.B. 223.
[45] *Associated Provincial Picture Houses Ltd v Wednesbury Corp* [1948] 1 K.B. 223.

remaining within the site set against those of its removal, the planning permission was quashed on the grounds that these conditions were repugnant to each other.[46]

(d) Contributions from the applicant

6.09   A condition cannot require payment of a monetary contribution by the applicant.[47] It would also be invalid for a condition to require the applicant to provide another form of contribution, such as relinquishing land for use by the public as open space[48] or parking.[49] For these purposes it is irrelevant that the applicant has agreed: validity cannot be conferred by consent.[50]

(e) Derogation from the benefit of permission

6.10   Although imposition of a condition necessarily alters the development proposed by the application, there must be a limit to such alteration. Conditions cannot be used to derogate from the benefit of the permission, with the result that the nature of the development permitted is significantly different to that proposed in the application for planning permission. In other words, the planning authority cannot seek to take away with one hand what it has granted with the other. This requirement derives from the statutory wording which subordinates the power to impose conditions to the power to grant permission. Use of conditions to alter radically the proposed development would leave no opportunity for the public to give their views on what would be a substantially different proposal.

It must always be a question of fact and degree whether a particular condition takes away the substance of the permission.[51] It is competent to impose conditions scaling down an application, but not to the extent of altering the substance of the development. A condition reducing the size of the proposed development from 35 acres and 420 dwellings to 25 acres and 250 dwellings was upheld on the basis that the result did not differ substantially from the development proposed in the original application.[52] This suggests a test of character: does the permitted development have a substantially different character from the development proposed in the original application? Conditions requiring "ancillary or incidental" development, such as the provision of children's play areas and open space in a housing development, have also been upheld.[53]

A grant of permission on appeal seeking to restrict the benefit of a permission previously granted for development of adjacent ground was held invalid.[54]

(f) Certainty

6.11   A condition must be capable of being understood so that the owner of the burdened property can comply with it. A planning condition is only void from

---

46 *R. v Essex CC Ex p. Tarmac Roadstone Holdings Ltd* [1998] J.P.L. B23.
47 *R. v Bowman* [1898] 1 Q.B. 663; *Att Gen v Wilts United Dairies.*
48 *MJ Shanley (In Liquidation) v Secretary of State for the Environment* [1982] J.P.L. 380.
49 *Westminster Renslade Ltd v Secretary of State for the Environment* [1983] J.P.L. 454.
50 *Birnie v Banff CC*, 1954 S.L.T. (Sh. Ct) 90.
51 *Kent CC v Secretary of State for the Environment* (1977) 33 P. & C.R. 70.
52 *Bernard Wheatcroft Ltd v Secretary of State for the Environment* [1982] J.P.L. 37. Discussed by Lord Jones in *Petition of The John Muir Trust* [2015] CSOH 163 at [103].
53 *Britannia (Cheltenham) Ltd v Secretary of State for the Environment* [1979] J.P.L. 534.
54 *North-East Fife DC v Secretary of State for Scotland*, 1992 S.L.T. 373.

uncertainty if it can be given no meaning or no sensible or ascertainable meaning, and not merely because it is ambiguous or leads to absurd results.[55] A Scottish judge has suggested that it would be equally invalid to impose a condition which produced an absurd result which was plainly not the one intended. This suggestion should be treated with caution, as it is not supported by previous decisions and was made in a case where the condition was void from uncertainty.[56]

The courts will take pains to find some meaning in the terms of a condition,[57] and have refused to construe the terms of a condition against the interest of the authority in favour of the applicant (contra proferentem).[58] Thus, mere ambiguity or doubtful instances will not render a condition invalid.[59] Even vagueness will probably not be sufficient to invalidate a condition. Terms such as "local"[60] and "surplus stock"[61] have been upheld even though incapable of precise definition. It is enough that such terms can be understood and applied. It would appear that there is effectively a presumption that a condition is certain in its wording, and this is emphasised by the few instances of successful challenges.[62] Implication is an appropriate technique for interpretation of conditions.[63]

Although the conditions imposed on a permission were not completely lucid, these conditions were not invalid because they were capable of being given a sensible and ascertainable meaning.[64] A condition imposed under the Environmental Protection Act 1990 that "[a]ll emissions to air from the process shall be free from offensive odour as perceived by an authorised officer of the Agency, outside the boundary" was held valid.[65] The court rejected the argument that the condition was void from uncertainty, on the grounds that the language of the condition was not ambiguous and there was nothing uncertain about what the condition was meant to achieve.

A condition that "leisure units should be completed and equipped for use before any shops commence trading" was challenged on the grounds that the use of the word "should" rather than "shall" or "must" rendered the condition invalid. It was held that there was nothing in this point, as it was plain that in the context of the conditions the word "should" was equivalent to "shall", and that the insistence on "shall" or "must" was over-exacting. Although one of the proposals granted permission subject to this condition did not contain a leisure component, the condition was held to mean no more than that in so far as the development contained leisure units, those units should be completed and equipped before any shops commenced trading.[66]

---

[55] *Fawcett Properties Ltd v Buckingham CC* [1960] 3 All E.R. 503 per Lord Denning at 517; [1961] A.C. 636. Discussed in *Trump International Golf Club v The Scottish Ministers* [2015] UKSC 74.
[56] *Eastwood DC v Mactaggart & Mickel Ltd*, 1994 S.L.T. 38; 1992 37 S.P.L.P. 76.
[57] *Kent CC v Kingsway Investments (Kent) Ltd* [1971] A.C. 72.
[58] *Crisp from the Fens v Rutland CC* [1950] 48 L.G.R. 210 per Singleton J.
[59] *Inverclyde DC v Inverkip Building Co Ltd*, 1983 S.L.T. 563; cf. *David Lowe & Sons Ltd v Musselburgh Town Council*, 1973 S.C. 130.
[60] *Alderson v Secretary of State for the Environment* [1984] J.P.L. 429.
[61] *R. v Wakefield MDC Ex p. Pearl Assurance* [1997] E.G. 32 (C.S.).
[62] *Eastwood DC v Mactaggart & Mickel Ltd*, 1994 S.L.T. 38; 1992 37 S.P.L.P. 76; *David Lowe & Sons Ltd v Musselburgh Town Council*, 1973 S.C. 130 is a doubtful authority.
[63] *Trump International Golf Club v The Scottish Ministers* [2015] UKSC 74 per Lord Carnwath at [60].
[64] *Aberdeen City Council v Secretary of State for Scotland*, 1997 G.W.D. 33-1692; 1997 64 S.P.E.L. 127.
[65] *Wheelan v Seed Crushers (Scotland) Ltd*, 1998 S.C.C.R. 293; 1998 68 S.P.E.L. 76.
[66] *Dumfries and Galloway RC v Secretary of State for Scotland*, 1996 G.W.D. 26–1558; 1996 58

(g) Enforceability

6.12   There are two senses in which a condition may be unenforceable: if it requires action that is outwith the control of the applicant, or if it is too vague to form the subject of enforcement action.

A condition which requires any action that is outwith the control of the applicant is unenforceable and therefore invalid because there are no steps that the applicant can take to secure the required result. As control of air traffic was the statutory responsibility of another body, a condition specifying the direction of aircraft flights was unenforceable because the applicant was unable to meet the requirements of the condition.[67] A condition relating to land that is neither within the application nor under the control of the applicant must be unenforceable, because the applicant will have no power to ensure compliance with the condition.[68] A condition requiring access to be by way of a specified road was held invalid because the road was neither within the application site nor under the control of the applicant and in consequence there were no steps which the applicant could take to secure or ensure that all vehicles used the prescribed route.[69] On similar reasoning, a condition may be unenforceable and invalid if it relates to land within the application site, but outwith the control of the applicant.[70] Where a condition prohibited storage or parking on the road of any vehicles left with or under the control of the applicant, compliance was within his control.[71]

Where it would be invalid to impose a condition requiring action outwith the control of the applicant, the same result can be achieved legitimately by using a negatively worded (or suspensive) condition (see para.6.28 below). The effect of such a condition is that the development cannot commence until the action is achieved. The obligation to be enforced would not be the obligation to achieve the result, but rather the lack of permission to start the development until the result was achieved. The decision to commence the development is under the control of the applicant.

The other sense of enforceability relates to the need for the meaning of a condition to be precise enough for enforcement action to be taken against any breach of its terms. Conditions that are so vague as to be incapable of definition, or physically incapable of performance, may be unenforceable. A condition requiring that the first opportunity to buy houses be given to local people was declared unenforceable because there was no indication of the method or terms upon which this opportunity was to be offered.[72] It is not enough that the condition is merely difficult to enforce.[73] Conditions may be valid even though breaches of the condition may be difficult to detect.[74]

A condition imposing a noise limit which did not indicate where the noise level was to be measured was unenforceable because it was impossible to ascertain

---

S.P.E.L. 118.
[67]   *BAA v Secretary of State for Scotland*, 1979 S.C. 200.
[68]   *Birnie v Banff CC*, 1954 S.L.T. (Sh. Ct) 90.
[69]   *Mouchell Superannuation Fund Trustees v Oxfordshire CC* [1992] 1 P.L.R. 97.
[70]   *R. v Rochdale MBC Ex p. Tew* [1999] 3 P.L.R. 74.
[71]   *Davenport v Hammersmith and Fulham LBC* [1999] J.P.L. 1122.
[72]   *MJ Shanley (In Liquidation) v Secretary of State for the Environment* [1982] J.P.L. 380.
[73]   *Chichester DC v Secretary of State for the Environment* [1992] 3 P.L.R. 49.
[74]   *Kent CC v Secretary of State for the Environment* (1977) 33 P. & C.R. 70.

whether or not it was being complied with.[75] However, the court was considering whether it was competent for the reporter to replace the condition, and not whether the condition itself was valid. In a subsequent case, legal arguments dealt with the issue of certainty and enforceability does not appear to have been raised as a separate issue.[76]

A condition relating to provision of affordable housing was quashed because it did not specify the type or form of the provision of the affordable housing, nor its location, and contained no compulsitor to achieving agreement on those points.[77]

The enforceability of a condition that, "leisure units should be completed and equipped for use before any shops commence trading" was challenged on the grounds that the use of the word "should" rather than "shall" or "must" rendered the condition unenforceable and invalid. It was held that there was nothing in this point, as it was plain that in the context of the conditions the word "should" was equivalent to "shall", and that the insistence on "shall" or "must" was over-exacting. Although one of the proposals granted permission subject to this condition did not contain a leisure component, the condition was held to mean no more than that in so far as the development contains leisure units, those units should be completed and equipped before any shops commence trading.[78]

If a condition can be certain enough for the applicant to understand the limits placed on his property rights, but open to challenge on the basis that it is unenforceable, it is difficult to resolve the requirements for certainty (see above) and enforceability of conditions,[79] and it has been suggested that there is no independent head of challenge to the validity of a condition relating to its enforceability.[80]

(h) Necessity

Following the introduction of the Human Rights Act 1998 (see para.1.11), art.8 (right to respect for private and family life) and First Protocol art.1 require any condition that interferes with those Convention rights to be necessary. An earlier Court of Session decision, which had declared that an unnecessary condition is invalid, had been criticised for taking the courts beyond questions of legality into the merits of a decision.[81]   **6.13**

If a condition is unnecessary because the application did not require it, then it should be caught by the "fairly and reasonably relates" test. The close link between the condition and the mischief caused by the development required by the concept of necessity appears to go further than the "fairly and reasonably relates" test and renders it redundant.

In a subsequent case, the Court of Session held that a condition preventing the

[75] *Dunfermline DC v Secretary of State for Scotland*, 1996 S.L.T. 89; 1995 52 S.P.E.L. 110.
[76] *Aberdeen City Council v Secretary of State for Scotland,*1997 G.W.D. 33-1692; 1997 64 S.P.E.L. 127.
[77] *Aberdeenshire Council v Scottish Ministers*, 2008 G.W.D. 12–230.
[78] *Dumfries and Galloway RC v Secretary of State for Scotland*, 1996 G.W.D. 26–1558; 1996 58 S.P.E.L. 118.
[79] This can be seen from the discussion in *Bromsgrove DC v Secretary of State for the Environment* [1988] J.P.L. 257 of the decisions in *MJ Shanley (In Liquidation) v Secretary of State for the Environment* [1982] J.P.L. 380; *Penwith DC v Secretary of State for the Environment* [1986] J.P.L. 432; *Bizony v Secretary of State for the Environment* [1976] J.P.L. 306.
[80] *Chichester DC v Secretary of State for the Environment* [1992] 3 P.L.R. 49.
[81] *BAA v Secretary of State for Scotland*, 1979 S.C. 200. Only TCPSA 1997 s.41(1) refers to conditions being "expedient".

erection of a gate until a public right of passage had been removed was unnecessary as any infringement of a legal right of passage is dealt with by other statutory and common law provisions.[82] However, the court was considering whether it was competent for the reporter to delete the condition, and not whether the condition itself was valid.

Validity of planning conditions: policy

6.14   In considering whether to impose conditions upon a grant of planning permission the planning authority is bound by the legal requirements for the validity of a condition. The authority must also have regard to the policy laid down by the Scottish Ministers. As this policy is used in the determination of any appeal, authorities anxious to avoid successful appeals against their decisions will give it careful consideration when applying conditions.

The Scottish Government policy is more restrictive than the legal requirements, stating that a condition must be necessary, relevant to planning, relevant to the development to be permitted, enforceable, precise and reasonable in all other respects.[83] The nature of the development permitted or its effect on the surroundings must call for the condition to be imposed. A greater burden is placed upon planning authorities to impose precise and clear conditions. The Scottish Ministers may find a condition unenforceable if breaches of the condition may be difficult to detect. The policy includes suggested models of acceptable conditions and indicates that conditions requiring the following results are not acceptable (the explanations in brackets have been added by the author).[84]

(a)   On policy grounds

6.15   (i)   Completion of a development within a specified time limit.

(ii)   Delaying the commencement of development until a future date.

(iii) Preventing the display of advertisements on the site (lack of planning purpose: there are separate statutory powers for control of advertisements—see Ch.9 below).

(iv)   Restricting occupation, for example, of flats, to a specified number of persons (difficult to enforce).

(v)   Construction of an ancillary road by the applicant as and when required by the planning authority (vague).

(b)   On legal grounds

6.16   (i)   That means of access shall be set back and splayed in agreement with the roads authority, when the latter is a third party (unenforceable—actions of third party).

(ii)   That the land in front of the building shall be made available for future road widening (cession of land).

(iii) A lay-by, having been constructed, should thereafter be assigned to the roads authority (cession of land).

---

[82] *South Lanarkshire Council v Secretary of State for Scotland*, 1997 S.L.T. 961; 1997 60 S.P.E.L. 34.

[83] Planning Circular 4/1998, Use of Conditions in Planning Permissions, Annex, para.12.

[84] Planning Circular 4/1998, Use of Conditions in Planning Permissions, para.1 and Planning Circular 18/1986, Use of Conditions in Planning Permissions (Scottish Development Department, 1986) Appendix B

(iv) Loading and unloading, and the parking of vehicles, shall not take place on the road in front of the premises (enforceability—road not under control of applicant).

(v) The site shall be kept tidy at all times (certainty/enforceability—vague).

(vi) The applicant shall comply with the byelaws and general statutory provisions in force in the district (lack of planning purpose).

(vii) Furnishing shall be of a fireproof material (lack of planning purpose).

(viii)Aircraft should only arrive or depart at an airfield on specified air traffic routes (lack of planning purpose—activity regulated by other statutory provisions; enforceability—outside control of applicant).

(ix) A shop window display to be maintained in an attractive condition (certainty/ enforceability—no criterion by which it could be enforced).

The list of model conditions should be consulted for forms of condition which may achieve these results validly.

Challenge of condition

There are several options available to the applicant for planning permission to challenge an unacceptable condition (see fig.6.1 below), most of which are described in more detail in Ch.8. The acceptability of the conditions should be considered before the permission is implemented (see Ch.5 above). **6.17**

(a) Negotiation

Formal procedures such as appeals are expensive and time-consuming for both the applicant and the planning authority, and negotiations must be in the interests of both parties. It may be possible to persuade the planning authority to dispense with the condition, with the result that permission is granted without the condition following a fresh application, or an application for permission to develop the land without compliance with the condition is approved (see para.6.21 below). Additional information may be produced which was not before the authority when it made the decision to impose the condition. Developers frequently complain that authorities do not appreciate the impact of conditions, especially their adverse financial impact, and these matters could be put to the authority. If valid grounds of appeal can be shown, the authority may be willing to negotiate a compromise to avoid losing an appeal. **6.18**

When negotiating, care must be taken that time limits for commencing a formal challenge do not expire.

(b) Appeal to the Scottish Ministers or application to local review body

Depending on whether the permission is granted by the councillors or an officer under delegated powers, there is a right of appeal to the Scottish Ministers, or to apply to the local review body (LRB), against a grant of permission with an unacceptable condition.[85] As part of the appeal/application, the planning merits of the condition and the facts of the case will be considered. The policy of the Scottish Ministers on imposition of conditions will be applied (see para.6.14 above). The Scottish Ministers/LRB may reverse or vary any part of the original decision, no **6.19**

---

matter what aspect is challenged. In consequence, there is a risk of losing the entire permission or being burdened with a more onerous condition.

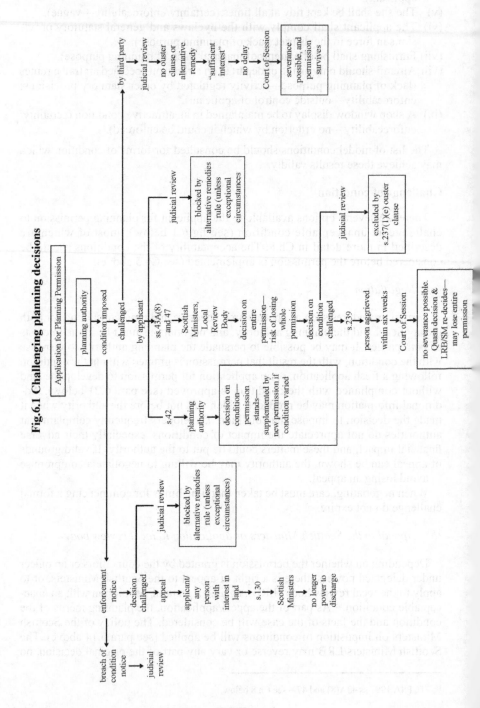

Fig.6.1 Challenging planning decisions

(c) Review by Court of Session

Review by the Court of Session (see Ch.8 below) relates to the legal validity of **6.20** the condition and not its planning merits. The legal requirements for validity will be applied and not the policy of the Scottish Ministers. A distinction must be drawn between statutory and common law judicial review:

(i) Statutory review is only competent for challenge of a decision by the Scottish Ministers or LRB on a condition.[86] The court has no power to sever the invalid condition from the remainder of the permission.[87] A successful challenge will therefore result in the permission being quashed and the matter being returned to the Scottish Ministers/LRB for re-decision. The Ministers/LRB may decide that without the condition, permission should be refused.

(ii) An application for judicial review at common law may be used to challenge a decision to impose a condition by either the planning authority or the Scottish Ministers. Unless there are exceptional circumstances, the existence of an alternative remedy will exclude an application for judicial review at common law. The applicant for permission therefore cannot utilise the common law judicial review procedure because of his statutory rights of appeal to the Scottish Ministers/application to the LRB against a decision by the planning authority, and review by the Court of Session of the decision by the Ministers/LRB.

Unlike statutory review, in the exercise of its common law judicial review jurisdiction the Court of Session has the power to sever an invalid condition with the result that the remainder of the permission stands shorn of the condition.[88]

There is no statutory test to determine whether a condition is severable, but several approaches can be identified from the cases. It is important to decide whether severance is a practical proposition. If the invalid condition is "inextricably interconnected" with the rest of the permission, severance may be impossible.[89] However, there is no absolute requirement for textual severability and the court may redraft a permission to retain the valid part.[90]

A distinction can be drawn between fundamental conditions which go to the root of the permission, and conditions that are unimportant or incidental, superimposed or collateral to the permission. Only conditions of the latter type can be severed. This test is essentially one of substance or character: can the condition be severed without changing the nature of the grant of permission? Another approach focuses on the intentions of the planning authority, asking whether it would have granted the permission without the offending condition. If not, the condition should not be severed and the whole permission should be quashed. It may be thought that a condition which does not fairly and reasonably relate to the permitted development is likely to be severable, but even in these circumstances the courts remain reluctant to alter the permission granted by the authority and prefer to quash the entire permission.

---

[86] TCPSA 1997 s.239.

[87] *BAA v Secretary of State for Scotland*, 1979 S.C. 200; *The Highland Council v Scottish Ministers* [2014] CSIH 74.

[88] *Mouchell v Oxfordshire CC* [1992] 1 P.L.R. 97; *R. (Midcounties Co-operative Ltd) v Wyre Forest DC* [2009] EWHC 964 (Admin).

[89] *R. v Secretary of State for Transport Ex p. Greater London Council* [1985] 3 All E.R. 300.

[90] *DPP v Hutchison* [1990] 2 All E.R. 836.

In consequence of the need to speculate on the intention of the planning authority in imposing the condition, the courts rarely declare a condition severable.[91] It is, therefore, unlikely that a successful application for judicial review at common law will result in anything other than invalidation of the whole permission.

(d)   Application for permission to develop land without compliance with condition

6.21   An application can be made to the planning authority for permission to develop the application site without complying with the conditions subject to which the permission was granted.[92] In deciding the application, the authority can only consider the conditions and there is no risk of losing the permission. If it decides permission should be granted subject to the same conditions, the application will be refused. If the application is successful permission will be granted subject to different conditions or unconditionally.

The disadvantage of this procedure is that the application is made to the same body that imposed the condition, although there is a right of appeal. Powerful arguments will be required to convince it that the condition should not have been imposed or should now be discharged. Using this procedure to challenge a condition may only be an option if circumstances have changed since the condition was imposed.

The Scottish Government note the following in relation to TCPSA s.42 applications[93]:

- The effect of granting permission is such that a new and separate permission exists for the development with different (or no) conditions attached. The previous planning permission remains unaltered by, and is not varied by, the decision on the s.42 application.
- The duration of the new permission is specified in the TCPSA. Alternatively, authorities may direct that a longer or shorter period applies.
- The need to attach to the new permission any of the conditions from the previous permission which it is intended should apply to the new planning permission.
- The need to secure any s.75 legal obligation (or other agreement) to the new permission, where it is intended this should still apply.

(e)   Ignore the condition

6.22   The applicant may choose to ignore the condition in the hope that the planning authority will not take enforcement action. A breach of condition becomes immune from enforcement action, and lawful, after 10 years (see Ch.7 below). Changes introduced in 2009 make this a riskier strategy, as there is no longer a right to appeal against an enforcement notice on the grounds that the condition ought to

---

[91]   *Allnatt London Properties v Middlesex CC* (1964) 15 P. & C.R. 288; *R. v St Edmundsbury BC Ex p. Investors in Industry* [1985] 3 All E.R. 234; *Elmbridge BC v Secretary of State for the Environment* [1989] J.P.L. 277; *R. (Midcounties Co-operative Ltd) v Wyre Forest DC* [2009] EWHC 964 (Admin).

[92]   TCPSA 1997 s.42; Town and Country Planning (Development Management Procedure) (Scotland) Regulations 2013 (SSI 2013/155) reg.11.

[93]   Planning Circular 3/2013, Development Management Procedures (Scottish Government, 2013) Annex I, para.2.

be discharged,[94] and retrospective planning permission cannot be granted if an enforcement notice has been issued.[95]

Also, authorities can use the power to serve a breach of condition notice where there is non-compliance with a condition regulating the use of land. There is no right of appeal against such a notice although it may be possible to seek judicial review at common law on the grounds that the condition which is the subject of the notice is invalid. If attempts to challenge the enforcement or breach of condition notice are unsuccessful, failure to comply with its terms is a criminal offence. The invalidity of the condition can be raised as a defence to any prosecution for failure to comply with a breach of condition notice,[96] but not in relation to an enforcement notice offence (see Ch.7 below).

(f) Application for retrospective permission

An application for retrospective permission may be made for development which **6.23** was carried out without complying with a condition subject to which permission was granted, provided no enforcement notice has been issued before the date of the application.[97] As part of the application, it would be necessary to convince the authority that there was no need for the condition. If no such application is made, the breach of condition will only become immune from enforcement action after 10 years.

Types of conditions

In addition to the two general statutory powers to impose planning conditions, **6.24** there are several more particular statutory powers relating to temporary and personal permissions, specification of use, and preservation and planting of trees (see para.6.04 above). Many other types of planning conditions have arisen in practice. Of these, four have been examined in particular detail by the courts: those relating to occupancy, restriction of use or development, avoidance of compensation payment, and the imposition of negative or suspensive conditions.

(a) Occupancy conditions

Prior to the introduction of the Human Rights Act 1998, the courts upheld the **6.25** validity of conditions that restricted occupancy to a particular occupier or class of occupier, provided the condition relates to a legitimate planning purpose. For example, a condition limiting occupation of a dwelling to persons employed in agriculture (agricultural occupancy condition) was validly imposed where the reason for the condition was the protection of the green belt from residential development.[98] Similarly, a condition restricting occupation of commercial or industrial property to local firms was imposed to restrict the entry of new industry into the area.[99] In contrast, an occupancy condition imposed to relieve the author-

---

94   TCPSA 1997 s.130(1)(a) has been repealed.
95   TCPSA 1997 s.33(4).
96   *Dilieto v Ealing London BC* [1998] 2 All E.R. 885.
97   TCPSA 1997 s.33.
98   *Fawcett Properties Ltd v Buckingham CC* [1961] A.C. 636.
99   *Slough Industrial Estates v Secretary of State for the Environment* [1987] J.P.L. 353.

ity of its statutory duty had no legitimate planning reason and was therefore invalid.[100]

It is likely that an occupancy condition will amount to interference with the Convention rights of the applicant for planning permission, either under art.8 (the right to respect for private and family life) and/or First Protocol art.1 (protection of property). The existence of an occupancy condition will restrict the opportunities to re-sell a property and therefore reduce its value for mortgage purposes. The planning authority will need to justify any interference with the applicant's Convention rights. For example, art.8(2) permits interference with rights "for the protection of the rights and freedoms of others", which includes environmental protection. This preserves the scope for using agricultural occupancy conditions to implement planning policies to protect the countryside. However, the planning authority will need to show that the condition is necessary (proportionate) in the circumstances of the particular case.[101] As the necessary/proportionality test raises similar issues as the "fairly and reasonably relates" test which has always applied to conditions (see para.6.07 above), it is possible that the introduction of Convention rights might not further restrict the use of occupancy conditions.

A refusal of planning permission also interferes with the Convention rights of the applicant. Use of an occupancy restriction might be a proportionate response, to avoid such a refusal of permission.

In considering whether an occupancy condition has been complied with, the relevant issue is occupancy and not use. A property subject to an agricultural occupancy condition had been occupied from May to September as holiday accommodation, and was empty from October to April. The decision to grant a certificate of lawful use on the grounds of 10 years' non-compliance with the condition was quashed on the grounds that the question of use had been improperly confused with the question of occupancy.[102]

An occupancy condition does not apply to a building which is not built in accordance with the planning permission. A bungalow which was about 90ft west of the permitted location was held not to be subject to the occupancy restriction imposed by the condition attached to the planning permission.[103] As the period for enforcement of development without planning permission is only four years in contrast to 10 years for a breach of planning condition, this is an important issue.

The Scottish Government guidance states that occupancy conditions should only be used when the need for special planning grounds can be demonstrated, and permission would otherwise be refused. Conditions restricting the occupancy of commercial or industrial premises to local firms should not be imposed. Similarly, occupancy conditions should be imposed on housing developments only in the most exceptional cases where there are clear and specific circumstances that warrant allowing an individual house (or extension) on a site where development would not normally be permitted. Agricultural occupancy conditions may be imposed where permission is granted for a house to be built to accommodate a worker engaged in agricultural or forestry employment on a site where residential development would not normally be permitted. Although conditions should not normally be used to control matters such as tenure, price or ownership, there may be circumstances in

---

[100]   *R. v Hillingdon LBC Ex p. Royco Homes Ltd* [1974] Q.B. 720.
[101]   *Gillow v UK* (1989) 11 E.H.R.R. 335.
[102]   *North Devon DC v Secretary of State for the Environment, Transport and the Regions* [1998] 4
        P.L.R. 46.
[103]   *Handoll v Warner Goodman and Streat* [1995] J.P.L. 930.

which it will be acceptable to use conditions to ensure that some of the housing built is occupied only by people falling within particular categories of need.[104]

(b) Restriction of use/development

The description of the development in the planning permission does not necessarily prevent a change of use, unless there is a specific condition.[105]   **6.26**

It is competent to impose a condition restricting changes of use, subject to satisfying the requirements of the Human Rights Act 1998 (see discussion above re occupancy conditions). This type of condition has the effect of restricting the freedom provided by the Use Classes Order (UCO) (see Ch.4 above), with the result that an application for planning permission may be required for any change from the permitted use. The condition may prohibit any change from the use permitted; alternatively, it may preclude specific alternative uses or restrict changes to specified classes of the UCO. For example, it may be valid to impose a condition preventing the change of use permitted by class 4 from light industrial to office use, provided the planning authority have valid planning reasons for imposing this restriction.[106] A condition stating "shall be for non-food sales only" was held to impliedly exclude the UCO.[107]

It is similarly possible to restrict permitted development rights under the Permitted Development Order (PDO).[108] For example, where permission is granted for erection of a dwellinghouse in the grounds of an existing dwellinghouse, it may be appropriate to restrict the permitted development rights which would otherwise be enjoyed by the new dwellinghouse. This would have the effect of requiring an application for planning permission to be made which would provide the planning authority with an opportunity to consider the effects of fresh development on the existing dwelling.

The Scottish Government guidance states that conditions limiting the provisions of the UCO or PDO should only be imposed in exceptional circumstances.[109] This type of condition requires to be carefully worded.[110]

(c) Liability to pay compensation

Where there is a choice of statutory powers, an authority can legitimately use the   **6.27**
power that carries no liability to payment of compensation. It is therefore competent to impose a condition for planning reasons which has the effect of avoiding the payment of compensation,[111] although avoidance of the payment of compensation is not

---

[104] Planning Circular 4/1998, Use of Conditions in Planning Permissions, Annex, paras 91–102.

[105] *I'm Your Man v Secretary of State for the Environment* (1999) 77 P. & C.R. 251; but see *Winchester CC v Secretary of State* [2015] EWCA Civ 563.

[106] Compare *Tower Hamlets LBC v Secretary of State for the Environment* [1990] J.P.L. 688 and *Camden LBC v Secretary of State for the Environment* [1989] J.P.L. 613.

[107] *Royal London Mutual Insurance Society v Secretary of State* [2013] EWHC 3597 Admin; *Coal Pension Properties Ltd v Scottish Ministers* [2015] CSIH 57.

[108] Town and Country Planning (General Permitted Development) (Scotland) Order 1992 (SI 1992/223) art.3(4); *Gill v Secretary of State for the Environment* [1985] J.P.L. 710.

[109] Planning Circular 4/1998, Use of Conditions in Planning Permissions, Annex, para.86.

[110] *Dunoon Developments v Secretary of State for the Environment* [1992] J.P.L. 936.

[111] *R. v Exeter City Council Ex p. JL Thomas & Co Ltd* [1991] 1 Q.B. 471; [1990] J.P.L. 129; cf. *Hall & Co Ltd v Shoreham-by-Sea Urban DC* [1964] 1 W.L.R. 240.

a planning consideration.[112] The Scottish Government policy is that conditions should not be imposed in order to avoid liability to pay compensation under other legislation, but that such conditions would not be illegal if justified on planning grounds.[113]

As with all conditions, any interference with the Convention rights of the applicant for planning permission will need to be justified by the planning authority. Although Convention rights do not create any general requirement for the payment of compensation, any entitlement to compensation is relevant in assessing whether the violation of Convention rights is disproportionate.[114]

(d) Negative/suspensive conditions

6.28   Permission for a proposed development often hinges on an element outside the applicant's control, such as the provision of adequate sewerage facilities by the sewerage authority. Since the result is outwith the applicant's control, any condition requiring him to achieve that result would be unenforceable (see para.6.12 above). The solution is to word the condition negatively so that it provides that development will not commence until the result has been achieved. It is competent to impose such negative or suspensive conditions, often referred to as "Grampian" conditions.[115] Use of this type of condition may avoid the necessity of entering into a planning agreement (see para.6.30 below), but is not appropriate where the development has already commenced.[116]

Until a decision of the House of Lords, it was trite law that it would be unreasonable and ultra vires to impose a negative condition on a grant of planning permission unless there was a reasonable prospect of the result being achieved.[117] In the absence of such a prospect, the authority would have granted a worthless permission.

In *British Railways Board v Secretary of State for the Environment*, the House of Lords overruled the reasonable prospect test.[118] If the negative condition is appropriate in light of sound planning principles, the fact that it appeared to have no reasonable prospects of being implemented did not mean that the grant of planning permission subject to it would be unlawful. What is appropriate depends on the circumstances and must be determined in the exercise of the discretion of the planning authority determining the application. The mere fact that a desirable condition appears to have no reasonable prospect of fulfilment does not mean that planning permission has to be refused.

The practical implications of this decision are uncertain. Authorities are likely to continue to regard the lack of a reasonable prospect of fulfilment as an important factor in their decision, albeit not a determining factor. It should be noted that the case before their Lordships concerned the imposition of negative conditions to solve ownership difficulties, where it was clear that those difficulties had no relevance to

---

112 *BAA v Secretary of State for Scotland*, 1979 S.C. 200 per Lord President Emslie at 218.

113 Planning Circular 4/1998, Use of Conditions in Planning Permissions, Annex, paras 20 and 22.

114 e.g. *James v UK* (1986) 8 E.H.R.R. 123; *Lithgow v UK* (1986) 8 E.H.R.R. 329.

115 *Grampian RC v Aberdeen DC*, 1984 S.L.T. 197; *Willis v Argyll and Bute Council* [2010] CSOH 122.

116 *Empress Car Co (Abertillery) Ltd v Secretary of State for Wales* [1995] E.G. 22 (C.S.).

117 *Norfolk House Group v Secretary of State for the Environment* [1990] J.P.L. 490; *Jones v Secretary of State for Wales* [1990] J.P.L. 907.

118 *British Railways Board v Secretary of State for the Environment* [1994] J.P.L. 32; [1993] 3 P.L.R. 125, followed in *Strathclyde RC v Secretary of State for Scotland*, 1996 S.L.T. 579; 1996 55 S.P.E.L. 51.

the determination of the planning application. One can speculate that a different approach might be taken where the problems concern more important matters such as necessary infrastructure.

The Scottish Government guidance indicates that there is no longer a legal requirement to satisfy a reasonable prospects test, and advises planning authorities to note the ruling by the House of Lords "and its implications for a less restrictive view in the use of negative conditions".[119]

Negative conditions can also be used to control the separate phases of a large development. For example, a condition may require provision of specified infrastructure works (roads, drains, etc.) before the development or a further phase of the development commences. Such conditions ensure the provision of expensive works which the developer might be tempted to defer for many years.

Negative conditions are not invalid where they relate to actions which might take place on land beyond the control of the applicant or depend on decisions taken by someone other than the planning authority.[120]

Conclusion

The court decisions on the use of the particular types of conditions discussed above do not show the expected degree of judicial concern to protect private rights of property against interference by way of conditions imposed on grants of planning permission.[121] Indeed, it seems that the courts generally favour the validity of conditions. Although the judges have developed a series of limitations on the exercise of the power to impose conditions, there are few instances where the courts have found conditions invalid. This may in part be due to the influence on the imposition of conditions of the Scottish/UK Government guidance on the use of conditions which is often more restrictive than the legal requirements.

6.29

PLANNING AGREEMENTS/OBLIGATIONS

Planning agreements are contracts entered into between the landowner and planning authority (and often with other parties). Agreements can be entered into at any stage of the planning process, but most commonly arise in connection with applications for planning permission. There are several statutory powers which enable local authorities to enter into agreements with developers. The widest and, therefore, most important is the power to enter into a s.75 obligation conferred by the TCPSA 1997 (previously s.50 of the Town and Country Planning (Scotland) Act 1972). Although many of the following points would apply to all forms of planning agreements, discussion will focus exclusively on s.75 obligations.[122]

6.30

---

[119] Planning Circular 4/1998, Use of Conditions in Planning Permissions, Annex, para.38. There is separate guidance for use of negative conditions for aviation radar in wind turbine permissions—Guidance on Dealing with Aviation and Associated Negative Conditions in Wind Turbine Consents (Scottish Government, 2012).

[120] *Strathclyde RC v Secretary of State for Scotland*, 1996 S.L.T. 579; 1996 55 S.P.E.L. 51.

[121] cf. McAuslan's thesis that the courts favour individual rights of private property at the expense of the public interest, thereby upholding individual challenges to the actions of planning authorities—Patrick McAuslan, *Ideologies of Planning Law* (Pergamon, 1980) and article of same name (1979) 2. U.L. & P. 1.

[122] Other powers include Local Government (Scotland) Act 1973 ss.69 and 85; Roads (Scotland) Act 1984 s.48; Local Government in Scotland Act 2003 s.20.

Studies have shown a wide variation in the use of s.75 obligations across Scotland.[123]

The Planning Etc. (Scotland) Act 2006 (PSA) substituted a new s.75. It introduced the power for a person to enter into a planning obligation unilaterally, in other words, to deliver the same result as a planning agreement, but without the requirement to obtain the participation of the planning authority in the drafting of the document. That is potentially useful where the planning authority do not support the proposed development, and the obligation might improve the chances of the appeal succeeding. These changes make the scope of the new s.75 power similar to the s.106 power in the English legislation.

Other provisions introduced by the PSA 2006 are the procedures for modification and discharge of planning obligations, including a right of appeal to the Scottish Ministers; the continuing liability of former owners[124]; and the power to enter into good neighbour agreements (see para.6.56 below).

Background

6.31   Section 75 obligations are often used where there are infrastructure deficiencies (discussed further below). In 1984 the Court of Session upheld the use of suspensive planning conditions (see para.6.28 above), to prevent developments from proceeding until the required infrastructure is provided. This approach facilitates grants of planning permission, but leaves uncertainty about when/if the infrastructure upgrade will be delivered, especially if the infrastructure has to be provided by a third party such as the roads authority. As public sector budgets shrank, developers explored ways to fund infrastructure improvements to unlock the development potential of their sites. So began the practice of planning gain, with developers offering to make financial contribution towards infrastructure works.

Initially these developer contributions were for road improvements, but as local authorities have become more experienced and sophisticated in their approach, planning gain has widened to include such varied issues as school improvements, dog waste bins and public art.

As planning conditions cannot be used to require monetary payments (see para.6.09 above), planning agreements have been used as the vehicle to deliver planning gain.[125]

New approaches have been proposed.[126] The planning gain supplement was a taxation device to provide funds to address such deficiencies. It would have imposed a levy on the uplift in value created by a grant of planning permission. The levy proceeds were to be used to pay for off-site infrastructure, leaving planning agreements to regulate on-site matters. The Westminster Government decided not to proceed with the planning gain supplement.

---

[123]   Scottish Government, *An Assessment of the Value of Planning Agreements in Scotland* (Scottish Government, 2008); also Ross, *Planning Agreements and Positive Planning for Sustainable Communities in Scotland* (Scottish Government, 2004) para.3.21, commenting on Colin Buchanan & Partners, Dundas & Wilson and Robert Turley Associates, *The Use and Effectiveness of Planning Agreements* (Scottish Executive, 2001). The Scottish Government Planning Performance Statistics, published quarterly, identify the number of planning applications which are subject to legal agreements.

[124]   TCPSA 1997 ss.75A–C.

[125]   e.g. PAN 2/2010, Affordable Housing and Housing Land Audits (Scottish Government, 2010) para.24 states that a s.75 agreement may be necessary if there is to be payment of a commuted sum.

[126]   For example: GVA, DLA Piper, Turner & Townsend and Steven Tolson, *The Potential of Development Charges in the Scottish Planning System* (Scottish Government, 2011).

In England and Wales, local authorities are empowered, but not required, to charge a Community Infrastructure Levy on new development in their area. The proceeds will be spent on local infrastructure. At the time of writing, there is no proposal for a Scottish equivalent of the Community Infrastructure Levy.

The advantage of a levy is the certainty provided to developers. A broadly similar approach has already been taken in some Scottish local development plans, which incorporate what is colloquially referred to as a "roof tax".[127] This enables a developer to calculate precisely how much will need to be paid.

Planning agreements are attractive to developers because of the potential to use a planning agreement to increase the likelihood of a grant of planning permission for a proposed development. This may be achieved by using an agreement to remove obstacles which would otherwise render the development unacceptable. Agreements can also be used to offer community benefits as a balance to offset the planning disadvantages of a proposed development. The development potential of a site can be unlocked through an agreement providing that the developer will undertake or pay for infrastructure improvements, such as roads and sewers, without which no development could be permitted on the site and which would otherwise be at the mercy of local government budgets. In the developer's eyes the agreement is a device to increase the likelihood of planning permission being granted. In consequence, it is essential to ensure that the planning authority may validly take into account the benefits promised in the agreement when determining the application for planning permission (see "Agreements as a Material Consideration" below).

Although planning agreements are entered into voluntarily, it must be acknowledged that developers are often left with no alternative but to agree.[128] If there are planning problems with the proposed development which can only be resolved through a planning agreement, planning permission cannot be obtained until the developer and the planning authority have negotiated the terms of the agreement. This places the planning authority in a position to dictate the terms, and possibly require the provision of planning gain. Without the agreement permission will be refused on appeal/review and the option of appealing to the Scottish Ministers, or applying to the local review body, against deemed refusal of planning permission (see Ch.8 below) is, therefore, not available to the developer. The Scottish Ministers/reporter/LRB has no power to impose an agreement on the planning authority. The developer must agree terms with the authority or abandon the proposed development. However, the developer's negotiating position need not be inherently weak. Considerations such as the number of jobs which would be created by the proposed development may cause the planning authority to be anxious to avoid its abandonment. In addition, in some circumstances, the Scottish Ministers/reporter/LRB may be able to grant planning permission without the agreement.[129]

The English courts have held that it was unreasonable for a highway authority, whose road safety objections had been fully heard and rejected on appeal, to maintain their original view and refuse to enter into an agreement with the developer.[130] However, it was not perverse for an updated assessment to be required before the agreement was concluded when the original study had been undertaken

6.32

---

[127] Ryden LLP, *Planning for Infrastructure* (Scottish Government, 2015).
[128] The new power to enter into an unilateral obligation will give developers more flexibility where agreement cannot be reached on the planning gain package.
[129] e.g. *Strathclyde RC v Secretary of State for Scotland*, 1996 S.L.T. 579; 1996 55 S.P.E.L. 51.
[130] *R. v Warwickshire CC Ex p. Powergen Plc* [1998] J.P.L. 131.

four years ago and there was evidence of changed traffic conditions in the area.[131]
It is unclear how far this principle may extend. For example, it could be argued that
it would be ultra vires for a planning authority to refuse to enter into a s.75 obligation where the Scottish Ministers/reporter/LRB has indicated that they are minded
to grant planning permission.

For planning authorities, agreements are an alternative means of controlling
developments. Agreements can be used to control matters clearly beyond the scope
of conditions. For example, conditions cannot validly require payment of money
or provision of infrastructure such as roads and sewers on land outside the application site which is not under the control of the applicant for permission, even where
the work is only necessary because of the proposed development. In addition, agreements can secure a degree of flexibility of control and management of development beyond the normal range of planning permission and conditions. Another at-
traction is the availability of contractual remedies for enforcement without the
procedural requirements of the planning enforcement regime (see Ch.7 below).

In consequence of the introduction of the procedure to apply to modify or
discharge a s.75 obligation (see para.6.45 below), there are appeal mechanisms for
both conditions and s.75 obligations. Previously agreements were a means of avoiding uncertainty regarding the validity of conditions and potential successful appeals against conditions.

The use of planning agreements is not without criticism.[132] The lack of public
scrutiny means that interests other than those of the negotiating parties may not
receive proper protection. Most importantly, there is concern that the advantages
(often referred to as "planning gain") accruing from the planning agreement may
affect the objectivity of the authority in evaluating the planning merits of the
scheme. In other words, that the process amounts to a sale of planning permission.[133]
Above all, the objection is that it is precisely because conditions cannot be imposed
that the applicant must "voluntarily" offer the benefit.[134] The legal restrictions placed
on the use of conditions are circumvented by using planning agreements to achieve
the desired objective. Criticism has focused on the use by planning authorities of
agreements to secure planning gain or benefit for the community which does not
form an essential part of the development.

Developers have cited more specific objections to the practice of using
agreements. Negotiating the terms of agreements is time-consuming and delays the
grant of planning permission. It is common for the first developer in an area to be
left with no choice but to agree to pay for the provision of infrastructure and
services which are then used by subsequent developers without any contribution to
the cost (the roof tax approach mentioned above can remove this inequality). A
frequent complaint is that restrictions proposed by planning authorities for inclusion in agreements exhibit a lack of understanding of the financial aspects of
development.

It is clear that there is some distrust of the use of planning agreements. Indeed,
it has been suggested that authorities should review their practices with a view to
utilising suspensive conditions in place of planning agreements wherever possible.
Nevertheless, it must be emphasised that the power to use agreements to achieve

---

131 *R. v Cardiff City Council Ex p. Sears Group Properties Ltd* [1998] 3 P.L.R. 55.
132 e.g. the Nolan Committee, Jean McFadden, "Nolan on Planning: the government's preliminary
response", 1998 68 S.P.E.L. 73; "The Nolan Committee on planning", 1997 63 S.P.E.L. 96.
133 Loughlin, "Planning Gain—Law, Policy and Practice" (1981) 1 O.J.L.S. 61.
134 Nathaniel Lichfield, "From Planning Gain to Community Benefit" [1989] J.P.L. 68.

objectives other than planning gain (as distinct from benefits related to the development) provides planning authorities with a flexible development management power.

Planning agreements have a useful role to play in the planning system in the interests of planning authority and developer alike.

Unilateral obligations

Most s.75 obligations are entered into with the planning authority as a signatory. However, the Planning etc. (Scotland) Act 2006 introduced the option for a s.75 obligation to be unilateral, ie. not signed by the planning authority.[135] The statutory provisions apply in the same way to unilateral obligations as to s.75 obligations signed by the planning authority.

6.33

Human rights

Since a planning agreement is essentially a contract, it cannot be assumed that all acts connected with a planning agreement are public and therefore regulated by the Human Rights Act 1998. It is likely that the Human Rights Act 1998 applies to the planning authority's decision to enter into the agreement; it is less clear whether it will apply to enforcement of the agreement thereafter.[136]

6.34

Scope of s.75 obligations

Two issues arise in any discussion of the scope of s.75 obligations: first, the limits to the power of planning authorities to enter into such agreements; and, secondly, the circumstances in which it would be illegal for the planning authority to take into account the provision of planning gain in terms of the agreement when determining an application for planning permission. Only the first issue truly concerns the scope of s.75 obligations; the second forms more a practical limit beyond which developers will be unwilling to venture although it provides scope for a rival developer to seek to reduce a grant of planning permission. It must be emphasised that it does not necessarily follow that where the provisions of an agreement cannot be validly considered when deciding an application, the planning authority must have exceeded its statutory power to enter into the planning agreement with the result that it is invalid.[137]

6.35

(a) Scope of the statutory power

As the term suggests, the power to enter into a s.75 obligation is conferred by statute.[138] If a planning authority exceeds the power conferred by statute, it is acting outwith its power (ultra vires) and, thus, illegally. The limits of the statutory power of a planning authority to enter into a s.75 obligation are therefore important.

The wording of s.75 refers to obligations "restricting or regulating the development or use of the land". It is difficult to identify what limits are placed on the scope

6.36

---

[135] TCPSA 1997 s.75(1)(b). Planning Circular 3/2012, Planning Obligations and Good Neighbour Agreements (Scottish Government, 2012), paras 46–48.
[136] Neil Collar, *Planning and Human Rights* (Edinburgh: W. Green, 2001), paras 7.22–7.37.
[137] *R. v South Northamptonshire DC Ex p. Crest Homes* [1994] 3 P.L.R. 47 per Henry L.J. at 56D–G.
[138] TCPSA 1997 s.75.

of agreements by this wording. It has been suggested that "restrict" refers to the prohibition or limitation of what is done on land, while "regulate" is more concerned with ensuring that something is done in a particular way.[139] The wording of s.75 does not permit the agreement to restrict or regulate the development or use of land, other than the land described in the agreement. Thus agreements cannot restrict off-site uses such as routes used by vehicles after leaving the site. An agreement requiring the developer to provide an access road to an adjacent development site was held to have been competently entered into by the planning authority.[140]

A s.75 agreement can require operations or activities to be carried out in, on, under or over the land, or require the land to be used in a specified way.[141]

The new, more specific provisions state that the obligation may be unconditional, or subject to conditions; require the payment of a specified amount or amount determined using a formula contained in the agreement, or periodic sums; and such incidental and consequential provisions as appear necessary or expedient. Any obligation in the agreement can be postponed to a later date.[142]

6.37   The first section of this chapter explored the limits on the power to impose planning conditions. Many of these limits have arisen from judicial interpretation of the statutory power. It had been suggested that if a condition would be invalid (ultra vires) then the same result could not be achieved through the use of a s.75 obligation.[143] This implied that the same restrictions had to apply to use of obligations under s.75 as applied to conditions. The House of Lords rejected that suggestion.[144]

Both the powers to impose planning conditions and to enter into s.75 obligations are provided by the TCPSA 1997, so there is a common requirement of a planning purpose.[145] As any consideration relating to the use and development of land can be a planning consideration,[146] this requirement should not unduly constrain the use of agreements. An agreement requiring the developer to provide an access road to an adjacent development site was held to have a sound and proper planning purpose.[147] Provisions restraining transfer of pollution control licences were unenforceable.[148]

Although most s.75 obligations are made in the context of applications for planning permission, agreements may be made in other situations. Unlike the power to impose conditions, the wording of s.75 does not connect the agreement to a grant of planning permission and the "fairly and reasonably relates" test therefore should

---

[139] Jeremy Rowan-Robinson and Eric Young, *Planning by Agreement in Scotland* (Edinburgh: W. Green, 1989) p.22.

[140] *McIntosh v Aberdeenshire Council*, 1999 S.L.T. 93

[141] TCPSA s.75(2). Previously there was uncertainty about whether a s.75 agreement could require that some positive obligation be undertaken, in other words that the developer agreed to do something, as opposed to not doing something.

[142] TCPSA 1997 s.75(3)–(4).

[143] Sir Graham Eyre QC in *Eagle Star Insurance Co v Secretary of State for the Environment* [1992] J.P.L. 434 at 440.

[144] *Tesco Stores Ltd v Secretary of State for the Environment* [1995] 2 All E.R. 636.

[145] *Good v Epping Forest DC* [1993] J.P.L. 127.

[146] *Stringer v Minister for Housing and Local Government* [1970] 1 W.L.R. 1281 per Cooke J.

[147] *McIntosh v Aberdeenshire Council*, 1999 S.L.T. 93.

[148] *Friends of Loch Etive v Argyll and Bute Council* [2015] CSOH 61.

not apply.[149] An agreement requiring provision of infrastructure beyond that required for the development has been upheld.[150]

While a fair and reasonable relation to the proposed development is not necessary for the agreement to be valid, some degree of relationship is necessary before the authority can take into account the terms of the agreement when determining the application for planning permission (see below).

The requirement of reasonableness or rationality is common to the exercise of all statutory discretionary powers by a public authority and applies both to conditions and agreements.[151] It may however be arguable that because a s.75 obligation is a contract this requirement should not apply.

From this brief examination, s.75 obligations appear to have greater scope than planning conditions because there is no requirement that for an agreement to be valid its provisions must "fairly and reasonably relate" to the development. This conclusion necessarily implies that s.75 obligations may be used to achieve a result that could not be legally achieved through imposition of a planning condition.[152] Indeed, this is one of the attractions of s.75 obligations in the eyes of planning authorities.

Where separate agreements are entered into with adjacent landowners, there might be a requirement for the planning authority to carry out a single process of consultation with all the landowners if apportionment of infrastructure costs is an issue.[153]

(b) Agreements as a material consideration

In most cases a developer enters into a s.75 obligation because the terms of the agreement will increase the likelihood of planning permission being granted. This objective will not be attained unless the terms of the agreement form a material consideration in the determination of the application for planning permission (see Ch.5 above). If the terms are not a material consideration, it would be illegal for the planning authority to take account of them when deciding the application for planning permission. In such circumstances, the developer would still be bound by the terms of the agreement, but the authority would be bound to ignore these terms when reaching its decision on the application. Any failure to ignore the agreement when deciding the application would expose any grant of planning permission to the risk of challenge by a competing developer or concerned member of the public. Similar comments apply to the relevance of the agreement to an appeal to the Scottish Ministers/application to the LRB.

Chapter 5 examines the circumstances in which the authority may take into account the agreement, which may give rise to planning benefits, when considering the application. A benefit which has nothing to do with the development will plainly not be a material consideration. If the benefit has some connection, then regard must be had to it. The extent to which it should affect the decision is a matter entirely within the discretion of the decision-maker. In exercising that discretion, he is

6.38

---

149 *Good v Epping Forest DC* [1994] 1 W.L.R. 376 CA.
150 *R. v Gillingham BC Ex p. F Parham Ltd* [1988] J.P.L. 336.
151 *R. v Wealden DC Ex p. Charles Church South East Ltd* [1989] J.P.L. 837, but this element is only included in the Lexis transcript.
152 *Good v Epping Forest DC* [1994] 1 W.L.R. 376 CA.
153 *R. v Lichfield DC Ex p. Lichfield Securities Ltd* [2001] 3 P.L.R. 33.

entitled to have regard to his established policy.[154] The courts have rejected the contention that the benefit must be necessary to overcome, remedy or alleviate planning objections to the proposed development.[155]

6.39　　It has been held that where residential development made additional infrastructure necessary or desirable, there was nothing wrong in the planning authority having a policy requiring major developers to contribute to the cost of infrastructure related to their development. The formula adopted by the authority, which was based on the enhanced value of the land, was not bad in law as insufficiently connecting the individual development with its associated infrastructure, as there was no suggestion that it would raise an amount disproportionate to what the developments required.[156]

The conflict underlying the scope of s.75 obligations should now be apparent. The wording of s.75 and, therefore, the legal validity of planning agreements, does not require any connection between the provisions of the agreement and the proposed development, but this connection is required before the provisions may be taken into account by the planning authority in deciding the planning application normally associated with the agreement.[157] It is not necessarily outwith the powers of a planning authority to enter into a s.75 obligation which it would be forced to ignore as an irrelevant consideration when determining an application for planning permission. It is up to the developer to resist provisions which are not sufficiently connected to the development to form material considerations for the planning application.

The connection required between the benefits offered by the agreement and the proposed development before the agreement can be deemed a material consideration may seem similar to the "fairly and reasonably relates" requirement applicable to conditions. However, the potential scope of agreements must inevitably result in a wider degree of connection than that permitted under the "fairly and reasonably relates" test, as agreements can, for example, require either contributions from developers or control off-site works on land outside the control of the developer.

(c)　Scottish Government guidance

6.40　　The Scottish Government has issued guidance on the use of planning agreements.[158] The guidance is an indication of the weight which will be given to the terms of a planning agreement in the course of determining an appeal to the Scottish Ministers against refusal of planning permission, or an application to the LRB. It can, therefore, be used by developers in the course of negotiating the terms of a s.75 obligation to resist excessive demands made by the planning authority. The guidance will also be a key consideration in determining an application/appeal seeking modification or discharge of a s.75 obligation.

The guidance indicates that s.75 obligations should only be used where all of the following tests are satisfied:

---

[154]　*Tesco Stores Ltd v Secretary of State for the Environment* [1995] 2 All E.R. 636.
[155]　*R. v Plymouth City Council Ex. p. Plymouth and South Devon Co-operative Society Ltd* [1993] J.P.L. 538 and (on appeal) [1993] 2 P.L.R 75; approved in *Tesco Stores Ltd v Secretary of State for the Environment* [1995] 2 All E.R. 636.
[156]　*R. v South Northamptonshire DC Ex p. Crest Homes Plc* [1994] 3 P.L.R. 47.
[157]　*R. v South Northamptonshire DC Ex p. Crest Homes* [1994] 3 P.L.R. 47 per Henry L.J. at 56D–G.
[158]　Planning Circular 3/2012, Planning Obligations and Good Neighbour Agreements.

- necessary to make the proposed development acceptable in planning terms;
- serve a planning purpose and, where it is possible to identify infrastructure provision requirements in advance, should relate to development plans;
- relate to the proposed development either as a direct consequence of the development or arising from the cumulative impact of development in the area;
- fairly and reasonably relate in scale and kind to the proposed development;
- reasonable in all other respects.

The guidance advises that wherever possible planning authorities should rely on planning conditions rather than using a planning agreement. A s.75 obligation is only necessary where successors in title need to be bound by the required obligation, for example where phased contributions to infrastructure are required.

The planning purpose test involves a judgment which should be rooted primarily in the development plan.

The relationship to proposed development test requires a link between the development and any mitigation offered as part of the developer's contribution. Planning authorities should not attach weight to offers made to undertake works, donate monies, or other incentives, including contributions to community trust funds, if these do not meet this test. Equally planning authorities should not be influenced by the absence of such offers.

The guidance also states that planning obligations must be related in scale and kind to the proposed development. In assessing any contributions, planning authorities may take into account the cumulative impact of a number of proposed developments and use obligations to share costs proportionately. The effect of such infrastructure investment may be to confer some wider community benefit but contributions should always be proportionate to the scale of the proposed development. Attempts to extract excessive contributions from developers towards the costs of infrastructure or to obtain extraneous benefits are unacceptable. Where the need to improve, upgrade or replace infrastructure does not arise directly from the proposed development, then planning authorities should not seek to address this through a planning obligation.

The reasonableness test is that the requirement in the obligation should be so directly related to the regulation of the proposed development that it should not be permitted without it. In the case of financial payments, these should contribute to the cost of providing necessary facilities required as a consequence of or in connection with the development.

The guidance indicates that planning authorities need to consider identifying infrastructure requirements in strategic and local development plans and the potential implications for the use of planning obligations, and more specific identification of expected contributions in supplementary guidance. Where standard charges and formulae are applied to individual developments, they should reflect the actual impacts of, and be proportionate to, the development and should comply with the general tests set out in the circular.

Effect of s.75 obligation

(a)   Relevance of obligation to planning application or appeal

The extent to which the provisions of a s.75 obligation form a material consideration in the determination of a planning application or appeal has already been   **6.41** discussed. There must be some relationship between the provisions of the agreement and the development proposed in the application. The absence of such a relationship may give a third party, such as a rival developer, grounds for seeking judicial review of the decision to grant planning permission.

(b) Fettering of discretion

6.42   In accordance with the general legal principle that decision-makers must not fetter their exercise of discretionary powers conferred by statute (see Ch.5 above), it is not competent for a planning authority to bind itself in a s.75 obligation to grant planning permission for a specified development.[159] Assuming that the terms of the agreement are a material consideration, the authority can take into account those terms when deciding the application. However, it must also take into account all other relevant considerations, which may dictate that permission should be refused.

In a similar way, the planning authority is obliged to take into account any material changes in circumstances arising between the time of the resolution to grant permission once a planning agreement is concluded and conclusion of that agreement, and may refuse to grant permission on the basis of these changes.[160]

(c) Binding on the land

6.43   The importance of s.75 obligations lies in the provisions allowing for recording of the completed agreement in the Register of Sasines or registration in the Land Register. Once the completed obligation has been recorded in the property register, its provisions bind in perpetuity the land to which it applies, applying to not only those persons who signed the obligation, but to all future parties who obtain an interest in the land notwithstanding their ignorance of the terms of the obligation, and it may be enforced against them by the planning authority. In this way, it is similar to a grant of planning permission which attaches to the land rather than to the person who made the application. Other forms of planning agreements merely bind the signatories to the agreement.

Positive obligations in the obligation—requiring operations or activities to be carried out in, on, under or over the land, or the land to be used in a specified way—can be enforced against the owner of the land.[161] Payment obligations can also be enforced against the owner. All other obligations in the agreement can be enforced against the owner or tenant of the land, or any other person having the use of the land. It also specifically states that it is immaterial whether the owner at the time of registration/recording was owner when the obligation was entered into. If more than one person comes within the description of owner, then "owner" means such person as has most recently acquired such right. Where a heritable creditor is in lawful possession of security subjects which comprise the land, then "owner" includes the heritable creditor.

The Planning etc. (Scotland) Act 2006 Act introduced a new s.75C, which states that an owner is still bound by obligations in the agreement even after ceasing to be the owner. This applies to positive obligations in the agreement—requiring operations or activities to be carried out in, on, under or over the land, or the land

---

[159] *Windsor and Maidenhead RBC v Brandrose Investments* [1983] 1 W.L.R. 509.

[160] *John G Russell (Transport) Ltd v Strathkelvin DC*, 1992 S.L.T. 1001.

[161] For the purposes of the new s.75, "owner" does not include a lessee under a lease with more than three years to run—TCPSA 1997 s.277.

to be used in a specified way, and also payment obligations. Liability for these obligations also transmits to any new owner, who is severally liable with the former owner, if the agreement is recorded/registered. If the new owner incurs expenditure in the performance of the obligation, he may recover the cost of that expenditure from the former owner. These provisions of s.75C are subject to the terms of the individual agreement, so it is possible for the parties to agree that s.75C does not apply (often referred to as "contracting out of s.75C").

The terms of the recorded obligation will not be enforceable against a third party who obtained an interest in the land in good faith prior to the obligation being recorded.[162] This will apply whether or not the title of the third party was recorded before the recording of the obligation. This protection extends to any person who derives title from the bona fide third party. In such circumstances, the obligation will only be effective against the parties who signed it and, therefore, of little value to the authority.

Any future grant of planning permission cannot override the provisions of a s.75 obligation.[163]

(d)   Enforcing the obligation

In the absence of any provision in the obligation regarding enforcement powers in the event of a failure to observe its terms, the obligation is treated as a contract and the normal contractual remedies are available to the planning authority without the necessity of following the enforcement procedures described in Ch.7.[164] For example, the authority may seek a court order for specific implement of the obligations of the developer under the obligation or for interdict preventing the developer from acting contrary to the restrictions contained in the obligation, and damages.[165] In England, a court order was granted to require demolition of a building in implement of an obligation,[166] and for refund to the developer of a sum paid to the planning authority, after the authority had failed to carry out highway improvements by the due date.[167] The provisions of the obligation have to be sufficiently precise before a court order will be granted.[168]

6.44

If there is a breach of an obligation, the planning authority have the power to carry out operations in, on, under or over the land, to enter the land and carry out the operations, and recover any expenses reasonably incurred from the person(s) against whom the obligation is enforceable. Not less than 21 days' notice must be given of the intention to exercise this power. It is an offence to wilfully obstruct someone who is exercising this power, with liability on summary conviction to a fine not exceeding level 3 on the standard scale.

---

[162] TCPSA 1997 s.75(6), which omits the previous requirement for the right to be acquired in good faith and for value. It also omits the specific protection for a person deriving title from the bona fide third party, although that protection is inherent in the deriving of that title.

[163] *R. v Tunbridge Wells BC Ex p. Blue Boys Development* [1990] 1 P.L.R. 55.

[164] *Avon CC v Millard* [1986] J.P.L. 211, *Newham LBC v Ali* [2013] EWHC 1715 (QB).

[165] Examples are mentioned in Jeremy Rowan-Robinson and Roger Durman, *Section 50 Agreements* (Scottish Office, 1992) para.17.2.

[166] *Wycombe DC v Williams* [1995] 3 P.L.R. 19.

[167] *Patel v Brent LBC* [2005] EWCA Civ 644.

[168] e.g. *R. v Maldon DC Ex p. Pattani* [1998] E.G. 135 (C.S.); *Wychavon DC v Westbury Homes (Holdings) Ltd* [2001] P.L.C.R 13

(e) Modification and discharge

6.45   Following recording in the property register, the provisions of the s.75 obligation bind the land in perpetuity.

Section 75A introduced the right to apply to the planning authority for modification or discharge of the planning obligation, and s.75B a procedure for appealing
to the Scottish Ministers against the decision by the planning authority or its failure
to reach a decision within a period to be prescribed.[169] The English Town and
Country Planning Act 1990 s.106A prohibits an application for modification or
discharge until five years after the agreement has been entered into, but s.75A
contains no equivalent prohibition.

On an application for modification, the planning authority can decide that the
obligation should continue without modification (ie. refuse to grant the application), or that the obligation should have effect subject to the modifications specified in the application (ie. grant the application).[170] The authority have no power to
decide that the obligation should have effect subject to different modifications.

The decision notice must be issued within two months of the date of validation.[171]
If the authority decide to discharge or modify the obligation, the decision notice is
recorded in the Register of Sasine or registered in the Land Register.[172]

(f) Challenge of obligation

6.46   Section 75A provides a right of appeal to the Scottish Ministers if the planning
authority refuse an application to modify or discharge a s.75 obligation. In addition, the provisions of an obligation may be a relevant consideration in an appeal
against the decision by the authority on an associated planning application.

It is unlikely that it will be competent for any party who signed the obligation
to apply to the Court of Session for judicial review of the obligation. Having
implemented an obligation, it was held that a developer could not competently apply to the court on the grounds that the council's exercise of its powers was invalid,
and it was a matter of private contract law, and not an issue for judicial review,
whether the obligations had been fulfilled.[173]

It may be competent for a third party to challenge the decision by the planning
authority to enter into or vary an obligation or decisions by the authority based on
the obligation.[174] Possible grounds of challenge are that the authority acted
unreasonably or that the obligation does not serve a planning purpose or that the
authority has exceeded the scope of its powers under s.75.

---

[169] Details of the procedure are specified in the Town and Country Planning (Modification and Discharge
of Planning Obligations) (Scotland) Regulations 2010 (SSI 2010/432). Previously, a s.75 agreement could only be discharged or varied if all the parties to the agreement or their successors in title
agreed. See *Tesco Stores Ltd v Perth & Kinross Council* [2014] CSOH 153 for an unsuccessful legal
challenge to a variation decision.

[170] TCPSA 1997 s.75A(4).

[171] Town and Country Planning (Modification and Discharge of Planning Obligations) (Scotland)
Regulations 2010 (Scottish SI 2010/432) reg.7, as amended by Town and Country Planning (Miscellaneous Amendments) (Scotland) Regulations 2015 (SSI 2015/249).

[172] TCPSA 1997 s.75A(6).

[173] *McIntosh v Aberdeenshire Council*, 1999 S.L.T. 93. That case predated the procedure to apply for
modification or discharge of an obligation.

[174] *Tesco Stores Ltd v Perth & Kinross Council* [2014] CSOH 153; *R. v Merton LBC Ex p. Barker*
[1998] J.P.L. 440; *R. v South Northamptonshire DC Ex p. Crest Homes* [1994] 1 P.L.R. 47.

The Lands Tribunal for Scotland has no jurisdiction to discharge or vary the obligations contained in a s.75 agreement.[175]

Drafting the obligation

A recorded obligation applies to the land in perpetuity, thus an overly restric- **6.47** tive or badly drafted obligation may adversely affect the value of the land. It is important for all parties to ensure that the obligation records fully what has been agreed and that it will be effective in securing performance.

In most cases the obligation will be drafted by the planning authority once the principal provisions have been agreed. Inevitably the draft will require some revision by the developer to avoid overly burdensome restrictions or obligations.

There is no prescribed form of planning obligation. The obligation must be expressed in clear and precise terms and any ambiguities avoided. In complex obligations, an interpretation clause defining the meaning of various key phrases is useful. To be accepted for recording in the property register, a s.75 obligation must identify the parties, the land, and the provisions agreed between the parties.

(a) Parties

Section 75 states that a person may enter into an obligation by agreement with **6.48** the planning authority, or unilaterally (see para.6.33 above), but acknowledges that where the owner is a party, it can be recorded in the Register of Sasines or registered in the Land Register of Scotland. It will therefore remain the case that the other principal party to the obligation is the person or persons who have sufficient legal interest in the site to bind the land. Without the signature of all such persons, the obligation cannot be recorded in the property registers and can only be enforced against the parties who have signed the obligation.

An "interest" in land must be such as to enable that person to enter into an obligation which will bind future owners of the land. Clearly the owner of the land (the proprietor of the heritable title) has sufficient interest for this purpose. The best practice must be to enter into s.75 obligations with persons who have a title to the land which is recorded in the Sasine Register or registered in the Land Register.

It would seem inadvisable to enter into a s.75 obligation with a person whose ownership is based on an executed, but unrecorded, disposition (ie. that person has not completed title to the land). Such a person has sufficient interest to bind the land, but until the disposition is registered in the property register there is a (slight) risk of a third party registering a title to the land before that disposition (and the s.75 obligation) is registered, rendering any s.75 obligation registered thereafter ineffective unless signed by that third party. Limited protection could be sought through a clause in the obligation prohibiting the party signing the obligation from selling the land prior to the registering of the obligation.

It is common for a sale of land to a developer to be agreed up to conclusion of missives, but the transfer of ownership not completed until planning permission is obtained. In such circumstances, the seller remains owner of the land until a signed disposition is delivered to the developer.[176] The only right available to the developer under concluded missives is the right to demand performance of the contractual

---

[175] Scottish Law Commission, *Real Burdens* (The Stationery Office, 1998) Scot. Law Com. Discussion Paper No.106.
[176] *Gibson v Hunter Home Designs Ltd*, 1976 S.L.T. 94 per Lord President Emslie at 96; but see *Sharp*

obligation to convey the land to him, and this is not an interest in land.[177] Thus a developer who has concluded missives, but has yet to complete the purchase, cannot enter into a s.75 obligation, other than as a consenter (see para.6.49 below). A person in this position may enter into an agreement with the planning authority undertaking to complete a s.75 obligation in specified terms as soon as a disposition in his favour has been delivered and registered. Alternatively, in order to give sufficient confidence for the purchase transaction to be completed, the planning authority may give an indication that planning permission will be forthcoming if a s.75 obligation is entered into (see para.6.54 below).

6.49   A lessee under a recorded/registered lease may also have a sufficient interest to enter into a s.75 obligation. In such circumstances, the landlord (and the owner if this is not the same person as the landlord) must consent to the obligation (see below). Thus s.75 obligations are often entered into with tenants and landlords under minerals leases in connection with applications for permission for mineral extraction, and similarly for wind farms.

A s.75 obligation is not enforceable against any third party who acquired right to the land prior to the registering of the obligation in the property registers, notwithstanding that the title of that third party has yet to be registered.[178] As a result, some persons who do not have sufficient interest to bind the land should be requested to sign the obligation as consentors. Their signature will have the effect of binding them by its terms even before the obligation is registered in the property register.

Possible consenting parties include heritable creditors, tenants, feudal superiors, parties with servitude rights over the site, purchasers under concluded missives and applicants for planning permission. Any restrictions contained in the obligation may significantly reduce the value of the land. Such a reduction in value may prejudice the interests of a bank or other financial institution which has lent money and been granted a security over the land. That occurred in England where one financial institution withdrew from lending because the terms of an obligation providing for "low-cost" housing would have made it difficult to sell the property if it ever came to be repossessed by the institution. Any heritable creditors should be asked to indicate their consent to the obligation by signing it as consentors.

If the owner has leased part of the land and the obligation affects the tenant's enjoyment of the land, the landlord may require the consent of the tenant depending upon the terms of the lease. The consent of those with servitude rights over the land may be required, depending on the provisions of the title to the land. If the owner of the land has concluded missives for its sale, the planning authority should consider seeking the purchaser's signature of the obligation as a consentor. The applicant for planning permission should sign the obligation.

In drafting (and revising) the obligation, it should be considered whether it is necessary for all signatories to be bound under all the obligations. In particular, if some parties have an interest in only part of the site, they should ensure that they are bound only by the obligations which apply to that part.

---

v Thomson, 1997 S.L.T. 636 HL.

[177] *Margrie Holdings Ltd v Customs and Excise Commissioners*, 1991 S.L.T. 38.

[178] TCPSA 1997 s.75(6), which does not require the third party to have acquired in good faith and for value.

(b)   The land

To be accepted for registering in the property register, the planning obligation **6.50** must contain a legal description of the land to which it is to apply. This description is prepared by reference to the previous title deeds, and may refer to a plan attached to the obligation. Unless the description is simple, it may be advisable for it to be contained in a separate schedule to the obligation.

(c)   The obligations

A wide range of obligations can competently form the basis of a s.75 obligation **6.51** and new examples will continue to emerge. The only legal requirements are the need for a planning purpose and a rational decision (see para.6.37 above).

For example, infrastructure improvements are a common subject. Developers often agree to pay the cost of the authority carrying out off-site infrastructure works in order to unlock the development potential of sites. Obligations can be used to phase-in parts of the development in conjunction with the provision of supporting infrastructure, or to prevent the construction of lucrative portions of the development ahead of parts of the development which the authority considers important to the community, for example, tying in provision of a school to occupancy of a housing development (although such phasing matters might be capable of being dealt with by condition).

Following the restrictions placed on the use of occupancy conditions, obligations can be used to regulate the occupancy of sheltered homes and retirement flats or provision of low-cost housing for local people. An obligation may contain restrictions on future sale of a property, for example, prohibiting the separate sale of farm cottages or granny flats.[179]

The obligation may revoke existing, but unimplemented, permission in return for a fresh grant of permission, or discontinue the existing use of premises once permission has been granted for the similar use of new premises. Where planning permission is granted for a replacement dwellinghouse, an obligation may be used to secure demolition of existing buildings.

Some forms of development have almost standard provisions. For example, authorities frequently require obligations for provision of restoration bonds in connection with mineral workings.

Some authorities have even used obligations to require the developer to observe a local employment or local contractor preference. However, it may be difficult to prove that such requirements fulfil a planning purpose.

It is important that the provisions of the obligation are sufficiently precise. The operation of a pharmacy within a superstore was held to fall within the terms of obligations restricting the use to the sale of food and associated household consumables and to use as a supermarket.[180]

(d)   Other matters

In addition to identifying the parties, the land and narrating the obligations, the **6.52** parties should consider the desirability of including other provisions.

---

[179] See guidance in Planning Circular 3/2012, Planning Obligations and Good Neighbour Agreements, paras 49-51.
[180] *R. v Maldon DC Ex p. Pattani*[1998] E.G. 135 (C.S.).

The developer should consider including a clause to the effect that it will only come into force if the grant of planning permission is implemented. This avoids the situation of the developer deciding not to proceed with the development, but the land remaining subject to the obligation.

If the obligation provides for a financial contribution to be paid, the purpose of the payment should be clearly specified and an obligation placed on the recipient to expend the money for that purpose. Provision should be made for a refund if this is not satisfied, either at all or within a specified period.

The normal contractual remedies are available to enforce the provisions of the obligation, but other remedies can be specified. For example, the obligation may empower the authority to carry out work and recover the cost from the developer if the work has not been commenced or completed within a specified time.[181] Obligations in connection with mineral workings normally provide for sums to be paid to the authority if the developer fails to carry out restoration works or goes into liquidation. These payments are guaranteed under bonds issued by banks or insurance companies.

Alternatively, the obligation may allow the authority to treat any failure to observe the terms of the obligation as a breach of planning control entitling it to use the powers conferred by the planning enforcement regime (see Ch.7 below). The legality of such provisions is uncertain and developers should carefully consider their position before agreeing to such a provision.

More importantly, the obligation may provide that on any breach of its terms by the developer, the authority can revoke the grant of planning permission without compensation. This would terminate the development and any change of use would have to cease. It is doubtful whether it is competent for permission to be revoked in this way, but developers should seek the deletion of such a provision during the revisal of the draft obligation. An alternative to this draconian measure is for the obligation to provide for the effect of the planning permission to be suspended until the breach is remedied.

6.53   In connection with powers to secure compliance with the terms of the obligation, ancillary powers should be provided. For example, planning officials should be given rights of entry to monitor compliance with the terms of the obligation and for the carrying out of any works upon which the developer has defaulted. Provision should be made for the authority to reclaim the cost of carrying out such works from the developer.

The obligation may provide that the planning authority is to be the sole judge of what constitutes a breach of the obligation, entitling it to exercise its enforcement powers under the obligation. Any provisions of this type, which give the planning authority complete discretion, should be resisted by the developer. An alternative is to provide for any disputes which arise in relation to the obligation to be settled through arbitration rather than legal action. An arbitration clause should be worded to include disputes relating to the interpretation as well as the level of compliance with the obligation. Careful consideration should be given to the profession from which the arbitrator(s) is to be selected. The decision of the arbitrator is normally declared to be final, although it may be challenged if the arbitrator makes a legal error in the course of the decision. Provision should be made for payment of expenses.

If subsequent subdivision of the site is likely, the obligation should be drafted

---

[181] TCPSA 1997 s.75(7) entitles the planning authority to carry out the operations and recover the cost.

to avoid future difficulties regarding the enforcement and the distribution of obligations.

Following registering in the property register, the provisions of the s.75 obligation bind the land in perpetuity. Formal discharges of obligations or parts of obligations (which will then be registered in the property register) should be obtained wherever possible to prevent legal difficulties arising in any future sale of the land. Positive obligations will usually be carried out shortly after the obligation is executed. In contrast, any restrictions on use will remain in force indefinitely, irrespective of any changes in circumstances, subject to a successful application/appeal for modification or discharge (see above).

The new s.75C will regulate the continuing liability of owners for breaches unless the obligation specifies different provisions, so consideration should be given to appropriate provisions.

Timing of obligation and associated planning permission

Most s.75 obligations are entered into in the context of applications for planning permission. The planning authority will be unwilling to grant planning permission until the obligation has been executed, but the developer will be wary of entering into an obligation unless he can be certain that planning permission will be granted. The Scottish Government guidance is that heads of terms for the obligation should be negotiated, where possible, during pre-application discussion.[182] If the authority is minded to grant planning permission subject to conclusion of the obligation, it should make clear the likely terms of the obligation at the date of the decision. The authority should consider delegating powers to officials to conclude the obligation. This approach is generally referred to as a "minded to grant" letter decision. There is no grant of planning permission until the decision notice is issued.[183] If there is a material change of circumstances in the period between the decision and completion of the obligation, the authority is obliged to take those circumstances into account and may refuse to grant the permission.[184] Any delay in concluding the obligation therefore risks losing the permission.

6.54

Proposal for obligation on appeal/review

Although there is no duty on them to do so, reporters/LRBs may encourage the parties to enter into negotiations with a view to concluding an obligation to remove an obstacle to a grant of planning permission, which cannot be removed by imposition of a condition. However, the reporter/LRB can play no part in the negotiations or specify the terms of the obligation (other than the heads of terms), and the developer may be unable to reach agreement with the authority (although a unilateral obligation could be used). There have been instances where permission has been granted on appeal despite the failure to conclude an obligation.[185]

The English courts have held that it was unreasonable for a highway authority, whose road safety objections had been fully heard and rejected on appeal, to maintain their original view and refuse to enter into an obligation with the

6.55

---

182 Planning Circular 3/2012, Planning Obligations and Good Neighbour Agreements, para.37.
183 *R. v West Oxfordshire DC Ex p. Pearce Homes* [1986] J.P.L. 523.
184 *John G Russell (Transport) Ltd v Strathkelvin DC*, 1992 S.L.T. 1001.
185 e.g. *Strathclyde RC v Secretary of State for Scotland*, 1996 S.L.T. 579; 1996 55 S.P.E.L. 51.

developer.[186] However, it was not perverse for an updated assessment to be required before the obligation was concluded when the original study had been undertaken four years ago and there was evidence of changed traffic conditions in the area.[187] It is unclear how far this principle may extend. For example, it could be argued that it would be ultra vires for a planning authority to refuse to enter into a s.75 obligation where the reporter has indicated that he is minded to grant planning permission.

Developers can sidestep unco-operative planning authorities by entering into a unilateral planning obligation to provide planning advantages.[188] This obviates the need to reach agreement with the planning authority. The obligation will have an equivalent effect to a bi-/multi-lateral obligation. Most importantly, it will be a material consideration during the determination of the application for planning permission and in any appeal against refusal or deemed refusal of planning permission.

GOOD NEIGHBOUR AGREEMENTS

6.56   The Planning etc. (Scotland) Act 2006 created a new power for a person to enter into an agreement, referred to as a good neighbour agreement, with a community body.[189] Given the wide-ranging powers to impose planning conditions and enter into planning agreements/obligations, it is unclear how good neighbour agreements will be used in the planning system, especially since the good neighbour agreement is entered into with a community body, not the planning authority. The writer is unaware of any good neighbour agreements being concluded so far.

Scope of good neighbour agreements

(a)   Scope of the statutory power

6.57   A good neighbour agreement may be entered into between any person and a community body. However, the land will only be bound if the owner is a party to the agreement. Although it is likely that most agreements will be made by an applicant for planning permission, agreements can be made in other situations. Unlike the new s.75 provisions, a good neighbour agreement cannot be made unilaterally, although most, if not all, of its provisions might be included in a unilateral obligation under s.75, obviating the need for a good neighbour agreement.

A good neighbour agreement can be entered into with the community council for the area in which the site is situated. It can also be entered into with any body or trust notified by the planning authority, whose members/trustees have a substantial connection with the land to which the application relates; and its object or function is to preserve or enhance the amenity of the neighbourhood in which is situated any part of the land to which the agreement relates.

The scope of the statutory power to enter into a good neighbour agreement is similar to a s.75 obligation:

"…[G]overning operations or activities relating to the development or use of land, either permanently or during such period as may be specified in the agreement."

---

[186] *R. v Warwickshire CC Ex p. Powergen Plc* [1998] J.P.L. 131.
[187] *R. v Cardiff City Council Ex p. Sears Group Properties Ltd* [1998] 3 P.L.R. 55.
[188] TCPSA 1997 s.75(1)(b). Guidance is provided in Planning Circular 3/2012, Planning Obligations and Good Neighbour Agreements.
[189] TCPSA 1997 s.75D–G.

In particular, it may require operations or activities specified in the agreement to be carried out in, on, under or over the land, or require the land to be used in a specified way. It may be unconditional or subject to conditions. There is specific reference to the potential for it to require the provision of information regarding the development and use of the site. In contrast to a s.75 obligation, there is a specific prohibition on it requiring the payment of money.

As the power to enter into a good neighbour agreement is conferred by the TCPSA 1997, the agreement must have a planning purpose. As any consideration relating to the use and development of land can be a planning consideration (see Ch.5 above), the need for a planning purpose is already reflected in the statutory scope of a good neighbour agreement—"governing operations or activities relating to the development or use of land ...".

(b)   Good neighbour agreements as a material consideration

As with s.75 obligations, in most cases a developer will enter into a good neighbour agreement because this will increase the likelihood of planning permission being granted. There is no statutory requirement for a good neighbour agreement to be taken into account as a material consideration. However, in consequence of the need for the agreement to have a planning purpose (see para.6.37 above), the agreement is likely to be a material consideration. **6.58**

Effect of good neighbour agreements

If the owner of the land is party to a good neighbour agreement, it can be recorded in the Register of Sasines or registered in the Land Register. The other effects are similar to those of s.75 obligations (see paras 6.41 to 6.46 above), with the exception that the community body does not have the power to enter the land and carry out operations and recover the cost. **6.59**

There is a procedure for applying to the planning authority for modification or discharge of a good neighbour agreement, with either party having a right of appeal to the Scottish Ministers.[190]

Drafting of good neighbour agreements

The approach to drafting good neighbour agreements will be similar to drafting s.75 obligations (see paras 6.47 to 6.53 above). **6.60**

Timing of good neighbour agreement and associated planning Permission

The timing issues are similar to s.75 obligations (see para.6.54 above). **6.61**

---

[190] TCPSA 1997 ss.75E and 75F; Town and Country Planning (Modification and Discharge of Good Neighbour Agreement) (Scotland) Regulations 2010 (SSI 2010/433).

CHAPTER 7

DEVELOPMENT MANAGEMENT IV—ENFORCEMENT

In order to control development effectively, planning authorities have sanctions **7.01**
to enforce planning control and prevent or stop unauthorised development. These
enforcement powers were strengthened following the overhaul of the statutory
enforcement system by the Planning and Compensation Act 1991 (amending the
Town and Country Planning (Scotland) Act 1997 (TCPSA)), which adopted many
of the recommendations of the Carnwath Report.[1] The procedures were simplified, tougher penalties introduced, loopholes removed, and new powers conferred
upon planning authorities.

A review of the practical operation of these provisions found that attitudes to the
effectiveness of the new and revised powers were very positive, but there were wide
variations in their use in practice. In particular, there was very limited use of breach
of condition notices, stop notices, direct action and interdict. There were continuing problems of delay in the enforcement process, principally caused by enforcement notice appeals and blatant and persistent transgression of planning control.
There were also continuing difficulties with prosecution of planning offences.[2]

Further changes were introduced by the Planning Etc. (Scotland) Act 2006
(PSA), including the definition of breach of planning control widened to include
initiating development without giving notice, and carrying out development without
displaying a site notice; the definition of taking enforcement action widened to
include service of a s.33A notice; removal of the right to appeal against an enforcement notice on the ground that planning permission should be granted; the introduction of fixed penalty notices for failure to comply with enforcement notices and
breach of condition notices; a new power to serve a temporary stop notice; and
enforcement charters.

HUMAN RIGHTS

Enforcement is one of the areas in which human rights issues are likely to be **7.02**
most relevant, because enforcement involves the planning authority interfering with
what is being done on land. Indeed, many of the decisions from the European Court
on the British planning system involve enforcement cases.[3]

It is unlawful for the planning authority to act, or fail to act, in a way that is

---

[1] Robert Carnwath, *Enforcing Planning Control* (HMSO, 1989).
[2] Edinburgh College of Art, Heriot Watt University and Brodies WS, *Review of Planning Enforce-
    ment* (Scottish Office Central Research Unit, 1997).
[3] For example, *Bryan v United Kingdom* [1996] 1 P.L.R. 47; *Buckley v United Kingdom* [1996] J.P.L.
    1018; *Chapman v United Kingdom* (2001) 33 E.H.R.R. 18; *Varey v United Kingdom* (2000) 30
    E.H.R.R. CD39.

incompatible with a Convention right.[4] In deciding whether to take enforcement action, the authority therefore has to take into account relevant Convention rights, for example, under art.6 (right to a fair trial), art.8 (right to respect for private and family life), and First Protocol art.1 (protection of property). Legislation must also be read and given effect to in a way that is compatible with Convention rights.[5] This creates the potential for the statutory provisions on enforcement to be interpreted to comply with Convention rights. The courts also need to take a fresh approach when considering whether to grant an interdict (see para.7.45 below).

Article 8 gives everyone the right to respect for private and family life, home and correspondence. It only permits a public authority to interfere with this right where this is in accordance with the law and necessary in a democratic society in the interests of national security, public safety or the economic well-being of the country, for the prevention of disorder or crime, for the protection of health or morals, or for the protection of the rights and freedoms of others. The planning authority can therefore take enforcement action, or not, even if this interferes with an individual's rights under art.8, provided it is acting within its legal powers, and can show that the interference is necessary within one of the categories specified in art.8. The European Court upheld the use of an enforcement notice against the siting of a gypsy caravan, because the reasons relied upon by the planning authorities were relevant and sufficient to justify the interference.[6] However, in another case there was a violation of art.8, because the enforcement action was disproportionate, as two inspectors (the English equivalent of reporters) had concluded that the proposed development would neither be visually intrusive nor prejudicially affect the green belt policy.[7] A decision not to take enforcement action can breach a neighbour's art.8 rights.[8] Similar comments apply in relation to rights under First Protocol art.1. The enforcement notice appeals system complies with art.6.[9]

UNDERLYING PRINCIPLES OF ENFORCEMENT POWERS

(a) Breach of planning control

7.03   The planning authority cannot exercise its enforcement powers unless there at least appears to have been a breach of planning control (a stricter requirement applies to the exercise of some powers). A breach of planning control occurs[10]:

(i)   when development is carried out without first obtaining the required planning permission (see Ch.4 above); or

(ii)   there is a failure to comply with any condition or limitation subject to which planning permission has been granted[11]; or

(iii)   development starts without notice being given to the planning authority (see Ch.5 above); or

---

4   Human Rights Act 1998 s.6.
5   Human Rights Act 1998 s.3; Scotland Act 1998 s.101.
6   *Buckley v United Kingdom* [1996] J.P.L. 1018. See also *Chapman v United Kingdom* (2001) 33 E.H.R.R. 18.
7   *Varey v United Kingdom* (2000) 30 E.H.R.R. CD39.
8   *Lopez-Ostra v Spain* (1995) 20 E.H.R.R. 277.
9   *Bryan v United Kingdom* [1996] 1 P.L.R. 47.
10   TCPSA 1997 s.123(1), as amended.
11   There is no statutory definition of "limitation". Previous Scottish Office guidance in Circular 36/1992 (Scottish Environment Circular 36/1992, Planning and Compensation Act 1991—Lawful Development and Enforcement (Scottish Office, 1992)) referred to the limitations which are imposed by the provisions for permitted development rights in the permitted development order (PDO) (see

(iv)   development is carried out without a site notice being displayed (only a requirement for specified types of development—see Ch.5 above).

(b) Enforcement action

Although there is a wide range of enforcement powers available to planning authorities, only service of the following notices constitutes taking enforcement action for the purposes of preventing a breach from becoming lawful development[12]:

  (i)   an enforcement notice;
  (ii)   a breach of condition notice;
  (iii) a notice under s.33A requiring application for planning permission for development already carried out.

7.04

(c) Lawful development (immunity from enforcement action)

A breach of planning control becomes lawful once the prescribed time limits (see para.7.07 below) for taking enforcement action have expired.[13] In consequence, there is no breach upon which to found enforcement action. In addition, permitted development rights under the Permitted Development Order (PDO) may be utilised. A certificate of lawfulness of existing use or development may be sought from the planning authority to establish conclusively the lawfulness of the use or development (see Ch.4 above).

7.05

The concept of lawful development does not extend to breaches of the statutory systems applicable to listed buildings, tree preservation, or advertisement control (see Ch.9 below). Breaches never become immune from enforcement action under these statutory systems, but may be immune from enforcement action under the planning system where there is an overlap in the statutory controls.

(d) Offences

A breach of planning control is not an offence in itself. In general, commission of an offence relates to a failure to comply with the requirements of a notice served by the authority in exercise of its enforcement powers against the breach. Individual offences are created in relation to each enforcement power, and are examined in the appropriate part of this chapter.

7.06

All enforcement offences are subject to a six-month time limit for commencing summary court proceedings.[14] This period runs from the occurrence of the contravention. In the case of a continuing contravention, the six-month period runs from the last date of the contravention. There is uncertainty about the application of the six-month period to planning offences. As enforcement offences do not relate to the breach of planning control, but to the non-compliance with the terms of the notice, the offence is a single one which can be charged by reference to a single day

---

Ch.4 above).

[12] TCPSA 1997 s.123(2), as amended.

[13] TCPSA 1997 s.150(2). Previously, a breach of planning control became immune from enforcement action after expiry of the time limit, but could never become lawful. As a result, permitted development rights could not be exercised and, in the event of compulsory purchase, there was no right to compensation for any value attributable to the activity.

[14] Criminal Procedure (Scotland) Act 1995 s.136; Brian Robertson, "Time-Limits for Criminal Prosecutions", 1994 45 S.P.E.L. 73.

or longer period. It is therefore arguable that the six-month period runs from the date of the expiry of the period specified in the notice for compliance with its terms, notwithstanding that the breach of planning control continues. However, it is possible that this argument only applies to a notice requiring positive action, i.e. something to be done. If it requires negative action, such as cessation of an activity, the failure to comply with the requirement is a continuing offence and the six-month time limit only runs from the date on which the activity ceases. This uncertainty can only be clarified by a court ruling or amendment of the law.

There is also provision for prosecution of second or subsequent offences if the contravention of the notice continues after conviction.

The penalties for individual offences vary, with a maximum fine of £20,000 following summary conviction, or an unlimited fine after conviction on indictment. In addition, the court is directed to have regard to any financial benefit which has accrued or appears likely to accrue to the person in consequence of the offence. For example, where an enforcement notice requires use of a building for retail purposes to be stopped, the court may take into account the profits made from that retail business following expiry of the period for compliance with the requirements of the notice until conviction. There is no provision for imprisonment following conviction for an enforcement offence.

This system of enforcement offences is not without its problems.[15] A planning authority intent on negotiating a solution to avoid the need for prosecution may fall foul of the six-month time limit. A substantial weight of corroborated evidence will be required to prove the case beyond reasonable doubt, including evidence on such prosaic matters as service of the notice upon the person charged with the offence. It is unclear whether the intent (mens rea) to commit the offence must be proved. A major hurdle is the apparent attitude of many procurators fiscal, who are responsible for prosecuting, and sheriffs, that planning offences are not true criminal matters. Indeed, the need to change this attitude was one of the underlying reasons for the increase in penalties for enforcement offences from £2,000 to £20,000. The hard-pressed fiscal with a heavy caseload of "real" criminal matters may decide that prosecution of an enforcement offence is not in the public interest and exercise his discretion not to prosecute. This decision is likely to be influenced by the generally low level of fines imposed by sheriffs in the few successful cases.

In 2009 a power was introduced to issue fixed penalty notices for non-compliance with enforcement notices and breach of condition notices (see paras 7.18 and 7.41 below).

In addition, a confiscation order can be obtained under the Proceeds of Crime Act 2002 for any property obtained as a result of the offence. For example, a confiscation order for £50,000 was imposed following destruction of a tree protected by a tree preservation order, for the increase in value of the property as the result of the removal of the tree.[16]

---

[15] Edinburgh College of Art, Heriot Watt University and Brodies WS, *Review of Planning Enforcement* (1997).
[16] *R v Davey (Neil)* [2013] EWCA Crim 1662.

ENFORCEMENT ACTION: TIME LIMITS

Enforcement action must be taken within the following time limits, otherwise the breach of planning control will become lawful development[17]:

7.07

Four-year time limit

(a) Building, engineering, mining or other operations (see Ch.4 above) undertaken without planning permission will become lawful development after four years from the date of substantial completion of the operations (such operations in breach of conditions or limitations are subject to the 10-year time limit). In deciding whether a building is substantially complete, regard should be had to the totality of the operations which the person intended to carry out, rather than whether the work to complete the building required planning permission.[18] A building operation was not substantially completed until removal of straw bales which were put there to conceal the dwelling while under construction.[19] Where an embankment was substantially completed within the four-year period, an enforcement notice requiring its demolition was upheld notwithstanding that parts of the embankment had been in place for over four years.[20] The Scottish Government guidance indicates that what is substantially complete must always be a matter of fact and degree and of the prevailing circumstances in any case. For example, a house would not be substantially complete until all the external walls, roof-tiling, woodwork, guttering and glazing are completed, but decorating or internal plastering wall need not have been done.[21]

7.08

(b) A change of use of any building to use as a single dwellinghouse will become lawful development after four years from the date of the change of use.[22] This applies even if the change of use is in breach of a planning condition.[23] It is irrelevant whether the building is converted into a single dwellinghouse or an existing dwellinghouse is subdivided into two or more separate dwellinghouses.[24] A house in multiple occupation with the occupants sharing facilities remains within the 10-year rule. It was held that former staff accommodation and outbuildings of a country house converted in breach of planning control into 10 self-contained units of residential accommodation for holiday lettings were used as single dwellinghouses and not as one planning unit, and were therefore subject to the four-year time limit.[25]

The infamous barn case illustrates the difficulties of interpreting these statutory

---

17 TCPSA 1997 s.124.
18 *Sage v Secretary of State for the Environment, Transport and the Regions* [2003] UKHL 22; [2003] J.P.L. 1299.
19 *Fidler v Secretary of State for Communities and Local Government* [2010] EWHC 143 (Admin).
20 *Ewen Developments v Secretary of State for the Environment* [1980] J.P.L. 404.
21 Planning Circular 10/2009, Planning Enforcement (Scottish Government, 2009), Annex A, para.6.
22 The Scottish Government guidance refers to a distinction between use as and being a dwelling-house—Planning Circular 10/2009, Planning Enforcement, Annex A, paras 7 and 8. Flats are used as dwellinghouses, but are excluded from the definition of "dwellinghouse" for the purposes of permitted development rights—see Ch.4 above.
23 *Arun DC v First Secretary of State* [2007] J.P.L. 237.
24 *Van Dyck v Secretary of State for the Environment; Doncaster BC v Secretary of State for the Environment* [1993] J.P.L. 565.
25 *Moore v Secretary of State for the Environment, Transport and the Regions* [1998] J.P.L. 877.

provisions.[26] Following the grant of planning permission for a barn, a building was constructed which from the outside looked like a barn, but internally was a dwelling-house. After the building was completed, it was occupied as a dwelling-house for 4 years. The local authority refused to grant a certificate of lawful use on the grounds that the 10-year period applied, but a planning inspector granted the certificate on appeal. That decision was overturned by the first instance judge; on appeal, the Court of Appeal upheld the certificate; the Supreme Court overturned that decision.

The Scottish Government suggest that a single, self-contained set of premises is used as a single dwellinghouse if it meets the following criteria[27]:

(i)   it comprises a unit of occupation, which can be regarded as a "planning unit" (see Ch.4 above) separate from any other part of a building containing it;

(ii)   it is designed or adapted for residential purposes, containing the facilities for cooking, eating and sleeping normally associated with use as a dwellinghouse;

(iii)   it is used as a permanent or temporary dwelling by a single person, or by persons living together as, or like, a single family.

Where the occupants of bed-sitting rooms share some communal facilities such as a bathroom, the Government indicate that the planning unit is likely to be the whole building, in use for the purpose of multiple residential occupancy, rather than each individual bed-sit room.

Ten-year time limit

7.09   All other breaches of planning control become lawful development after 10 years from the date of the breach. This will include all material changes of use, and breaches of planning conditions, other than those relating to change of use of a building to a single dwellinghouse.[28] Where a house was built about 90ft west of the permitted location, the occupancy condition was held not to apply, and the breach of planning control related to development without planning permission rather than failure to comply with the condition.[29]

Enforcement action against a change of use can require restoration of the land to its state prior to the change, thereby undoing any incidental operational development which may in itself not require planning permission or be lawful development. The laying of hardcore was an integral part of an unauthorised change of use for the parking of lorries and enforcement action against that change of use could validly require removal of the hardcore notwithstanding that it had been laid more than four years previously and was therefore immune from enforcement action in itself.[30] However, it is not sufficient if the works were integral to the present

---

[26] *Welwyn Hatfield Council v Secretary of State for Communities and Local Government* [2011] UKSC 15.

[27] Planning Circular 10/2009, Planning Enforcement, Annex A, para.8.

[28] It would also appear to include the operation of a marine fish farm in the circumstances specified in TCPSA 1997, s.26AA, which was added to the definition of "development" in s.26 in 2007 (see Ch.4 above), but is not specifically referred to in s.124.

[29] *Handoll v Warner Goodman and Streat* [1995] 1 P.L.R. 40; [1995] J.P.L. 930.

[30] *Murfitt v Secretary of State for the Environment* [1980] J.P.L. 598.

unauthorised use of land if the works were undertaken for a different, and lawful use, and could be used for that lawful use even if the unauthorised use ceased.[31]

Further action outwith time limits

If an enforcement notice has been served within the time limit and is still in effect, it is competent for the planning authority to serve a breach of condition notice in respect of the same breach of planning control, notwithstanding that the time limit for enforcement action has expired.[32]   **7.10**

Further enforcement action is also possible where the planning authority have taken or purported to take enforcement action against the breach within the previous four years.[33] This extends the time limit for a further four years to allow a planning authority to issue a fresh enforcement or breach of condition notice where the previous notice was withdrawn or found to be null.

Where the purpose of two enforcement notices was the same, to stop multiple occupancy of the premises, the reporter was entitled to find that the notices purported to relate to the same breach. The phrase in the statute, "purported to take enforcement action" clearly included the possibility that the first notice contained some defect. The second notice was not therefore time barred.[34] This "second-bite" provision only applies if the previous actual or purported enforcement action was timeous, otherwise the planning authority could issue a first notice out of time, withdraw it and issue a further notice.[35] The power could be used where a notice under s.33A, requiring submission of a retrospective planning application, has been ignored and the planning authority considers it necessary to issue an enforcement notice.[36]

Enforcement Powers

All enforcement powers are discretionary and the planning authority can choose not to take enforcement action. Equally, the authority may choose to under-enforce by taking enforcement action against only part of the breach. Such decisions can only be challenged by applying to the Court of Session for judicial review on the grounds that the decision is unreasonable (in the special legal sense, see Ch.8 below).[37]   **7.11**

It is unlawful for the planning authority to act, or fail to act, in a way that is incompatible with a Convention right.[38] In deciding whether to take enforcement action, the authority therefore has to take into account relevant Convention rights, for example, under art.6 (right to a fair trial), art.8 (right to respect for private and family life) and First Protocol art.1 (protection of property).

The Scottish Government guidance states that in considering any enforcement action the planning authority should have regard to the development plan, and consider whether the breach of control would affect unacceptably public amenity

---

[31] *Bowring v Secretary of State for Communities and Local Government* [2013] EWHC 1115 (Admin).
[32] TCPSA 1997 s.124(4)(a).
[33] TCPSA 1997 s.124(4)(b).
[34] *Barn Properties Ltd v Secretary of State for Scotland*, 1995 S.C.L.R. 113; 1995 49 S.P.E.L. 52.
[35] *William Boyer (Transport) Ltd v Secretary of State for the Environment* [1996] 1 P.L.R. 103.
[36] Planning Circular 10/2009, Planning Enforcement, Annex A, para.15.
[37] e.g. *R. v Flintshire CC Ex p. Somerfield Stores Ltd* [1998] E.G. 53 (C.S.).
[38] Human Rights Act 1998 s.6.

or the use of land and buildings meriting protection in the public interest. Enforcement action should always be commensurate with the breach of planning control to which it relates.[39] This guidance does not refer explicitly to Convention rights, presumably on the grounds that Convention rights do not add anything to the existing planning issues.

The first phase of enforcement action is likely to be service of a planning contravention notice requiring provision of further information. Planning officers may exercise rights of entry to ascertain whether there has been a breach. If a breach of planning control appears to have occurred, the person responsible for the apparent breach may be encouraged to apply for retrospective planning permission (see Ch.5 above) or a certificate of lawfulness of existing use or development (see Ch.4 above) with a view to regularising the position. If the person refuses, or the case is serious, the authority may take further enforcement action to require the breach to be remedied.

Only service of an enforcement or breach of condition notice, or s.33A notice, within the prescribed time limits prevents a breach of planning control becoming lawful development (see para.7.04 above).

The methods of serving notices are dealt with at the end of this chapter.

If there is failure to comply with the requirements of the notice, the planning authority may report the matter to the procurator fiscal for a decision on prosecution, or take direct action to carry out the requirements and recover the cost from the recipient of the notice (this power to take direct action only arises following failure to comply with an enforcement or wasteland notice).

Enforcement charters

7.12   The planning authority are required to prepare an enforcement charter, which is a document setting out a statement of the authority's policies on taking enforcement action; an account of how members of the public are to notify the authority of any alleged breach of planning control; and an account of procedures for making and dealing with any complaint made to the authority about enforcement action.[40] The authority must have regard to any guidance issued by the Ministers.[41] The authority must keep their enforcement charter under review, and update and republish it at least every two years, or if required to do so by the Scottish Ministers.

Planning contravention notices

7.13   The power to serve a planning contravention notice is intended to enable planning authorities to seek information where there is a suspected breach of planning control. The notice should also encourage discussion with the planning authority by acting as a warning of enforcement action, and provide an opportunity to regularise the situation. The power to serve a planning contravention notice may in practice replace the more general power to seek information as to interests in land.[42]

A planning contravention notice may be served by the planning authority where it appears that there may have been a breach of planning control (see para.7.03

---

39   Planning Circular 10/2009, Planning Enforcement, para.7.
40   TCPSA 1997 s.158A.
41   A model charter has been published on the Scottish Government website.
42   TCPSA 1997 s.272.

above) in respect of any land.[43] A mere suspicion of a breach, following upon a complaint by a member of the public, may be enough. The absence of even a suspicion of a breach is likely to invalidate the notice.[44] Service of this notice does not affect any other power exercisable in respect of any breach of planning control. It is not an essential prerequisite to enforcement action that a planning contravention notice has been served.

The notice is served on the owner or occupier or any person with another interest in the land, or any person carrying out operations on the land or using it for any purpose.

The notice may require the person on whom it is served to give information so far as he is able about any specified operations, uses or activities being carried out on the land (the requirement to specify these matters should act as an obstacle to a planning authority using the notice as a fishing expedition for information). It may also require provision of information regarding any matter relating to conditions or limitations imposed upon a grant of planning permission. These requirements are complied with by giving information in writing to the planning authority.

For example, the notice may require the person to state whether or not the land is being used for any specified purpose or any operations or activities are being or have been carried out on the land. It may also require him to state when any use, operations or activities began, and to give the name and address of any person known to him to use or have used the land for any purpose or to be carrying out, or have carried out, any operations or activities on the land. In addition, it may require any information he holds as to any planning permission for any use or operations or any reason for planning permission not being required for any use or operation. He may also be required to state the nature of his interest (if any) in the land and the name and address of any other person known to him to have an interest in the land.

The notice must inform the person on whom it is served of the likely consequences of his failing to respond to the notice, and, in particular, that enforcement action may be taken. It must also inform the person that failure to respond to the notice may result in the loss of the right to compensation following service of a stop notice (see para.7.32 below). The notice may also give notice of a time and place at which the authority will consider any representations which may be made in connection with the notice. This will give an opportunity for negotiation with the planning authority to avoid enforcement action.

Failure to comply with a planning contravention notice within 21 days of its service is an offence carrying liability on summary conviction to a fine not exceeding level 3 on the standard scale.[45] This offence may be committed in the space of a day or over a longer period of time and a person may be convicted again if he fails to comply with the notice following conviction. It will be a defence to prove that there was a reasonable excuse for failing to comply with the requirement.

Article 6 of the European Convention includes the right to silence, sometimes also known as the right against self-incrimination. In the absence of any mention of this right in the planning contravention notice provisions, it may be that the issue has to be considered at any subsequent criminal trial when determining whether

---

[43] TCPSA 1997 s.125.
[44] *R. v Teignbridge DC Ex p. Teignmouth Quay Co* [1995] J.P.L. 828.
[45] TCPSA 1997 s.126. Appendix I contains details of the standard scale for fines.

the answers are admissible in evidence.[46] The right against self-incrimination is only relevant in criminal proceedings, so the planning authority are free to use the information obtained through a planning contravention notice in taking enforcement action such as service of an enforcement notice.

It is also an offence knowingly or recklessly to make a statement purporting to comply with a requirement of the notice, which is false or misleading in a material particular. A person convicted of this offence will be liable on summary conviction to a fine not exceeding level 5 on the standard scale.

There is no statutory right of appeal to the Scottish Ministers against a planning contravention notice. However, a petition for judicial review may be brought before the Court of Session alleging that the notice is invalid.[47] Alternatively, the notice may be ignored and any prosecution defended on the basis that the notice is invalid.

Rights of entry for enforcement purposes

7.14   A person duly authorised in writing by the planning authority has the right to enter any land at any reasonable hour if there are reasonable grounds for entering for the purpose in question. This right of entry may be exercised to ascertain whether there is or has been a breach of planning control, determine whether and how any enforcement powers should be exercised, or ascertain whether there has been compliance with any requirement imposed as a result of the exercise of enforcement powers.[48] The right of entry extends to neighbouring land, whether or not it is in the same ownership or occupation. Where admission is sought to a dwellinghouse, 24 hours' notice of the intended entry must be given to the occupier. Where admission has been refused, or a refusal is reasonably apprehended, or the case is one of urgency, a warrant authorising entry may be issued by a sheriff.

The land should be left as effectively secured against trespassers as when entry was taken. Compensation is payable for any damage caused. It is an offence to disclose details of manufacturing processes or trade secrets obtained while exercising the right of entry, other than in the course of duty. It is an offence wilfully to obstruct exercise of the right of entry, punishable on summary conviction by a fine not exceeding level 3 (see Appendix 1 below).

Enforcement notices

7.15   Service of an enforcement notice prevents a breach of planning control becoming lawful development (see para.7.04 above) and therefore is one of the main enforcement powers (the others being service of a breach of condition notice or notice under s.33A). Service of an enforcement notice may be combined with a stop notice (see para.7.27 below).

Enforcement notices remain the main enforcement power used by planning authorities. There is concern about the scope for delaying the effects of an enforcement notice by utilising the right of appeal to the Scottish Ministers against the

---

[46] *R. v Hertfordshire CC Ex p. Green Environmental Industries Ltd* [2000] 2 A.C. 412; [2000] 1 P.L.R. 108; *Brown v Stott* [2003] 1 A.C. 681; 2001 S.L.T. 59.
[47] *R. v Teignbridge DC Ex p. Teignmouth Quay Co* [1995] J.P.L. 828.
[48] TCPSA 1997 ss.156–158. The list of powers in s.156(1)(b) does not include interdict.

notice. There are approximately 60–100 planning enforcement appeals each year, with a success rate of 33 per cent in 2014–15.[49]

(a) Power to serve enforcement notice

An enforcement notice may be issued by the planning authority where it appears that there has been a breach of planning control (see para.7.03 above) and that it is expedient to issue the notice, having regard to the provisions of the development plan and to any other material considerations (see Ch.5 above).[50] The authority therefore has the discretion to ignore a breach of planning control, or underenforce (see para.7.20 below). In deciding whether to issue a notice, the authority must act in accordance with the provisions of the development plan unless material considerations indicate otherwise. [51] If the development which has led to the breach of planning control requires environmental impact assessment, the planning authority should consider issuing a s.33A notice requiring submission of a planning application.[52]

7.16

The Scottish Ministers also have a default power to serve an enforcement notice.[53]

One enforcement notice may be served in respect of several breaches of planning control.[54] Following service of an invalid enforcement notice, the authority may serve a fresh notice, subject to the prescribed time limits (see para.7.07 above).[55]

Planning authorities have the power to withdraw an enforcement notice, or waive or relax any requirement of such a notice.[56] In particular, the time limit for taking steps to comply with the notice may be extended. This power to vary or withdraw may be exercised whether or not the notice has taken effect. The planning authority is required to give notice of the variation or withdrawal to every person served with a copy of the enforcement notice, and to any person who would be served with a copy if the notice was re-issued. Withdrawal of an enforcement notice will not prejudice the power of the planning authority to issue a further notice within the prescribed time limits (see para.7.07 above).

(b) Effect of enforcement notice

The enforcement notice must specify the date upon which it will take effect.[57] Any appeal against the enforcement notice must be lodged prior to that date. Lodging an appeal prevents the notice taking effect until the appeal has been determined or withdrawn.[58]

7.17

Once the enforcement notice comes into effect, it will apply permanently to the land (unless withdrawn), even if there has been full compliance with its

---

49 Directorate for Planning and Environmental Appeals, *Annual Review 2014/15* (DPEA, 2015), Tables 2 and 4A.
50 TCPSA 1997 s.127.
51 TCPSA 1997 s.25. See Ch.3 above.
52 Planning Circular 10/2009, Planning Enforcement, Annex G, para.39.
53 TCPSA 1997 s.139.
54 *Valentina of London v Secretary of State for the Environment* [1992] J.P.L. 1151.
55 *R. v Wychavon DC Ex p. Saunders* [1992] J.P.L. 753.
56 TCPSA 1997 s.129.
57 TCPSA 1997 s.128(8).
58 TCPSA 1997 s.131(3).

requirements. Thus any requirement to discontinue a use will operate as a permanent restriction, and any resumption of the discontinued use will be in contravention of the notice and, therefore, an offence. In particular, any reinstatement or restoration of buildings demolished or altered in compliance with an enforcement notice, will be in contravention of that notice notwithstanding that its terms are not apt for this purpose. A person who carries out such reinstatement or restoration shall be guilty of an offence and liable on a summary conviction to a fine not exceeding level 5 on the standard scale (see Appendix 1 below).[59]

The notice will cease to have effect in so far as it is inconsistent with a planning permission granted after the service of the notice for any development carried out before the grant of the permission, i.e. retrospective permission.[60] To avoid uncertainty, it would be advisable for the notice to be withdrawn or varied when the permission is granted.

In certain limited circumstances, compliance with the terms of an enforcement notice results in a deemed grant of planning permission. Where the planning authority chooses to under-enforce by requiring only partial remedying of the breach of planning control and all the requirements of the enforcement notice have been complied with, planning permission is deemed to have been granted in respect of any construction of buildings or carrying out of activities in respect of which the authority could have taken enforcement action. In addition, where an enforcement notice requires construction of a replacement building and all the requirements of that notice have been complied with, planning permission is deemed to have been granted in respect of that construction.[61]

There are three potential consequences for failure to comply with an enforcement notice: criminal prosecution; fixed penalty notice; and/or direct action by the planning authority.

Various offences may be committed once an enforcement notice has taken effect. The owner of the land, or lessee under a lease with at least three years still to run, commits an offence if the period specified in the enforcement notice for complying with its requirements has expired without those requirements being satisfied in full.[62] This offence also includes any failure to cease a specified activity. It is a defence to show that he did everything he could be expected to do to secure compliance with the notice. This permits financial and physical incapacity to be taken into account.[63] If the occupier is preventing the owner from carrying out work required by an enforcement notice, a sheriff may issue a warrant authorising the owner to go on to the land and carry out the work.[64]

It is also an offence for any other person who has control of or an interest in the land to carry on, or cause or permit to be carried on, after the end of the period for compliance any activity which an enforcement notice requires to be ceased. Occupiers, lessees and other persons (conceivably even heritable creditors) may therefore be guilty of an offence. However, only the owner/lessee can be prosecuted for failing to take the active steps required by the notice, such as demolition of a building. The liability of other parties is confined to failing to cease an activity which the notice required to be discontinued.

---

[59] TCPSA 1997 s.138.
[60] TCPSA 1997 s.137; *Cresswell v Pearson* [1997] J.P.L. 860.
[61] TCPSA 1997 s.128(13) and (14).
[62] TCPSA 1997 s.136.
[63] *Kent CC v Brockman* [1996] 1 P.L.R. 1.
[64] TCPSA 1997 s.135(5).

The offences may be committed in the course of a single day or any longer period. A person may be convicted of a second or subsequent offence if he continues the failure to comply with the requirements of the notice following conviction. It is a defence that the person was unaware of the existence of the notice, but only if that person was not served with a copy and the notice was not contained in the register of enforcement notices which must be kept by the planning authority (see para.7.19 below).[65] Summary prosecution for these offences must commence within six months (see para.7.06 above).

The decision to prosecute and the choice of summary or solemn procedure lies with the procurator fiscal. On summary conviction, a fine not exceeding £20,000 may be imposed, but an unlimited fine may be imposed following conviction on indictment. In determining the level of fine, the court must have regard to any financial benefit which has accrued or appears likely to accrue to the person in consequence of the offence. For example, where an enforcement notice requires use of a building for retail purposes to be stopped, the court may take into account the profits made from that retail business following expiry of the period for compliance with the requirements of the notice. The court must also have regard to the means of the offender.[66]

7.18

A fixed penalty notice can be served by the planning authority within the six months which immediately follows the compliance period in the enforcement notice, if they have reason to believe that the person is in breach of the enforcement notice.[67] A fixed penalty notice cannot be served after the person has been charged with an offence in relation to breach of the enforcement notice. Service of a fixed penalty notice is at the discretion of the planning authority, applying the principle that any action should be commensurate to the nature and scale of the breach.[68]

The fixed penalty notice offers the person the opportunity to pay to the planning authority, within the period of 30 days which immediately follows the day on which that notice is served, a penalty of the prescribed amount specified in the notice.[69] If payment is made within the first 15 days of that period the amount payable is reduced by 25 per cent. If the amount is paid timeously, that discharges any liability to conviction for an offence in relation to breach of the enforcement notice. No prosecution can be commenced during the 30-day period after the notice is served.

The fixed penalty notice must identify the step specified in the enforcement notice which has not been taken, or the activity so specified which has not ceased. It is not competent to serve more than one fixed penalty notice in relation to a particular step or activity. However, there could be several fixed penalty notices issued, if there are different steps or activities involved.

The weakness of the fixed penalty notice is that, although it penalises the recipient for the breach, it does not directly require the recipient to remedy that breach. However, the planning authority retain the power to take direct action (see below).

There is no right of appeal against a fixed penalty notice and no power to withdraw or vary the notice. If the recipient disputes the accuracy or validity of the

---

65 TCPSA 1997 s.147.
66 Criminal Procedure (Scotland) Act 1995 s.211(7); *R. v Browning* [1996] 1 P.L.R. 61.
67 TCPSA 1997 s.136A.
68 Planning Circular 10/2009, Planning Enforcement, Annex K, para.5.
69 Currently £2,000—Town and Country Planning (Amount of Fixed Penalty) (Scotland) Regulations 2009 (SSI 2009/52).

fixed penalty notice, the notice could simply be ignored, as it does not impose any requirement to pay, in contrast to a parking ticket. The only difficulty might be a situation where, because of a defect in the notice, the recipient is deprived of an opportunity to discharge liability to conviction by paying the financial penalty. Judicial review might be the remedy in such circumstances.

The planning authority also have the power to take direct action. If the steps detailed in the enforcement notice have not been taken within the specified period, the planning authority may take those steps, including action to discontinue a use, and recover any expenses reasonably incurred from the person who is then the owner or lessee of the land.[70] It is an offence to obstruct the authority from taking such steps. If that person failed to exercise his right to appeal to the Scottish Ministers against the notice (see para.7.22 below), he is prevented from disputing the validity of any such action taken in accordance with the notice by the authority. The planning authority is also given the power to sell any materials removed by it from the land, unless claimed by the owner within three days. Where the owner, lessee or occupier incurs expenses for the purpose of complying with an enforcement notice or reimburses the expenses of the planning authority, these sums may be recovered from the person by whom the breach of planning control was committed.[71]

It was held not to be unreasonable for a planning authority to take direct action to demolish a building notwithstanding a pending appeal to the Court of Appeal in relation to the decision to dismiss the enforcement notice appeal. The authority had concluded that the appeal had little chance of success, which was not unjustified.[72] However, where the planning authority ignored a pending planning permission appeal, its decision to take direct action was disproportionate.[73]

(c) Service of enforcement notice

7.19   Copies of the notice must be served in the required manner on the following persons within 28 days after its date of issue and at least 28 days before the date on which it is to take effect[74]:

   (i)   the owner of the land, which includes a lessee under a lease with at least three years left to run[75];
   (ii)   the occupier of the land—whether a person is an occupier is a question of facts and circumstances, and squatters have been considered occupiers by virtue of the length of their occupation[76]; and
   (iii)   any other person having an interest in the land which the planning authority believes is materially affected by the notice, for example, heritable creditors and landlords.

---

[70] TCPSA 1997 s.135. Research in 1997 indicated that only two planning authorities had used the direct action power to any significant extent. The principal reason for the reluctance to use the power stemmed from concerns about the likelihood of recovering the costs involved. One of these main user authorities achieved approximately a 35 per cent success rate in recovering its costs—Edinburgh College of Art, Heriot Watt University and Brodies WS, *Review of Planning Enforcement* (1997).

[71] TCPSA 1997 s.135(4).
[72] *R. v Chiltern District Council, Ex p. Dyason* [1997] E.G. 147 (C.S.).
[73] *R. (on the application of O'Brien) v Basildon DC* [2006] EWHC 1346 (Admin).
[74] TCPSA 1997 s.127(2) and (3).
[75] TCPSA 1997 s.277(1).
[76] *Scarborough BC v Adams* [1983] J.P.L. 673.

Thus the enforcement notice is directed against the persons who may have the power to secure the result required by the notice and all other parties who have an interest in the land which requires that they be made aware of the notice. The latter parties may have the ability to force the former to comply with the terms of the notice, for example, through the terms of a lease. A planning contravention notice may be used to establish the identity of these parties (see para.7.13 above).

In an appeal to the Scottish Ministers against an enforcement notice, any failure to serve the notice on the appellant or another person may be disregarded if no substantial prejudice has been caused by the failure to serve.[77] An enforcement notice was not null where the failure was the result of a mistaken belief that another party served with the notice was the owner.[78] In contrast, failure to serve an enforcement notice on a person known by the authority to be the owner of the land rendered the notice null.[79] If a failure to serve renders the notice null, the planning authority can serve a fresh enforcement notice on all parties, subject to the prescribed time limits.

Details of the notice should also be recorded in the register available for public inspection. Failure to do so may create a defence to any prosecution (see para.7.17 above).

(d) Content of enforcement notice

Prior to the changes introduced by the Planning and Compensation Act 1991, the **7.20** requirements governing the content of enforcement notices were a happy hunting ground for lawyers seeking to challenge notices. The overhauled system was designed to reduce the legal complexity surrounding the content of enforcement notices, coupled with increased powers for planning authorities and reporters on appeal to vary or correct notices. As a result of these changes, much of the previous case law on the content of enforcement notices must now be treated with caution. However, the courts are still prepared to take a restrictive approach to the interpretation of enforcement notices in appropriate cases.[80]

There is no prescribed form of enforcement notice, but each notice must state the following[81]:

(i) the matters which appear to the planning authority to constitute the breach (or breaches) of planning control, but only in sufficient detail or with sufficient precision to enable the recipient to know what these matters are;

(ii) which of the four categories of breach of planning control (see para.7.03 above) the breach falls within: thus the notice need only identify the general nature of the alleged breach;

(iii) the steps required to be taken or the activities which must cease in order to wholly or partly remedy the breach or remedy any injury to amenity which has been caused by the breach: this is considered in detail below;

---

[77] TCPSA 1997 s.132(4).
[78] *R. v Greenwich LBC Ex p. Patel* [1985] J.P.L. 851.
[79] *McDaid v Clydebank DC*, 1984 S.L.T. 162; [1984] J.P.L. 579, but see the compulsory purchase case of *Martin v Bearsden and Milngavie DC*, 1987 S.L.T. 300.
[80] e.g. *Browning v Tameside MBC* (1998) 75 P. & C.R. 417.
[81] TCPSA 1997 s.128.

(iv)   the date on which the notice is to take effect, which must be at least 28 days after the last date of service of the enforcement notice[82];

(v)   the period at the end of which any steps are required to have been taken or any activities ceased; different periods may be specified for different steps or activities; and

(vi)   the reasons why the planning authority considers it expedient to issue the notice, and a description of the precise boundaries of the land to which the notice relates, by reference to a plan or otherwise. The enforcement notice must be accompanied by an explanatory note giving prescribed information as to the right of appeal.[83]

A failure to include any of this information could render the notice a nullity and of no effect (see para.7.21 below).

In most cases, the land to which the notice is directed will be the planning unit (see Ch.4 above) within which the alleged breach has taken or is taking place. However, the notice may be validly directed against a greater or lesser area than the planning unit.[84] The only requirement is that the area involved be sufficiently identified to tell the recipient what he has done wrong and what he must do to remedy that wrong.

Remedying the breach will involve making the developer comply with the terms and conditions of any planning permission by discontinuing any use of the land or by restoring the land to its condition before the breach took place, or remedying any injury to amenity which has been caused by the breach. The steps should not strike at an activity which is not part of the breach. An enforcement notice requiring discontinuation of a retail use went too far as it prevented continuation of the ancillary retail use attached to the previous main agricultural use.[85] The steps may include reversal of any development integral to the breach, notwithstanding that the development would not require planning permission in its own right or is lawful.[86] Where an enforcement notice required discontinuance of multiple occupancy of a dwellinghouse, the notice could not require the restoration of its use for single family occupation.[87]

The required steps may include the alteration or removal of any buildings, the carrying out of building or other operations, or the modification of contours of a deposit of refuse or waste materials by altering the gradient of its sides. The notice may specify restrictions on the carrying on of activities on the land. If the breach of planning control consisted of demolition of a building, the notice may require construction of a replacement building as similar as possible to the demolished building. Once the replacement building has been constructed in compliance with the enforcement notice, planning permission is deemed to have been granted for its construction.

Care will still require to be taken to describe precisely the steps to be taken to remedy the breach, and avoid exceeding what is necessary for this purpose, particularly in light of the potential criminal liability attached to the notice. Requiring the installation of "satisfactory soundproofing of a compressor and for all pos-

[82]   TCPSA 1997 s.127(3)(b).
[83]   Town and Country Planning (Enforcement of Control) (No.2) (Scotland) Regulations 1992 (SI 1992/2086) regs 3 and 4.
[84]   *Rawlins v Secretary of State for the Environment* [1990] 1 P.L.R. 110.
[85]   *Mansi v Elstree Rural DC* (1965) 16 P. & C.R. 153.
[86]   *Murfitt v Secretary of State for the Environment* [1980] J.P.L. 598.
[87]   *Barn Properties Ltd v Secretary of State for Scotland*, 1995 S.C.L.R. 113; 1995 49 S.P.E.L. 52.

sible action to be taken to minimise the effects created by acrylic paint" was held to be hopelessly imprecise.[88] An enforcement notice requiring removal of stone from the foreshore was invalid because it was impossible to tell from the notice which of the stone was to be removed.[89] Instances where rights under the PDO have been exceeded require careful consideration.[90]

In addition to the discretion to ignore a breach of planning control and not serve an enforcement notice, the authority may decide to underenforce by serving an enforcement notice requiring only partial remedying of the breach. This allows the authority to take a practical view of what can be achieved through issuing an enforcement notice. Underenforcement is not without consequences. If an enforcement notice could have required the removal of any buildings or cessation of activity, but the authority chose to under-enforce, as soon as the requirements of the enforcement notice have been complied with planning permission is deemed to have been granted for the development consisting of the construction of the buildings or carrying out of the activities.[91] Thus an ill-considered enforcement notice will prevent any future enforcement action. Planning authorities must therefore be sure to identify the full extent of breaches of planning control prior to issuing an enforcement notice.

(e) Nullity and invalidity of enforcement notice

There is a distinction between a notice which is null, and one which is invalid. **7.21** Where there is an obvious flaw in the notice, it is null and of no effect; if there is an underlying flaw which can only be proved on the facts, the notice is invalid but has effect until it is quashed. As a result, if on appeal to the Scottish Ministers the notice is found to be null, the appeal should be dismissed because there is no notice to appeal against.

Grounds of nullity have been identified by the courts. A notice which fails to specify the required information (see "Content of enforcement notice", at para.7.20 above) is likely to be null.[92] For example, if the notice fails to specify the date upon which it is to take effect, it cannot take effect, and must therefore be null. The failure to specify the steps required to remedy the breach renders the notice a nullity.[93] A notice which is hopelessly ambiguous and uncertain might also be a nullity.[94] Mistaken allegations of fact do not render a notice null.[95] It has been held that an enforcement notice which was not served on a person known to the planning authority to be the owner of the land rendered the notice a nullity, but this decision is likely to have been influenced by the expiry of the time limit for any appeal to the Scot-

---

[88] *Metallic Protectives v Secretary of State for the Environment* [1976] J.P.L. 166.

[89] *McNaughton v Peter McIntyre (Clyde) Ltd*, 1981 S.P.L.P. 15.

[90] *Attorney General's Reference (No.1 of 1996)* [1997] J.P.L. 749; [1996] E.G. 164 (C.S.).

[91] TCPSA 1997 s.128(13). Permission is not granted if the notice is a nullity—*Tandridge DC v Verrechia* [1999] 3 P.L.R. 27.

[92] *Miller-Mead v Minister of Housing and Local Government* [1963] 1 All E.R. 459, per Upjohn L.J. at 470G.

[93] *Tandridge DC v Verrechia* [1999] 3 P.L.R. 27, unsuccessfully argued in *Barn Properties Ltd v Secretary of State for Scotland*, 1995 S.C.L.R. 113; 1995 49 S.P.E.L. 52.

[94] *Miller-Mead v Minister of Housing and Local Government* [1963] 1 All E.R. 459, per Upjohn L.J. at 470I.

[95] *Miller-Mead v Minister of Housing and Local Government* [1963] 1 All E.R. 459, per Diplock L.J. at 479D.

tish Ministers prior to the owner becoming aware of the notice, and is unlikely to be given wide application.[96]

A notice which has no obvious flaws is not a nullity, but may be shown to be invalid on proof of the facts. Where development without planning permission is alleged and it is found that no permission is required, the notice is invalid and may be quashed.[97] The following statutory grounds of appeal to the Scottish Ministers relate to issues of validity:

(i)   the matters stated in the notice have not occurred;
(ii)   these matters do not amount to a breach of planning control;
(iii)   at the date when the notice was issued no enforcement action could be taken against the breach of planning control;
(iv)   copies of the enforcement notice were not served as required by the TCPSA 1997.

The distinction between nullity and invalidity is important. A notice which is null cannot be the foundation for any further enforcement action or prosecution, even if the recipient has not submitted an appeal against the notice. In contrast, an invalid notice remains valid until it is quashed. The validity of an enforcement notice on the grounds outlined above can only be challenged in an appeal to the Scottish Ministers.[98] Issues of validity, such as allegations that the planning authority has acted in bad faith and been motivated by immaterial considerations, cannot be raised as a defence to a prosecution, but could be the subject of a petition for judicial review in so far as the allegations do not fall within the grounds of appeal to the Scottish Ministers.[99] There is also scope for the Scottish Ministers to amend an invalid notice as part of the appeal proceedings, for example by exercising the power to correct any defect, error or misdescription in the notice.[100]

(f)   Appeal against enforcement notice

7.22   At any time before the date specified in the notice on which it will take effect, any person served with a copy of the notice or any other person having an interest in the land may appeal to the Scottish Ministers against the enforcement notice.[101]

Lodging an appeal prevents the enforcement notice coming into force on the date specified in the notice.[102] As a result, until the enforcement notice is upheld on appeal there is no requirement to take the steps specified in the notice to remedy the breach of planning control. Exercise of the right of appeal may therefore provide a further period for negotiation to resolve any dispute between the planning authority and the landowner, during which the alleged breach may continue. Most authorities would prefer to agree a solution, thereby avoiding the necessity of continuing with an appeal. Submission of an appeal would also provide sufficient time to lodge an application for retrospective planning permission or apply for a certificate of lawfulness of existing use or development.

---

[96] *McDaid v Clydebank DC*, 1984 S.L.T. 162; [1984] J.P.L. 579; but see *Martin v Bearsden and Milngavie DC*, 1987 S.L.T. 300 and *R. v Greenwich LBC Ex p. Patel* [1985] J.P.L. 851.
[97] *Miller-Mead v Minister of Housing and Local Government* [1963] 1 All E.R. 459 per Upjohn L.J. at 470G.
[98] TCPSA s.134; *James Barrie (Sand & Gravel) Ltd v Lanark DC*, 1979 S.L.T. 14.
[99] *R. v Wicks* [1997] 2 All E.R. 801.
[100] *Barn Properties Ltd v Secretary of State for Scotland*, 1995 S.C.L.R. 113; 1995 49 S.P.E.L. 52.
[101] TCPSA 1997 ss.130–133.
[102] TCPSA 1997 s.131(3).

7.23 The right of appeal is open to abuse by persons seeking to continue a profitable activity, which is in breach of planning control, for as long as possible. Appeals may take several months to be determined. Such abuses can be prevented by the planning authority serving a stop notice with the enforcement notice, with the effect that the use or operation is prohibited from continuing pending determination of the appeal. Most authorities are reluctant to serve stop notices because of the potential liability to pay compensation. Alternatively, an interdict could be sought to prevent the activity from continuing, but the authority could be liable to pay damages if the interdict was wrongfully obtained (see para.7.45 below).

The grounds of appeal are[103]:

(i) the matters stated in the notice as constituting the breach of planning control have not occurred;

(ii) these matters do not amount to a breach of planning control, including development which has become lawful because no enforcement action has been taken within the prescribed time limits (see para.7.07 above)[104];

(iii) at the date when the notice was issued no enforcement action could be taken against the breach of planning control: this either refers to lawful development or to the time limit for further enforcement action (see para.7.05 above);

(iv) copies of the enforcement notice were not served as required by the TCPSA 1997;

(v) the requirements of the notice exceed what is necessary to remedy any breach of planning control or to remedy any injury to amenity which has been caused by any such breach;

(vi) any period specified in the notice for compliance with its requirements falls short of what should reasonably be allowed.

It is not competent to appeal on the grounds that planning permission ought to be granted in respect of the breach of planning control constituted by the matters specified in the notice, or the condition or limitation concerned ought to be discharged.[105]

The explanatory notes accompanying the enforcement notice explain how an appeal is lodged. Written notice must be given to the Scottish Ministers before the date specified in the enforcement notice as that on which it is to take effect. The appeal will have been lodged timeously if the notice was sent in a properly addressed and pre-paid envelope posted in sufficient time for it to be delivered before that date in the ordinary course of the post (overturning a court ruling that the effective date is the date of receipt and not the date of posting). Alternatively, notice can be sent by electronic communications at such time that, in the ordinary course of transmission, it would be delivered to the Ministers before that date.[106]

7.24 In addition to specifying the grounds of appeal, the appellant must also submit a statement of appeal on the form obtained from the Directorate for Planning and Environmental Appeals (DPEA) giving information on all matters which the appellant intends to raise in the appeal; the name and address of the appellant; a copy of the notice against which the appeal is made; the name and address of the representative of the appellant (if any) and whether any notice or other correspondence to be sent to the appellant should be sent to the representative instead; and a

---

[103] TCPSA 1997 s.130(1), as amended.
[104] For example, *Doonin Plant v Scottish Ministers* [2011] CSOH 3.
[105] PSA 2006 Sch.1 para.1, repealed s.130(1)(a).
[106] TCPSA 1997 s.130(2), as amended.

note of what matters the appellant considers require determination and by what procedure (or combination of procedures) the appellant wishes the appeal to be determined. The statement of appeal is to be accompanied by copies of all documents, materials and evidence which the appellant intends to rely on in the appeal.[107] There are restrictions on the appellant raising any matters not set out in the statement of appeal or documents, materials and evidence.[108]

When giving notice of appeal to the Ministers, the appellant must at the same time send the planning authority copies of the notice of appeal, statement of appeal, and all documents, materials and evidence which accompanied the notice of appeal. The planning authority must submit a statement ("the planning authority's response") within 21 days of receiving notification of the appeal, and send a copy to the appellant. This statement includes a response to each ground of appeal, and an indication of what matters the authority consider require determination and by what procedure or combination of procedures the authority wish the appeal to be conducted. The authority must also send copies of documents which were before the authority and which were taken into account in reaching its decision to issue the notice which is the subject of the appeal.[109] If the authority fails to submit the statement within the time limit, the Scottish Ministers may proceed with the appeal and quash the enforcement notice.[110]

The appellant has 14 days from the date of receipt of the planning authority's response to submit any comments on matters raised in that response.[111]

Within 14 days of receiving notification of the appeal, the planning authority must give notice to each person (other than the appellant) on whom the enforcement notice was served. The notice states that representations on the appeal may be made within a specified period which must be at least 14 days from the date of the notice.[112]

In determining an appeal against an enforcement notice, the Ministers have power to[113]:

(i)   correct any defect, error or misdescription in the notice, or vary its terms, if they are satisfied that the correction or variation will not cause injustice to the appellant or the planning authority (previously this power was limited to correcting any non-material informality, defect or error)[114];

(ii)   disregard the failure to serve a copy of the notice on any person, if neither the appellant or that person has been substantially prejudiced by this failure;

(iii)   give directions to give effect to the decision on the appeal, including directions for quashing the notice;

(iv)   determine whether on the date on which the appeal was made, any existing use of the land, operations, or any matter constituting a failure to comply with a condition or limitation attached to a grant of planning permission, were lawful, and grant a certificate of lawfulness of existing use or development accordingly.

---

[107] Town and Country Planning (Appeals) (Scotland) Regulations 2013 (SSI 2013/156) (TCPASR) reg.14.
[108] TCPASR reg.14(4).
[109] TCPASR reg.15.
[110] TCPSA 1997 s.132(3)(b).
[111] TCPASR reg.15(3).
[112] TCPASR reg.16.
[113] TCPSA 1997 ss.132 and 133.
[114] e.g. *Barn Properties Ltd v Secretary of State for Scotland*, 1995 S.C.L.R. 113; 1995 49 S.P.E.L. 52.

The Ministers no longer have the following powers: grant planning permission in respect of any of the matters stated in the enforcement notice as constituting a breach of planning control; discharge any condition or limitation subject to which planning permission was granted, and substitute any other condition or limitation; grant permission for such other development on the land to which the enforcement notice relates as appears appropriate.[115]

The statutory grounds of appeal do not include the manner of the exercise of the planning authority's discretion to take enforcement action, and this should not be considered in the determination of the appeal.[116] It is competent for the notice to be upheld where there is no longer any breach of planning control once the appeal is determined, if the situation might change and the notice would prevent such change.[117]

7.25

Aside from the grounds of appeal, the Scottish Ministers may find that the enforcement notice is a nullity. If the notice is a nullity, it does not exist and there is no notice upon which to determine the appeal (see para.7.21 above).

Where an appeal against an enforcement notice is upheld on the grounds that the matters stated in the notice do not amount to a breach of planning control, this is a conclusive determination which cannot be re-opened in subsequent proceedings.[118]

Any person aggrieved by the decision of the Scottish Ministers on appeal may challenge the validity of that decision in the Court of Session.[119] This right of challenge is subject to a six-week time limit from the date of the decision letter. The court is only concerned with the validity (or legality) of the decision and will not interfere with its merits (see Ch.8 below). The decision must therefore be challenged on the grounds that it is null or invalid as outwith the powers (ultra vires) of the Ministers. For example, the Ministers may have misused their statutory powers by failing to take into account a relevant factor. An appeal decision was quashed because the reporter failed in his duty to give reasons.[120]

As part of an appeal to the Court of Session it is competent to seek interim suspension of the decision of the Ministers, for example, to prevent the enforcement notice from taking effect. It is unclear whether the statutory provision that the notice, "shall be of no effect pending the final determination or the withdrawal of the appeal"[121] extends to an appeal to the Court of Session. Although a decision of the English Court of Criminal Appeal indicates that this provision does apply, the relevant statutory provisions in England are different.[122]

(g)   Challenge of enforcement notice in the courts

Any person aggrieved by the decision of the Scottish Ministers on an appeal against an enforcement notice may challenge the validity of that decision in the Court of Session (see para.7.25 above).

7.26

The availability of the right of appeal to the Scottish Ministers against an enforce-

---

[115] TCPSA 1997 s.133(1)(a)–(c) and (4)–(11) have been repealed
[116] *Parkes v Secretary of State for Scotland*, 1998 G.W.D. 6-292; 1998 67 S.P.E.L. 55; *Tarn v Secretary of State for Scotland*, 1997 G.W.D. 9-394; 1997 62 S.P.E.L. 81.
[117] *Parkes v Secretary of State for Scotland*, 1998 G.W.D. 6-292; 1998 67 S.P.E.L. 55.
[118] *Hammond v Secretary of State for the Environment* [1997] J.P.L. 724.
[119] TCPSA 1997 ss.237(3)(d) and 239.
[120] *Bennett v Gordon*, 2008 G.W.D. 11-219. See also *Doonin Plant v Scottish Ministers* [2011] CSOH 3.
[121] TCPSA 1997 s.131(3).
[122] *R. v Kuxhaus* [1988] 2 All E.R. 705.

ment notice will in most instances mean that judicial review procedure will not be appropriate for challenging the legality of the notice. There is a statutory prohibition on any legal challenge to the validity of a notice where the grounds of challenge fall within the grounds of appeal to the Scottish Ministers (see para.7.25 above). This extends to a challenge to an anticipated enforcement notice.[123] However, it may be possible to raise judicial review proceedings on the grounds that the notice is null or invalid on other grounds, such as that it was beyond the powers of the authority to issue the notice.

The invalidity of the notice cannot be raised as a defence to a prosecution if the alleged invalidity falls within the grounds of appeal to the Scottish Ministers. Even if the statutory prohibition does not apply, it may be appropriate for the alleged invalidity to be challenged by judicial review rather than in the criminal courts.[124]

Stop notices

(a) Power to serve stop notice

7.27   The power to serve a stop notice may be exercised only in association with service of an enforcement notice, where the planning authority considers it expedient that any activity (or ancillary or associated activity), which the enforcement notice requires to be ceased, should cease before the expiry of the period for compliance with the enforcement notice.[125] A stop notice may be served at the same time as the enforcement notice or at any time thereafter until the enforcement notice takes effect. Lodging an appeal against an enforcement notice will prevent that notice from taking effect, leaving the planning authority with the option of serving a stop notice. Scottish Government guidance states that planning authorities should ensure that the requirements of a stop notice prohibit only what is essential to safeguard amenity or public safety in the neighbourhood, or to prevent serious or irreversible harm to the environment in the surrounding area.[126]

The effect of a stop notice is to prohibit the carrying out of the activity on the land to which the enforcement notice relates or on any part of the land specified in the stop notice. The stop notice can also require cessation of activities which are ancillary to or associated with the activity struck at by the enforcement notice, in other words, activities associated with (but not part of) the breach of planning control.

The stop notice may prohibit some but not all of the activities which the enforcement notice requires to cease, or particular aspects of a single activity. It may also require cessation of activity on part but not all of the land specified in the enforcement notice. This ability to under-enforce by selecting which of the activities specified in the enforcement notice should be prohibited by the stop notice enables the planning authority to prevent a clear breach of planning control from continuing, pending an appeal against the enforcement notice, but avoid liability to pay compensation for preventing an activity which is less obviously a breach.

A stop notice cannot prohibit use of any building as a dwellinghouse. However,

---

[123] *James Barrie (Sand & Gravel) Ltd v Lanark DC*, 1979 S.L.T. 14.
[124] *R. v Wicks* [1997] 2 All E.R. 801; but see *Badcock v Hertfordshire CC* [2002] EWCA Crim 1941.
[125] TCPSA 1997 s.140. The Scottish Ministers can also serve a stop notice—s.142. Edinburgh College of Art, Heriot Watt University and Brodies WS, *Review of Planning Enforcement*, 1997, found very low use of stop notices, with almost half of the planning authorities serving no stop notices in the period 1992–96, and only two authorities making regular use of the stop notice powers. The principal reason appeared to be concerns about liability for compensation.
[126] Planning Circular 10/2009, Planning Enforcement, Annex H, para.6.

the restriction on prohibiting use of a residential caravan has been removed.[127] A stop notice also cannot prohibit any use carried out (whether continuously or not) for more than four years prior to the date of service of the notice. In calculating the four years, no account is taken of any period during which the use was authorised by planning permission, such as a temporary permission. This four-year rule applies to uses and does not extend to building, engineering, mining or other operations or the deposit of refuse or waste materials.

The effect of serving a stop notice underlines the limitations of enforcement notices. An enforcement notice takes at least 28 days to come into effect and provides a further period for compliance with its terms, during which time the breach of planning control may continue. Lodging an appeal to the Scottish Ministers against the enforcement notice suspends its effect until the determination or withdrawal of the appeal. Service of a stop notice prevents the breach of planning control from continuing until the enforcement notice comes into effect.

Stop notices have their own limitations. A stop notice has a negative character **7.28** and can only be used to prohibit activity rather than to achieve positive action or remedy the breach of planning control. As the effect of a stop notice is limited to requiring complete cessation of an activity, stop notices cannot be used to keep an activity within reasonable bounds. In addition, unlike an interdict, a stop notice cannot be used to prohibit a threatened breach: it can only be served with or after an enforcement notice once there appears to have been a breach of planning control. The usefulness of the power to serve a stop notice is reduced further by the potential liability for compensation (see para.7.32 below).

A stop notice ceases to have effect once the period for compliance with the enforcement notice has expired and an offence is thus committed for non-compliance with the terms of the enforcement notice. It also ceases to have effect if the enforcement notice to which it relates is withdrawn or quashed on appeal. Where the enforcement notice is varied so that it no longer relates to an activity prohibited by the stop notice, the stop notice will cease to have effect in relation to that activity. A stop notice is not invalidated by any failure to serve the enforcement notice on all parties, provided the planning authority shows that it took all reasonably practicable steps to effect proper service.[128]

The stop notice may be withdrawn at any time by the planning authority without prejudicing its power to serve a fresh notice. Withdrawal is effected by giving notice to all persons served with a copy of the stop notice and displaying this notice in place of any site notices.[129] There is no statutory power to vary a stop notice.

It is an offence for a person to contravene, or cause or permit contravention of, the provisions of a stop notice after a site notice has been displayed or the notice has been served on him.[130] This offence may be committed in the course of a day or a longer period of time. Continued contravention of the stop notice following conviction is also an offence. It will be a defence for the accused person to prove that the stop notice was not served on him and that he had no reasonable cause to believe that the activity was prohibited by the stop notice. Display of a site notice (see para.7.29 below) may be an important factor in determining reasonable cause. The decision to prosecute and the choice of procedure rests with the procurator fis-

---

[127] *R. (on the application of Wilson) v Wychavon DC* [2007] J.P.L. 1158 upheld this as compatible with Convention rights.
[128] TCPSA 1997 s.141.
[129] TCPSA 1997 s.140(9).
[130] TCPSA 1997 s.144.

cal, with liability to a fine not exceeding £20,000 on summary conviction and an unlimited fine following conviction on indictment. In determining the level of fine the court will have regard to any financial benefit which has accrued or appears likely to accrue to the person in consequence of the failure to comply with the stop notice.

(b) Service of stop notice

7.29   A stop notice may be served on any person who appears to the planning authority to have an interest in the land or be engaged in activities which constitute or involve the breach of planning control alleged in the enforcement notice.[131] In comparison, the enforcement notice is served on the owner and occupier of the land. The stop notice may be served at the same time as the enforcement notice or at a later date before the enforcement notice takes effect.

The planning authority may also display a site notice on the land, stating the requirements of the stop notice, the persons on whom it has been served, and the consequences of contravening the stop notice.[132] Display of a site notice may widen the categories of persons against whom prosecution for contravening the notice may be successful (see para.7.28 above).

(c) Content of stop notice

7.30   There is no prescribed form of stop notice, but it must specify the date upon which it is to take effect.[133] In normal circumstances, this date must be between three and 28 days after the date of service. However, a stop notice may take earlier effect if the planning authority considers that there are special reasons why an earlier date should be specified. The Scottish Government guidance gives as an example the need to protect areas of great landscape value or conservation areas from harmful operational development.[134] For the notice to take earlier effect in this way, the authority must serve a statement of these special reasons along with the notice. There is no longer a requirement that the stop notice refer to and enclose a copy of the enforcement notice, but it is recommended by the Scottish Government guidance.[135]

Where there is a need to stop an activity with immediate effect, a temporary stop notice (see para.7.33) is likely to be more effective, as it enables the activity to be stopped from the point at which the temporary stop notice is displayed on the site.

As penal consequences arise from a stop notice, its terms must be strictly construed, and it is not permissible to look at the enforcement notice associated with the stop notice in order to ascertain what is prohibited.[136]

(d) Challenge of stop notice

7.31   There is no statutory right of appeal to the Scottish Ministers or the Court of Session against a stop notice. However, a petition for judicial review may be brought

---

[131] TCPSA 1997 s.140(8).
[132] TCPSA 1997 s.141(3).
[133] TCPSA 1997 s.140(7).
[134] Planning Circular 10/2009, Planning Enforcement, Annex H, para.12.
[135] Planning Circular 10/2009, Planning Enforcement, Annex H, para.11.
[136] *R. v Dhar* [1993] 2 P.L.R. 60.

before the Court of Session alleging that the notice is invalid on legal grounds (see Ch.8 below). Failure to follow the Scottish Government guidance is unlikely to be sufficient for a successful judicial review.[137] It may be difficult to obtain an interdict to prevent service of a stop notice or to suspend its effect pending the decision of the court, as there is a right to compensation if the stop notice is eventually quashed.[138] An alternative but risky option to applying for judicial review is to ignore the notice and defend any prosecution on the basis that the notice is invalid.

(e) Compensation and stop notices

The potential liability to pay compensation has acted as a deterrent to use of stop **7.32** notices. Compensation is payable where a stop notice has ceased to have effect (see para.7.28 above) in the following circumstances[139]:

(i) the enforcement notice is quashed on appeal as invalid; or

(ii) the enforcement notice is varied to omit the requirement to cease the activity prohibited by the stop notice; or

(iii) the enforcement notice is withdrawn, other than in consequence of a grant of planning permission by the planning authority for the development to which the notice relates; or

(iv) the stop notice is withdrawn.

No compensation is therefore payable where the stop notice prohibits any activity which at any time when the stop notice is in force constitutes or contributes to a breach of planning control. Thus, even if the enforcement notice fails, the ludicrous situation will not arise of the planning authority being liable to pay compensation for prohibiting an activity which is a breach of planning control. The right to compensation is also excluded where any loss or damage suffered could have been avoided if the claimant had provided information sought under statutory powers, such as a planning contravention notice (see para.7.13 above), or had otherwise co-operated with the planning authority when responding to the notice. Finally, no compensation is payable if the planning authority decides to grant planning permission and, therefore, withdraws the enforcement notice.

Compensation may be claimed by a person who had an interest in the land to which the stop notice related when it was served. There is no requirement that the person must have been served with a copy of the notice. Interests in land will include those of an owner or occupier and possibly other parties such as lessees and heritable creditors who had a legal interest in the land.

Compensation is payable in respect of any loss or damage directly attributable to the prohibition contained in the notice, including any sum payable in respect of a breach of contract caused by taking action necessary to comply with the prohibition. The initial claim for compensation in respect of a stop notice must be submitted within six months, but will be valid for 20 years.[140] Except in so far as may be otherwise provided by any regulations, any question of disputed compensation can be referred to and determined by the Lands Tribunal.

---

[137] *R. v Elmbridge BC Ex p. Wendy Fair Markets Ltd* [1995] J.P.L. 928.

[138] *Central RC v Clackmannan DC*, 1983 S.L.T. 666; contrast *Shanks & McEwan (Contractors) Ltd v Gordon DC*, 1991 32 S.P.L.P. 15.

[139] TCPSA 1997 s.143.

[140] *Holt v Dundee DC*, 1990 S.L.T. (Lands Tr.) 30.

Temporary stop notice

7.33   The power to serve a temporary stop notice was introduced in 2009.[141] It enables action to be taken immediately without the need for an enforcement notice:

(a)   Power to serve temporary stop notice

7.34   A temporary stop notice may be issued where the planning authority consider that:

(i)   there has been a breach of planning control (see para.7.03 above) in relation to any land;

(ii)   the breach consists in engagement in an activity; and

(iii)   it is expedient that the activity (or any part of the activity) is stopped immediately.

The notice prohibits engagement in the activity (or in so much of the activity as is specified in the notice). It has effect from the time a copy of it is first displayed (see below).

Scottish Government guidance states that a temporary stop notice could be used to stop an activity that would, in the planning authority's view, cause damage to the environment and/or local amenity. It should only be used when the authority is satisfied there is a clear and immediate need for such action.

The use of temporary stop notices is subject to similar restrictions as stop notices: a temporary stop notice cannot prohibit use of any building as a dwellinghouse, or any use carried out (whether continuously or not) for more than four years prior to the date of display of the notice. In calculating the four years, no account is taken of any period during which the use was authorised by planning permission, such as a temporary permission. This four-year rule applies to uses and does not prevent a temporary stop notice prohibiting building, engineering, mining or other operations, or activity incidental to those operations, or the deposit of refuse or waste materials. There is also provision for activities to be prescribed which cannot be prohibited by a temporary stop notice. Unlike stop notices, a temporary stop notice cannot be used to prohibit stationing of a caravan on land provided the caravan is stationed on the land immediately prior to the issue of the temporary stop notice and it is at that time occupied by a person as his/her main residence.[142]

Temporary stop notices also have similar limitations to stop notices: the notices can only be used to prohibit activity rather than to achieve positive action or remedy the breach of planning control; they can only require complete cessation of an activity, so cannot be used to keep an activity within reasonable bounds; they cannot be used to prohibit a threatened breach; and there is potential liability for compensation (see para.7.38 below). However, unlike a stop notice, a temporary stop notice can be served without an enforcement notice.

A difference from stop notices is that a second or subsequent temporary stop notice must not be issued in respect of the same activity unless the planning authority have in the meantime taken some other enforcement action in relation to the breach.

The temporary stop notice ceases to have effect 28 days after it is first displayed,

---

[141] TCPSA 1997 ss.144A–D; Planning Circular 10/2009, Planning Enforcement, Annex I.

[142] Town and Country Planning (Temporary Stop Notice) (Scotland) Regulations 2009 (SSI 2009/213).

unless a shorter period is specified in the notice, or the notice is withdrawn by the planning authority before it ceases to have effect.

As with stop notices, it is an offence for a person to contravene, or cause or permit contravention of, the provisions of a temporary stop notice after it has been served on him, or a copy has been displayed. This offence may be committed in the course of a day or a longer period of time. Continued contravention of the temporary stop notice following conviction is also an offence. It will be a defence for the accused person to prove that the temporary stop notice was not served on him and he did not know, and could not reasonably have been expected to know, of its existence. The decision to prosecute and the choice of procedure rests with the procurator fiscal, with liability to a fine not exceeding £20,000 on summary conviction and an unlimited fine following conviction on indictment. In determining the level of fine the court will have regard to any financial benefit which has accrued or appears likely to accrue to the person in consequence of the failure to comply with the notice.

(b) Service of temporary stop notice

A temporary stop notice may be served on any person who appears to the plan-   **7.35**
ning authority to be engaged in the activity, and/or to have an interest in the land (whether as an owner or occupier or otherwise).

Unlike a stop notice, the display of a site notice is mandatory. The planning authority must display on the site a copy of the notice and a statement explaining the offence provisions. The notice has effect from the time the copy is first displayed on the site.

(c) Content of temporary stop notice

The temporary stop notice must be in writing and specify the activity, prohibit   **7.36**
engagement in the activity (or in so much of the activity as is specified in the notice), and set out the authority's reasons for issuing the notice. As penal consequences arise from a temporary stop notice, its terms are likely to be strictly construed, and external sources cannot be used to ascertain what is prohibited.[143]

(d) Challenge of temporary stop notice

A temporary stop notice can only have effect for a maximum of 28 days, but there   **7.37**
might be circumstances in which the recipient wishes to challenge the notice, especially if further enforcement action is likely at the end of that period. There is no statutory right of appeal to the Scottish Ministers or the Court of Session against a temporary stop notice. However, a petition for judicial review may be brought before the Court of Session alleging that the notice is invalid on legal grounds (see Ch.8 below). Failure to follow the Scottish Government guidance is unlikely to be sufficient for a successful judicial review.[144] It may be difficult to obtain an interdict to prevent service of a temporary stop notice or to suspend its effect pending the decision of the court, as there is a right to compensation if the temporary stop notice

---

[143] See re stop notices: *R. v Dhar* [1993] 2 P.L.R. 60.
[144] See re stop notices: *R. v Elmbridge BC Ex p. Wendy Fair Markets Ltd* [1995] J.P.L. 928.

is eventually quashed.[145] An alternative but risky option to applying for judicial review is to ignore the notice and defend any prosecution on the basis that the notice is invalid.

(e)   Compensation and temporary stop notices

7.38   Although the notice can be served on any person engaged in the activity, entitlement to compensation is limited to a person with an interest, whether as owner or occupier or otherwise, in the land to which the notice relates. There is no requirement that the person must have been served with a copy of the notice. Interests in land might include other parties such as lessees and heritable creditors who had a legal interest in the land.

The entitlement to be compensated by the planning authority is for any loss or damage directly attributable to the prohibition effected by the notice, provided either:

(i)   the activity prohibited by the notice is authorised by planning permission granted on or before the date on which the notice is first displayed; or

(ii)   a certificate of lawfulness of existing use or development is granted in relation to the activity; or

(iii)   the notice is withdrawn, other than following a grant of planning permission by the planning authority for the activity to which the notice relates.

Unlike a stop notice, the authority are therefore liable to pay compensation if they withdraw the notice. However, in common with stop notices, no compensation is payable where the notice prohibits any activity which at any time when the notice is in force constitutes or contributes to a breach of planning control, or where any loss or damage suffered could have been avoided if the claimant had provided information sought under statutory powers, such as a planning contravention notice (see para.7.13 above), or had otherwise co-operated with the planning authority when responding to the notice.

Breach of condition notice

7.39   The Carnwath Report recommended that there should be a remedy to enforce a condition without enabling the merits to be reopened in an enforcement notice appeal. This recommendation led to the introduction of the breach of condition notice, which joined the enforcement notice as the other main form of enforcement action which prevents a breach of planning control from becoming lawful development.[146]

As a result of the lack of a right of appeal against a breach of condition notice, a grant of planning permission should not be implemented until consideration has been given to the appropriateness of any conditions attached to the permission. Any purchase of land should involve careful scrutiny of planning conditions and warranties should be obtained from the seller that no conditions have been breached.

---

[145] See re stop notices: *Central RC v Clackmannan DC*, 1983 S.L.T. 666; contrast *Shanks & McEwan (Contractors) Ltd v Gordon DC*, 1991 32 S.P.L.P. 15.

[146] Carnwath, *Enforcing Planning Control* (1989). Since 2009 a s.33A notice also prevents a breach of planning control from becoming lawful development. Between 1992–1996 over 300 breach of condition notices were served, with a 73 per cent compliance rate—Edinburgh College of Art, Heriot Watt University and Brodies WS, *Review of Planning Enforcement* (1997).

(a) Power to serve breach of condition notice

7.40

A breach of condition notice may be served by the planning authority where there is non-compliance with any of the conditions or limitations regulating the use of land imposed upon a grant of planning permission. [147] Thus, a notice may be served only if there is actual non-compliance (an objective test), whereas an enforcement notice may be served where it "appears" to the authority that there has been a breach of planning control (a subjective test). This suggests that more proof will be required before the breach of condition notice may be served.

Enforcement action can be taken against a breach of planning condition for up to 10 years from the date of breach. In addition, a breach of condition notice can be served if an enforcement notice is in effect, or in the preceding four years the planning authority have taken or purported to take enforcement action in respect of the breach.[148]

The Scottish Government guidance states that the decisive issue should be whether public amenity or the use of land or buildings meriting protection in the public interest is unacceptably affected. A breach of condition notice should only be served where the condition is legally valid and enforceable, satisfies the policy criteria for the imposition of conditions, and has clearly been breached, on the available evidence (see Ch.6 above).[149] In dismissing an application for judicial review of a decision not to take enforcement action, the court acknowledged that although there had not been strict compliance with the terms of a condition, it had in substance been complied with.[150]

The planning authority has power to withdraw the notice without prejudicing its power to serve a fresh notice within the prescribed time limits. There is no specific power to vary the notice. However, the time limit for compliance may be extended.

(b) Effect of breach of condition notice

7.41

In contrast to an enforcement notice, a breach of condition notice comes into effect on the date of service. If, after the period allowed for compliance has expired, any of the conditions specified in the notice are not complied with and the steps specified in the notice have not been taken or the activities have not ceased, the person served with a copy of the notice is in breach of its terms and guilty of an offence. It is not clear whether compliance with the terms of the notice has the effect of discharging the notice, or whether a breach of condition notice has a similar effect to an enforcement notice and will remain in force to catch any future breaches following compliance.

Where a condition prevented occupation of a dwelling until a sewage treatment plant was installed, and the breach of condition notice required installation of the plant, no offence was committed when occupation commenced without installation of the plant, as cessation of use was not a step specified in the notice.[151]

---

[147] TCPSA 1997 s.145.
[148] TCPSA 1997 s.124(3) and (4).
[149] Planning Circular 10/2009, Planning Enforcement, Annex J, paras 4, 5 and 17.
[150] *R. v Flintshire CC Ex p. Somerfield Stores* [1998] E.G. 53 (C.S.).
[151] *Quinton v North Cornwall DC* [1994] C.L.Y. 4315.

Any person found guilty of such an offence shall be liable on summary conviction to a fine not exceeding level 3 on the standard scale (see Appendix 1 below).[152] This offence may be committed in the course of a day or over a longer period. Further offences will be committed if there is non-compliance with the notice following conviction. It will be a defence to prove that all reasonable measures were taken to secure compliance with the conditions specified in the notice, or that the accused no longer had control of the land where the notice was purportedly served upon him as the person having control thereof.

In 2009 planning authorities were given the power to serve a fixed penalty notice within the six months which immediately follows the compliance period in the breach of condition notice, if they have reason to believe that the person is in breach of the notice.[153] A fixed penalty notice cannot be served after the person has been charged with an offence in relation to breach of the notice. Service of a fixed penalty notice is at the discretion of the planning authority, applying the principle that any action should be commensurate to the nature and scale of the breach.[154]

The fixed penalty notice offers the person the opportunity to pay to the planning authority, within the period of 30 days which immediately follows the day on which that notice is served, a penalty of the prescribed amount specified in the notice.[155] If payment is made within the first 15 days of that period the amount payable is reduced by 25 per cent. If the amount is paid timeously, that discharges any liability to conviction for an offence in relation to breach of the notice. No prosecution can be commenced during the 30-day period after the notice is served.

The fixed penalty notice must identify the step specified in the breach of condition notice which has not been taken, or the activity so specified which has not ceased. It is not competent to serve more than one fixed penalty notice in relation to a particular step or activity. However, there could be several fixed penalty notices issued, if there are different steps or activities involved.

The weakness of the fixed penalty notice is that, although it penalises the recipient for the breach, it does not directly require the recipient to remedy that breach.

There is no right of appeal against a fixed penalty notice and no power to withdraw or vary the notice. If the recipient disputes the accuracy or validity of the fixed penalty notice, the notice could simply be ignored, as it does not impose any requirement to pay, in contrast to a parking ticket. The only difficulty might be a situation where, because of a defect in the notice, the recipient is deprived of an opportunity to discharge liability to conviction by paying the financial penalty. Judicial review might be the remedy in such circumstances.

A breach of condition notice will cease to have effect where the condition is discharged, or so far as the notice is inconsistent with a subsequent grant of retrospective planning permission.[156] However, this will not affect liability for a previous failure either to comply or to secure compliance with the notice.

There is no provision enabling the planning authority to take the steps specified in a breach of condition notice and recover its expenses from the person served with the notice.

---

[152] In *Stott v Reclip Ltd*, 2004 G.W.D. 10-238 a fine of £1,000 was imposed.
[153] TCPSA 1997 s.145A. There is a similar provision for enforcement notices in s.136A.
[154] Planning Circular 10/2009, Planning Enforcement, Annex K, para.5.
[155] Currently £300—Town and Country Planning (Amount of Fixed Penalty) (Scotland) Regulations 2009 (SSI 2009/52).
[156] TCPSA 1997 s.137.

(c) Service of breach of condition notice

The breach of condition notice may be served upon any person who is carrying out or has carried out the development, or who has caused or permitted another to do so. In the case of conditions regulating the use of the land, the notice may be served upon the person who has control of the land. Thus, unlike an enforcement notice which is served on the owner and occupier, the objective seems to be that a breach of condition notice is served upon the person responsible for the breach of condition or the person who can secure compliance with the condition. It also seems that the planning authority has an element of discretion in deciding the person(s) to be served with a breach of condition notice.

7.42

The example given by the Scottish Government guidance is a condition requiring completion of a landscaping scheme in association with a housing development.[157] This type of condition does not regulate the use of land. Thus a breach of condition notice cannot be served upon the individual homeowners (it would be possible to serve enforcement notices), but must be served upon the original developer.

(d) Content of breach of condition notice

The notice must specify the planning permission to which it relates, the conditions which have not been complied with (which need not be all the conditions), and the steps which the authority consider ought to be taken, or the activities which the authority considers ought to cease, to secure compliance with these conditions. The period for compliance must be at least 28 days from the date of service of the notice, as specified in the notice.

7.43

In consequence of the potential criminal liability, the notice must be clearly drafted. A breach of condition notice was held invalid because it did not specify sufficiently steps to be taken to secure compliance. In repeating the terms of the condition, the notice specified the result to be achieved, not the means to achieve it.[158]

It may be within the discretion of the planning authority to ignore non-compliance with some or all of the conditions imposed upon a grant of planning permission. However, unlike the power to serve an enforcement notice, the statutory wording does not explicitly permit service of a breach of condition notice requiring partial, and not full, compliance with a condition.

(e) Challenge of breach of condition notice

There is no statutory right of appeal to the Scottish Ministers or the Court of Session against a breach of condition notice. It will therefore be impossible to challenge the merits of the notice, but may be possible to challenge its validity. An invalid notice could be ignored and its invalidity raised as a defence to any prosecution for non-compliance with its terms.[159] Alternatively, a petition for common law judicial review may be submitted to the Court of Session on the ground that the notice is beyond the powers (ultra vires) of the planning authority to serve (see Ch.8

7.44

---

[157] Planning Circular 10/2009, Planning Enforcement, Annex J, para.8.
[158] *Scottish Coal Co Ltd v East Lothian Council*, 2001 S.L.T. 495; [2001] 1 P.L.R. 1.
[159] *Dilieto v Ealing LBC* [1998] 2 All E.R. 885.

below).[160] The Court of Session may refuse a petition for judicial review on the ground that the statutory procedures for challenging conditions should have been utilised (see Ch.6 above). Invalidity of the notice will not prevent the planning authority serving a fresh notice within the prescribed time limits. Where the conditions had not been breached, the decision to issue a breach of condition notice was based on an error of law and was accordingly flawed.[161]

The option of negotiating with the planning authority must always be borne in mind. Negotiations may lead to submission of an application for planning permission without compliance with the condition (see Ch.5 above).

Interdict

7.45   Planning authorities have a statutory power to seek interdict from the sheriff court or the Court of Session to restrain or prevent any actual or apprehended breach of planning control.[162] Interdict is a court order requiring an activity to be stopped or preventing an activity from starting. It has a negative character and is not appropriate for requiring an activity or works to be carried out, unlike injunctions in England and Wales which can have negative ("stop") and positive ("do") requirements. Breach of interdict amounts to contempt of court and may result in a fine and/or imprisonment.

It is irrelevant to the exercise of this power that the authority has exercised or proposes to exercise other enforcement or planning powers. Interdict can, therefore, be used in conjunction with other enforcement action, for example, to prevent the lodging of an appeal from delaying the requirement of an enforcement notice to cease an unauthorised activity. This power may be used to avoid the potential liability for compensation which follows service of a stop notice in such a situation (see para.7.32 above). However, planning authorities should note that interim interdict is granted *periculo petentis*, with the result that there will be liability to pay compensation in the form of damages if the interim interdict is later proved to be excessive. An interdict may be sought in circumstances where a stop notice cannot be served, such as before there has been an actual breach of planning control, or after an enforcement notice has come into effect.

Application for interdict may be made to either the sheriff court or the Court of Session. The choice of court will depend on factors such as the seriousness of the case, convenience and cost. The court may grant such interdict as it thinks appropriate for the purpose of restraining or preventing the breach.[163] Refusal of the application for interdict will continue to be within the discretion of the court. For example, it is possible that the court may refuse to grant an interdict in circumstances where a stop notice could be served, on the grounds that the more specific power provided by Parliament should be exercised, especially since it carries provisions for payment of compensation.

Where a caravan site was being used in breach of planning conditions, the sheriff granted interim interdict to the planning authority preventing the landowners from permitting caravans, keeping caravans, or residing in caravans on their land, and from wilfully obstructing the council from exercising their power to take direct ac-

---

[160] *Scottish Coal Co Ltd v East Lothian Council*, 2001 S.L.T. 495; [2001] 1 P.L.R. 1

[161] *R. v Ealing LBC Ex p. Zainuddin* [1995] J.P.L. 925.

[162] TCPSA 1997 s.146.

[163] *City of London Corp v Bovis Construction Ltd* [1989] J.P.L. 263 shows the circumstances in which the courts in England and Wales will grant an injunction.

tion to enforce an enforcement notice. The balance of convenience favoured the grant of interim interdict as there was no colourable argument that the defenders had the right to do what they were alleged to have been doing. Although the defenders might have a justifiable sense of grievance at the way in which they had been treated, this was not a relevant consideration to the grant of interdict.[164]

In an odour nuisance case, the Court of Session refused to grant an interim interdict to prevent the sewerage authority from operating the sewage treatment plant adjacent to the premises occupied by a manufacturing company, on the grounds that the balance of convenience did not favour the granting of the interdict, which would result in untreated sewage overflowing into nearby watercourses.[165]

Although injunction is a wider remedy, useful principles can be drawn from **7.46** English cases decided following the introduction of the Human Rights Act 1998, especially those involving removal of unauthorised caravans occupied by gypsies. The leading case indicates that proportionality requires not only that the injunction be appropriate and necessary for the attainment of the public interest sought—the safeguarding of the environment—but also that it does not impose an excessive burden on the individual whose private interests—the gypsy's private life and home and the retention of his ethnic identity—are at stake. The judge must consider all questions of hardship for the defendant and his family. Questions of the family's health and education are relevant. The judge also has to take into account countervailing considerations such as the need to enforce planning control in the general interest and the planning history of the site. The degree and flagrancy of the breach of planning control may well prove critical. If conventional enforcement measures have failed over a prolonged period of time to remedy the breach, the court would be readier to use its own powers. Conversely, the court might well be reluctant to use its powers in a case where enforcement action has never been taken. Other potential considerations include urgency in the situation sufficient to justify the pre-emptive avoidance of an anticipated breach of planning control, and health and safety. Preventing a gypsy moving on to the site might involve him in less hardship than moving him out after a long period of occupation.[166]

Interdicts are rarely sought as planning authorities are concerned about the costs involved. However, in 1992–96, 90 per cent of interdicts sought were granted.[167]

Notice requiring proper maintenance of land

The planning authority has power to serve a notice (previously referred to in the **7.47** Town and Country Planning (Scotland) Act 1972 as a "waste land notice") where it appears that the amenity of any part of its district or of an adjoining district is adversely affected by the condition of any land or buildings within the district. Unlike the other enforcement powers, this power may be exercised in the absence of a breach of planning control. The notice is served on the owner, lessee and occupier of the land or building, and requires specified steps to be taken to abate the

---

[164] *Perth and Kinross Council v Lowther*, 1996 58 S.P.E.L. 119.

[165] *Barr & Stroud Ltd v West of Scotland Water Authority*, 1996 G.W.D. 36-2126; 1997 62 S.P.E.L. 83; cf. *Glasgow City Council v Cannell*, 1998 G.W.D. 33-1722; 1999 71 S.P.E.L. 15 (listed building control).

[166] *South Buckinghamshire DC v Porter* [2002] 1 All E.R. 425, [2002] J.P.L. 608, upheld by the House of Lords in *Wrexham BC v Berry* [2003] 2 A.C. 558; [2003] J.P.L. 1412.

[167] Edinburgh College of Art, Heriot Watt University and Brodies WS, *Review of Planning Enforcement* (1997).

adverse effect. The effect of the notice is similar to an enforcement notice. An appeal against the notice may be submitted to the Scottish Ministers at any time until the notice takes effect. Failure to comply with the requirements of the notice is not declared to be an offence. If the required steps are not taken, the only sanction available to the authority is to enter the site and take those steps itself, recovering the costs of doing so from the owner or lessee of the site.[168]

Discontinuance order

7.48   The planning authority has power to require discontinuance of any use of land, alteration or removal of any buildings or works, or to impose conditions on the continuance of a use of land.[169] This power is exercised in the interests of the proper planning of its area (including the interests of amenity). Regard must be had to the development plan and to any other material considerations, and the decision made in accordance with the provisions of the development plan unless material considerations indicate otherwise.[170] The order will not take effect until confirmed by the Scottish Ministers.[171] There is provision for a hearing to be held at the request of the owner, lessee or occupier of the land, or any other person affected by the order. If the order is confirmed, there is a right to compensation for depreciation of the value of an interest in land, or disturbance in the enjoyment of the land.[172] The cost of carrying out works in compliance with the order can also be recovered from the planning authority. It is an offence not to comply with the order.[173] If any step required by the order has not been taken within the period specified in the order, the planning authority may enter the land, take the required step and recover their reasonable expenses from the owner of the land.[174]

OTHER ENFORCEMENT MATTERS

Service of notices

7.49   Service of a notice is achieved by delivering it to the person, by leaving it at their usual or last known place of abode, or by sending it by recorded delivery or registered mail to that address. Where the valuation roll shows a person to have an interest in the land, the notice should be served at the address on the roll for that person. Service on companies is effected by delivery to the secretary or clerk of the company at its registered or principal office, or by registered letter/recorded delivery addressed to the secretary or clerk at that office. If the planning authority is unable to identify after reasonable enquiry the persons entitled to service, the notice may be addressed to "the owner", "the lessee", or "the occupier" of the land and served as above. If any part of the land is unoccupied, the notice may be addressed to "the owners and any lessees and occupiers" and affixed in a conspicuous manner to some object on the land, but must be served upon any person who has given to the author-

---

[168] TCPSA 1997 ss.135 and 179; *Russell v Scottish Ministers* unreported 20 December 2002 OH.
[169] TCPSA 1997 s.71.
[170] TCPSA 1997 s.25.
[171] TCPSA 1997 s.72.
[172] TCPSA 1997 s.83.
[173] TCPSA 1997 s.148.
[174] TCPSA 1997 s.149.

ity an address for service.[175] Most notices relating to enforcement cannot be served using electronic communications.[176]

Register of notices

Prescribed details of every s.179 notice (notice requiring proper maintenance), **7.50** enforcement notice, breach of condition notice, notices under s.33A, stop notices, and temporary stop notices, served in relation to land in its district must be entered by the planning authority into a register as soon as practicable and, in any event, within nine days. The register must be available for public inspection at all reasonable hours. Provision is made for removal of entries following withdrawal of a notice, a decision on appeal to quash the notice, or its reduction by the Court of Session.[177]

Personal bar

There are certain limited circumstances in which the planning authority will be **7.51** personally barred from exercising its enforcement powers (the equivalent principle in English law is estoppel).

Where an appeal has been upheld on the substantive issues, the legal principle of res judicata (finality of determination) applies and it is not open to the planning authority to serve fresh notices alleging similar breaches of planning control based on the same facts and circumstances. [178] However, this principle does not prevent service of a fresh notice within the time limits where a previous notice was quashed on procedural grounds or as a nullity.[179]

The other instance in which personal bar may be an issue is where a planning officer indicates that planning permission is not required for a proposed development. The problem is whether such a statement can personally bar the planning authority and prevent it from taking enforcement action against the development, which has commenced without permission in reliance upon this indication. Previously it could be argued that where the authority had delegated powers to the officer to make decisions on its behalf, a written statement in this form amounted to a s.51 determination which bound the authority. With the replacement of the formal procedure for obtaining certificates of lawfulness of proposed use or development (CLOPUD) for the informal s.51 determinations, there is no longer a mechanism for obtaining informal but binding decisions. In the absence of delegated powers, statements by its planning officers do not bind the authority.[180] However, the ostensible or apparent authority of the officer to make the decision may prevent the authority from taking enforcement action.[181] In light of this uncertainty, it is clearly unsafe to rely upon any assurances from planning officers regarding the need for planning permission and consideration should be given to applying for a CLOPUD.

---

[175] TCPSA 1997 s.271.

[176] TCPSA 1997 s.271(1)(cc) and (5), added by Town and Country Planning (Electronic Communications) (Scotland) Order 2004 (SSI 2004/332).

[177] TCPSA 1997 ss.147 and 181 and the Town and Country Planning (Enforcement of Control) (No.2) (Scotland) Regulations 1992 (SI 1992/2086) reg.7, as amended.

[178] *Thrasyvoulou v Secretary of State for the Environment* [1990] 2 A.C. 273; *Hammond v Secretary of State for the Environment* [1997] J.P.L. 724.

[179] *R. v Wychavon DC Ex p. Saunders* [1992] J.P.L. 753.

[180] *Western Fish Products v Penwith DC* [1981] 2 All E.R. 204; *R. (on the application of Repratech (Pebsham) Ltd) v East Sussex CC* [2002] J.P.L. 821.

[181] *Camden LBC v Secretary of State for the Environment* [1993] J.P.L. 1049; *Postermobile Plc v Brent*

LBC, The Times, 8 December 1997. See also Ch.8, "Sue for Negligence or Breach of Contract", below.

CHAPTER 8

CHALLENGE OF PLANNING DECISIONS

Prior to embarking on a challenge of a planning decision, it is essential to identify **8.01** the result that is sought and determine which, if any, procedure could achieve this result. For example, despite a successful judicial review petition, the Scottish Ministers or planning authority in re-deciding the matter may be free to reach the same decision, provided the decision is taken in the correct manner. Judicial review is, therefore, not always the most appropriate procedure for challenging decisions.

Other relevant factors in deciding which procedure to use include the existence of time limits and the availability of the remedies in the circumstances. The degree to which professional assistance will be necessary, with the resultant cost implications, will be an important consideration. None of the procedures discussed in this chapter necessarily require such assistance, and indeed some are deliberately informal to avoid intimidating non-professionals, but many persons will be unwilling to act without professional advice. The likelihood of a successful challenge using the procedure must also be assessed.

This chapter concentrates upon the options available to a person who wishes to challenge a decision upon a planning application, either at first instance or on appeal. However, procedures for challenging the exercise of other planning powers share the same general characteristics.

In 2009, significant changes were introduced to the procedures for challenging planning application decisions, followed by minor changes in 2013. Previously, all decisions by planning authorities on planning applications were subject to a right of appeal to the Scottish Ministers. Since 2009, a decision taken on an application for planning permission by a planning officer acting under certain delegated powers is subject to a right of review by a local review body (LRB), and the right of appeal to the Scottish Ministers is only available for other decisions by planning officers and for decisions taken by councillors. The decision by the LRB is final subject only to appeal to the Court of Session on points of law.[1]

Other changes introduced in 2009 include a reduction in the time limit for lodging an appeal/review from six to three months; a restriction on lodging new material as part of the appeal/review; and the removal of the right of the parties to dictate the type of procedure adopted for hearing the appeal/review.

---

[1] In *Sally Carroll v Scottish Borders Council* [2015] CSIH 73 none of the parties suggested that the statutory provisions relating to LRBs are incompatible with Convention rights or EU law; the Court held that the requirements of the Public Participation Directive (Directive 2003/35/EC providing for public participation in respect of the drawing up of certain plans and programmes relating to the environment and amending with regard to public participation and access to justice Council Directives 85/337/EEC and 96/61/EC OJ L156) had been satisfied.

NEGOTIATION/MEDIATION

8.02   Chapter 5 commenced with a reminder of the importance of consulting the planning authority for its views in advance of submitting a planning application. It is equally advisable to explore the possibility of negotiating a solution with the planning authority before formally challenging a decision. Formal procedures are expensive and time-consuming for both challenger and planning authority, and each should recognise the importance of compromise and avoidance of appeals. Mediation might be appropriate.[2]

If valid grounds of challenge can be shown, the planning authority may be willing to negotiate a compromise. Alternatively, the authority may be willing to give an informal indication that a revised proposal may be successful. Such an indication would enable submission of a fresh application for planning permission rather than a challenge to the original decision. Additional information not before the planning authority at the time of the decision may also provide scope for negotiation.

The procedures to commence a challenge may begin during negotiations to place more pressure on the planning authority to agree a compromise. However, such action carries the risk that the authority will withdraw from further negotiations. Whatever tactics are employed, care must be taken to ensure that any time limit for commencing the challenge does not expire. If necessary, a challenge can be commenced to prevent expiry of the time limit while the negotiations continue. If negotiations will be lengthy, the parties can agree that the challenge be sisted (suspended) in the meantime, although sists are harder to obtain now. It was once common to submit duplicate applications, enabling an appeal to be lodged in connection with one application while continuing negotiations with the authority on the other application, but this practice has fallen away (see Ch.5 above).

As a result of the inability of the planning authority to revoke a grant of planning permission without paying compensation or re-determine the matter in the absence of a fresh planning application, for all practical purposes negotiation with the authority is not a worthwhile option for third parties wishing to challenge a decision on a planning application. Such parties may, however, wish to seek reassurance on future decisions or that compliance with conditions attached to a grant of permission will be monitored and enforcement action taken against any breaches.

---

[2]   Scottish Government, *A Guide to the Use of Mediation in the Planning System in Scotland* (Scottish Government, 2009).

Fig.8.1 Planning appeals

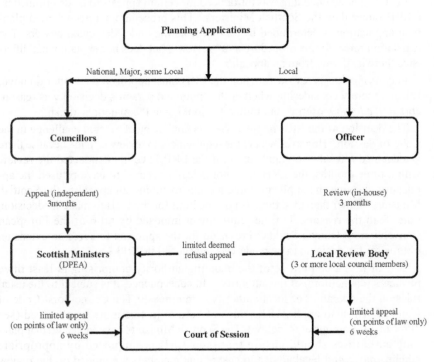

Reproduced by permission of Brodies LLP.

TYPES OF CHALLENGE

Although there are several different types of challenge mentioned in this chapter, **8.03** in general there is not a choice, as the circumstances of each case will mean that only one type of challenge is available.

The principal types of challenge discussed in this chapter are:

LRBs— these hear challenges to most decisions by local authority officers on applications for planning permission or for consent, agreement or approval.

Appeal to Scottish Ministers/reporter— this right of appeal is available for other decisions by local authority officers or councillors on planning applications and other planning decisions/orders.

Court of Session— the court hears appeals against decisions by LRBs and the Scottish Ministers/reporter. It can also review decisions by local authorities, but not where the decision can be reviewed by the LRB or appealed to the Scottish Ministers/reporter. As there is no third party right of appeal in Scotland, the only remedy available to a person other than the applicant for planning permission is to seek judicial review by the Court of Session.

LOCAL REVIEW BODY

8.04   In 2009 a new procedure was introduced for certain appeals to be determined by a LRB rather than the Scottish Ministers.[3] This procedure applies where a planning application is determined by an officer acting under delegated powers. The legislation refers to this procedure as a "review", but does not explain what difference there is, if any, from an appeal.[4]

In carrying out its review function the LRB must approach the matter do novo. It is not merely considering whether the appointed person's decision was reasonable in *Wednesbury* terms, but rather it is looking at the materials afresh.[5]

The decision of the LRB on the review is final, subject to legal challenge in the Court of Session.[6] However, where the requirement to review is made because there is a deemed refusal of an application, if the LRB have not conducted the review within three months, the LRB are automatically deemed to have refused the application, leaving the applicant three months to submit an appeal to the Scottish Ministers.[7] Other than this, there is no time limit for the LRB to make its decision, other than the reasonable time requirement imposed by art.6 of the European Convention on Human Rights.[8] Provision for the applicant to agree an extension of time for the decision to be made was introduced in 2013.[9]

The LRB is a committee of the planning authority comprising at least three members (councillors) of the authority.[10] In consequence, it is subject to the usual rules on the operation of local authority committees.[11] The Councillors' Code of Conduct will also apply.[12] The rules of natural justice must be observed (see "Procedural Impropriety", below). The Scottish Ministers have indicated that planning authorities should ensure that their LRB is supported by appropriate administrative and legal advice to ensure that members are guided on the review

---

[3]   See Ferguson and Watchman, *Local Planning Reviews in Scotland* (Edinburgh: Avizandum, 2015). Best Practice Guidance Notes for LRBs are published on the Scottish Government website (see *http://www.gov.scot/topics/built-environment/planning/aboutappeals/bestpractice* [Accessed 11 April 2016]).

[4]   In *Sally Carroll v Scottish Borders Council* [2015] CSIH 73 at [56], the Court indicated that the LRB should apply a similar level of scrutiny or consideration as an appeal reporter. See also letter from Chief Planner to all heads of planning dated 29 July 2011, confirming the Scottish Government's view that the "de novo" approach should be adopted in determining cases brought before LRBs (see *http://www.gov.scot/Topics/Built-Environment/planning/Roles/Scottish-Government/Guidance/ChiefPlannerLetters* [Accessed 11 April 2016]).

[5]   *Sally Carroll v Scottish Borders Council* [2015] CSIH 73 at [55(6)].

[6]   Town and Country Planning (Scotland) Act 1997 (TCPSA) ss.47(1A), 237(3A) and 239(4).

[7]   TCPSA 1997 s.43A(17) and Town and Country Planning (Schemes of Delegation and Local Review Procedure) (Scotland) Regulations 2013 (LRPR) (SSI 2013/157) reg.8(3). Note the LRB are automatically deemed to have refused the application, whereas in other situations it is at the option of the applicant that the application is deemed to have been refused. The time limit was previously two months.

[8]   *Lafarge Aggregates Ltd v Scottish Ministers*, 2004 S.C. 524.

[9]   TCPSA 1997 s.43A(8), as amended by Public Services Reform (Planning) (Local Review Procedure) (Scotland) Order 2013 (SSI 2013/24).

[10]   LRPR 2013 (SSI 2013/157) reg.7.

[11]   Local Government (Scotland) Act 1973 Pt IIIA, "Access to meetings and documents of local authorities, committees and subcommittees".

[12]   Standards Commission Scotland, *Code of Conduct for Councillors* (Scottish Government, 2010). The National Park Authorities have separate Codes of Conduct for their members.

process, and that those administrative arrangements respect the principles of fairness and transparency that must underpin the operation of the new system.[13]

Meetings at which the LRB decides the manner in which the review is to be conducted, or as to how the case under review is to be determined, are to be held in public.[14] However, there is no automatic right for the applicant or any other person to make oral representations (see para.8.19 below).

Availability

The applicant (and no other person) has a right to require the LRB to review a case where the planning application is decided by a planning officer acting under s.43A delegated powers.[15] The right to require a review applies where the officer:

8.05

(a) refuses an application for planning permission or for consent, agreement or approval[16];

(b) grants it subject to conditions (procedures for challenging planning conditions are examined in Ch.6)[17];

(c) is deemed to have decided to refuse the application because the officer has not determined it within the period prescribed (see para.8.06 below).[18]

Decisions by officers on other types of planning applications, for example, for major or national developments, or for other types of permission, such as listed building consent, conservation area consent, hazardous substances consent or advertisement consent, remain subject to rights of appeal to the Scottish Ministers.[19]

If there is any doubt about whether the decision is subject to review by the LRB or appeal to the Scottish Ministers/reporter, clarification should be sought well within the relevant time limit. There have been instances of decision notices issued by planning authorities containing erroneous information on review/appeal procedures.

---

[13] Planning Circular 5/2013, Schemes of Delegation and Local Reviews (Scottish Government, 2013) para.31.

[14] LRPR 2013 (SSI 2013/157) reg.7(2).

[15] TCPSA 1997 s.43A(8) and (9). The officer is appointed by the scheme of delegation (see Ch.5 above). The right to review by the LRB only applies to delegation under a s.43A scheme of delegation, not under the powers conferred by the Local Government (Scotland) Act 1973.

[16] For example, an approval required under the Permitted Development Order (PDO) (see Ch.4 above)

[17] This includes review of the time period imposed for the commencement of development TCPSA 1997 ss.58(3) and 59(6), as amended by the Planning Etc. (Scotland) Act 2006 (Consequential Amendments) Order 2009 (SSI 2009/256) art.5.

[18] Where the requirement to review is made under this ground, if the planning authority have not conducted the review within three months beginning with the date on which the requirement to review is made, the authority are deemed to have decided to refuse the application, and the applicant can submit an appeal to the Scottish Ministers—TCPSA 1997 s.43A(17) and LRPR 2013 (SSI 2013/157) reg.8(3).

[19] A development might require applications for planning permission and other consents such as listed building consent. If all these applications are determined by the same officer using different delegated powers, the applicant would require review of the planning application decision by the LRB and submit an appeal(s) to the Scottish Ministers on the other decisions. A practical answer might be for the appeals to be sisted pending the outcome of the review. Planning Circular 5/2013, Schemes of Delegation and Local Reviews, para.17 says that it is for the planning authority to determine the most effective route to determine related applications.

Time limit

8.06   The notice of review must be lodged within three months of[20]:

(a)   the notice of the decision on the application; or

(b)   in the case of a deemed refusal, two months after the validation date (four months for a development which requires environmental impact assessment)[21]; or

(c)   the expiry of any extended period agreed in writing between the applicant and the planning officer.[22]

This time limit is absolute and any notice of review lodged late will be rejected as invalid.

These statutory provisions are similar to those for planning appeals. The guidance for planning appeals (see para.8.11 below) is that the appeal must be submitted before the end of the third month. For example, if the date of the planning authority's decision notice is 1 September, the appeal must be submitted on or before 30 November.

Grounds of challenge

8.07   The notice of review must include a statement setting out the applicant's reasons for requiring the LRB to review the case.[23] All matters which the applicant intends to raise in the review must be set out in or accompany the notice of review (see "Procedure", below).

Although the LRB are required to determine the review in accordance with the provisions of the development plan unless material considerations indicate otherwise (see para.5.42), the statutory provisions prohibit any person raising a matter which was not before the planning officer at the time the determination reviewed was made, unless that person can demonstrate that the matter could not have been raised before that time, or that its not being raised before that time was a consequence of exceptional circumstances.[24] This is discussed further below (see para.8.14).

The notice of review will indicate the reasons why planning permission ought to be granted for the proposed development or granted on different terms from those imposed by the planning officer. Unlike a challenge in the courts, these reasons may involve discussion of the planning merits of the application and other factual matters. The planning merits of a proposed development stem from the provisions of the development plan and other material considerations (see Ch.5 above). Appropriate reference can therefore be made to relevant law, policies in the development plans, any other relevant policies of the planning authority, and the advice given to planning authorities by the Scottish Ministers through circulars and other documents (see Ch.2 above).

The applicant may wish to stress the reasons why permission should be granted

---

[20]   LRPR 2013 (SSI 2013/157) reg.9(2).
[21]   LRPR 2013 (SSI 2013/157) reg.8, as amended by the Town and Country Planning (Miscellaneous Provisions) (Scotland) Regulations 2015 (SSI 2015/249) reg.8.
[22]   TCPSA 1997 s.43A(8), as amended by Public Services Reform (Planning) (Local Review Procedure) (Scotland) Order 2013 (SSI 2013/24).
[23]   LRPR 2013 (SSI 2013/157) reg.9(4).
[24]   TCPSA 1997 s.43B.

for the proposed development, by reference to development plan policies and the material considerations outlined in Ch.5. Alternatively, or in addition, the applicant can argue that the reasons given by the planning officer for the decision are wrong, based on erroneous information, or insufficient to overcome the presumption in favour of development. There is no single correct approach, but all matters must be stated in the notice of review.

Procedure

As there are similarities in the review and appeal procedures, these are considered together below (para.8.13).

8.08

APPEAL TO THE SCOTTISH MINISTERS

Applicants for planning permission have a statutory right of appeal to the Scottish Ministers in respect of the decision on their application by the planning authority (other than decisions which are subject to review by LRB, see above).[25] There are rights of appeal to the Scottish Ministers in connection with other forms of planning decisions. Unless otherwise stated, these follow a similar procedure.[26] In most cases, the power of the Scottish Ministers to determine appeals has been delegated to full-time qualified officials known as reporters (equivalent to the inspectors in England and Wales).[27] The Scottish Ministers retain the power to recall for decision exceptional or important cases within the classes of delegated appeals. These cases, together with non-delegated appeals, are decided by the Scottish Ministers after consideration of the report made by the reporter who heard the appeal. The administration of planning appeals is handled by the Scottish Government Directorate of Planning and Environmental Appeals (DPEA).

8.09

The Scottish Ministers/reporter may deal with the appeal as though it were an application made to him/her in the first instance.[28]

The Scottish Ministers/reporter may not necessarily be an independent and impartial tribunal as required by art.6 of the European Convention on Human Rights, but the statutory right of appeal to the Court of Session against the decision by the Ministers/reporter satisfies art.6.[29]

Article 6 also requires the Ministers/reporter to determine the appeal within a reasonable time.[30]

Availability

The applicant (and no other person) has a right of appeal to the Scottish Ministers against:

8.10

    (a) a refusal of permission by the planning authority, or against any condi-

---

[25] TCPSA 1997 s.47; Town and Country Planning (Appeals) (Scotland) Regulations 2013 (TCPASR) (SSI 2013/156).

[26] TCPASR 2013 extends these appeals procedures to listed building and conservation area controls and advertisements—reg.1. Planning Circular 4/2013, Planning Appeals (Scottish Government, 2013) paras 12–14 list the statutory provisions to which the appeal procedures apply.

[27] TCPSA 1997 Sch.4; Town and Country Planning (Determination of Appeals by Appointed Persons) (Prescribed Classes) (Scotland) Regulations 2010 (SI 2010/467), as amended.

[28] TCPSA 1997 s.48(1).

[29] *County Properties Ltd v Scottish Ministers*, 2001 S.L.T. 1125.

[30] *Lafarge Redland Aggregates Ltd v Scottish Ministers*, 2000 S.L.T. 1361.

tions imposed on the grant of permission (procedures for challenging planning conditions are examined in Ch.6);

(b) a refusal by the planning authority of an application for any consent, agreement or approval required by a condition imposed on a grant of planning permission, or against any conditions imposed on such consent, agreement or approval;

(c) a refusal by the planning authority of an application for any approval required under any development order (for example, the PDO, see Ch.4 above), or against any conditions imposed on such approval;

(d) a deemed refusal of permission, where the planning authority has failed either to notify the applicant of its decision on the application, or give notice that it has exercised its power to decline to determine the application, or that the application has been called in by the Scottish Ministers for decision (see Ch.5 above)[31];

(e) a deemed refusal of permission by the LRB on a review, but only where the requirement to review is made because the officer is deemed to have refused the application.[32]

There is no right of appeal to the Ministers against:

(a) decisions which are subject to review by LRB (see above);

(b) a decision of a LRB on a review (see above). The relevant procedure for challenge is appeal to the Court of Session.[33]

The introduction of LRBs in 2009 means that decisions on different types of planning application are subject to different procedures for challenge. Broadly, where the application is decided, or due to be decided, by a planning officer acting under delegated powers, the procedure for challenge is to seek review by the LRB. Decisions on other types of planning applications, for example, for major or national developments, or for other types of permission, such as listed building consent, conservation area consent, hazardous substances consent or advertisement consent, remain subject to rights of appeal to the Scottish Ministers. Where a development requires applications for planning permission and other consents such as listed building consent, these applications might be determined by the same officer but using different delegated powers, with the result that the planning application decision is subject to review by the LRB and the other decisions are subject to appeal to the Scottish Ministers, despite the issues being related and overlapping.[34]

If there is any doubt about whether the decision is subject to review by the LRB or appeal to the Scottish Ministers/reporter, clarification should be sought well within the relevant time limit. There have been instances of decision notices issued by planning authorities containing erroneous information on review/appeal procedures.

---

[31] TCPSA 1997 s.47.
[32] TCPSA 1997 s.43A(17) and LRPR 2013 (SSI 2013/157) reg.8(3).
[33] TCPSA 1997 ss.43A(16), 47(1A) and 237(3A).
[34] A practical answer might be for the appeals to be sisted pending the outcome of the review. Planning Circular 5/2013, Schemes of Delegation and Local Reviews, para.17 says that it is for the planning authority to determine the most effective route to determine related applications.

Time limit

The notice of appeal must be lodged within three months of[35]:   **8.11**

(a) the notice of the decision of the planning authority on the application; or
(b) in the case of a deemed refusal, the expiry of two months from the date of
     validation of the application (four months for national or major develop-
     ments (see "Hierarchy of Developments", Ch.5 above), or if the applica-
     tion includes an environmental statement), or the expiry of any extended
     period agreed upon in writing by the applicant and the planning authority.[36]

This time limit is absolute and any appeal lodged late will be rejected as invalid.

The guidance from DPEA is that the appeal must be submitted before the end of
the third month. For example, if the date of the planning authority's decision notice
is 1 September, the appeal must be submitted on or before 30 November.[37]

Grounds of challenge

The notice of appeal must include a statement setting out full particulars of the   **8.12**
appeal including a note of what matters the appellant considers require to be taken
into account in determining the appeal. All matters which the appellant intends to
raise in the appeal must be set out in or accompany the notice, or be in the documents which accompany the notice of appeal. There is a general prohibition on raising any other matters.[38] All documents, materials and evidence which the appellant intends to rely on must also accompany the notice.

Although the appeal must be determined in accordance with the provisions of the
development plan unless material considerations indicate otherwise (see para.5.42),
the statutory provisions prohibit any person raising a matter which was not before
the planning authority at the time the determination appealed against was made, unless that person can demonstrate that the matter could not have been raised before
that time, or that its not being raised before that time was a consequence of
exceptional circumstances.[39] This is discussed further below (see para.8.14).

There is also a prohibition on varying the application after the appeal has been
submitted.[40]

In most appeals to the Scottish Ministers there is essentially only one ground of
challenge: that planning permission ought to be granted for the proposed
development. It would be competent but inadvisable for the appellant to do no more
than state this ground. The Scottish Ministers (or their reporter) have power to deal
with the application afresh, as if it had been made to them in the first instance.[41] The

---

35 TCPASR 2013 (SSI 2013/156) reg.3(3). Previously the time limit was six months.
36 TCPASR 2013 (SSI 2013/156) reg.3(2). The extension must be agreed prior to the expiry of the
    initial two or four-month period—*Vattenfall Wind Power Ltd v Scottish Ministers*, 2009 S.L.T. 516.
37 DPEA, *Notes for Appellants—PPA* (Scottish Government, 2015).
38 TCPASR 2013 (SSI 2013/156) reg.3(6). Further matters and documents, materials or evidence can
    be submitted if permitted by reg.4 (comment on planning authority's response); reg.5 (comment on
    representations by interested parties); reg.11 (further representations in response to procedure notice);
    the Hearing Session Rules; and the Inquiry Session Rules.
39 TCPSA 1997 s.47A.
40 TCPSA 1997 s.32A(3).
41 TCPSA 1997 s.48(1). For example, *Dalfaber Action Group v Scottish Ministers*, 2007 G.W.D. 39-
    688, in which it was held that the reporter was not limited to granting permission for the develop-
    ment as it stood or refusing permission.

planning merits of the application may, therefore, be assessed without any further input from the appellant other than the information which appears in the planning application. This is the inevitable result of the presumption in favour of development (see Ch.5 above), which is the usual starting point for grounds of appeal.

It is advisable for the appellant to expand on the reasons why planning permission ought to be granted to ensure that all the relevant points are put before the reporter. Rather than rely on the presumption in favour of development, the appellant may wish to stress the reasons why permission should be granted for the proposed development, by reference to the policies in the development plan and the material considerations outlined in Ch.5. Alternatively, or in addition, the appellant can argue that the reasons given by the planning authority for its decision are wrong, based on erroneous information, or insufficient to overcome the presumption. There is no single correct approach, but all the grounds of appeal must be stated on the form before the appeal is submitted.

Unlike a challenge in the courts, the grounds of appeal may involve discussion of the planning merits of the application and other factual matters. The planning merits of a proposed development stem from the provisions of the development plan and other material considerations (see Ch.5 above). Appropriate reference can therefore be made to relevant law, policies in the development plan, any other relevant policies of the planning authority, and the advice given to planning authorities by the Scottish Ministers through circulars and other documents (see Ch.2 above). The report to the planning committee on the application, prepared by the planning officer and obtainable by members of the public through the access to information rules, is a useful starting point for gathering this information. The complexity or importance of the proposed development will dictate how much reference to such documents is required.

APPEAL/REVIEW PROCEDURE

8.13   Although there are separate statutory provisions, the procedures for appeals and reviews are very similar. The following section therefore considers the procedures together. Reference is made to the "appellant" for appeal procedures and the "applicant" for review procedures.

Fundamental changes were made to the procedures in 2009 and further changes in 2013. In addition to the introduction of the review procedure, the procedures have been "frontloaded", with a requirement that full details of the case are submitted at the beginning of the procedure rather than in the lead-up to an hearing or inquiry. There are also general prohibitions on raising a matter which was not before the planning officer/authority at the time the determination appealed/reviewed was made (see para.8.14 below), and on varying a planning application after an appeal has been made (see para.8.12 above).

In most instances, appeals are decided by the "appointed person", normally a reporter acting under powers delegated by the Scottish Ministers.[42] The same procedures apply whether the planning appeal is decided by the appointed person,

---

[42]   TCPSA 1997 Sch.4 para.1.

or by the Ministers after considering his/her report.[43] Similar procedures also apply to applications called-in by the Ministers (see para.5.91).[44]

Electronic communication can be used for any notice, consent, agreement, decision, representation, statement, report or other information or communication, providing the recipient consents to receive it electronically. Where a person uses electronic communication, that person is taken to have agreed to the use of electronic communications, unless and until the person gives notice to revoke the agreement.[45]

Until the appeal/review is determined, the planning authority must make available for inspection at their office the papers in relation to the appeal/review, and afford any person who requests the opportunity to inspect and, where practicable, take copies.[46]

(a) Notice of appeal/notice of review

Each procedure is initiated by the applicant serving notice.[47]   **8.14**

The notice of appeal uses a form obtained from the Scottish Ministers, and the notice of review uses a form obtained from the planning authority. The notice must include the name and address of the appellant/applicant for review; the date and reference number assigned by the planning authority to the application being appealed/reviewed; the name and address of the representative of the appellant/applicant (if any) and whether any notice or other correspondence should be sent to the representative instead of the appellant/applicant.

The notice of appeal must include a statement setting out full particulars of the appeal including a note of what matters the appellant considers require to be taken into account in determining the appeal. The notice of review must include a statement setting out the applicant's reasons for requiring the LRB to review the case. Notices of appeal and review both require to indicate the procedure (or combination of procedures) the appellant/applicant wishes the appeal/review to follow. However, it is the reporter/LRB which makes the decision on the procedure to be used, and it is not bound to follow the appellant/applicant's request (see para.8.19 below).

The determining issues in selecting which further procedure, if any, to request are the complexity and importance of the issues involved, any dispute as to the facts, and the suitability of written or oral submissions for deciding these issues. It may also be relevant that the written submissions procedure is quicker. If the appellant/applicant is paying for professional advice or assistance, written submissions procedure will also be cheaper. In appeals, inquiry procedure is appropriate where the disputed issues are best explored through cross-examination.

All matters which the appellant/applicant intends to raise in the appeal/review must be set out in the notice or in the accompanying documents. There is a general prohibition on raising a matter which was not before the planning officer/authority

---

43   TCPASR 2013 (SSI 2013/156) reg.26.
44   TCPASR 2013 (SSI 2013/156) reg.24.
45   TCPASR 2013 (SSI 2013/156) reg.32; LRPR 2013 (SSI 2013/157) reg.23.
46   TCPASR 2013 (SSI 2013/156) reg.6; LRPR 2013 (SSI 2013/157) reg.11 and definition of "review documents" in reg.2.
47   TCPASR 2013 (SSI 2013/156) reg.3; LRPR 2013 (SSI 2013/157) reg.9.

at the time the determination appealed/reviewed was made.[48] There is a general prohibition on raising any other matters not included in the notice of appeal/review.[49] The Scottish Government guidance interprets "matter" as "issue", permitting new information on an existing issue to be submitted.[50] All documents, materials and evidence which the appellant/applicant intends to rely on must also accompany the notice.[51]

The appellant is required to send the planning authority a copy of the notice of appeal; a list of all documents, materials and evidence which accompanied the notice of appeal; and a copy of all such documents, materials and evidence listed which have not already been provided to the planning authority in connection with the application.[52] There is no similar requirement in review procedure (the LRB is a committee of the planning authority, so the notice of review is submitted to the planning authority).

(b) Notice by planning authority/LRB

8.15   Within 14 days following notification of the appeal/review, the planning authority must give notice of the appeal to each interested party,[53] which means any statutory consultee which lodged representations on the application with the planning authority which were not subsequently withdrawn, and any other person who submitted representations on the application within the prescribed period. Notice may be given by post or newspaper advertisement, depending on the circumstances.[54]

The notice states that copies of the representations previously made on the application will be taken into account in the determination of the appeal/review, but includes information on how any further representations may be made. An interested party has 14 days from the date on which notice is given to make further representations to the Ministers/LRB as appropriate. The Ministers/LRB are to send the appellant/applicant a copy of such representations and give the appellant/applicant at least 14 days to make comments on the representations. In an appeal, the Ministers must also send the planning authority a copy of the representations

---

48   TCPSA 1997 s.47A for appeals, and s.43B for reviews. However, the appeal/review must be determined in accordance with the provisions of the development plan unless material considerations indicate otherwise, which suggests scope for raising "new" development plan issues or material considerations.

49   TCPASR 2013 (SSI 2013/156) reg.3(6); LRPR 2013 (SSI 2013/157) reg.9(5). Further matters and documents, materials or evidence can be submitted if permitted by TCPASR 2013 (SSI 2013/156) reg.4 (comment on planning authority's response); reg.5 (comment on representations by interested parties); reg.11 (further representations in response to procedure notice); the Hearing Session Rules; and the Inquiry Session Rules; or, for reviews, if permitted by LRPR 2013 (SSI 2013/157) reg.15 (written submissions) and the Hearing Session Rules.

50   Planning Circular 4/2013, Planning Appeals, para.22; Planning Circular 5/2013, Schemes of Delegation and Local Reviews, para.25 uses the term "matter", but appears to provide similar guidance. See also DPEA, Reporter Guidance Note 16: *New matters and the submission of documents, materials or evidence* (Scottish Government, 2014).

51   Documents which are to be referred to in evidence were previously known as productions. These can include plans, maps and diagrams, photographs, models, video and audio recordings.

52   TCPASR 2013 (SSI 2013/156) reg.4.

53   "Interested party" is defined by TCPASR 2013 (SSI 2013/156) reg.2; LRPR 2013 (SSI 2013/157) reg.2.

54   TCPASR 2013 (SSI 2013/156) reg.5(2); LRPR 2013 (SSI 2013/157) reg.10(2).

and give them at least 14 days to make comments.[55] In a review, there is no requirement for the LRB to send a copy of the representations to the planning officer whose decision is being reviewed.

The LRB has additional duties: within 14 days following notification of the review, the LRB must send an acknowledgment to the applicant and inform the applicant how documents related to the review may be inspected[56]; and if any neighbour notification or consultation procedures on the planning application have not been undertaken or completed, the LRB must undertake or complete those procedures.[57]

(c) Responses to appeal/review

The planning authority's response to the appeal must be sent to the Scottish Ministers and the appellant within 21 days from the date of receipt of the notice of appeal.[58] In practice, this is referred to as the PARF. The response must set out the matters the planning authority consider require to be taken into account in determining the appeal and by what procedure (or combination of procedures) the authority wish the appeal conducted. The authority must also send copies of: any documents not specified on the appellant's list which were before the planning authority and which were taken into account in reaching their decision; any report on handling prepared in respect of the application; and the conditions (if any) which the planning authority presently consider should be imposed in the event that the Ministers/reporter decide that permission should be granted.

8.16

In a review, there is no requirement for the applicant or LRB to send a copy of the notice of review to the planning officer whose decision is being reviewed, so no procedure is specified by the statutory provisions for the planning officer to submit comments.

An interested party has 14 days from the date on which notice is given to that party by the Ministers/LRB to make further representations to the Ministers/LRB as appropriate. There is no provision for representations by other persons.

(d) Counter responses from appellant/applicant

The appellant has 14 days from date of receipt of the planning authority's response to send to the Ministers and the planning authority comments on any matters raised in the response which had not been raised in the decision notice on the application; and any documents, materials or evidence on which the appellant intends to rely in relation to such comments.[59] In a review, the statutory procedures do not refer to a planning authority response, so there is no procedure specified for a response by the applicant.

8.17

The appellant/applicant also must be given at least 14 days to make comments on representations submitted by an interested party.

---

55 TCPASR 2013 (SSI 2013/156) reg.5; LRPR 2013 (SSI 2013/157) reg.10, "interested party" is
    defined by reg.2 in both sets of regulations.
56 LRPR 2013 (SSI 2013/157) reg.10(1)(a).
57 LRPR 2013 (SSI 2013/157) reg.20.
58 TCPASR 2013 (SSI 2013/156) reg.4(2).
59 TCPASR 2013 (SSI 2013/156) reg.4(3).

There are no specific rights for any party to make further comments or responses, but the appointed person/LRB can request further submissions (see para.8.19 below).

(e)   Determination without further procedure

8.18   In an appeal, the Scottish Ministers will appoint a person, usually a reporter, either to determine the appeal or to provide them with a report enabling them to determine the appeal. Where the appointed person considers that no further representations or information is required to enable the appeal to be determined, he/she may determine the appeal without further procedure.[60] The LRB have the same power where they consider that the review documents provide sufficient informa- tion to enable them to make their decision.[61] This is a departure from the pre-2009 appeal procedures which gave the appellant and/or the planning authority the right to require a oral hearing.[62]

(f)   Further procedure—procedure notice

8.19   The appointed person/LRB can at any stage of the appeal/review decide that further representations should be made or further information should be provided to enable the appeal/review to be determined. The appeal/review can be conducted by one or a combination of the following procedures: written submissions; the hold- ing of one or more hearing sessions; the holding of one or more inquiry sessions (appeals only); and a site inspection.[63] A pre-examination meeting can be held to consider the manner in which the appeal/review or any stage of the appeal/review is to be conducted.[64] The Scottish Ministers anticipate that pre-examination meet- ings will only be required in complex cases.[65]

There is no government guidance on the relevant factors in selecting the further procedure(s).[66] Potential factors include the complexity and importance of the is- sues involved, any dispute as to the facts or competing expert opinion, and the suit- ability of written or oral submissions for deciding these issues. In appeals, inquiry procedure is appropriate where the disputed issues are best explored through cross- examination.

The further procedure is initiated by service of a procedure notice.[67] Only mat- ters specified in the procedure notice are to be considered in the written submis- sions or hearing or inquiry session. This is a change from the former appeals procedure, and requires a degree of focus from the appointed person/LRB about what the determining issues appear to be, what amongst these issues requires further

---

[60]   TCPASR 2013 (SSI 2013/156) reg.7.
[61]   LRPR 2013 (SSI 2013/157) reg.12.
[62]   Although the Scottish Ministers anticipate no further procedure in the majority of reviews (Plan- ning Circular 5/2013, Schemes of Delegation and Local Reviews, paras 37 and 38), they do not com- ment on how often this might apply to appeals, presumably because appeals will generally involve more significant/complex cases.
[63]   TCPASR 2013 (SSI 2013/156) reg.9; LRPR 2013 (SSI 2013/157) reg.13.
[64]   TCPASR 2013 (SSI 2013/156) reg.10; LRPR 2013 (SSI 2013/157) reg.14.
[65]   Planning Circular 4/2013, Planning Appeals, para.42; Planning Circular 5/2013, Schemes of Delega- tion and Local Reviews, para.39.
[66]   But see DPEA, Reporters Guidance Note 8: *Deciding Further Procedure* (Scottish Government, 2014).
[67]   Defined by TCPASR 2013 (SSI 2013/156) and LRPR 2013 (SSI 2013/157) reg.2.

discussion, and what may have been adequately covered in the documents already submitted.

In planning appeals, the appointed person can write to interested parties seeking their confirmation that they wish to be involved in the further procedure.[68] At least 14 days must be allowed for them to serve an opt-in notice.

(g) Written submissions

The written submissions procedure is initiated by the procedure notice, served **8.20** by the appointed person/LRB. It sets out the matters on which such further representations or information is requested; specifies the date by which the representations/information is to be sent to the appointed person/LRB; and provides the name and address of any other body or person to whom a similar request has been made.[69]

The procedure notice is served on the appellant/applicant, the planning authority (appeal only) and any other body or person from whom the appointed person/ LRB wishes to receive further representations or information. There is no requirement for the procedure notice to be copied to other bodies or persons who submitted representations in response to the notice of appeal/review.

The recipient of the procedure notice sends the requested representations/ information to the appointed person/LRB on or before the specified date, and sends a copy to the appellant/applicant, the planning authority (in an appeal only) and to such other bodies or persons specified in the notice. This is referred to as the procedure notice response. There is 14 days from receipt of the copy to send comments in reply..

If the reply includes any new evidence, the appointed person/LRB must provide recipients of the procedure notice with an opportunity of making representations.[70] It is unclear how this interacts with the general prohibitions on raising any matter not before the planning officer/authority at the time the determination appealed/ reviewed was made, and on raising any matters not included in the notice of appeal/ review.[71]

A site inspection can be made in conjunction with this written submissions procedure (see para.8.25 below).

(h) Hearings

The Hearings Session Rules apply to a hearing.[72] **8.21**

The hearing is initiated by the appointed person/LRB serving a procedure notice on the appellant/applicant; the planning authority (appeal only); any interested party who made representations in relation to the specified matters set out in the procedure notice; and any other body or person from whom the appointed person/LRB wishes

---

68 TCPASR 2013 (SSI 2013/156) reg.8. Planning Circular 4/2013, Planning Appeals, para.39 explains the aim is to avoid repeatedly sending information about the progress of an appeal to people who, though they may be interested in the case and want their original views to be considered, do not want to be involved in any further appeal procedure.

69 TCPASR 2013 (SSI 2013/156) reg.11; LRPR 2013 (SSI 2013/157) reg.15.

70 TCPASR 2013 (SSI 2013/156) reg.13; LRPR 2013 (SSI 2013/157) reg.17.

71 TCPSA 1997 s.47A for appeals, and s.43B for reviews; TCPASR 2013 (SSI 2013/156) reg.3(6); LRPR 2013 (SSI 2013/157) reg.9(5).

72 TCPASR 2013 (SSI 2013/156) regs 2, 9(5)(b) and Sch.1; LRPR 2013 (SSI 2013/157) regs 2, 13(5)(b) and Sch.1.

to receive further representations or to provide further information on specified matters at the hearing session. There is no requirement for the procedure notice to be copied to other bodies or persons who submitted representations in response to the notice of appeal/review.

The notice sets out the matters which are to be considered at the hearing. No other matters are to be considered at the hearing.

An assessor may be appointed to sit with the appointed person/LRB at a hearing session to advise on such matters arising as the Ministers/LRB may specify. Every person entitled to appear at the hearing session must be notified of the name of the assessor and of the matters on which the assessor is to advise. After the close of the hearing, the assessor may make a written report to the appointed person/LRB on the matters on which he/she was appointed to advise.[73]

Recipients of the procedure notice have 14 days from date of the notice to inform in writing the appointed person/LRB of their intention to appear at the hearing.

The persons entitled to appear at hearings are the appellant/applicant; and any other person or body, who in response to a procedure notice, has informed the appointed person/LRB of their intention to appear at the hearing. The planning authority have the right to appear at an appeal hearing, but not a review hearing. No other person or body is entitled to participate in the hearing. The review hearing must be held in public, so any person can attend, but there is no requirement for an appeal hearing to be open to the public.

The date, time and place of the hearing is determined, and may subsequently be varied, by the appointed person/LRB. Reasonable notice of the date, time and place must be given to the persons entitled to appear at the hearing.

It is open to the appointed person/LRB to require parties to submit a hearing statement, and, if they intend to refer to or rely on any documents when presenting their case, a list of all such documents and a copy of every document (or the relevant part) on that list which is not already available for inspection. Different dates can be specified for submission of the hearing statement and the documents.[74] The statement and any documents must be sent to the appointed person/LRB, the appellant/applicant, the planning authority (appeals only) and such other persons entitled to appear at the hearing session as the appointed person/LRB may specify in the notice. The planning authority must afford to any person who requests a reasonable opportunity to inspect and, where practicable, take copies of any hearing statement or other document submitted in connection with the hearing.

A hearing statement is a written statement which sets out fully the case relating to the matters specified for the hearing which a person proposes to put forward at the hearing session. It also contains a list of documents (if any) which the person putting forward the case intends to refer to or rely on; and a list of any other persons who are to speak at the hearing session in respect of the case, any matters which such persons are particularly to address and any relevant qualifications of such persons to do so.[75] There is no requirement to mention that the person intends to be represented by a lawyer at the hearing.

---

[73] TCPASR 2013 (SSI 2013/156) reg.30; LRPR 2013 (SSI 2013/157) reg.21. Planning Circular 5/2013, Schemes of Delegation and Local Reviews, para.53 and Planning Circular 4/2013, Planning Appeals, para.102 indicate that appointment of an assessor will be infrequent.

[74] For planning inquiries, the usual practice is for documents to be submitted in advance of witness statements (precognitions), which enables comments to be included in the statements about the contents of the documents.

[75] Such persons are in effect being called as witnesses.

There is no prohibition in the rules against evidence being given at the hearing on matters not mentioned in the hearing statement but, if those matters are sufficiently material and new, natural justice may require the hearing to be adjourned to provide the other parties with an opportunity to address those matters.

The appointed person/LRB can require by notice in writing any person who has served a hearing statement to provide such further information about matters contained in the statement as the appointed person/LRB may specify.

The procedure at the hearing is determined by the appointed person/LRB, except as otherwise provided in the Hearing Session Rules. In the absence of the adversarial procedures of an inquiry, the appointed person/LRB has an inquisitorial burden to investigate the facts, and failure to take the necessary steps to inform him/themselves of the case could mean that the decision is invalid because the appellant/applicant was not given a fair hearing.[76] There is an overriding legal requirement to provide natural justice (see "Procedural Impropriety" below)—in particular, each party must be given an opportunity to present their case and respond to the case presented by other parties.

The appointed person/LRB must state at or before the commencement of the hearing the procedure which they propose to adopt, having considered any submission by the persons entitled to appear at the hearing. In particular, the appointed person/LRB are to state: the order in which the specified matters are to be considered; and the order in which the persons entitled to appear are to be heard in relation to a specified matter (a different order may be chosen for different specified matters).

The hearing takes the form of a discussion led by the appointed person/LRB. Cross-examination is not permitted in an appeal hearing, but in a review hearing the LRB can permit cross-examination if it is required to ensure a thorough examination of the issues.[77] A person entitled to appear at a hearing may appear on their own behalf or be represented by another person. Where there are two or more persons having a similar interest in the issues being considered, the LRB/appointed person may allow one or more persons to appear on behalf of some or all of any persons so interested. The hearing can proceed in the absence of any person entitled to appear.

The LRB may refuse to permit the giving or production of evidence, cross-examination, or the presentation of any other matter, which the LRB consider to be irrelevant or repetitious.

The appointed person/LRB may from time to time adjourn the hearing. Notice of the date, time and place of the adjourned hearing session can be announced before the adjournment; if not, reasonable notice of the date, time and place must be given to the persons entitled to appear.

A site inspection may be made by the appointed person/LRB before, during or after the hearing (see para.8.25 below).

---

[76] *Dyason v Secretary of State for the Environment, Transport and the Regions* [1998] J.P.L. 778.

[77] The Scottish Ministers anticipate that it would only be exceptionally that cross-examination would be required, Planning Circular 5/2013, Schemes of Delegation and Local Reviews, para.45; for example, where the reliability of expert evidence is being disputed—*Errington v Wilson*, 1995 S.C. 550.

(i) Inquiries

8.22   In appeals, but not reviews, an inquiry may be held.[78] At an inquiry the issues are presented through the giving of evidence by and cross-examination of witnesses.

The parties need to decide which witnesses to call to deal with the matters set out in the procedure notice. The objective is to call witnesses who can provide evidence which will persuade the appointed person. Although there is no requirement to call expert witnesses, such as planning consultants, landscape architects, and transportation engineers, the testimony of an expert witness is often more persuasive on a technical issue.

Expert witnesses are entitled to express their professional opinion on the issues involved in the appeal which are within the area of their expertise.[79] However, this can be a double-edged sword. During cross-examination an expert witness can be asked for his/her professional opinion on a point, and will be forced to voice this opinion even if it is contrary to the case being pursued by the party who called the witness to give evidence. Questioning during the cross-examination of an expert witness may therefore provide support for the opposing case.

The planning authority will normally call the planning officer who dealt with the application (or his/her superior) as the main witness. However, if the decision reached on the application was contrary to that recommended by the planning officer in the report on the application (see Ch.5 above), the Royal Town Planning Institute (RTPI) advises the officer to refuse to appear as a witness as this would involve supporting a decision contrary to his recommendation. In the absence of a planning officer, one option is to call a member of the planning committee as a non-expert witness.

Significant changes were made to the inquiry procedures in 2009. The absolute right of parties to require an inquiry to be held was removed, and it is for the appointed person to decide whether or not an inquiry should be held. Also, the inquiry will not consider the whole appeal, only the matters specified by the appointed person. Entitlement to participate in the inquiry is limited to the persons who made representations in relation to those specified matters. Pre-2009, copies of documents only had to be lodged in the run-up to the inquiry, but the new procedures require parties to submit full details of their cases, including all documents, in the early stages of the procedures (see above).

The Inquiry Session Rules apply to an inquiry.[80] All inquiries are based on the principles of natural justice, broadly defined as openness, fairness and impartiality. The Court of Session may quash the appeal decision if there has been a failure to comply with the procedural rules which has caused substantial prejudice or a breach of natural justice (see para.8.49 below). Compliance with the rules does not necessarily prevent a breach of natural justice; and failure to comply with the rules is not necessarily a breach of natural justice.

The inquiry is initiated by the appointed person serving a procedure notice on the appellant; the planning authority; any interested party who made representations in relation to the specified matters set out in the procedure notice; and any other body or person from whom the appointed person wishes to receive further representations or to provide further information on specified matters at the inquiry session.

---

78   TCPSA 1997 s.265 and Sch.4 para.6; TCPASR 2013 (SSI 2013/156) reg.9(3), (4)(c).
79   John M. Watchman, "An Expert's Obligations", 1996 54 S.P.E.L. 25.
80   TCPASR 2013 (SSI 2013/156) regs 2, 9(5)(c) and Sch.2.

There is no requirement for the procedure notice to be copied to other bodies or persons who submitted representations in response to the notice of appeal. The appointed person has the power to require a witness to attend.[81]

The procedure notice sets out the matters which are to be considered at the inquiry. No other matters are to be considered at the inquiry. This is a significant change, as pre-2009 inquiries generally heard evidence on all development plan policies and material considerations.

An assessor may be appointed to sit with the appointed person at an inquiry session to advise on such matters arising as Ministers may specify. Every person entitled to appear at the inquiry session must be notified of the name of the assessor and of the matters on which the assessor is to advise. After the close of the inquiry, the assessor may make a written report to the appointed person on the matters on which he/she was appointed to advise.[82]

Recipients of the procedure notice have 14 days from date of the notice to inform in writing the appointed person of their intention to appear at the inquiry.

The persons entitled to appear at inquiries are the appellant; the planning authority; and any other person or body, who in response to a procedure notice, has informed the appointed person of their intention to appear at the hearing. No other person or body is entitled to participate in the inquiry. There is a general rule that oral evidence at planning inquiries should be heard in public and that documentary evidence be open to public inspection.[83]

The date, time and place of the inquiry is determined, and may subsequently be varied, by the appointed person. There is no requirement for the appointed person to obtain agreement from the parties to the date, time and place. The practice is for the inquiry to be held in a venue near to the appeal site. Reasonable notice of the date, time and place must be given to the persons entitled to appear at the inquiry. The appointed person may also require the planning authority to publicise the inquiry session, either by notice in a local newspaper and on a website; and/or by serving notice on persons or classes of persons specified by the appointed person.

The appointed person can require parties to submit an inquiry statement, documents and precognitions. Different dates can be specified for submission of these papers.[84] The papers must be sent to the appointed person, the appellant, the planning authority and such other persons entitled to appear at the inquiry session as the appointed person may specify in the notice. The planning authority must afford to any person who requests a reasonable opportunity to inspect and, where practicable, take copies of any of these papers submitted in connection with the inquiry.

8.23

An inquiry statement is a written statement containing particulars of the case relating to the matters specified for the inquiry which a person proposes to put forward at the inquiry session. It also contains a list of documents (if any) which the person putting forward the case intends to refer to, rely on or put in evidence[85]; and a list of witnesses, specifying the persons to be called to give evidence at the inquiry, the matters on which such persons are to give evidence and the relevant

---

81 TCPSA 1997 s.265(4).
82 TCPASR 2013 (SSI 2013/156) reg.30. Planning Circular 4/2013, Planning Appeals, para.102 indicates that appointment of an assessor will be infrequent.
83 TCPSA 1997 s.265A.
84 It is common practice to require documents to be submitted four weeks before the inquiry, and precognitions two weeks before the inquiry.
85 There is only a limited right to submit documents which were not submitted with the notice of appeal—TCPASR 2013 (SSI 2013/156) reg.3(5), discussed above.

qualifications of such persons to do so. There is no requirement to mention that the person intends to be represented by a lawyer at the inquiry.

There is no prohibition in the rules against evidence being given at the inquiry on matters not mentioned in the inquiry statement but, if those matters are sufficiently material and new, natural justice may require the inquiry to be adjourned to provide the other parties with an opportunity to address those matters. Evidence on the matters may be prevented by the prohibition on raising matters not raised in the notice of appeal, or the prohibition against raising a matter which was not before the planning officer/authority at the time when the determination appealed was made.[86]

The precognition is a written statement of the evidence which it is proposed that a witness will give to the inquiry session. The rules state that a precognition must not contain more than 2,000 words, unless the appointed person so agrees.

A precognition generally starts by identifying the person giving evidence and narrating any relevant qualifications and experience. The evidence in the precognition can consist of facts and expert opinions relating to the case deriving from the witness's own professional or local knowledge. The evidence must be relevant to the subject-matter of the inquiry, and avoid being repetitious. Reference should be made to the relevant documents lodged, giving the appropriate reference number. For ease of reference, the precognition should have page numbers and numbered paragraphs.

The procedure at the inquiry is determined by the appointed person, except as otherwise provided in the Inquiry Session Rules. There is an overriding legal requirement to provide natural justice (see "Procedural impropriety", below)—in particular, each party must be given an opportunity to present their case and respond to the case presented by other parties.

The appointed person must state at or before the commencement of the inquiry the procedure which they propose to adopt, having considered any submission by the persons entitled to appear at the inquiry. In particular, the appointed person is to state: the order in which the specified matters are to be considered; and the order in which the persons entitled to appear are to be heard in relation to a specified matter (a different order may be chosen for different specified matters).

The usual format for an inquiry is a morning session between 10.00 and 13.00, followed by an afternoon session from 14.00 until 16.30. This timing may vary to avoid breaks in the evidence of a witness. More frequent breaks may be taken during long inquiries. Participants are normally free to enter and leave the room when the inquiry is sitting. It is normal for a long inquiry not to sit on a Monday.

8.24 The evidence on behalf of the appellant is normally heard first, followed by evidence from any party supporting the appeal. Evidence is then heard from parties opposing the appeal usually first from the planning authority. Closing statements are often made in reverse order, enabling the appellant to respond during his closing statement to the closing statements made by the other parties, although closing statements are generally submitted in writing and not read out at inquiry. In some instances, the evidence is heard on a topic-by-topic basis, with all parties' witnesses being heard on a topic, and the inquiry then moving on to hear all witnesses on the next topic.

Evidence is given through testimony of witnesses. It is normal practice for each witness to give evidence by reading their precognition, although the parties might

---

[86] TCPASR 2013 (SSI 2013/156) reg.3(5), and TCPSA 1997 s.47A.

agree to take the precognition as read. Once the evidence of the witness has been heard (what lawyers refer to as the examination-in-chief), the other parties participating in the inquiry are given the opportunity to cross-examine the witness. The witness can be cross-examined on any point in the precognition and on any relevant matter within his/her knowledge. Cross-examination is not limited to matters covered in examination-in-chief and may include matters favourable to the case of the party cross-examining the witness. Cross-examination is normally restricted to opposing parties, although a witness on behalf of a supporting party may be cross-examined either to clarify matters raised or where parts of the witness's evidence are hostile to the cross-examining party. Cross-examination is used to clarify issues, highlight areas of agreement, and undermine the credibility of the evidence by exposing weakness or flaws. Expert evidence may be undermined by exposing incomplete research or faulty conclusions. The appointed person may prohibit further cross-examination of a witness which would lead to undue repetition.

Following cross-examination by the other parties, the appointed person will normally ask any questions he/she might have, although he/she can do this at any time. The witness may then be re-examined by the party on whose behalf the witness is giving evidence. Re-examination cannot be used to introduce matters which were not raised in the course of the witness's evidence or cross-examination. The purpose of re-examination is to clear up difficulties or ambiguities which arose during the cross-examination, and repair any flaws in the evidence. The next witness is then called and the procedure repeated.

The rigid evidential rules applicable to court procedures do not apply to inquiries. Witnesses are not normally put on oath. Corroboration of evidence is not required. Hearsay evidence, such as a report of a conversation which the witness did not hear but which was reported to him/her, or written evidence from a person who is not called as a witness, will be admissible even though it cannot be tested by cross-examination.[87] Comments can be made which are not supported either by documentary evidence or any expertise or experience claimed by the witness. However, less weight may be attributed to such evidence as a result.

The appointed person has the discretionary power to require appearance of witnesses or production of evidence, either on the request of any party or of his/her own accord. However, any person may refuse to answer a question or produce evidence on the ground of the legal rules relating to privilege or confidentiality. The appointed person may administer oaths and examine witnesses on oath and may accept, in lieu of evidence on oath by any person, a statement in writing by that person.[88]

A person entitled to appear at an inquiry may appear on their own behalf or be represented by another person. Where there are two or more persons having a similar interest in the issues being considered, the appointed person may allow one or more persons to appear on behalf of some or all of any persons so interested. The inquiry can proceed in the absence of any person entitled to appear.

Any person entitled to appear at the inquiry is entitled to call evidence and to cross-examine persons giving evidence and to make closing statements. The appointed person may refuse to permit the giving or production of evidence, cross-examination, or the presentation of any other matter, which he/she considers to be irrelevant or repetitious.

---

[87] *TA Miller v Minister for Housing and Local Government* [1968] 1 W.L.R. 992.
[88] TCPSA 1997 s.265.

The appointed person must not require or permit the giving or production of any written or oral evidence which would be contrary to the public interest. This may include information relating to the estimated profitability of the proposed development.[89] A representative of the Scottish Ministers or government department cannot be required to answer a question which is, in the opinion of the appointed person, directed to the merits, as opposed to the facts, of government policy. Such a question should be disallowed by the appointed person as Parliament is the proper forum for raising such questions. However, this principle should not preclude discussion at the inquiry of whether a policy should be departed from in the particular circumstances of the appeal.

The appointed person may from time to time adjourn the inquiry. Notice of the date, time and place of the adjourned session can be announced before the adjournment; if not, reasonable notice of the date, time and place must be given to the persons entitled to appear.

A site inspection may be made by the appointed person before, during or after the inquiry (see below).

(j) Site inspection

8.25   The appointed person/LRB may make a site inspection for any appeal/review, whether or not further written submissions have been requested or a hearing or inquiry held.[90] The inspection can be unaccompanied or in the presence of the parties to the appeal/review.

An unaccompanied inspection of the land to which the appeal/review relates may be made at any time, but the appointed person/LRB must inform the appellant/applicant that they propose to do so. The appointed person must also inform the planning authority.

For an accompanied inspection, reasonable notice must be given of the date and time of the inspection. Notice is given to the appellant/applicant, the planning authority (appeal only) and any person or body given notice of the appeal/review. The inspection can proceed if any person to whom notice was given is not present at the time appointed. The statutory provisions do not specify how an accompanied site inspection should be conducted. The usual practice of reporters is not to allow discussion of the issues, and to limit the inspection to clarifying, in the presence of the parties, the physical characteristics of the site. The appointed person/LRB must avoid creating a suspicion of bias in its dealings with the parties during the site inspection (see "Procedural impropriety", below).

If the appointed person/LRB propose to take into consideration any new evidence from the site inspection, an opportunity of making representations on that new evidence must be given to the parties.[91]

(k) Decision

8.26   If the appellant appears to be responsible for undue delay in the progress of the appeal, whether by the written submission procedure, hearing or public local inquiry, the Scottish Ministers/appointed person may give the appellant notice at any time before or during the determination of the appeal that it will be dismissed,

---

89   *Wordie Property Co Ltd v Secretary of State for Scotland*, 1984 S.L.T. 345.
90   TCPASR 2013 (SSI 2013/156) regs 9 and 12; LRPR 2013 (SSI 2013/157) regs 13 and 16.
91   TCPASR 2013 (SSI 2013/156) reg.13; LRPR 2013 (SSI 2013/157) reg.17.

unless the appellant takes specified steps for the expedition of the appeal within a specified time limit.[92] For example, the notice may require the appellant to agree an inquiry date. The Scottish Ministers/appointed person have a discretionary power to dismiss the appeal if these steps are not taken within the time limit. As planning authorities would then have the power to decline to determine any similar application within the next two years (see Ch.5 above), appellants should comply with these notices. There is no equivalent provision for reviews.

If after the conclusion of any further procedure, the appointed person/LRB propose to take into consideration any new evidence which is material to the determination of the appeal/review, the appointed person/LRB must not reach a decision without first offering specified parties an opportunity of making representations on such new evidence. For an appeal, the opportunity must be offered to the appellant and the planning authority; for a review, to the applicant. Where the evidence relates to a specified matter considered at a hearing or inquiry session, the opportunity must be offered to any person entitled to appear at that session; if it relates to matters in respect of which further written representations or information was sought by a procedure notice, the opportunity must be given to any person to whom the procedure notice was sent.[93]

The appeal may be allowed or dismissed, and any part of the decision of the planning authority may be reversed or varied, irrespective of what aspect of the decision is challenged.[94] However, an opportunity to make representations must be given to the planning authority and appellant if the Scottish Ministers/appointed person proposes to reverse or vary any part of the decision to which the appeal does not relate. If planning permission could not have been granted by the planning authority or could not have been granted without the conditions imposed by it, the Scottish Ministers/appointed person may decline to determine the appeal or to proceed with the determination.[95]

The Scottish Ministers/appointed person may intimate to the parties, before issuing the decision letter, that they are minded to grant planning permission if a s.75 obligation is concluded (see Ch.6 above). This gives the parties an opportunity to enter into such an obligation, but this will require the co-operation of the planning authority which may be unforthcoming, given the expectation that the appeal will be dismissed if no obligation can be put in place (although there is now provision for unilateral obligations). English case law suggests that a planning authority which refuses to enter into an obligation in these circumstances may be acting ultra vires.[96]

The LRB may uphold, reverse or vary a determination reviewed by them.[97] Where the requirement to review is made because the officer is deemed to have refused the application, if the LRB have not conducted the review within two months beginning with the date on which the requirement to review is made, the authority are deemed to have decided to refuse the application, and the applicant can submit an appeal to the Scottish Ministers.[98] If the LRB decide to grant planning permission, it is unclear whether they require to notify the Scottish Ministers

---

92 TCPSA 1997 s.48(8).
93 TCPASR 2013 (SSI 2013/156) reg.13; LRPR 2013 (SSI 2013/157) reg.17.
94 TCPSA 1997 s.48(1).
95 TCPSA 1997 s.48(7).
96 *R. v Warwickshire CC Ex p. Powergen Plc* [1998] J.P.L. 131, but see *R. v Cardiff CC Ex p. Sears Group Properties Ltd* [1998] 3 P.L.R. 55.
97 TCPSA 1997 s.43A(15).
98 TCPSA 1997 s.43A(17) and LRPR 2013 (SSI 2013/157) reg.8(2).

if the development falls within the categories requiring notification by the planning authority (see Ch.5 above).

In consequence of the powers of the appointed person and LRB, an applicant challenging a planning permission that has been granted, takes the risk of either losing the entire permission, or being burdened with a more onerous condition. Duplicate planning applications (see Ch.5 above) were used for a time to enable the decision on one application to be appealed in the knowledge that it was possible to fall back on the decision on the second application if the appeal was unsuccessful, but that approach is no longer frequent.

A decision notice must be issued by the appointed person/LRB to the appellant/applicant; the appointed person must also issue a decision notice to the planning authority. Every person who made representations in respect of the appeal/review must be notified by the appointed person/LRB that a decision on the appeal/review has been made, and advised of where a copy of the decision notice is available for inspection.[99] Various matters must be contained in the decision notice from the LRB, including the terms in which the planning authority have decided the case reviewed, and the reasons on which the authority based that decision.[100] There are no equivalent requirements for appeal decision notices.

8.27 In relation to appeals, the courts have indicated that the written reasons should be proper, intelligible and adequate. They should deal with the substantial points raised in the appeal and enable the reader to know what conclusion the decision-maker has reached on the principal controversial issues, and understand on what grounds the appeal has been decided. The degree of particularity required will depend entirely upon the nature of these issues. Decision letters should not be construed as if they were Acts of Parliament and should be read as a whole. The central question is whether the deficiency of the reasons given has caused substantial prejudice.[101] An LRB is entitled to confine itself to the determining issues, and so long as its reasons are intelligible and accurate, it is entitled to express them concisely.[102]

Where the determination of the appeal is delegated to the appointed person, he/she prepares the decision letter. If the determination is not delegated, the appointed person makes a report in writing to the Scottish Ministers which includes findings-in-fact, conclusions and recommendations or reasons for not making any recommendations. The appointed person is not required to make a finding-in-fact on every disputed issue.[103] The full report is submitted to the Scottish Ministers who will use it to decide the appeal. The Ministers are not bound to follow the recommendation made by the appointed person.[104]

In reaching these conclusions, the appointed person is entitled to make use of his/her planning experience and expertise. A reporter was entitled to refuse to grant planning permission on road safety grounds contrary to the views of the Director

---

[99] TCPASR 2013 (SSI 2013/156) reg.31; LRPR 2013 (SSI 2013/157) reg.22.
[100] TCPSA 1997 s.43A(12); LRPR 2013 (SSI 2013/157) reg.22 and Sch.2.
[101] *J Sainsbury Plc v Secretary of State for Scotland*, 1997 S.L.T. 1391; 1997 63 S.P.E.L. 108; *Save Britain's Heritage v Secretary of State for the Environment* [1991] 2 All E.R. 10; *Wordie Property Co Ltd v Secretary of State for Scotland*, 1984 S.L.T. 345.
[102] *Carroll v Scottish Borders Council* [2015] CSIH 73 at [55(7)].
[103] *London & Clydeside Properties Ltd v Aberdeen DC*, 1984 S.L.T. 50.
[104] e.g. *London & Midland Developments v Secretary of State for Scotland*, 1996 G.W.D. 14-861; 1996 55 S.P.E.L. 52.

of Highways.[105] In common with the planning authority, the reporter is obliged to take account of all material considerations and not merely those raised by the parties at the inquiry or in their written submissions.[106] However, where the reporter identifies a planning issue which he/she considers may be material to the decision on the appeal, but which has not been addressed by either party, the reporter is not entitled to reach a conclusion on that issue and found upon it as a factor material to his determination of the appeal, without giving the parties an opportunity of commenting on it.[107] The weight to be attached to the material put before him is a matter for the reporter and he/she is not bound to accept evidence presented by a party even though it is not contested.[108] The decisions of the courts on challenges to reporters' decisions emphasise the breadth of the reporter's powers, and hence the narrowness of the courts' power to intervene, and give considerable leeway in interpreting their decision letters.[109] It is relatively rare for a reporter's decision to be successfully challenged. In 2014–15 there were 12 decisions by reporters challenged in the Court of Session; six were withdrawn; three decisions were upheld; with three cases still to be decided.[110]

The decision of the appointed person/LRB on the appeal/review is final.[111] Any person aggrieved by the decision has six weeks from the date of the decision to raise a legal challenge in the Court of Session (see para.8.30 below).

(l) Expenses

Unlike court cases, expenses do not follow success and the parties involved in a planning appeal/review are normally expected to meet their own expenses. However, expenses can be awarded in an appeal, but not a review, if there has been unreasonable behaviour which has caused the party applying for the award to incur unnecessary expense, either because it should not have been necessary for the case to come before the Scottish Ministers for determination or because of the manner in which the party against whom the claim is made has conducted his/her part of the proceedings.[112]

8.28

What amounts to unreasonable behaviour will depend on the circumstances of each case. Appellants risk an award of expenses against them if the planning authority can show that the proposed development is contrary to a policy in an approved or adopted development plan which is both up to date and consistent with Scottish Government guidance, and the appellant produces no substantial evidence to support the contention that there are material considerations which might justify an exception to the policy. Planning authorities risk an award of expenses against them

---

[105] *Castle Rock Housing Association v Secretary of State for Scotland*, 1995 S.C.L.R. 850.
[106] But see *Anwar v Secretary of State for Scotland*, 1992 S.C.L.R. 875.
[107] TCPASR 2013 (SSI 2013/156) reg.12. *Bancon Developments Ltd v Scottish Ministers* [2011] CSOH 137; *Anduff Holdings Ltd v Secretary of State for Scotland*, 1992 S.L.T. 696; cf. *Ladbroke Racing Ltd v Secretary of State for Scotland*, 1990 S.C.L.R. 705; *Ecotricity v Secretary of State* [2015] EWHC 801 (Admin).
[108] *Narden Services Ltd v Secretary of State for Scotland*, 1993 S.L.T. 871.
[109] e.g. *Edinburgh City Council v Secretary of State for Scotland*, 1998 S.L.T. 120; *Glasgow DC v Secretary of State for Scotland*, 1997 S.C.L.R. 711; *Parkes v Secretary of State for Scotland*, 1998 G.W.D. 6-292.
[110] DPEA, *Annual Review 2014/15* (Scottish Government, 2015).
[111] TCPSA 1997 s.48(6) and Sch.4 para.2(7); s.43A(16).
[112] TCPSA 1997 ss.265(9) and 266; Circular 6/1990, Awards and Expenses in Appeals and Other Planning Proceedings and in Compulsory Purchase Order Inquiries (Scottish Office, 1990).

by applying policies which are out of date or inconsistent with Scottish Government guidance and not substantiating sound reasons for refusal on appeal.

Some of the other examples given in the Scottish Government guidance of unreasonable behaviour on the part of the planning authority include failing to give complete, precise and relevant reasons for refusal of an application; reaching its decision without reasonable planning grounds for doing so; refusing an application because of local opposition, where that opposition is not founded upon valid planning reasons; refusing an application where it is clear from the decision on an earlier appeal against the refusal of a similar application that no objection would be seen to a revised application in the form submitted; and failing to take account of relevant statements of government policy in departmental circulars or of relevant precedents of which the planning authority was aware.

Unreasonable behaviour on the part of the appellant may include pursuing an appeal in circumstances where there is no reasonable likelihood of success, for example as a result of a previous appeal decision in respect of a similar development on the same site; withdrawing the appeal without giving sufficient time for reasonable notice of the cancellation of the inquiry to be given to the parties; and deliberately unco-operative behaviour, including refusing to explain the grounds of appeal or refusing to discuss the appeal.

Unreasonable behaviour on the part of either party may include introducing a new matter at a late stage in the proceedings; refusing either to supply adequate grounds of appeal, or to co-operate in settling agreed facts or supplying relevant information all of which unnecessarily prolongs the proceedings; failing to comply with the requirements of any statutory procedural rules (account will be taken of the extent to which an appellant has taken professional advice); and failure to comply with procedural requirements to the serious prejudice of the other party and leading to the adjournment of the inquiry (an award may be made relating to the extra expense arising from the adjournment).

8.29   In exceptional circumstances, such as unreasonable conduct at a public inquiry which causes unnecessary expense, awards of expenses may be made in favour of or against parties other than the appellant and planning authority. In general, third parties will not be eligible to receive expenses where unreasonable behaviour by one of the main parties relates to the substance of that party's case.

Application for expenses should be made to the appointed person prior to conclusion of the hearing or inquiry, to enable him/her to hear the parties' arguments on the application. In the case of an appeal by written submissions, application may be made at any time until submission of the party's final written submission. The decision on the application for expenses will be taken on the basis of a further exchange of written submissions. In either procedure, later applications will only be entertained if good reason can be shown for not submitting the application earlier.

The application for an award of expenses does not require to specify the amount of the expenses claimed or contain any details of the expenses. Once a full or partial award of expenses has been made, the parties must agree the amount of expenses incurred in relation to the appeal. If they fail to agree, the matter is referred to the Auditor of the Court of Session for decision. A decision to award expenses can only be challenged by judicial review.[113]

In 2014–15, 60 requests for awards of expenses were made, 57 of which were

---

[113] *Aberdeen DC v Secretary of State for Scotland*, 1993 S.L.T. 1149.

by main contacts against planning authorities, and the other three were by planning authorities against main contacts. Only 18 were successful—all against planning authorities.[114]

CHALLENGE IN THE COURT OF SESSION—REVIEW PROCEEDINGS

The Court of Session in Edinburgh has jurisdiction to hear challenges of planning decisions or actions, either by way of the statutory appeal procedure or under its common-law (non-statutory) judicial review procedure. The statutory right of appeal satisfies the European Convention on Human Rights art.6 requirement for an independent and impartial tribunal, even where an earlier decision-maker such as the Scottish Ministers are not independent and impartial.[115]   **8.30**

Although an application for review is often referred to as an appeal, there are important legal differences between review by the Court of Session and an appeal/review decided by the Scottish Ministers/appointed person/LRB. In deciding an appeal/review, the Scottish Ministers/appointed person/LRB has the power to declare the original decision wrong, whether as a matter of policy or on the merits of the case, and substitute a decision in place of that originally reached. In essence, the appeal/review involves a rehearing and re-decision of the application. In contrast, the Court of Session has no power to rule on the merits or correctness of the original decision. The judges can only decide whether or not the decision was made in a legal manner, and have no power to intervene where a "wrong" decision has been made in a legal manner. Even where a decision is held to be illegal and quashed, the Court of Session has no power to substitute its own decision and must refer the case back to the decision-maker for a fresh decision to be reached. At this stage it is open to the decision-maker to reach the same decision, but in a legal manner. A successful challenge in the Court of Session may, therefore, be a pyrrhic victory.

Unlike an inquiry or hearing (see paras 8.21 and 8.22 above), a challenge by review procedure will be subject to the legal rules of evidence and procedure common to all court actions.

Common law petitions for judicial review are heard by a single judge in the Outer House, with a right to appeal (reclaim) to the Inner House and thereafter the Supreme Court (which has replaced the House of Lords). Challenges under the statutory review procedure are heard by three judges in the Inner House, but the Rules of Court were amended in 1996 to provide for such challenges to be remitted to a single Outer House judge, with a right to reclaim to the Inner House against the decision of that judge.[116] The case may be remitted by the court at its own instance, after hearing the parties, or on the motion of any of the parties to the case. There is a right to appeal from the decision of the Inner House to the Supreme Court.

---

[114] DPEA, *Annual Review 2014/15*, Table 7.
[115] *County Properties Ltd v Scottish Ministers*, 2001 S.L.T. 1125. For LRB, see—*Sally Carroll v Scottish Borders Council* [2015] CSIH 73.
[116] Act of Sederunt (Rules of the Court of Session 1994) 1994 (RCS) (SI 1994/1443) r.41.45.

STATUTORY REVIEW

8.31   The term statutory review is used here to denote the review powers of the Court of Session conferred by the TCPSA 1997.

Types of challengeable decision

8.32   There is a statutory right of challenge in the Court of Session against the decision of the LRB on a review,[117] and against the decision of the Scottish Ministers/appointed person on a planning permission appeal.[118]

There is also a statutory right of challenge in the Court of Session against orders[119]:

(a)   revoking or modifying planning permission (see Ch.5 above);
(b)   requiring discontinuance of use or alteration or removal of buildings or works (see Ch.7 above);
(c)   prohibiting resumption of or suspending the winning and working of minerals (see Ch.9 below);
(d)   tree preservation orders (see Ch.9 below);
(e)   defining areas of special control of advertisements (see Ch.9 below); and
(f)   revocation of listed building consent (see Ch.9 below).

The right of statutory challenge in the Court of Session also extends to decisions by the Scottish Ministers/appointed person in connection with:

(a)   an application for planning permission for the operation of a marine fish farm;
(b)   a called-in application for planning permission (see Ch.5 above);
(c)   appeals against waste land notices (see Ch.7 above), enforcement notices (see Ch.7 above), tree enforcement notices, and listed building enforcement notices (see Ch.9 below), and against the refusal or partial refusal of a certificate of lawful use or development (see Ch.4 above);
(d)   confirmation of a completion notice (see Ch.5 above);
(e)   appeals seeking modification or discharge of s.75 obligations or good neighbour agreements (see Ch.6 above);
(f)   an application for hazardous substances consent (see Ch.9 below);
(g)   an application for consent under a tree preservation order or advertisement control regulations, or relating to any certificate or direction under any such order or regulations, whether his decision is made on appeal or on an application referred to him for determination in the first instance (see Ch.9 below);
(h)   confirmation or refusal to confirm a purchase notice or listed building purchase notice (see Ch.5 above and Ch.9 below);
(i)   an application for listed building consent referred to him for decision or on an appeal (see Ch.9 below); and
(j)   an application for planning permission for urgent Crown development.

---

[117] TCPSA 1997 ss.47(1A), 237(3A) and 239(4). *Sally Carroll v Scottish Borders Council* [2015] CSIH 73.
[118] TCPSA 1997 ss.237(3)(b) and 239.
[119] TCPSA 1997 s.239 and Planning (Listed Buildings and Conservation Areas) (Scotland) Act 1997 s.58.

The statutory review procedure also extends to challenges relating to both strategic development and local development plans.[120] These challenges share many of the characteristics discussed below, but the particular issues involved are examined in Ch.3.

Standing—persons who may challenge

Standing (locus standi) is the legal term used to describe the classes of person who have a legal right to challenge a decision. If a person has no standing in connection with the court action, the court will refuse to consider his challenge.   **8.33**

The statutory review procedure can be used by the planning authority directly concerned with one of the decisions/orders specified above, and by any person "aggrieved" by the decision/order.[121] In the absence of any statutory definition, it is impossible to identify all the instances of when persons can be aggrieved.[122] It is clear, however, that mere dissatisfaction is not enough and some connection to the decision or order will be required, most commonly through participation in the process leading up to that decision or order. Persons who can be "aggrieved" by an appeal decision include persons who have been given notice of a public local inquiry in connection with the appeal, have submitted observations to a public local inquiry and who would have been entitled to participate in the inquiry.[123] Where adjacent proprietors, the planning authority which decided the application, and the regional council, as water and drainage authority, had participated in a public local inquiry, they were held to be persons aggrieved.[124] In an appeal against an agricultural occupancy condition, "person aggrieved" included the owner of the access to the appeal site.[125]

In England, "person aggrieved" included the appellant; someone who took a sufficiently active role in the planning process, i.e. a substantial objector, not just somebody who objected and did no more about it; and someone who has a relevant interest in the land.[126] A person whose dwelling would be 260m from the proposed building but who had not objected nor taken an active role was not a "person aggrieved".[127]

The Court of Session has taken a broad approach to the question of when a person is aggrieved. A third party who had not objected to an application was held to be a person aggrieved by the appeal decision in relation to the application in the exceptional circumstances where the application and newspaper advertisement failed to give full notice of the proposed development and deprived the third party of his opportunity to make representations.[128]

To identify persons aggrieved, some assistance may be sought from the deci-

---

[120] TCPSA 1997 s.238.
[121] TCPSA 1997 s.239(1), (2); Eric Young, "'Aggrieved Persons' in Planning Law", 1993 S.L.T. (News) 43.
[122] See discussion by Supreme Court in *Walton v The Scottish Ministers* [2012] UKSC 44 at [83]-[87].
[123] *Strathclyde RC v Secretary of State for Scotland (No.2)*, 1990 S.L.T. 149 at 154E.
[124] *North East Fife DC v Secretary of State for Scotland*, 1992 S.L.T. 373.
[125] *Bannister v Secretary of State for the Environment* [1994] 2 P.L.R. 90.
[126] *Eco-Energy (GB) Ltd v First Secretary of State* [2004] EWCA Civ 1566.
[127] *Historic Buildings and Monuments Commission for England v Secretary of State for Communities and Local Government* [2009] EWHC 2287 (Admin).
[128] *Cumming v Secretary of State for Scotland*, 1993 S.L.T. 228.

sions on title and interest for the purposes of common law judicial review (see below), and on "persons aggrieved" for challenges to local plans (see Ch.3 above).

Time limits

8.34   Application to the Court of Session for statutory review of an order or action must be made within six weeks from the date on which the order is confirmed or the action taken.[129] In relation to a decision of the Scottish Ministers/appointed person, the period commences from the date on which the letter recording the decision is typed, signed and date-stamped, and not when notification of the decision is received by the parties.[130] Christmas day and bank holidays are included within the six-week period.[131]

Grounds of challenge

8.35   The validity of the order or action can be challenged on either of two grounds[132]:

(a)   that the order or action was not within the statutory powers; or

(b)   that the interests of the challenger have been substantially prejudiced by a failure to comply with any of the relevant requirements in relation to that order or action.[133] This is a reference to the requirements of the TCPSA 1997 and the Tribunals and Inquiries Act 1992, and any rules made under those Acts, including the statutory procedures applicable to planning appeals.

Interpretation of these grounds has proved a problem for the courts. However, it is now accepted that under the first ground of challenge[134]:

"... [T]he court can interfere with the Minister's decision if he has acted on no evidence; or if he has come to a conclusion to which, on the evidence, he could not reasonably come; or if he has given a wrong interpretation to the words of a statute; or if he has taken into consideration matters which he ought not to have taken into account, or vice versa; or has otherwise gone wrong in law."[135]

This wide approach has been summarised into a checklist of four principles known as the Ashbridge formula:

(a)   The decision-maker must not act perversely. In other words, the decision may be overturned if the court considers that no reasonable person in the position of the Scottish Ministers/appointed person/LRB, properly directing himself on the relevant material, could have reached the conclusion which he did reach.

(b)   He must not take into account irrelevant material or fail to take into account that which is relevant. Provided the Scottish Ministers/appointed person/LRB takes account of a matter, the court will not interfere with the

---

[129]   TCPSA 1997 s.239(3). The court has no power to extend this time limit—*Collins v Scottish Ministers*, 2004 S.L.T. 228.

[130]   *Griffiths v Secretary of State for the Environment* [1983] 1 All E.R. 439; [1983] J.P.L. 237.

[131]   *Stainer v Secretary of State for the Home Department* [1994] J.P.L. 44.

[132]   TCPSA 1997 s.239(1)(a), (b).

[133]   TCPSA 1997 s.239(5)(b).

[134]   *Ashbridge Investments v Minister of Housing and Local Government* [1965] 1 W.L.R. 1320 per Lord Denning at 1326.

[135]   Per Forbes J. in *Seddon Properties Ltd v Secretary of State for the Environment* [1978] J.P.L. 835; and see *Wordie Property Co Ltd v Secretary of State for Scotland*, 1984 S.L.T. 345 per Lord President at 347–8.

weight he gives to that matter in the decision, partly because the court has no opportunity to hear the witnesses or re-examine the evidence.

(c)   He must abide by statutory procedures.

(d)   He must not depart from the principles of natural justice.

In addition, in non-delegated appeals (see para.8.09 above) to differ from the reporter in a finding-of-fact, the Scottish Ministers must have sufficient material.[136]

The decision-maker must give proper and adequate reasons for the decision, which are clear and intelligible and deal with the substantial points which have been raised.[137] The decision letter should not be subjected to the rigorous interpretation appropriate to the determination of the meaning of a contract or statute.[138]

The Ashbridge formula closely corresponds to the common law grounds for judicial review. The first ground of statutory challenge will, therefore, be used to review all errors of law which are reviewable under the common law judicial review procedure (see para.8.45 below).

As a result of the width of the first ground of challenge, the second ground is only likely to be used where there is a procedural defect which does not amount to an error of law and is, therefore, not reviewable under the first ground (or the common law judicial review procedure), such as breach of a non-mandatory procedural requirement[139] or failure to give reasons as required by statute or regulations.[140] For a successful challenge under the second ground, the interests of the challenger must have been substantially prejudiced as a result of the failure to comply with the relevant requirements.[141] It seems that any defect in procedure which is more than a technical or insignificant defect will be assumed to have caused substantial prejudice.[142] It is not necessary for the challenger to show that the decision would have been different if the statutory requirements had been complied with—"the loss of a chance of being better off" will be enough to constitute substantial prejudice.[143] Where a local plan was challenged on the grounds that there was a lack of reasoned justification for taking no account of the possible implementation of a planning permission for a site, there was no substantial prejudice to the landowner as there was no imminent risk that the permission would expire and the balance of convenience was therefore against ordering interim suspension of the local plan.[144]

A decision of the House of Lords illustrates the approach of the courts to challenges to planning decisions. Their Lordships held that, provided the decision-maker took the relevant factors into account, the weight to be given to those fac-

---

[136]   *Coleen Properties Ltd v Minister of Housing and Local Government* [1971] 1 W.L.R. 433.

[137]   *Uprichard v Scottish Ministers* [2013] UKSC 21 at [47]. In *Eadie Cairns Ltd v Fife Council* [2013] CSIH 109, a local plan was part quashed because of failure to give adequate reasons. *Petition of The John Muir Trust* [2015] CSOH 163 per Lord Jones at [259]–[272].

[138]   *Sally Carroll v Scottish Borders Council* [2015] CSIH 73 at [55(7)].

[139]   For discussion of mandatory and directory requirements, see *London & Clydeside Estates Ltd v Aberdeen DC* [1980] 1 W.L.R. 182, e.g. per Lord Hailsham LC at 189H; *James v Secretary of State for Wales* [1966] 1 W.L.R. 135 per Lord Denning MR at 142.

[140]   *Wordie Property Co Ltd v Secretary of State for Scotland*, 1984 S.L.T. 345.

[141]   *Ampliflaire v Secretary of State for Scotland*, 1999 S.L.T. 937; 1998 68 S.P.E.L. 77. See also discussion in *Walton v Scottish Ministers* [2012] UKSC 44 at 110–112.

[142]   *Wordie Property Co Ltd v Secretary of State for Scotland*, 1984 S.L.T. 345 per Lord President Emslie at 356.

[143]   *Hibernian Property Co v Secretary of State for the Environment* (1974) 27 P. & C.R. 197 per Browne J. at 218.

[144]   *Mackenzie's Trustees v Highland RC*, 1994 S.C.L.R. 1042. Contrast *Eadie Cairns Ltd v Fife Council* [2013] CSIH 109.

tors was a matter for the judgment of the decision-maker, and the courts should only intervene where the decision reached was irrational or perverse.[145] The success rate of legal challenges is low. For example, in 2014–15 there were 12 decisions by reporters challenged in the Court of Session; six were withdrawn; three decisions were upheld; with three cases still to be decided.[146]

Powers of the court

8.36   The Court of Session has the power to suspend, by interim order, the operation of the order (except a tree preservation order) or action which is the subject of challenge until the final determination of the proceedings.[147]

If the court determines that the order or action in question is not within the powers of the Act or that the interests of the applicant have been substantially prejudiced by a failure to comply with any of the relevant requirements, it has the discretion to quash that order or action.[148] The court may decide not to quash the order or action on the grounds that the same decision would have been reached in any case, or that the decision was correct but for the wrong reasons.[149] With the exception of tree preservation orders and orders designating areas of special control, the court has no power to quash only part of the whole order or action.[150]

Following the quashing of a decision, the matter is referred back to the decision-maker for a fresh decision to be reached. There is no requirement for the court to order the whole process to start again.[151] Where a fundamental error of law has been made, it may be necessary to start the decision-making process afresh.[152] Any new evidence or circumstances which have arisen in the meantime, such as the adoption of different policies, must be considered and new arguments can be raised by the parties. However, a fresh start may not always be required. For example, if the challenger has not been given an opportunity to make representations on a point, it may be sufficient to give the challenger that opportunity and to allow the other parties an opportunity to comment on those representations.

The powers of the court expose the limitations of statutory review proceedings for challenging planning orders or actions. Even if the decision is challenged successfully, the court may refuse to exercise its discretionary power to quash the decision. If the court quashes the decision, it is open to the decision-maker to reach the same decision as before, but in a legal manner. It is, therefore, possible that the challenger may be able to achieve nothing more than obtaining further time for negotiation.

Expenses

8.37   Unlike planning appeals (see para.8.28 above), the successful party in the Court of Session will normally be awarded his expenses against the other party (expenses

---

[145] *Tesco Stores Ltd v Secretary of State for the Environment* [1995] 2 All E.R. 636.
[146] DPEA, *Annual Review 2014/15*.
[147] TCPSA 1997 s.239(5)(a); e.g. *Mackenzie's Trustees v Highland RC*, 1994 S.C.L.R. 1042.
[148] TCPSA 1997 s.239(5)(b). Discussed in *Walton v Scottish Ministers* [2012] UKSC 44 at 102–140.
[149] *Glasgow DC v Secretary of State for Scotland*, 1982 S.L.T. 28.
[150] *British Airports Authority v Secretary of State for Scotland*, 1979 S.C. 200; *The Highland Council v Scottish Ministers* [2014] CSIH 74. Contrast TCPSA 1997 s.238(2)(b) which provides for a development plan to be quashed in part—see Ch.3.
[151] *Hallam Land Management Ltd v City of Edinburgh Council*[2011] COSH 75.
[152] *Kingswood DC v Secretary of State for Environment* [1988] J.P.L. 248.

follow success), although the scale used to calculate these expenses results in only one-half to two-thirds of the actual expenses being recovered. Before commencing court action, the challenger must consider whether, if his challenge is unsuccessful, he can afford to pay the costs incurred by the other party (or parties) in relation to the court action. However, the costs of preparing for court action and the danger of liability to pay the costs of a successful challenger may persuade the decision-maker to negotiate a compromise.

Protective expenses orders can be granted by the court, capping potential liability to pay expenses.[153]

JUDICIAL REVIEW

In addition to the statutory review jurisdiction discussed above, the Court of Session has a common-law supervisory jurisdiction to review decisions of inferior courts, tribunals and other administrative and public bodies to ensure that they do not exceed or abuse their statutory jurisdiction, powers or authority. This jurisdiction also allows the court to insist upon standards of rationality and fairness of procedure (for example, the rules of natural justice), in addition to what is expressly required by statute. In the exercise of this jurisdiction, as with statutory review, the court acts as a review body and cannot substitute its own decision for the decision which is challenged (the distinction between review and appeal procedure is discussed above).[154]

8.38

The supervisory jurisdiction of the court is exercised through decisions on petitions for judicial review. This judicial review procedure offers a quick decision on the challenge, and a wider range of remedies than is available to the court under the statutory review procedure. However, there are limitations on the availability of judicial review procedure. If there is a statutory remedy available to the challenger, judicial review may be excluded as a result of a statutory ouster clause or the duty to exhaust a statutory remedy. Any person seeking to use judicial review procedure must also establish that they have sufficient standing to challenge the decision and that they have not delayed in making their challenge.

Changes to judicial review procedures were introduced in 2015, including a time limit (see para.8.43 below) and procedure for obtaining permission (see para.8.54 below).

Types of decision

Planning is a statutory function, with powers conferred upon planning authorities and the Scottish Ministers by statute and exercised for the public benefit. Planning decisions are, therefore, a prime example of decisions which are susceptible to judicial review under the common law supervisory jurisdiction. In general, all forms of planning decisions, orders and actions are susceptible to judicial review, although a petition for judicial review must always satisfy the restrictions examined below.

8.39

---

[153] RCS (SI 1994/1443) r.58A—for example, *Sally Carroll v Scottish Borders Council* [2014] CSOH 30; *Petition of Friends of Loch Etive* [2014] CSOH 116; *John Muir Trust v Scottish Ministers*, 2015 G.W.D. 1–20. At common law—*McGinty, Petitioner* [2010] CSOH 5; *Road Sense v Scottish Ministers* [2011] CSOH 10; *Newton Mearns Residents Flood Protection Group v East Renfrewshire Council* [2013] CSIH 70.

[154] *West v Secretary of State for Scotland*, 1992 S.L.T. 636.

However, a petition for judicial review of a planning agreement has been dismissed as incompetent, as the petitioner, having entered into the agreement and implemented its terms, could not competently apply to the court on the grounds that the planning authority's exercise of its powers was ultra vires. It was a matter of private contract law whether the obligations under the agreement had been fulfilled.[155]

Ouster clauses: exclusion of judicial review

8.40   Where provisions in Acts of Parliament have sought to oust completely the jurisdiction of the court by precluding the courts from entertaining a challenge at any time (such provisions are known as ouster clauses), the courts have been willing to resist the exclusion of their judicial review powers and find jurisdiction to hear the challenge. In contrast, where a statutory review procedure offers the courts a limited opportunity to review the decision, the courts have accepted restrictions on their common law jurisdiction. This latter approach has been consistently taken by both the Scottish and English courts towards challenges of planning decisions.

As well as providing a statutory review procedure, the TCPSA 1997 states that the orders and actions which may be challenged under that procedure cannot be questioned in any other legal proceedings.[156] As a result, any common law judicial review proceedings to question the validity of such an order or action will not be competent, whether or not the six-week time limit for commencement of statutory review proceedings has expired.[157] For these purposes, it is irrelevant that the challenger had no knowledge of the matter complained of during that six-week period.[158]

Duty to exhaust alternative remedies

8.41   Even in the absence of an ouster clause, the existence of a statutory procedure to challenge a decision may exclude any petition for judicial review of that decision.[159] The well-established principle that failure to exercise a statutory remedy bars resort to the common law supervisory jurisdiction of the Court of Session, is incorporated into its rules governing judicial review procedure.[160] As a result, judicial review procedure is generally unavailable where there is a statutory right of appeal.[161]

This strict position means that any petition for judicial review will be incompetent where a statutory remedy exists. For example, the applicant for planning permission has a statutory right of appeal against the decision of the planning authority on the application. Thus, any challenge attempted under judicial review procedure would be incompetent as the applicant must first exhaust the statutory

---

155   *McIntosh v Aberdeenshire Council*, 1998 S.C.L.R. 435; 1998 67 S.P.E.L. 56. There is now power to apply for variation or discharge of a s.75 obligation—see Ch.6.
156   TCPSA 1997 s.237(1).
157   *Pollock v Secretary of State for Scotland*, 1993 S.L.T. 1173; 1993 38 S.P.L.P. 19.
158   *Martin v Bearsden and Milngavie DC*, 1987 S.L.T. 300.
159   See generally, Neil Collar, "Judicial Review: The Significance of an Alternative Remedy" (1991) 36(8) J.L.S.S. 299.
160   RCS (SI 1994/1443) r.58.3(1).
161   *Bellway Ltd v Strathclyde RC*, 1979 S.C. 92; 1980 S.L.T. 66.

remedy.[162] Third parties have no statutory right to challenge the decision of the authority and are, therefore, free to apply for judicial review. An extreme example of the strictness of this position is that judicial review of the decision to serve a stop notice is incompetent, notwithstanding the lack of a statutory means of appealing, on the grounds that there is a right to compensation for loss due to the stop notice.[163]

An exception is made to this duty to exhaust all alternative remedies in "exceptional circumstances".[164] The extent of this exception is uncertain and the decisions of the court on this point very much depend upon the facts and circumstances of each case. The seriousness of the alleged illegality and the effectiveness of the statutory procedure to remedy the illegality may be important factors. However it is clear that the "exceptional circumstances" test creates a strong presumption in favour of exhaustion of the statutory remedy.

Standing/sufficient interest

The petitioner must have standing before the court has jurisdiction to hear the challenge. In 2011 the Supreme Court clarified the approach to the question of standing, to put an end to the unduly restrictive approach which had been taken.[165] The petitioner must have sufficient interest. In many contexts it will be necessary for a person to demonstrate some particular interest in order to demonstrate that he is not a mere busybody. Not every member of the public can complain of every potential breach of duty by a public body. But there may also be cases in which any individual, simply as a citizen, will have sufficient interest to bring a public authority's violation of the law to the attention of the court, without having to demonstrate any greater impact upon himself than upon other members of the public.[166] The court should have regard to the provisions of the Aarhus Convention on access to justice.[167]

8.42

Time limits

In 2015 a three-month time limit was introduced for making an application for judicial review.[168] The court can substitute such longer period as it considers equitable having regard to all the circumstances.

8.43

The three-month period begins with the date on which the grounds giving rise to the judicial review application first arise. Where there is a delay between the decision to grant permission and the issue of that permission, for example while a s.75 obligation is concluded, it is the issue of the permission which should be challenged.[169]

8.44

---

162 *Wallace v East Lothian Council* [2012] CSOH 195.
163 *Central RC v Clackmannan DC*, 1983 S.L.T. 666; *Earl Car Sales (Edinburgh) Ltd v Edinburgh DC*, 1984 S.L.T. 8; cf. *Shanks & McEwan v Gordon DC*, 1991 32 S.P.L.P. 15.
164 Collar, *"Judicial Review: The Significance of an Alternative Remedy"* (1991).
165 *AXA General Insurance Ltd v HM Advocate* [2011] UKSC 46; [2012] 1 A.C. 868; 2011 S.L.T. 1061.
166 *Walton v Scottish Ministers* [2012] UKSC 44 per Lord Reed at [89]–[95]. This can affect the remedy sought—*Petition of The John Muir Trust* [2015] CSOH 163 per Lord Jones at [105].
167 e.g. *Forbes v Aberdeenshire Council* [2010] CSOH 01.
168 Court of Session Act 1988 s.27A, inserted by Courts Reform (Scotland) Act 2014 s.89. The equivalent time limit in England is six weeks.
169 *R. (On the application of Burkett) v Hammersmith & Fulham LBC* [2002] UKHL 23; *Bova v The Highland Council* [2011] CSOH 140.

Grounds for judicial review

8.45   The grounds for judicial review are based upon ultra vires (literally "beyond powers") conduct, where the decision-maker has acted illegally by acting outwith its powers. The grounds for judicial review frequently overlap and new grounds are always developing.[170] Indeed, it is often difficult to identify the particular grounds at issue in a court case. Traditionally, the grounds for judicial review were classified under three heads: jurisdiction, discretion and natural justice, but have been reclassified under the heads of illegality, irrationality, and procedural impropriety.[171]

(a) Illegality

8.46   The decision-maker must understand the law that regulates its decision-making power and give effect to it, including the rights conferred by the European Convention on Human Rights, the need to keep within its jurisdiction and not act outwith its statutory powers, the need to avoid acting in bad faith, and the requirement that any statutory discretionary power be exercised properly.

Many planning powers are discretionary and seem to confer unfettered power upon decision-makers. However, limits to the exercise of these powers have been developed by the courts, allowing them to intervene to prevent abuse of discretionary powers. For example, when determining applications for planning permission, planning authorities have the statutory power to impose "such conditions as they think fit". Although the wording of this statutory power would seem to give authorities absolute discretion, the courts have evolved a series of legal restrictions on the exercise of this power (see Ch.6 above).

Each individual exercise of discretion must be free and not pre-judged. It is well-established that each planning application must be decided upon its individual merits. The concept of precedent, whereby the planning authority is bound to act in accordance with previous similar decisions, has no place in planning law (although consistency in decision-making is encouraged by the Scottish Government). Similarly, the decision-maker may formulate a policy for dealing with future decision-making, but the possibility of making an exception to that policy must be considered in each case, otherwise the policy has fettered the exercise of discretion. Thus although planning applications must be determined according to the policies expressed in development plans, provision is made for material planning considerations in individual cases to overcome this presumption (see Ch.5 above). In addition, unless authorised by statute, the decision-maker must not delegate its discretion and must always make the final decision itself (see Ch.5 above). A planning authority cannot bind itself in a s.75 obligation to grant planning permission (see Ch.6 above).

8.47   Discretionary powers must also be exercised reasonably, in the special legal sense of *Wednesbury* reasonableness.[172] This requires the decision-maker to take into account all material considerations and ignore all irrelevant matters or ulterior motives. Powers conferred by the planning legislation must, therefore, be exercised for a planning purpose, otherwise an ulterior motive has been taken into account. For example, the discretionary power to impose conditions upon a grant of plan-

---

[170] For example, the general public sector equality duty (see Ch.3).

[171] Per Lord Diplock in the GCHQ case—*Council of Civil Service Unions v Minister for the Civil Service* [1985] A.C. 374 at 410–411.

[172] *Associated Provincial Picture Houses Ltd v Wednesbury Corp* [1948] 1 K.B. 223.

ning permission was illegally exercised when a condition was imposed upon a housing development requiring that the houses should first be occupied by persons on the council's housing waiting list, because the power was exercised to require the developer to assume the duty of the council at his own expense.[173]

The court will quash the decision only if the consideration which was ignored or the irrelevant factor which was taken into account influenced the decision, and the same decision would not have been reached for other valid reasons.[174] However, the consideration need not have been the dominant reason for the decision; provided it was not an insignificant or insubstantial factor in the decision reached, there will be no requirement to prove that a different conclusion would have been reached had it not been taken into account.[175]

The House of Lords (now the Supreme Court) have emphasised that, provided the decision-maker takes the relevant factors into account, the weight to be given to those factors is a matter for the judgment of the decision-maker, and the courts should only intervene where the decision reached is irrational or perverse.[176]

The Supreme Court have also indicated that misinterpretation of the development plan is an error of law, rejecting the proposition that the meaning of the development plan was a matter to be determined by the planning authority, unless the view taken by the planning authority was perverse or irrational. The correct approach is for development plans to be interpreted objectively in accordance with the language used, read in its proper context.[177]

The interpretation and application of Scottish Government guidance appears to be a matter for the judgment of the decision-maker.[178] If the decision-maker decides not to follow that guidance, sufficient reasons must be given.[179] In some instances there is a statutory requirement for regard to be had to guidance.[180]

Where reports had been lodged by consultants acting for the applicants and objectors, and these reports contained conflicting views regarding the applicable law, the Director of Planning should have advised the planning committee on the correct view of the law and approach to be taken. Since his report appeared to favour the wrong approach, there was a real risk that the committee were misled as to the correct approach. The report also materially misrepresented the facts in respect of the reduction between the previous and present proposals. Since the report appeared to place importance on the comparison between those proposals, it was likely that the committee took into account irrelevant considerations concerning the extent of the reduction.[181] However, the courts will not submit a report to committee to detailed textual analysis as if it were a statute or conveyancing deed.[182]

Where a reporter incorrectly held that a building was not listed, this was an error of law and his decision on this issue was quashed.[183]

Where a statutory consultee's view was so obviously material to the decision,

173 *R. v Hillingdon LBC Ex p. Royco Homes Ltd* [1974] 2 All E.R. 643.
174 *R. v Broadcasting Complaints Commission Ex p. Owen* [1985] Q.B. 1153.
175 *Simplex GE (Holdings) Ltd v Secretary of State for the Environment* [1988] 3 P.L.R. 25.
176 *Tesco Stores Ltd v Secretary of State for the Environment* [1995] 2 All E.R. 636.
177 *Tesco Stores v Dundee City Council* [2012] UKSC 13 per Lord Reed at 18.
178 *Petition of The John Muir Trust* [2015] CSOH 163 per Lord Jones at [192]–[198].
179 *Scottish Housebuilders Association v Secretary of State for Scotland*, 1995 S.C.L.R. 1039; 1995 52 S.P.E.L. 109.
180 For example, guidance on sustainable development, discussed in Ch.3.
181 *Campbell v Edinburgh City Council*, 1998 G.W.D. 17–877; 1998 69 S.P.E.L. 99.
182 *Sally Carroll v Scottish Borders Council* [2015] CSIH 73 at [55(7)].
183 *Edinburgh City Council v Secretary of State for Scotland*, 1998 S.L.T. 120; 1998 65 S.P.E.L. 11.

particularly when the planning authority was expressing what was, in effect, the opposite view, not to give direct consideration to it would not be in accordance with the intention of the relevant Regulations.[184]

The decision-maker must give proper and adequate reasons for the decision, which are clear and intelligible and deal with the substantial points which have been raised.[185]

(b) Irrationality

8.48　"Irrationality" is defined as:

> "...[A] decision which is so outrageous in its defiance of logic or of accepted moral standards that no sensible person who applied his mind to the question to be decided could have arrived at it."[186]

Previously this formed part of the concept of *Wednesbury* reasonableness "a conclusion so unreasonable that no reasonable authority could ever have come to it".[187] The requirement for such an extreme degree of unreasonableness should act as a safeguard to prevent the court from interfering with the merits of a decision.

Where the planning authority has refused earlier applications for the same site, it is not necessarily irrational for them to grant a subsequent identical application.[188] One judge observed that while there might be grounds for thinking that the view formed by the decision-maker was surprising, that did not mean that it was perverse.[189] Where on the facts it was clear that the proposed development covered a floor area greater than that available at the existing site, it was irrational for the reporter to find that the existing site was suitable for, or could accommodate, the proposed development.[190]

(c) Procedural impropriety

8.49　The supervisory jurisdiction allows the court to insist on standards of procedural fairness beyond what is expressly required by statute. Judicial review on this ground does not relate to the content of the decision, rather to the manner in which it was reached. The decision is tainted by a flaw in the decision-making process. Judicial development of this area of the law has given rise to suggestions that there is a duty to act fairly.[191] The degree of procedural fairness required varies depending upon the circumstances of each decision. For example, an oral hearing cannot be demanded in every circumstance.

Included under the head of "procedural impropriety" are failures to observe statutory procedural rules, and breaches of the rules of natural justice, which form a procedural code implied by the common law and supplementing any statutory provisions. There are two limbs to the rules of natural justice: the right to be heard and the rule against bias.

184　*Petition of The John Muir Trust* [2015] CSOH 163 per Lord Jones at [214].
185　*Petition of The John Muir Trust* [2015] CSOH 163 per Lord Jones at [259]–[272].
186　*CCSU v Minister for the Civil Service* [1985] A.C. 374 per Lord Diplock at 410G.
187　*Associated Provincial Picture Houses Ltd v Wednesbury Corp* [1948] 1 K.B. 223.
188　*Moore v East Renfrewshire Council*, 2005 G.W.D. 30-584; *R. v Aylesbury Vale DC Ex p. Chaplin* [1996] E.G. 126 (C.S.).
189　*Wyre Forest DC v Secretary of State for the Environment* [1995] E.G. 115 (C.S.).
190　*Lidl UK GmbH v Scottish Ministers* [2006] CSOH 165.
191　Per Lord Roskill in *CCSU v Minister for the Civil Service* [1985] A.C. 374 at 414; *Lakin Ltd v Secretary of State for Scotland*, 1988 S.L.T. 780.

The right to be heard (*audi alteram partem*) includes the right to have the op-   **8.50**
portunity to present your case and know the basis of the case presented by the other
side, as well as the right to a fair hearing—each party should have a "fair crack of
the whip".[192] Some planning authorities give applicants the opportunity either to
respond formally to objections made to a proposed development or to amend the
application to counter the objections. It may be arguable that such an opportunity
must be offered to ensure that the applicant is given a fair hearing. Similarly, if the
application is amended, but not to such an extent that the planning authority require
a fresh application to be submitted, there may be a duty to inform all those who
lodged objections to the original application of the amendments and allow them to
make further representations.[193] The law has not evolved to the extent that definite
limits may be expressed. The only safe course is for the planning authority to assess at each stage in the progress of the application whether it has acted fairly in
respect of all parties. In one case, by representing to the councillors determining the
application that the outstanding problem had been resolved, without drawing attention to the representations maintained by an objector, the planning officers had not
allowed a fair opportunity for the objections to be considered.[194] There was a breach
of natural justice where a reporter imposed a replacement noise condition without
giving the parties an opportunity to express their views as to the acceptable noise
level.[195] It was a breach of natural justice for the reporter to decide that the existing site could accommodate the proposed development without giving the parties
an opportunity of being heard on that issue.[196]

In a hearing, a failure by the appointed person/LRB to take the necessary steps
to inform himself of the case could mean that the appellant/applicant is not given
a fair hearing.[197] The written submissions procedure (see para.8.20 above) provides
a good example of the procedures necessary to ensure that each party is given a fair
hearing. Where an appeal was determined on issues not raised by either party and
no opportunity was offered for submissions to be made by the parties on these issues, there was held to be a breach of natural justice.[198]

The other limb to natural justice is the rule against bias (*nemo judex in re sua*).   **8.51**
Mere suspicion of bias influencing the decision may be sufficient for the decision
to be declared illegal[199]: justice must not only be done, but be seen to be done. An
example of this principle can be seen in the non-statutory code of conduct whereby
any councillor who has an interest, financial or otherwise, in a planning application, should declare the existence of the interest and take no part in the discussion
and determination of that application (see Ch.2 above). This system is voluntary and
individual councillors must decide whether their interest in the application is sufficiently close to warrant self-disqualification. Inevitably, in smaller communities
it is more difficult to avoid conflicts of interest arising and this may have to be
recognised when assessing suspicion of bias. There may be a suspicion of bias

192 *Fairmount Investments Ltd v Secretary of State for the Environment* [1976] 2 All E.R. 865.
193 *Lochore v Moray DC*, 1992 S.L.T. 16; cf. *Walker v Aberdeen City Council*, 1997 S.C.L.R. 425 and
   Burgon v Highland Council [2007] CSOH 70. See para.5.35.
194 *Castelow v Stirling DC*, 1992 G.W.D. 19–1139.
195 *Dunfermline DC v Secretary of State for Scotland*, 1996 S.L.T. 89; 1995 52 S.P.E.L. 110.
196 *Lidl UK GmbH v Scottish Ministers*[2006] CSOH 165.
197 *Dyason v Secretary of State for the Environment, Transport and the Regions* [1998] J.P.L. 778.
198 *Anduff Holdings Ltd v Secretary of State for Scotland*, 1992 S.L.T. 696; *Bancon Developments Ltd
   v Scottish Ministers* [2011] CSOH 137.
199 *Steeples v Derbyshire CC* [1984] 3 All E.R. 468; *Simmons v Secretary of State for the Environment* [1985] J.P.L. 253.

where a councillor is a business competitor of the applicant and, therefore, has an interest in the failure of a business-related planning application, although the courts have ruled that it would be going too far to say that this necessarily disqualifies him.[200] There was no real danger of bias where a councillor with a pecuniary interest in a development was present when the decision was made, but had declared his interest, vacated his chair and taken no part in the discussions or voting.[201] Involvement with the local Conservative Association or membership of the rugby club on whose land the development was proposed was held to be insufficient to invalidate the decision.[202] Where predisposition in favour of a proposal arose from performance of other council duties of a councillor, this did not of itself prevent the councillor from sitting on the planning committee, provided the councillor did not have a closed mind and considered the proposal on its planning merits.[203] A licensing decision was quashed when, following a site visit, the chair made a private visit to adjoining premises of an objector and was seen giving the objector a friendly wave.[204]

The rule against bias does not prevent the grant of planning permission for development of land owned by the planning authority, even in circumstances where the authority has agreed to lease the land to the applicant if the planning application is successful.[205] Special procedural rules apply to proposals for development by the planning authority (see Ch.9 below).

The decision-maker must avoid giving the appearance of a closed mind. Where a Minister was alleged to have said in advance of a committee meeting that he was, "going to go with the inspector's report", that did not indicate a closed mind.[206]

The reporter hearing a planning appeal, and the LRB undertaking a review, must also avoid creating any suspicion of bias. A conversation between a reporter and officials of the planning authority following the close of an inquiry created such a suspicion and, therefore, amounted to a breach of natural justice.[207] Allegations of such conduct might justify the exceptional step of requiring the reporter to appear as a witness before the court.[208] Where the reporter and both parties indulged in a drink after the inquiry, it was considered inadvisable for the reporter to remain for a fresh drink after the departure of one party, although there was no breach of natural justice.[209] Similarly, there was doubtful wisdom in a reporter lunching with and travelling to the site visit with a planning authority witness, even with the consent of the appellant.[210] A decision was quashed where the inspector had proceeded with a site inspection with a representative of the planning authority but in the absence of the appellant.[211] Where an appeal involved the development of social housing to be funded by the Scottish Ministers, there was no real possibility

[200] *R. v Holderness BC Ex p. James Roberts Developments Ltd* (1993) 66 P. & C.R. 46.
[201] *R. v Bristol City Council Ex p. Anderson* [1998] P.L.C.R. 314.
[202] *R. v Secretary of State for the Environment Ex p. Kirkstall Valley Campaign Ltd* [1996] 3 All E.R. 304; 1996 55 S.P.E.L. 55.
[203] *R. v Hereford and Worcester CC Ex p. Wellington Parish Council* [1996] J.P.L. 573.
[204] *Mahmood v West Dunbartonshire Licensing Board*, 1998 S.C.L.R. 843.
[205] *R. (on the application of Lewis) v Redcar and Cleveland BC* [2008] EWCA Civ 746; *R. v St Edmundsbury BC Ex p. Investors in Industry Commercial Properties* [1985] 3 All E.R. 234; cf. *Steeples v Derbyshire CC* [1984] 3 All E.R. 468.
[206] *R. (on the application of Condron) v National Assembly for Wales* [2006] EWCA Civ 1573.
[207] *Simmons v Secretary of State for the Environment* [1985] J.P.L. 253.
[208] *Jones v Secretary of State for Wales* (1995) 70 P. & C.R. 211.
[209] *Cotterell v Secretary of State for the Environment* [1991] J.P.L. 1155.
[210] *Fox v Secretary of State for the Environment* [1993] J.P.L. 448.
[211] *R. (On the application of Tait) v Secretary of State* [2012] EWHC 643 (Admin).

of bias even although the reporter is appointed by the Ministers.[212] There was a real possibility of bias where the inspector deciding the demolition of a former bus station had been responsible for transport planning in the local county council.[213]

Allegations of bias by the Scottish Ministers have also been unsuccessful.[214]

As part of the requirement for procedural fairness, the law protects legitimate expectations.[215] A legitimate expectation is normally equated with a right to be heard or a duty to consult, although the concept is wider.[216] Legitimate expectations can be created by promise or by an established practice which it is reasonable to expect will continue.[217] If a planning authority undertakes to consult a person on a planning application or has always consulted that person on similar applications, that person may have a legitimate expectation of being consulted prior to determination of the application. Failure to fulfil that expectation may result in a challengeable decision.[218] It is unfortunate that diligent planning authorities, which consult widely to gauge public reaction to planning proposals, may create enforceable legitimate expectations of consultation, whilst authorities which rarely consult any persons other than statutory consultees will avoid creating such expectations.

8.52

If the decision-maker creates an express legitimate expectation that a policy will be followed, then the policy cannot be changed without giving an opportunity to discuss this change to those with the expectation. However, the courts have rejected the argument that this could extend to a legitimate expectation that the Scottish Ministers would follow previous indications of policy and grant planning permission.[219] The expectation does not prevent a change in policy, but merely requires the decision-maker to consult with the person holding the legitimate expectation before making the change and to allow representations to be made regarding the change.[220] An appeal decision was quashed on the ground of unfairness where, by reason of the decision-maker's inconsistency in the interpretation and application of his policy, a person dealing with him had been taken by surprise and had had no adequate opportunity to meet the new approach before the relevant decision was made.[221] Even if there has been a previous understanding between the local authority and the community that a community hall would be part of a development of a site, in determining the planning application, the authority were bound to have regard to the current planning policy.[222]

Legitimate expectation is a developing area of the law and the courts have yet to issue a judgment explaining its limits in planning. Clearly much will depend on the circumstances of individual cases. From recent decisions, it seems that legitimate expectations overlap with the duty of fairness. Where applicants for plan-

---

[212] *McDonald v Scottish Ministers*, 2008 G.W.D. 10–198.
[213] *R. (on the application of Ortona Ltd) v Secretary of State for Communities and Local Government* [2009] EWCA Civ 863.
[214] *Packard, Petitioner* [2011] CSOH 93; *Trump International Golf Club Scotland Ltd v Scottish Ministers* [2015] CSIH 46.
[215] Ian Loveland, "Legitimate Expectations and Local Authority Autonomy" [2009] J.P.L. 1422.
[216] *R. v Secretary of State for the Home Department Ex p. Ruddock* [1987] 2 All E.R. 518.
[217] *Devine v McPherson*, 2002 S.L.T. 213 —there was no legitimate expectation where the local authority's practice was to regard holding a hearing as a matter within their discretion.
[218] *Gerber v Wiltshire Council* [2015] EWHC 524 (Admin).
[219] *R. v Secretary of State for the Environment Ex p. Barratt (Guildford) Ltd* [1990] J.P.L. 25. See also *R. v Great Yarmouth BC Ex p. Botton Bros Arcades* [1988] J.P.L. 18.
[220] *R. v Secretary of State for Health Ex p. United States Tobacco International Inc* [1992] 1 Q.B. 353.
[221] *Barnet Meeting Room Trust v Secretary of State for the Environment* [1993] J.P.L. 739.
[222] *R. (On the application of Godfrey) v Southwark LBC* [2012] EWCA Civ 500.

ning permission failed to carry out their legal duty to notify a neighbour of the application, the neighbour drew this to the attention of the planning authority and indicated that he wished to object to the application, but reserved the statement of his reasons until he had been properly notified. The applicants then submitted an amended application in respect of which the neighbour was not notifiable and for which the planning authority granted permission two days later. This grant of planning permission was declared illegal because the planning authority had prejudiced the legitimate expectation of the neighbour of being able to lodge an objection against the application.[223]

8.53   An applicant, whose appeal against refusal of planning permission was pending, sought to challenge the Secretary of State's decision not to call in another superstore application. The court held that the applicant had been deprived of its legitimate expectation of having its appeal determined at a public local inquiry and the Secretary of State had pre-judged the issue and pre-empted the appeal. In considering the merits of the alternative site, which was the subject of the applicants' appeal, the Secretary of State failed to give them a fair hearing and, therefore, acted illegally.[224] The decision would probably have been valid if the Secretary of State had ignored the existence of alternative sites completely, even although this would still have effectively pre-judged the outcome of the applicant's appeal. This is supported by the decision in a subsequent case that any prejudice caused to the appellant was inherent in the planning process because of the absence of a right of appeal against the grant of permission to a rival applicant, and that the Secretary of State did not act illegally in not calling in a rival application when he recalled an appeal for his determination.[225]

Where a previous application for residential development of the same site had been treated as a major one, with consequent procedural implications, this did not constitute a regular practice which the local residents could reasonably have expected to continue.[226]

Persons who had lodged objections to a finalised local plan unsuccessfully argued that a decision to grant planning permission which effectively pre-judged their objections unfairly deprived them of their legitimate expectation of having their objections considered at a local plan inquiry. The court held that the planning authority could competently grant planning permission provided the objections were taken into account in the determination of the planning application.[227]

In response to a letter from the planning authority objectors confirmed their intention to speak at the committee meeting and asked for confirmation of the date and time of the meeting. The objectors did not provide their telephone number. No contact was made by the planning authority. The meeting took place in the absence of the objectors, who challenged the grant of permission on the grounds that they had been given a reasonable expectation. The court held that although the leaflet provided by the planning authority to the objectors could be read as placing the onus on the objectors to obtain the information about the meeting, the leaflet had to be

---

[223]   *Lochore v Moray DC*, 1992 S.L.T. 16.
[224]   *Lakin Ltd v Secretary of State for Scotland*, 1988 S.L.T. 780.
[225]   *ASDA Stores Ltd v Secretary of State for Scotland*, 1998 S.C.L.R. 246; 1998 66 S.P.E.L. 33.
[226]   *Campbell v Edinburgh City Council*, 1998 G.W.D. 17–877; 1998 69 S.P.E.L. 99.
[227]   *Watson v Renfrew DC*, 1995 S.C.L.R. 82; 1995 50 S.P.E.L. 68. See also *Land Securities Group Plc v North Lanarkshire Council* [2005] CSOH 116.

read through the eyes of the objectors, and the authority should have informed them by letter of the date, time and place of the meeting.[228]

As the concept of legitimate expectation demonstrates, the boundaries of the grounds for judicial review are continually developing.

Procedure

An application for judicial review is made by petition to the Court of Session. **8.54** There is a special accelerated procedure intended to promote flexibility and rapid decisions where required.[229]

In 2015 a permission stage was introduced: the application can only proceed if[230]:

(a)   the applicant can demonstrate a sufficient interest (discussed at para.8.42 above) in the subject matter of the application; and
(b)   the application has a real prospect of success.

The previous first (and occasionally second) hearings are replaced by procedural and substantive hearings.

Powers of the court

The discretionary powers of the Court of Session under judicial review procedure **8.55** are wider than its statutory review powers (see para.8.36 above). In addition to quashing an illegal decision, either in whole or in part, judicial review procedure allows the court to prevent an illegal decision being made or restrain illegal conduct (by interdict), to force a body to carry out a stated duty (by specific implement), to declare the true legal position (make a declaration), and to award damages.[231] It also has power to make any interim order which it thinks fit, pending determination of the action.[232]

In considering motions for interim suspension of a planning permission and interim interdict against implementing that permission, the court held that the principal issue was whether the petitioner had demonstrated that she had a prima facie case and, if so, whether, in light of that prima facie case, the balance of convenience favoured the granting of the motions. It was for the petitioner to demonstrate there is a likelihood of harm, especially where there had been environmental assessment of the environmental effects of the development. There were no averments of significant changes to the ecology of the site as a result of the works. The balance of convenience did not therefore favour the granting of the motions, as the works were already underway, and there would be financial consequences to the developer if the works had to stop.[233]

In deciding whether to quash a decision to grant consent, the court took into account the prejudice to members of the public.[234] Where there had been a breach of the relevant Regulations, the court exercised its discretion to refuse to grant relief,

---

[228] *R. v Alnwick DC Ex p. Robson* [1997] E.G. 144 (C.S.).
[229] RCS (SI 1994/1443) Ch.58, first introduced in 1985.
[230] Court of Session Act 1988 s.27B, inserted by Courts Reform (Scotland) Act 2014 s.89.
[231] RCS, r.58.13.
[232] e.g. interim interdict—*Bonnes v West Lothian DC*, 1994 G.W.D. 31-1888.
[233] *Forbes v Aberdeenshire Council* [2010] CSOH 01.
[234] *Petition of The John Muir Trust* [2015] CSOH 163 per Lord Jones at [105]–[106].

because the same decision would have been reached even if the correct process was followed.[235]

Expenses

8.56   The normal rule of expenses following success applies: the successful challenger will normally obtain an order of expenses against the decision-maker, while the unsuccessful challenger will be liable to pay the costs of the other parties involved in the court action, in addition to his own.

Protective expenses orders can be granted by the court, capping potential liability to pay expenses.[236]

OTHER METHODS OF CHALLENGE

Ombudsman

8.57   Complaints relating to decisions and actions of planning authorities on planning applications can now be made direct to the Scottish Public Services Ombudsman (SPSO).[237] The SPSO can only consider a complaint if a member of the public suffered hardship or injustice as a result of maladministration or service failure in the provision of a public service. Although the SPSO has substantial powers of investigation, there is no power to enforce his/her decisions or recommendations. However, recommendations for compensation or redress are frequently implemented by planning authorities.

Sue for negligence or breach of contract

8.58   Planning authorities are subject to the ordinary law of delict and contract. Thus, where an individual has suffered harm as a consequence of either the unlawful actions or the omissions of a public official or public body, an action for damages may be available. However, the current trend is to deny any liability in negligence of public authorities for the exercise of their statutory powers.[238] Where a person fails to fulfil the conditions of a s.75 obligation, the normal remedies for a breach of contract will be available to the other parties to the obligation (see Ch.6 above).

Human rights

8.59   Chapter 2 outlines the relevance of the European Convention on Human Rights.

---

[235] *R. (on the application of Champion) v North Norfolk DC* [2015] UKSC 52.
[236] RCS (SI 1994/1443) r.58A—for example, *Sally Carroll v Scottish Borders Council* [2014] CSOH 30; *Petition of Friends of Loch Etive* [2014] CSOH 116; *John Muir Trust v Scottish Ministers*, 2015 G.W.D. 1-20. At common law—*McGinty, Petitioner* [2010] CSOH 5; *Road Sense v Scottish Ministers* [2011] CSOH 10; *Newton Mearns Residents Flood Protection Group v East Renfrewshire Council* [2013] CSIH 70.
[237] See *http://www.spso.org.uk* [Accessed 2 February 2016].
[238] *R. v Hounslow LBC Ex p. Williamson* [1996] E.G. 27 (C.S.); *Tidman v Reading BC* [1994] 3 P.L.R. 72; *Ryeford Homes Ltd v Sevenoaks DC* [1990] J.P.L. 36; 1989 27 S.P.L.P. 53; cf. *Lambert v West Devon BC* (1998) 75 P. & C.R. 282; *Welton v North Cornwall DC* [1997] 1 W.L.R. 570.

CHAPTER 9

PARTICULAR CONTROLS

The provisions of Acts examined in the previous chapters generally have   **9.01**
universal application. The Town and Country Planning (Scotland) Act (TCPSA)
1997 and related Acts also contain particular controls which apply to items of
special significance, such as listed buildings, or to designated areas, such as
conservation areas, or to specific forms of development, such as mineral extraction, or to classes of developers, such as the Crown and planning authorities. The
following examination of these often complex controls necessarily takes the form
of an overview rather than a complete and detailed exposition.

LISTED BUILDINGS

The statutory provisions on listed buildings are contained in the Planning (Listed   **9.02**
Buildings and Conservation Areas) (Scotland) Act 1997, as amended by the Planning Etc. (Scotland) Act (PSA) 2006, and the Historic Environment (Amendment) Scotland Act 2011.

On 1 October 2015, Historic Environment Scotland (HES) was launched, a new
lead public body to investigate, care for and promote Scotland's historic
environment.[1] It takes over the responsibilities of Historic Scotland[2] and The Royal
Commission on Ancient and Historic Monuments.

HES have the power to compile lists of buildings of special architectural or
historic interest, referred to as listed buildings.[3] There are currently some 47,000
listed buildings in Scotland. Policy is set out in the Scottish Historic Environment
Policy (SHEP).[4]

The term "building" includes any structure or erection, and items such as
telephone boxes and bridges have been designated as listed buildings. Any object
or structure fixed to the listed building, or which falls within its curtilage and has

---

[1] Historic Environment (Scotland) Act 2014. Historic Environment Circular 1 (2015—available on
  the HES website) explains the changes introduced by the 2014 Act and secondary legislation—
  Appendix 1 summarises the key changes.
[2] Historic Scotland was an executive agency of the Scottish Government. The Scottish Ministers were
  therefore not an independent and impartial tribunal when they determined a called-in listed building consent application or appeal, if Historic Scotland objected to the application or appeal. However,
  the existence of a right of appeal to the Court of Session was sufficient to satisfy the requirements
  of art.6 of the European Convention on Human Rights—*County Properties Ltd v Scottish Ministers*
  2000 S.L.T. 965 (OH); 2001 S.L.T. 1125 (IH).
[3] Planning (Listed Buildings and Conservation Areas) (Scotland) Act (PLBCASA)1997 s.1(1), as
  amended by the Historic Environment Scotland Act 2014; Listed Buildings (Notification and
  Publication) (Scotland) Regulations 2015 (SSI 2015/241).
[4] See *http://www.historic-scotland.gov.uk/index/heritage/policy/shep.htm* [Accessed 2 February 2016].

formed part of the land since before 1 July 1948, is treated as part of the building.[5] The primary test of what is listed is the circumstances of the site at the date of statutory listing.

New statutory provisions enable aspects to be specified as excluded from the listing.[6]

Importantly, listing covers the interior as well as the exterior of the building irrespective of whether the list contains a detailed interior description.

Determining whether an object or structure is fixed to the building depends on the degree to which it can be said to be annexed to the building and the purpose for which it was put there.[7]

There is no statutory definition of "curtilage", but this term broadly includes any land or building used for the comfortable enjoyment of the listed building or serving its purpose in some necessary or reasonably useful way, although not marked off or enclosed in any way (see Ch.4 above). A listed building may, therefore, include stables, mews blocks or garden walls within its grounds, notwithstanding that these have passed into separate ownership since the date of listing, but not buildings erected within its curtilage since 1 July 1948.[8] The curtilage of a building need not always be small, and the question of what falls within the curtilage of a building is one of fact and degree.[6]

The courts can quash a decision where the list has been misconstrued, for example where the decision-maker has erroneously decided that a building is not listed.[9]

It is open to planning authorities or any person or body to suggest to HES that a building be listed. The HES policy on listed buildings is in the SHEP, which was updated in 2011.[10] When considering whether to list a building, HES may take into account not only the building itself, but also the contribution of its exterior to the architectural or historic interest of any group of buildings of which it forms part. They may also consider the desirability of preserving any feature of the building on the ground of its architectural or historic interest. Before compiling or approving the list, persons or bodies with special knowledge or interest in buildings of architectural or historic interest are consulted.

In 2015, a right of appeal to the Scottish Ministers was introduced against decision by HES to list a building or to amend an entry on the list.[11]

Listed buildings may be removed from the list, either following representations by an interested party or the demolition or alteration of the building.

Listed buildings are divided into three non-statutory categories according to merit:

A   buildings of national or international importance; either architectural or historic, or fine, little-altered examples of some particular period, style or building type;

---

5   PLBCASA 1997 s.1(4), as amended by Historic Environment Scotland Act 2014. For example, *Glasgow City Council v Cannell*, 2000 S.L.T. 1023 where interim interdict was granted to prohibit the sale of stained glass panels.
6   PLBCASA 1997 s.1(4A), inserted by Historic Environment Scotland Act 2014.
7   *R. v Secretary of State for Wales Ex p. Kennedy* [1996] 1 P.L.R. 97; [1996] J.P.L. 645.
8   *Morris v Wrexham CBC* [2002] 2 P. & C.R. 7.
9   *Edinburgh City Council v Secretary of State for Scotland*, 1998 S.L.T. 120; 1998 65 S.P.E.L. 11.
10   SHEP, paras 2.17–2.36 and Annex 2, "Criteria for Determining Whether a Building is of 'Special Architectural or Historic Interest' for Listing".
11   PLBCASA 1997 s.5B, inserted by Historic Environment Scotland Act 2014.

B   buildings of regional or more than local importance; or major examples of
     some particular period, style or building type;
C   buildings of local importance; lesser examples of any period, style or build-
     ing type, as originally constructed or altered; and simple, traditional build-
     ings, which group well with others.

These categories have no legal effect, but are used as a guide to the importance
of the listed building and might, therefore, suggest the degree of difficulty which
may be anticipated in obtaining listed building consent in relation to the building.

After the list has been compiled and approved, notification must be served on the
owner, and occupier of the building and the local authority for the area.[12] Copies
of the list of such buildings must also be made available for public inspection.

Listed building control

(a)   Listed building consent

Listed building consent is required in advance for demolition of a listed build-   **9.03**
ing or its alteration or extension in any manner which would affect its character as
a building of special architectural or historic interest.[13] A substantial structure
erected close to the façade of the building may so affect its character or appearance that it constitutes an alteration or extension.[14] Works to Crown listed buildings now require consent.[15]

Whether works are demolition or alteration is a question of fact in each case, but
the demolition of part of a listed building is an alteration and not a demolition.[16] The
need for listed building consent is not satisfied by a grant of planning permission,
nor an express or deemed consent under the control of advertisement regulations.
It is an offence to carry out demolition or such works without listed building
consent, or to fail to comply with conditions attached to such a consent (see
para.9.08 below). An application may be made for retrospective consent to authorise
works already done.[17] Unlike planning permission, a failure to obtain listed building consent can never become immune from enforcement action through the passage of time. An owner can be liable for works carried out by a previous owner.[18]

The requirement for consent extends to objects or structures which are fixed to
a listed building, or come within its curtilage and have done so since before 1 July
1948. In consequence, buildings which were originally ancillary to the listed building, but are now under separate ownership, can continue to be regarded as listed
buildings on the basis of location within the curtilage of the principal building (see
para.9.02 above).

It is important to note that, unlike planning permission, consent may be required
for internal alterations to a listed building irrespective of whether the internal
features are described in the listing.

Listed building consent is not required (although it may be necessary to obtain

---

[12]   PLBCASA 1997 s.1A, inserted by Historic Environment (Scotland) Act 2014; Listed Building
       (Notification and Publication) (Scotland) Regulations 2015 (SSI 2015/241).
[13]   PLBCASA 1997 ss.6 and 7.
[14]   *Ampliflaire Ltd v Secretary of State for Scotland*,1998 S.C.L.R. 565; 1998 68 S.P.E.L. 77.
[15]   PLBCASA 1997 s.73A.
[16]   *Shimizu (UK) Ltd v Westminster City Council* [1997] 1 All E.R. 481; [1997] J.P.L. 523.
[17]   PLBCASA 1997 s.7(3).
[18]   *Braun v Secretary of State for Transport, Local Government and the Regions* [2003] J.P.L. 1536.

planning permission)[19]:

    (i)   if the building is an ecclesiastical building used for ecclesiastical purposes (other than wholly or mainly as a residence for a minister);

    (ii)   if the building is included in the schedule of monuments (scheduled monument consent is required instead);

    (iii) for the erection of a modern, free-standing building in the curtilage of a listed building, or for works to objects or structures which have been within its curtilage only since 1 July 1948 and are not physically attached to the building.[20]

9.04   Application for listed building consent is made to the planning authority, on the form obtainable from the authority.[21] It is not competent to apply for consent in principle (referred to as outline consent), and full details of the proposed works must be given in the application. If planning permission is also required for the work (see Ch.4 above), application for both consents is normally made on the same form. The applications can be processed simultaneously, but separate decisions must be issued.

    When applying for listed building consent, the applicant is required to complete a certificate stating either that he is the owner of the building or any part of the building to which the application relates, or has served notice of the application on the owner(s) named in the certificate or, despite taking specified steps, has been unable to trace any or all of the owners (see Ch.5 above). Copies of the form of notice to be served upon the owners are included with the application form obtained from the planning authority. In contrast to planning applications, there is no form of neighbour notification for listed building consent applications.

    The planning authority has the power to decline to determine an application in certain circumstances where a similar application was refused previously.[22]

    The planning authority must advertise the application in both a local newspaper and the *Edinburgh Gazette*, and display a site notice for at least seven days. The advertisement and site notice must include a description of the works and name a place where plans of the works can be inspected. The application cannot be determined until 21 days after the date of the advertisement or the posting of the notice.

    The authority must consult HES where the application is submitted by the planning authority, or is for demolition of a listed building, or for works to a Category A or B listed building.[23] In contrast to planning applications, the authority is not obliged to consult other appropriate bodies for their views, although this may be done as a matter of good practice.

    In determining the application, the authority must take into account any representations relating to the application received during the 21-day period and, in particular, any representations made by a person who satisfies them that he is owner of part of the building. Special regard must be paid to the desirability of preserving the building or its setting or any features of special architectural or

---

[19] PLBCASA 1997 ss.54 and 55.

[20] But see *Amplifaire Ltd v Secretary of State for Scotland*, 1998 S.C.L.R. 565; 1998 68 S.P.E.L. 77.

[21] Planning (Listed Building Consent and Conservation Area Consent Procedure) (Scotland) Regulations 2015 (SSI 2015/243), repealing the Town and Country Planning (Listed Buildings and Buildings in Conservation Areas) (Scotland) Regulations 1987 (SI 1987/1529).

[22] PLBCASA 1997 s.10A, inserted by Historic Environment (Amendment) (Scotland) Act 2011.

[23] Planning (Listed Building Consent and Conservation Area Consent Procedure) (Scotland) Regulations (PLBCCACPSR) 2015 (SSI 2015/243) reg.7.

historic interest which it possesses (see para.9.11 below).[24] The policy on listed building consent is in the SHEP.[25] It includes a presumption against demolition or other works that adversely affect the special interest of a listed building or its setting, which can be overcome if there will be significant benefits for economic growth or the wider community.

If the planning authority is minded to grant consent, contrary to advice from HES, or the authority does not propose to impose any condition recommended by HES, the planning authority must notify the Ministers of that intention.[26] That gives the Scottish Ministers the opportunity to consider whether to call in the application for their determination.

Listed building consent may be granted subject to conditions, for example reserving specified minor details of the work for subsequent approval of the planning authority; preserving particular features of the building; requiring the making good, after the works are completed, of any damage caused to the building by the works; or providing for the reconstruction of the building or any part of it following the execution of any works, with the use of original materials so far as practicable and with specified alterations to its interior. It is also competent for the authority to impose a condition preventing demolition of the listed building until it is satisfied that the site will be redeveloped in accordance with a current planning permission, either through a s.75 agreement/obligation (see Ch.6 above) and/or the placing of contracts for redevelopment work.[27] Any person with a legal interest in a listed building may apply to the planning authority for variation or discharge of conditions attached to a grant of listed building consent.[28]

9.05

Where consent has been granted for demolition of a listed building, work cannot commence until at least three months after HES has been notified by the applicant (the appropriate form should be sent to the applicant by the planning authority along with the grant of consent). HES must either have been given access to record the building, or have stated in writing that its recording is complete or that it does not wish to record it.[29]

A listed building consent lapses after three years from the date of the consent (previously five years), unless the works permitted by the consent have begun. The planning authority when granting the consent can specify a different period.[30] The date of the grant of listed building consent by the authority is the date on which the decision notice bears to have been signed.

The applicant has a right of appeal to the Scottish Ministers against[31]:

(i)   a refusal of listed building consent or of approval of subsequent details required in terms of a condition attached to the original grant of consent, or the grant of consent or approval subject to conditions;

(ii)   a refusal of an application to vary or discharge conditions, or any fresh conditions imposed following such an application; and

(iii)   a failure of the planning authority to determine the application, or give

---

24 PLBCASA 1997 s.14(2).
25 SHEP, paras 3.39–3.53.
26 The Planning (Listed Buildings and Conservation Areas) (Notification of Applications) Direction 2015.
27 PLBCASA 1997 s.15.
28 PLBCASA 1997 s.17.
29 PLBCASA 1997 s.7(2), as amended by Historic Environment Scotland Act 2014.
30 PLBCASA 1997 s.16, as amended by the PSA 2006 s.20(3).
31 PLBCASA 1997 s.18.

notice that the application has been called in by the Scottish Ministers, within two months of the date of receipt of the application or any extended period agreed in writing with the applicant (known as a deemed refusal appeal).

The appeal must be submitted within three months (previously six months) of notice of the decision or expiry of the two-month period.[32] The procedure is similar to that for planning appeals described in Ch.8.[33] In addition to the normal grounds of appeal, the appellant may allege that the building is not of special architectural or historic interest and, therefore, ought not to be listed. In determining the appeal, the Scottish Ministers may reverse or vary any part of the decision by the authority, whether the appeal relates to that part or not, and may deal with the application as if it had been made to him in the first instance. As part of the appeal decision, the Scottish Ministers can also "de-list" the building by directing HES to remove it from the list.[34]

The Scottish Ministers' decision on the merits of the appeal or called-in application is final. However, the legality of the decision may be challenged in the Court of Session under the statutory review procedure, but only within six weeks of the decision (see Ch.8 above).

(b) Enforcement

9.06   Where there is a failure to obtain listed building consent, the planning authority may serve a listed building enforcement notice, and/or may seek interim interdict.[35] A stop notice can be served in conjunction with the enforcement notice.[36] The planning authority also have power to serve a temporary stop notice.[37]

A listed building enforcement notice may be served where it appears to the planning authority, or the Scottish Ministers, that any works have been or are being executed to a listed building in contravention of the requirement to obtain listed building consent, or of the conditions attached to a consent. In making its decision, the authority has regard to the effect of the works on the character of the building as one of special architectural or historic interest.[38] A failure to obtain listed building consent can never become immune from enforcement action through passage of time, unlike work carried out without planning permission. An owner can be liable for works undertaken by a previous owner.[39]

The notice specifies the alleged contravention and, either the works to cease and/or the steps required, within a given period, to restore the building to its former state, or to bring it to the state in which it would have been if the terms and conditions of any listed building consent for the works had been complied with. Alternatively, where it appears to the authority that complete restoration of the building to its former state is undesirable or not reasonably practical, the notice can

---

[32] Town and Country Planning (Appeals) (Scotland) Regulations 2013 (SSI 2013/156) reg.17

[33] Discussed in Historic Environment Circular 1/2015, paras 131–204.

[34] PLBCASA 1997 ss.19 and 20, as amended by PSA 2006 and Historic Environment Scotland Act 2014.

[35] *Glasgow City Council v Cannell*, 2000 S.L.T. 1023.

[36] PLBCASA 1997 s.41A, inserted by Historic Environment (Amendment) (Scotland) Act 2011.

[37] PLBCASA 1997 s.41F, inserted by Historic Environment (Amendment) (Scotland) Act 2011.

[38] PLBCASA 1997 ss.34 and 41, as amended by Historic Environment (Amendment) (Scotland) Act 2011.

[39] *Braun v Secretary of State for Transport, Local Government and the Regions* [2003] J.P.L. 1536.

specify steps to alleviate the effects of works executed without listed building consent, in a manner acceptable to it. The notice must specify the date upon which it is to take effect, and the period within which the steps are required to be taken. Different periods may be specified for different steps.

A copy of the listed building enforcement notice is served on the current owner, lessee and occupier of the building and on any other person who has an interest in the building which, in the opinion of the planning authority, is materially affected by the notice. (Methods of service are discussed in Ch.7.) Details of the building in respect of which the notice has been served must be entered in a list available for public inspection.

Withdrawal of the notice by the planning authority is competent at any time, whether or not it has taken effect, and without prejudice to its power to serve another. The authority may also waive or relax any requirement of the notice and, in particular, extend any period for taking the steps specified in the notice. Notification of its withdrawal, or any waiver or relaxation of its terms, must be given to every person served with the notice.

The owner of the land is guilty of an offence if at the end of the period for compliance with the notice, any step required to be taken in terms of the notice has not been taken, or any works required to cease have not ceased.[40] Such an offence may be charged by reference to any day or longer period of time. It is a defence to show that everything was done that could be expected to secure that all the required steps were taken, or that the owner was not served with a copy of the notice and was not aware of it. On summary conviction, there is liability to a maximum fine of £20,000, and to an unlimited fine following conviction on indictment. In determining the level of fine the court shall in particular have regard to any financial benefit which has accrued or appears likely to accrue to the person in consequence of the offence. Following conviction, further offences are committed if there is a continuing failure to take any step.

The planning authority have power to serve a fixed penalty notice where there is a breach of a listed building enforcement notice.[41]

If the steps required by the listed building enforcement notice have not been taken within the specified period, the planning authority may enter the land and take those steps, recovering any expenses reasonably incurred in this process from the person who is then the owner or lessee of the land. Such expenses are deemed to have been incurred on behalf of the person who carried out the unauthorised works, but there is no specific provision for recovery from that person. It is an offence to wilfully obstruct the exercise of this right of entry.[42]

Any person on whom the notice was served or any other person having an interest in the building to which it relates may lodge an appeal to the Scottish Ministers against the notice.[43] Such an appeal follows a similar procedure to an appeal against a planning enforcement notice (see Ch.7 above) and prevents the requirements of the notice from coming into force pending determination or withdrawal of the appeal. Written notice of the appeal must be lodged with Directorate of Planning and Environmental Appeals (DPEA) before the notice takes effect (on the expiry of the period specified in the notice), or sent in a properly addressed and pre-paid

---

[40] PLBCASA 1997 s.39, as amended by Historic Environment (Scotland) Act 2011.
[41] PLBCASA 1997 s.39A, inserted by Historic Environment (Scotland) Act 2011.
[42] PLBCASA 1997 s.38.
[43] PLBCASA 1997 s.35.

envelope posted at such a time that, in the ordinary course of post, it would be delivered before that date, or sent using electronic communications at such time that, in the ordinary course of transmission, it would be delivered to them before that date.

9.07   The grounds of appeal are:

(i)   that the building is not of special architectural or historic interest;

(ii)   that the matters alleged to constitute a contravention of the requirements to obtain listed building consent, or of the conditions of a consent, do not involve such a contravention;

(iii)   that those matters (if they occurred) do not constitute such a contravention;

(iv)   that the works were urgently necessary in the interests of safety or health or for the preservation of the building, and it was not practicable for this purpose to carry out repairs or works for affording temporary support or shelter, and that the works were limited to the minimum measures immediately necessary;

(v)   that listed building consent ought to be granted for the works, or any relevant condition of such consent which has been granted ought to be discharged or different conditions substituted;

(vi)   that the notice was not served in accordance with the statutory provisions;

(vii)   that the requirements of the notice exceed what is necessary for restoring the building to its condition before the works were carried out;

(viii) that the period specified in the notice as the period within which any steps required thereby are to be taken falls short of what should reasonably be allowed;

(ix)   that the steps required by the notice to be taken would not serve the purpose of restoring the character of the building to its former state;

(x)   cessation of any works required by the notice exceeds what is necessary to remedy the contravention;

(xi)   that the steps specified exceed what is necessary to bring the building to the state it would have been in if the listed building consent had been complied with;

(xii)   that the steps specified exceed what may reasonably be required to alleviate the effects of works executed without listed building consent.

In the course of the appeal, the Scottish Ministers may correct any defect, error or misdescription in the notice, or vary its terms, provided they are satisfied that the correction or variation will not cause injustice to the appellant or planning authority. They may also disregard a failure to serve the notice on any person where that person has not suffered material prejudice as a result. In deciding the appeal, the Scottish Ministers may either quash the notice and grant listed building consent for the works to which the notice relates, or discharge any condition subject to which such consent was granted and substitute any other condition, whether more or less onerous, or uphold the notice. In addition, the Ministers may de-list the building by directing HES to remove it from the list of buildings of special architectural or historic interest. The legality of the decision of the Scottish Ministers on the appeal may be challenged in the Court of Session using the statutory review procedure (see Ch.8 above).[44]

(c) Offences

It is an offence to carry out demolition or works which require listed building consent without obtaining such consent, or to fail to comply with conditions attached to a consent. It is a defence to show that the works were urgently necessary in the interests of safety or health or for the preservation of the building, and that it was not practicable to secure these interests by repair works or works providing temporary support or shelter, that the works were limited to the minimum measures immediately necessary and written notice justifying the need for the works was given to the planning authority as soon as reasonably practicable.[45] A person guilty of such an offence is liable on summary conviction to imprisonment for up to six months and/or a maximum fine of £50,000 (previously £20,000), and for conviction on indictment up to two years' imprisonment and/or an unlimited fine. In determining the level of fine to be imposed, the court is directed to have regard to any financial benefit which has accrued or appears likely to accrue to that person in consequence of the offence.[46]

9.08

Failure to comply with a listed building enforcement notice is also an offence (see para.9.06 above), together with doing or permitting to be done any act, other than that authorised by a grant of planning permission and/or listed building consent, which causes or is likely to result in damage to a listed building with the intention of causing such damage (see para.9.13 below).

Other consequences of listing

(a) Permitted development

The permitted development rights conferred by the Permitted Development Order (PDO) (see Ch.4 above) apply more restrictively to listed buildings, with the result that planning permission is required for a wider scope of activities. For example, permitted development rights for painting the exterior of a building do not apply to listed buildings, with the result that planning permission will be required for the painting work if the external appearance of the listed building will be materially affected as a result of that work.[47]

9.09

(b) Consultation with HES

Planning authorities must consult HES on any application for planning permission for a development which may affect a Category A listed building or its setting.[48] If the planning authority propose to grant planning permission for development

9.10

---

44 For example, *Edinburgh City Council v Scottish Ministers*, 2002 S.L.T. 1243; [2003] J.P.L. 903, in which the reporter's decision to grant listed building consent was quashed.
45 *Secretary of State for Scotland v Highland Council*, 1998 S.L.T. 222; 1997 63 S.P.E.L. 104.
46 PLBCASA 1997 s.8, as amended by Historic Scotland (Amendment) (Scotland) Act 2011.
47 Town and Country Planning (General Permitted Development) (Scotland) Order (PDO 1992) 1992 (SI 1992/223) Sch.1 Class 9(2); TCPSA 1997 s.26(2)(a).
48 Town and Country Planning (Development Management Procedure) (Scotland) Regulations (DMPR) 2013 (SSI 2013/155) reg.25 and Sch.5 para.17, inserted by Town and Country Planning (Historic Environment Scotland) Amendment Regulations 2015 (SSI 2015/237).

of a Category A listed building contrary to the advice received from HES, the authority must notify the Scottish Ministers prior to granting the permission (see Ch.5 above).

(c) Protection of setting

9.11   If the planning authority considers that the setting of a listed building would be affected by a development for which an application for planning permission has been made, the application should be advertised in a local newspaper and a site notice displayed for at least seven days, and 21 days allowed for representations to be lodged. When deciding whether to grant planning permission for such a development, the planning authority must take into account any representations received following the advertisement and site notice.[49]

In considering whether to grant permission for a development which affects a listed building or its setting, the authority must have special regard to the desirability of preserving the building or its setting or any features of special architectural or historic interest which it possesses.[50]

Where HES have been consulted on development affecting a Category A listed building or its setting, and advised against the grant of planning permission or recommended conditions which the planning authority does not propose to attach to the planning permission, the Scottish Ministers must be notified before the permission is granted.[51]

(d) Intimation of notices

9.12   Where a building owned, leased or occupied by the planning authority has been listed, various statutory notices, orders or proposals relating to demolition or the carrying out of works affecting the building must be intimated in writing to the Scottish Ministers. Written intimation may be dispensed with in cases where public safety requires demolition or other work to be carried out without delay, but intimation, even if initially oral, must be given as soon as possible before commencement of the demolition or works.[52]

(e) Offences

9.13   It is an offence to carry out demolition or works without listed building consent, or contrary to the conditions of a consent (see para.9.08 above). It is also an offence to do or permit to be done any act, other than that authorised by a grant of planning permission and/or listed building consent, which causes or is likely to result in damage to a listed building (other than those buildings exempted from the provisions relating to listed building consent), with the intention of causing such damage. On summary conviction a person guilty of such an offence is liable to a fine not exceeding level 3 on the standard scale (see Appendix 1 below).

Following conviction, a further offence is committed by failure to take such

---

49 PLBCASA 1997 s.60; TCPSA 1997 s.37(3).
50 PLBCASA 1997 s.59. *Simson v Aberdeenshire Council*, 2007 S.L.T. 244; *Barnwell Manor Wind Energy Ltd v East Northamptonshire DC* [2014] EWCA Civ 137.
51 The Town and Country Planning (Neighbouring Planning Authorities and Historic Environment) (Scotland) Direction 2015.
52 PLBCASA 1997 s.56.

reasonable steps as may be necessary to prevent any damage or further damage resulting from the offence, with a maximum fine of one-tenth of level 3 for each day on which the failure continues.[53]

(f)   Urgent works for preservation

If it appears to the planning authority (or the Scottish Ministers) that any works are urgently necessary for the preservation of a listed building, it may execute those works after giving not less than seven days' written notice to the owner of the building.[54] This power does not extend to an ecclesiastical building in ecclesiastical use, other than a minister's residence, or to a scheduled monument. The works may include erection of scaffolding for support or a temporary roof covering, and preventative works necessary to limit any deterioration of the building. If the building is occupied, works may be carried out only to those parts which are not in use.

    9.14

A similar power may be applied by direction of the Scottish Ministers to an unlisted building in a conservation area which should be preserved to maintain the character or appearance of the conservation area.

Notice may also be given to the owner rendering him liable to pay the expenses of these works unless within 28 days of the date of the notice he lodges an objection with the Scottish Ministers on the grounds that some or all of the works are unnecessary for the building's preservation, that temporary arrangements for support or shelter have continued for an unreasonable length of time, or that the amount specified in the notice is unreasonable, or that recovery of it would cause him hardship. The Scottish Ministers consider the justification for such an objection and give notice of their decision to the owner and the planning authority, if it carried out the works, together with a statement of the reasons for the decision and the amount recoverable.[55]

The notice of liability for expenses procedure can be used to make a new owner severally liable with the former owner for the expenses.[56]

(g)   Repairs notices and compulsory purchase

A repairs notice may be served at any time on the owner of a listed building by the planning authority or the Scottish Ministers specifying the works considered reasonably necessary for its proper preservation, and explaining the effect of the compulsory purchase provisions.[57] The notice may be withdrawn at any time, by serving notice of the withdrawal upon any person served with a copy of the notice. The landowner may not be able to challenge the repairs notice in the courts until a compulsory purchase order has been served.[58]

    9.15

Compulsory purchase proceedings can be initiated two months after service of a repairs notice, even if the building was demolished following service of the notice. The Scottish Ministers may authorise compulsory purchase if they are satisfied that reasonable steps are not being taken for properly preserving the listed building, and that it is expedient to make provision for its preservation and to authorise its

---

53   PLBCASA 1997 s.53.
54   PLBCASA 1997 s.49, as amended by Historic Environment (Amendment) (Scotland) Act 2011 s.25.
55   PLBCASA 1997 s.50. *Ramzan Bibi v Scottish Ministers* [2006] CSOH 152.
56   PLBCASA 1997 s.50A–G, inserted by Historic Environment (Amendment) (Scotland) Act 2011.
57   PLBCASA 1997 s.43.
58   *Prestige Assets Ltd v Renfrewshire Council*, 2003 S.L.T. 679.

compulsory purchase for that purpose.[59] The compulsory purchase order may include any land required for preserving the building or its amenities, or for giving access to it for its proper control or management. This compulsory purchase power does not extend to an ecclesiastical building in ecclesiastical use, other than a minister's residence, or to a scheduled monument. Any person with an interest in the building has 28 days after service of a compulsory purchase order to apply to the sheriff for an order prohibiting further proceedings upon it. Such an order will only be granted if the sheriff is satisfied that reasonable steps have been taken to preserve the building.

Where the planning authority or the Scottish Ministers are satisfied that the building has been deliberately allowed to fall into disrepair for the purpose of justifying its demolition and the development of the site, a direction may be made for the payment of minimum compensation, which ignores the redevelopment value of the land.[60]

(h) Listed building purchase notices

9.16   A listed building purchase notice may be served on the planning authority by the owner or lessee where the land has become incapable of reasonably beneficial use in its present state and listed building consent has been refused, granted subject to conditions, revoked or modified.[61] The notice has the effect of requiring the authority to purchase the interest in the land. The procedure is similar to that for planning purchase notices (see Ch.5 above).

(i) Rights of entry

9.17   HES and the planning authority has the right to enter land in specified circumstances in connection with listed buildings,[62] including to ascertain whether work is being carried out without listed building consent, or contrary to a condition attached to a consent, and whether the building is being maintained in a proper state of repair. Entry to land which is occupied cannot be demanded as of right unless 24 hours' notice of the intended entry has been given to the occupier. A warrant authorising entry may be sought from a sheriff if admission to the land has been refused or a refusal is reasonably apprehended, or the case is one of urgency.

Building preservation notices

9.18   Service of a building preservation notice extends the protection afforded to listed buildings to an unlisted building, on a temporary basis, while HES consider whether it should be listed. This notice may be served where it appears to the planning authority that the building is of special architectural or historic interest and is in danger of demolition or alteration in such a way as to affect its character. It is not competent to serve a building preservation notice in respect of an ecclesiastical building in use for ecclesiastical purposes, other than a minister's residence, or a

---

59   PLBCASA 1997 s.42.
60   PLBCASA 1997 s.45.
61   PLBCASA 1997 s.28.
62   PLBCASA 1997 ss.76–78, as amended by Historic Environment (Amendment) Scotland Act 2011 and Historic Environment Scotland Act 2014.

scheduled monument.[63] While the notice is in force, the building is treated as a listed building, except that an act causing or likely to cause damage to the building will not be an offence.

The notice states that the building appears to be of special architectural or historic interest and that the planning authority has requested HES to consider listing it, and explains its effect. The notice comes into force as soon as it has been served by the planning authority on the owner, lessee and occupier of the building. In urgent circumstances personal service may be dispensed with and the notice takes effect once it has been affixed conspicuously to some object on the building. The notice remains in force for six months from the last date of service, but is discharged within this period by the listing of the building or written notification to the planning authority from the HES that they do not intend to list the building.

If HES decide not to list the building the notice is discharged and this decision must be intimated forthwith to the owner, lessee and occupier of the building by the planning authority. Following a decision not to list the building, the planning authority cannot serve another building preservation notice in respect of the building within the following 12 months. Any enforcement proceedings will lapse, although liability will remain for non-compliance with a listed building enforcement notice committed while the notice was in force.

If the building preservation notice ceases to have effect without the building becoming listed, any person who at the time when the notice was served had an interest in the building shall be entitled to be paid compensation by the planning authority in respect of any loss or damage directly attributable to the effect of the notice.[64]

Certificate of intention not to list

HES may, on the application of any person, issue a certificate stating that it does not intend to list a building. Such a certificate prevents the building from being either listed or having a building preservation notice served for the subsequent five years.[65]   **9.19**

CONSERVATION AREAS

The planning authority has a duty to determine periodically which parts of its district are areas of special architectural or historic interest, the character or appearance of which it is desirable to preserve or enhance. Such areas should be designated as conservation areas.[66] HES have a reserve power to intervene and designate a conservation area. Notice of the designation, and any variation or cancellation of a designation, is given to the Scottish Ministers and advertised in the *Edinburgh Gazette* and a local newspaper. Individual owners and occupiers of property within the area do not require to be notified. No formal confirmation of the designation is   **9.20**

---

63 PLBCASA 1997 s.3, as amended by Historic Environment Scotland Act 2014.
64 PLBCASA 1997 s.26.
65 PLBCASA 1997 s.5A, as amended by Historic Environment (Amendment) Scotland Act 2011 and Historic Environment Scotland Act 2014. Discussed in SHEP Annex 11.
66 PLBCASA 1997 s.61(1) as amended by Historic Environment Scotland Act 2014. SHEP Annex 3 sets out the criteria which Scottish Ministers expect to be taken account of in designation. Advice is given in Planning Advice Note (PAN) 71, Conservation Area Management (Scottish Executive, 2004).

required from the Scottish Ministers. The authority must compile and make available for public inspection a list of particulars of conservation areas within its district. There are almost 600 conservation areas in Scotland.

Conservation area consent

9.21   Conservation area consent is required for demolition of a building in a conservation area, with exceptions including[67]:

(a)   a listed building (listed building consent will be required);

(b)   an ecclesiastical building in ecclesiastical use, other than a minister's residence;

(c)   a scheduled monument (scheduled monument consent will be required);

(d)   a building (but not a part of a building) with a total cubic content not exceeding 115 cubic m;

(e)   any gate, wall, fence or railing which is less than 1m high where abutting a road used by vehicular traffic or an open space, or 2m high in any other case; and

(f)   any building required to be demolished in terms of a discontinuance order or enforcement notice, or by virtue of a condition of a planning permission or provision of a s.75 agreement.

Consent may only be required where the whole building is to be demolished.[68]

Consent is obtained from the planning authority. The procedure for applying for consent and the powers of enforcement are the same as those applicable to applications for listed building consent (see para.9.04 above). In considering the application, the planning authority must pay special attention to the desirability of preserving or enhancing the character or appearance of the conservation area (see para.9.23 below). The importance of the building to the character and appearance of the conservation area are key considerations. If the site is to be redeveloped, consent should in general only be given where there are acceptable proposals for the new building.[69]

A number of the provisions applicable to listed building control (see paras 9.03 to 9.08 above) are applied to conservation area consent. Conditions similar to those for listed building consents may be imposed upon the grant of conservation area consent. If consent is granted for demolition of the building, HES must be given an opportunity to record the building. Enforcement action may be taken against any failure to obtain conservation area consent, and there is a right of appeal to the Scottish Ministers in respect of that action. It is an offence to demolish a building without the required conservation area consent.

---

[67]   The full list of exceptions appears in PLBCASA 1997 s.66, as amended by Historic Environment (Amendment) (Scotland) Act 2011 and Historic Environment Scotland Act 2014, and s.67, and Direction, "Exemption from Demolition Control in Conservation Areas", attached to Circular 17/1987, New Provisions and Revised Guidance relating to Listed Buildings and Conservation Areas (Scottish Office, 1987) Annex IV. The equivalent requirement in the English legislation was removed in October 2013, but still applies in Wales.

[68]   *Shimizu (UK) Ltd v Westminster City Council* [1997] 1 All E.R. 481; [1997] J.P.L. 523; Michael Brainsby and Howard Carter, "Shimizu: Part II: The Implications for Conservation Area Controls" [1997] J.P.L. 603.

[69]   SHEP paras 3.58–3.59.

Permitted development rights

Under the PDO (see Ch.4 above) permitted development rights for develop- **9.22**
ment in conservation areas are restricted, with the result that planning permission
is required for a wider range of development. For example, permitted development rights for painting the exterior of a building do not apply to buildings situated in conservation areas, with the result that planning permission will be required
for the painting work if the external appearance of such a building will be materially affected as a result of that work.[70] Further restrictions may be placed on permitted development rights within conservation areas by the use of art.4 directions[71] (see
para.9.27 below).

Planning applications—preservation of character and appearance

If the planning authority believes that a proposed development would affect the **9.23**
character or appearance of a conservation area, the application must be advertised
in a local newspaper and a site notice displayed for at least seven days. Any comments received within 21 days of the advertisement or display of the notice must
be taken into account when the application is determined.[72]

In addition, the planning authority must pay special attention to the desirability
of preserving or enhancing the character or appearance of a conservation area when
exercising its planning powers in relation to any buildings or land in that area,
including the determination of planning applications.[73] This will include looking at
such matters as scale, bulk, height, materials, colour, vertical or horizontal emphasis
and design and must be the first consideration for the authority.[74] The character or
appearance of a conservation area is preserved not only by a positive contribution
to preservation, but also by development which has a neutral effect and leaves the
character or appearance unharmed.[75] Where a development simultaneously causes
both enhancement and some detriment, the detrimental effect is a material
consideration.[76] This requirement may lead planning authorities to insist on applications for detailed rather than planning permission in principle for development
within conservation areas. A development can harm the character or appearance
even if there have already been extensive alterations in the vicinity.[77]

Protection of trees

With some exceptions, it is an offence to cut down, top, lop, uproot, wilfully dam- **9.24**
age or wilfully destroy a tree in a conservation area, even if it is not protected by a
tree preservation order, unless the planning authority was given six weeks' notice
of the proposed work or consented to it (see para.9.30 below).

---

[70] PDO 1992 (SI 1992/223) Sch.1 Class 9(2); TCPSA 1997 s.26(2)(a).
[71] PDO 1992 (SI 1992/223) art.4.
[72] PLBCASA 1997 s.65; TCPSA 1997 s.37(3).
[73] PLBCASA 1997 s.64. *Campbell v Edinburgh City Council*, 1999 S.L.T. 1009; 1999 69 S.P.E.L. 99;
Uprichard v Fife Council [2009] CSOH 170; *Eildon v Scottish Ministers* [2010] CSOH 102.
[74] *Bath Society v Secretary of State for the Environment* [1991] 1 W.L.R. 1303.
[75] *South Lakeland DC v Secretary of State for the Environment* [1992] 2 A.C. 141.
[76] *Bath Society v Secretary of State for the Environment* [1991] 1 W.L.R. 1303.
[77] *R. (on the application of University College London) v First Secretary of State* [2004] EWHC 2846
(Admin).

Urgent works for preservation

9.25   The Scottish Ministers may direct that the power to undertake works which are urgently necessary for the preservation of a listed building be extended to apply to a building in a conservation area, if satisfied that its preservation is important for maintaining the character or appearance of the area.[78]

If the building is occupied, works may be carried out only to those parts which are not in use.

Proposals for preservation and enhancement

9.26   There is a duty placed on planning authorities to formulate and publish proposals for the preservation and enhancement of conservation areas.[79] There is some criticism that planning authorities largely ignore this duty and use the conservation area designation as a device to achieve greater control over development.

Article 4 directions

9.27   The requirement for conservation area consent only applies to demolition of certain classes of buildings (see para.9.21 above). The planning authority can achieve greater control over development within a conservation area (and elsewhere) by means of an art.4 direction.[80] The effect of such a direction is to remove permitted development rights under the PDO (see Ch.4 above) for specified classes of development, with the result that planning permission must be obtained from the planning authority for those classes of development. The direction may apply to specified classes of development within a conservation area or other geographical areas or any particular development within a class, other than a small list of developments which cannot be restricted by an art.4 direction.

An art.4 direction may be made by the planning authority (or the Scottish Ministers), if it is satisfied that it is expedient to restrict permitted development rights in this way. In most cases the direction must be submitted to the Scottish Ministers for approval. Notice of the direction made or approved by the Scottish Ministers is published by the planning authority in the *Edinburgh Gazette* and at least one local newspaper.[81] The notice must specify any particular geographical area affected by the direction and contain a concise statement of the effect of the direction and name a place where a copy may be inspected. In the case of a direction specifying any particular development, notice must be served on the owner and occupier of the land affected. The direction comes into force on the date of publication of the first notice or date of service on the occupier or, if there is no occupier, on the owner. There is a right to compensation if an application for planning permission is refused and a development cannot proceed which but for the direction would not have required permission.[82]

An art.4 direction made by a planning authority may be cancelled without the ap-

---

[78] PLBCASA 1997 s.68.

[79] PLBCASA 1997 s.63.

[80] PDO 1992 (SI 1992/223) art.4. For information on the use of art.4 directions, see Scottish Office Development Department, *Research on the General Permitted Development Order and Related Mechanisms* (Scottish Office, 1998), pp.32 et seq.

[81] PDO 1992 (SI 1992/223) art.5.

[82] TCPSA 1997 s.77.

proval of the Scottish Ministers, although a notice must be published or served on the owner and occupier affected by the cancelled direction.

World Heritage Sites

The United Nations Education, Scientific and Cultural Organisation (UNESCO)   **9.28**
designates World Heritage Sites. Scotland currently has six World Heritage Sites: the Forth Bridge, the Antonine Wall, St Kilda, Edinburgh's Old and New Towns, New Lanark and the Heart of Neolithic Orkney.

A planning authority must consult HES before determining a planning application for a development which may affect a World Heritage Site.[83] Where HES have advised against the grant of planning permission or have recommended conditions which the planning authority does not propose to attach to the planning permission, the Scottish Ministers must be notified before the permission is granted.[84]

The Scottish Government guidance states that where a development proposal has the potential to affect a World Heritage Site, or its setting, the planning authority must protect and preserve its outstanding universal value.[85]

Permitted development rights are restricted within World Heritage Sites.[86]

Battlefields

The Scottish Government guidance states that planning authorities should seek   **9.29**
to protect, conserve and where appropriate, enhance the key landscape characteristics and special qualities of sites in the inventory of historic battlefields.[87]

A planning authority must consult HES before determining a planning application for a development (other than a householder development) which may affect a historic battlefield.[88] Where HES have advised against the grant of planning permission or have recommended conditions which the planning authority does not propose to attach to the planning permission, the Scottish Ministers must be notified before the permission is granted.[89]

Permitted development rights are restricted within historic battlefields.[90]

Trees

The planning authority and the Scottish Ministers have a duty when granting   **9.30**
planning permission to ensure that adequate provision is made for the preserva-

---

[83] DMPR 2013 (SSI 2013/155) Sch.5(17), as amended by theTown and Country Planning (Historic Environment Scotland) Amendment Regulations 2015 (SSI 2015/237).
[84] The Town and Country Planning (Neighbouring Planning Authorities and Historic Environment) (Scotland) Direction 2015.
[85] *Scottish Planning Policy* (SPP) (Scottish Government, 2014), para.147.
[86] For example, PDO 1992 (SI 1992/223) Class 9C.
[87] SPP, para.149.
[88] DMPR 2013 (SSI 2013/155) Sch.5(17), as amended by the Town and Country Planning (Historic Environment Scotland) Amendment Regulations 2015 (SSI 2015/237).
[89] The Town and Country Planning (Neighbouring Planning Authorities and Historic Environment) (Scotland) Direction 2015.
[90] For example, PDO 1992 (SI 1992/223) Class 9C.

tion or planting of trees.[91] This duty is normally discharged by imposing appropriate conditions upon the grant of permission, or making tree preservation orders. The courts have held that the statutory procedures for tree preservation orders (TPOs) comply with the European Convention on Human Rights.[92]

Tree preservation orders may be made by the planning authority either where it appears expedient in the interests of amenity to make provision for the preservation of trees, or woodlands in the district and/ or the trees or woodlands are of cultural or historical significance.[93] The TPO will specify the particular tree, groups of trees or woodlands to which it applies and include a map showing their position. It may also provide for the prohibition of the cutting down, topping, lopping, uprooting, wilful damage, or wilful destruction of the trees without the consent of the planning authority, which consent may be given subject to conditions. A TPO can secure the replanting, in a specified manner, of any part of a woodland area which is felled in the course of forestry operations. Where planning permission is granted subject to conditions requiring the planting of trees it is possible for a TPO to take effect from the time when those trees are planted. Nothing in a TPO prohibits the uprooting, felling or lopping of any tree if this work is urgently necessary in the interests of safety or is necessary for the prevention or abatement of a nuisance, or is carried out in compliance with a development consent or in compliance with any obligation imposed by an Act of Parliament, provided written notice of the proposed work is given to the planning authority as soon as may be after the necessity for the operation arises.[94]

The making of the TPO must be advertised, notice served on specified persons, and a copy of the order and map made available for public inspection.[95] The planning authority have power to enter the land and fix a copy of the TPO to the trees, if it appears to them that the trees may be in imminent danger of being cut down, topped, lopped, uprooted, wilfully damaged or wilfully destroyed.[96]

The TPO takes effect on the date specified in the order, but expires after six months unless it has been confirmed by the planning authority.[97] It is competent for the TPO to be confirmed subject to modifications. Following its confirmation, the TPO is recorded in the Register of Sasines or the Land Register (the property register) by the planning authority, thereby becoming enforceable against all subsequent owners of the land on which the trees stand.

There is a duty is on the planning authority to review TPOs from time to time to consider whether the TPOs should be varied or revoked.[98]

An application for consent to the carrying out of any act prohibited by a TPO must be made to the planning authority and must specify the operations for which

---

91 TCPSA 1997 s.159.
92 R. (on the application of Brennon) v Bromsgrove DC [2003] J.P.L. 1444.
93 TCPSA 1997 s.160 as amended by the PSA 2006 s.28(2); Town and Country Planning (Tree Preservation Order and Trees in Conservation Areas) (Scotland) Regulations 2010 (SSI 2010/434), which revoke the Town and Country Planning (Tree Preservation Order and Trees in Conservation Areas) (Scotland) Regulations 1975 (SI 1975/1204). The Scottish Ministers' policy is contained in Planning Circular 01/2011, Tree Preservation Orders (Scottish Government, 2011).
94 Perrin v Northampton BC [2008] 1 W.L.R. 1307; [2008] J.P.L. 809.
95 Town and Country Planning (Tree Preservation Order and Trees in Conservation Areas) (Scotland) Regulations 2010 (SSI 2010/434).
96 TCPSA 1997 s.161A, inserted by the PSA 2006 s.28(4).
97 TCPSA 1997 s.161, as amended by PSA 2006 s.28(3). TCPSA s.163 has been repealed.
98 TCPSA 1997 s.159(c), inserted by the PSA 2006 s.28(1)(d).

consent is sought; give reasons for carrying out such operations; and identify the protected tree or trees which would be affected by such operations.[99]

Where a tree protected by a TPO is removed, uprooted or destroyed in contravention of the TPO, the owner of the land must plant another tree of an appropriate size and species in the same place as soon as reasonably possible.[100] The TPO will apply to the new tree as it applied to the original tree.[101] This replanting obligation also applies where the uprooting or felling is authorised only as being urgently necessary in the interests of safety. In the case of trees in a woodland, it is sufficient to replace the trees with the same number of trees either on or near the land on which the trees previously stood or on such other land as may be agreed with the planning authority. It is possible to apply to the planning authority to dispense with the requirement to replant trees.

The protection conferred by a TPO extends to trees in conservation areas which are not the subject of a TPO, with exceptions. These include the uprooting, felling or lopping of a tree not exceeding 75mm or the uprooting or felling in a woodland of a tree having a diameter not exceeding 100mm where this is done to improve the growth of other trees.[102]

In any prosecution relating to trees in conservation areas which are not the subject of a TPO, it will be a defence to prove that notice of the intention to do the act was served upon the planning authority and the authority consented to the work, or six weeks was allowed for them to respond before the work was carried out (there is a two-year time limit from giving such notice to do the work).[103] The six-week period is intended to give the authority time to consider making a TPO. The planning authority must keep a register of such notices and make it available for public inspection. The replanting obligation applies.

The planning authority has the power to serve a notice on the owner of the land requiring him to plant a tree or trees of specified size and species within a specified period, in enforcement of the general replanting obligations or any conditions of a consent given under a TPO requiring replanting.[104] The notice must be served within two years of the date on which the failure to comply came to the knowledge of the authority. The notice takes effect after the expiry of the period specified in the notice, which must be at least 28 days from the date of service, unless the person on whom notice is served has appealed to the Scottish Ministers.[105] The procedure for such an appeal is similar to appeals against enforcement notices (see Ch.7 above).

The grounds of appeal are that:

(a)   the replanting obligation or the conditions of a consent given under a TPO have been complied with;

(b)   in the circumstances of the case the replanting obligation should be dispensed with;

---

[99]   Town and Country Planning (Tree Preservation Order and Trees in Conservation Areas) (Scotland) Regulations 2010 (SSI 2010/434) reg.9.

[100] TCPSA 1997 s.167.

[101] *Brown v Michael B Cooper Ltd*, 1990 S.C.C.R. 675; TCPSA 1997 s.168(3A) applies this to a tree (s) replanted following service of a notice by the planning authority.

[102] TCPSA 1997 s.172; Town and Country Planning (Tree Preservation Order and Trees in Conservation Areas) (Scotland) Regulations 2010 (SSI 2010/434) reg.8.

[103] TCPSA 1997 s.172

[104] TCPSA 1997 s.168(1).

[105] The grounds of appeal are specified in TCPSA 1997 s.169.

(c) the requirements of the notice are unreasonable in respect of the period or the size or species of trees specified therein;

(d) the planting of a tree or trees in accordance with the notice is not required in the interests of amenity or would be contrary to the practice of good forestry;

(e) the place on which the tree(s) is required to be planted is unsuitable for that purpose.

There is provision for recovery of the expenses incurred by the owner in complying with the notice from any person responsible for the cutting down, destruction or removal of the original tree or trees.[106] If the steps required by the notice are not taken, the planning authority has the power to enter the land and take those steps. It is an offence to obstruct wilfully the exercise of this power.[107]

It is an offence to cut down, uproot or wilfully destroy a tree, or wilfully damage, top or lop a tree in such a manner as to be likely to destroy it, in contravention of a TPO or where the tree is situated in a conservation area.[108] Following summary conviction a fine not exceeding £20,000 may be imposed, and an unlimited fine if convicted on indictment. In determining the amount of the fine the court is directed to have regard to any financial benefit which has accrued or appears likely to accrue to the offender in consequence of the offence. Any other contravention of a TPO, for example damaging a tree short of destruction, is an offence punishable on summary conviction by a fine not exceeding level 4 of the standard scale (see Appendix 1 below).

High hedges

9.31   Local authorities have power to require high hedges to be cut back.[109]

ADVERTISEMENT CONTROL

9.32   The display of advertisements is restricted and regulated by a separate set of controls.[110] No advertisement may be displayed without an express consent granted either by the planning authority or the Scottish Ministers, or a deemed consent. As with a grant of planning permission, the consent attaches to the site rather than to the applicant, and can be utilised by future persons with an interest in the site. Planning permission is deemed to have been granted for the display of an advertisement which is in accordance with the advertisement control requirements.[111]

Definition of "advertisement"

9.33   An advertisement is defined to include any word, letter, model, sign, placard, board, notice, awning, blind, device or representation, whether illuminated or not, in the nature of an advertisement, announcement or direction, and which is employed wholly or partly for that purpose. This includes anything used or designed or adapted principally for use, for the display of advertisements, such as a hoarding or similar structure, or a balloon. Anything employed wholly or partly as a

---

[106] TCPSA 1997 s.170(4).
[109] High Hedges (Scotland) Act 2013.
[110] TCPSA 1997 ss.182–187; Town and Country Planning (Control of Advertisements) (Scotland) Regulations (CAR) 1984 (SI 1984/467), as amended.
[111] TCPSA 1997 s.184.

memorial or as a railway signal is excluded.[112] This definition should embrace any form of advertisement, and remove any doubt that canopies installed at shops carrying manufacturers or brand names are subject to advertisement control.[113] Similarly, anything designed or adapted principally for use as an advertisement is controlled, which will include hoardings, rotating panels, gantry or pylon signs, and free-standing structures, such as drums. Items used to draw attention to a business, such as national flags displayed on flagpoles and searchlights, can therefore be advertisements.[114]

Advertisement control does not apply to advertisements[115]:

(a) displayed within a building (with some exceptions);

(b) on or in a vehicle normally employed as a moving vehicle, except during periods when it is being used primarily for the display of advertisements;

(c) incorporated in and forming part of the fabric of a building (which does not necessarily include advertisements affixed or painted on the building), unless the building is used principally for the display of advertisements or a hoarding or similar structure;

(d) displayed on land wholly or mainly enclosed by a hedge, fence, wall or similar screen and not readily visible from outside or from any part of the enclosed land over which there is public right of way or public access: this includes any railway station together with its yards and forecourts whether enclosed or not, but not public parks, public gardens or other land held for the use or enjoyment of the public, or any railway line;

(e) displayed on or consisting of a balloon flown at a height of more than 60m above ground level;

(f) displayed on or consisting of a balloon, provided the site is not within an area of special control (see para.9.38 below), a conservation area (see para.9.20 above), or other area designated for the purpose of conserving the natural beauty and amenity of the countryside, for example a national scenic area (see para.9.45 below): no more than one such advertisement may be displayed at any one time on the site, and the site may not be used for the display of such advertisements on more than 10 days in total in any one calendar year, irrespective of which part of the site is used or who is using it for this purpose; and

(g) displayed on an article for sale or on the container or dispenser in or from which an article is sold, provided the advertisement is not illuminated and does not exceed 0.1sq m in area.

Deemed consent

There are six classes of advertisements for which consent is deemed to be granted without application to the authority, provided the specified conditions relating to matters such as height and area are observed (but other statutory consents may still be required).[116] Reference must be made to the statutory provisions for full details, but these classes are:

9.34

---

[112] TCPSA 1997 s.277(1); CAR 1984 (SI 1984/467) reg.2(1), as amended.

[113] *Glasgow DC v Secretary of State for Scotland*, 1989 S.L.T. 256.

[114] *Taylor v Secretary of State for Scotland*, 1997 S.L.T. 535; 1997 59 S.P.E.L. 15; *Great Yarmouth BC v Secretary of State for the Environment* [1997] J.P.L. 650.

[115] CAR 1984 (SI 1984/467) reg.3.

[116] CAR 1984 (SI 1984/467) reg.10 and Sch.4, as amended.

I   Functional advertisements of local authorities, community councils, statutory undertakers, the Crown and public transport undertakers.
II   Advertisements relating to the land on which they are displayed (including identification and direction signs, and advertisements in relation to business on the premises where the advertisement is displayed).
III Advertisements of a temporary nature (including for sale boards, and builders' signs on sites).
IV   Advertisements displayed on business premises (including references to the goods sold or services provided, and the name and qualification of the person carrying on the business).
V   Advertisements within buildings (if not exempt from advertisement control).
VI   Illuminated advertisements (displayed on business premises wholly with reference to the business, goods sold or services provided, and qualifications of the person carrying on the business).
VII Advertisements on ground based housing for electronic communications apparatus.

Deemed consent also extends to advertisements relating specifically to elections, statutory advertisements, and traffic signs. There is also deemed consent for advertisements on sites used for the display of advertisements on 16 August 1948. The deemed consent for such sites does not necessarily expire if the use of the site for advertising is interrupted, and is not extinguished by an application for express consent.[117]

In addition to the conditions attached to each class of deemed consent and the standard conditions applicable to the display of all advertisements (see para.9.37 below), deemed consent is subject to an implied condition preventing siting or display of an advertisement so as to obscure or hinder the ready interpretation of any road traffic sign, railway signal or aid to navigation by water or air, or so as otherwise to render hazardous the use of any road, railway, waterway (including coastal waters) or airfield.[118]

There are several ways in which deemed consent can be lost or removed. Where there is deemed consent for display of an advertisement, submission of an application for express consent removes the right to display the advertisement with deemed consent, irrespective of whether the application is successful.[119] The Scottish Ministers have the power to remove deemed consent for the display of advertisements of a specified class or description in any particular area or in any particular case.[120]

It is also open to the planning authority to require discontinuance of the display of an advertisement with deemed consent (other than election and statutory advertisements and traffic signs), by serving a discontinuance notice, where it considers it expedient to do so to remedy a substantial injury to the amenity of the locality or a danger to members of the public.[121] The notice is served upon the person who himself, or by his servant or agent, undertakes or maintains the display of the advertisement, and on the owner, lessee and occupier of the land on which

---

[117] *Parker v Secretary of State for Scotland*, 1998 S.L.T. 299; 1997 63 S.P.E.L. 103.
[118] CAR 1984 (SI 1984/467) reg.6 and Sch.1.
[119] CAR 1984 (SI 1984/467) reg.10(2), (3). But see *Parker v Secretary of State for Scotland*, 1998 S.L.T. 299; 1997 63 S.P.E.L. 103.
[120] CAR 1984 (SI 1984/467) reg.11.
[121] CAR 1984 (SI 1984/467) reg.14, as amended.

it is displayed. It specifies the advertisement or the site to which it relates, the period within which the display or use of the site is to be discontinued, and the reasons why the authority considers it expedient, in the interests of amenity or public safety, that the display or use of the site should be discontinued. The notice takes effect on the date specified therein, which must be not less than 28 days after the date of service. The authority may withdraw the notice at any time until it takes effect, or, where no appeal is pending, vary its terms to extend the period before it takes effect (in contrast to most other enforcement powers, where the right to withdraw or vary a notice has been extended beyond the time when the notice takes effect).

There is a right of appeal to the Scottish Ministers against a discontinuance notice.[122] Submission of an appeal prevents the notice from taking effect until the appeal has been determined. The procedure is similar to that for enforcement notice appeals (see Ch.7 above). The Scottish Ministers may dismiss the appeal, quash the notice, or vary its terms in favour of the appellant.

Express consent

In the absence of deemed consent for the display of an advertisement, an applica- **9.35** tion for express consent must be submitted to the planning authority on the form available from the authority.[123] A register of the particulars of all such applications must be maintained for public inspection by the authority. The decision of the authority on the application must be notified to the applicant within two months from either the date of receipt or any longer period agreed in writing with the applicant. If consent is refused or granted subject to conditions other than the standard conditions (see para.9.37 below), written reasons must be given for the decision.

Unlike normal planning powers, advertisement control can only be exercised in the interests of amenity and public safety.[124] Consent cannot be refused because the planning authority consider the advertisement to be unnecessary or offensive to public morals, and any consent granted cannot limit or restrict the subject matter, content or design of the advertisement. In the interest of amenity, the authority may determine the suitability of the use of the site for the display of advertisements in light of the general characteristics of the locality, including the presence of any features of historic, architectural, cultural or similar interest. The presence of existing advertisements in the locality should be ignored. On the grounds of public safety, the authority should have regard to the safety of persons who may use any road, railway, waterway (including coastal waters), dock, harbour or airfield which is likely to be affected by the proposed advertisement display. In particular, it should consider whether the display is likely to obscure or hinder the ready interpretation of any road traffic sign, railway signal or aid to navigation by water or air. The authority should also have regard to any material change of circumstances likely to occur within the period for which the consent is required, and any other material factor.

Consent may be granted subject to the standard conditions (see para.9.37 below) and such additional conditions as the authority thinks fit, or refused (but only on the grounds of amenity and/or public safety). Consent may be granted for display of a

---

[122] CAR 1984 (SI 1984/467) reg.21, as amended.
[123] CAR 1984 (SI 1984/467) reg.5.
[124] CAR 1984 (SI 1984/467) reg.4.

particular advertisement or specify the use of a particular site for the display of advertisements in a particular manner, by reference to the number, siting, size or illumination of the advertisements or the structures intended for such display, or the design or appearance of any such structure. A temporary consent may be granted, with a condition requiring removal of the advertisement following expiry of a specified period. Retrospective consent may be granted for the display of advertisements begun prior to the date of application or for the retention of advertisements displayed prior to the application.

Where the application relates to display of an advertisement within one of the deemed consent classes (see para.9.34 above), consent cannot be refused or more restrictive conditions imposed, unless required to prevent or remedy a substantial injury to the amenity of the locality or a danger to members of the public.

9.36   Consent may be granted for the temporary display on unspecified sites within the authority's district of placards, posters or bills relating to the visit of a travelling circus, fair or similar travelling entertainment.[125] Such a consent is subject to a set of conditions which apply in addition to the standard conditions. There is no right of appeal against the decision of the planning authority on an application for this form of consent.

Every grant of express consent expires after five years, or such other period as is specified in the consent.[126] This time limit may be specified as running from the date of commencement of the display of the advertisement or from a date not later than six months after the date consent is granted, whichever is the earlier. The consent may be renewed at any time within six months before its expiry. Unless prohibited by a condition or where an application for renewal is refused, the display may continue after the time limit by virtue of a deemed consent on the same terms and conditions, subject to service of a discontinuance notice (see para.9.34 above).[127]

An express consent may be revoked or modified by the planning authority on grounds of amenity or public safety, but only before the display of the advertisement commences or building or other operations involved in the display have been completed. The confirmation of the Scottish Ministers is required. A written claim for compensation may be served upon the authority within six months after confirmation of the revocation or modification order.[128]

Following a refusal of express consent or grant subject to conditions, the applicant has a right of appeal to the Scottish Ministers. There is also a right of appeal against a deemed refusal, where the authority has failed to notify its decision within two months of the date of receipt of the application, or any longer period agreed with the applicant.[129] The appeal procedure is similar to planning appeals, except that no provision is made for using the written submissions procedure, and the reforms to the planning appeal procedures have not been extended to advertisement consent appeals (see Ch.8 above). Advertisement consent appeals have been delegated by the Scottish Ministers to reporters for decision, although some advertisement appeals may continue to be decided by the Scottish Ministers.[130] The Scottish Ministers/reporter may allow or dismiss the appeal, or reverse or vary any

---

125 CAR 1984 (SI 1984/467) reg.27.
126 CAR 1984 (SI 1984/467) reg.18.
127 CAR 1984 (SI 1984/467) reg.19.
128 CAR 1984 (SI 1984/467) regs 22 and 23.
129 CAR 1984 (SI 1984/467) regs 20 and 21, as amended.
130 Town and Country Planning (Determination of Appeals by Appointed Persons) (Prescribed Classes)

part of the decision by the authority whether or not the appeal relates to that part, dealing with the application as though it was made to him in the first instance. The decision on the merits of the appeal is final, but its legality may be challenged in the Court of Session using the statutory review procedure (see Ch.8 above), subject to a six-week time limit.

Standard conditions

The display of all advertisements is subject to implied conditions requiring, to the reasonable satisfaction of the planning authority[131]:

    9.37

(a) maintenance in a clean and tidy condition of the advertisement (other than an election notice) and the land upon which it is displayed;

(b) maintenance in a safe condition of any hoarding, similar structure or sign, placard, board or other device used principally for displaying the advertisement;

(c) removal of the advertisement when required under the regulations;

(d) advance permission for display of the advertisement (other than statutory advertisements) to be obtained from the owner of the land or other person entitled to grant permission.

Areas of special control

The planning authority has the power to designate Areas of Special Control, within which stricter standards of advertisement control apply.[132] This power is exercised in the interests of amenity, having regard to the general characteristics of the area, including the presence of any feature of historic, architectural or cultural interest. The designation must be approved by the Scottish Ministers, who have indicated that it is not normally enough for the area to be a conservation area (see para.9.20 above), but that this stricter control is wholly appropriate in rural areas. Once the area comes into operation, advertisements already displayed in the area (with some exceptions) may continue to be displayed for a further six months or for the remainder of the term of any express consent, whichever is longer, and then for a further two months, after which the advertisement must be removed unless express consent is granted for its continued display.[133]

    9.38

Enforcement

An enforcement notice may be served by the planning authority where it appears that any advertisement has been displayed without the necessary consent, or without compliance with a condition or limitation attached to a consent, whether express or deemed.[134] Unlike planning control, a breach of advertisement control can never become immune from enforcement action.[135] The notice is served upon the owner, lessee and occupier of the land and on any other person known to the authority to be displaying the advertisement. The notice requires specified steps to

    9.39

(Scotland) Regulations 2010 (SSI 2010/467).

[131] CAR 1984 (SI 1984/467) reg.6 and Sch.1.

[132] CAR 1984 (SI 1984/467) reg.8. The procedure is described in Sch.2.

[133] CAR 1984 (SI 1984/467) reg.9(3)(c).

[134] CAR 1984 (SI 1984/467) reg.24, as amended.

[135] *Torridge DC v Jarrad* [1998] J.P.L. 954.

be taken, within a given period, to restore the land to the condition it was in before the display began or to secure compliance with the condition or limitation. In addition, it may specify as an alternative steps to be taken to bring the display up to an acceptable condition. The notice takes effect on the date specified in the notice which must be 28 days from the date of the latest service of the notice, or seven days in certain limited circumstances. Any provision in the notice requiring the use of land to be discontinued operates as a permanent restriction, notwithstanding compliance with the notice. The resumption of that use after its discontinuance will, therefore, be in contravention of the notice. Similarly, where the notice requires either demolition or alteration of buildings or works, the notice will strike at any reinstatement of those buildings or works, notwithstanding that its terms are not apt for this purpose.

Where any of the steps required by the notice have not been taken within the specified period, the planning authority may enter the land and take those steps (other than discontinuance of any use), recovering its expenses from the owner or lessee of the land.[136] The validity of this action cannot be disputed by any person who failed to exercise his right of appeal to the Scottish Ministers (see below). Any sums incurred by the owner, lessee or occupier in complying with the enforcement notice, or in payment of the expenses of the planning authority in taking the steps required by the notice, may be recovered from the person by whom the display was carried out.

At any time prior to the notice taking effect, any person on whom the notice is served may appeal in writing to the Scottish Ministers.[137] The notice has no effect until the appeal is either determined or withdrawn. The appeal procedure is similar to the procedure for planning enforcement appeals (see Ch.7 above). The grounds of appeal are that:

(a) the matters alleged in the notice do not constitute a display of an advertisement without the necessary consent or a failure to comply with any condition or limitation;
(b) the notice was not served as required;
(c) the specified period for compliance with the notice falls short of what should be reasonably allowed;
(d) the steps required by the notice exceed what is necessary for its purpose.

In the course of the appeal the Scottish Ministers may correct any non-material informality, defect or error in the notice, and disregard any failure to serve the notice if neither the appellant nor the person served with the notice have been substantially prejudiced by that failure. In determining the appeal, the notice may be quashed or its terms varied in favour of the appellant. Amenity and public safety are not relevant.[138]

Offences

9.40   Display of an advertisement in contravention of advertisement control is an offence, with a maximum fine on summary conviction of level 3 on the standard scale (see Appendix 1 below), with a further offence carrying a fine of one-tenth of level 3 for each day during which the offence continues after conviction. The persons li-

---

[136] CAR 1984 (SI 1984/467) reg.26.
[137] CAR 1984 (SI 1984/467) reg.25, as amended.
[138] *Site Projects Ltd v Scottish Ministers*, 2008 S.L.T. 445.

able for such an offence are the owner and occupier of the land upon which the advertisement is displayed, or the person whose goods, trade, business or other concerns are publicised by the advertisement. It is a defence to show that the advertisement was displayed without the knowledge or consent of the accused person.[139] If the contravention of advertisement control consists of a failure to observe any condition relating to maintenance of the advertisement or its site, or to the unsatisfactory removal of the advertisement, a person whose goods, trade, business or other concern is publicised by the advertisement only commits an offence if he has failed to comply with the requirements of an enforcement notice served on him.[140]

Power to remove or obliterate placards and posters

The planning authority has the power to remove or obliterate any placard or   **9.41**
poster displayed in its area in contravention of advertisement control, unless it is displayed within a building to which there is no public right of access.[141] This power is aimed at the nuisance caused by flyposting.

Where the placard or poster identifies the person who displayed it or caused it to be displayed, the authority must give that person written notice of its intention to remove or obliterate it on expiry of a period specified in the notice which must be not less than two days from the date of service of the notice. This notice period is intended to give an opportunity to convince the authority that the placard or poster is not displayed in contravention of advertisement control. Written notice is not required if the placard or poster does not give the address of the person and the authority does not know it and is unable to ascertain it after reasonable inquiry. There is a right of entry on to the land at any reasonable time, provided the land is unoccupied and it would be impossible to exercise the power without entering it.

ENTERPRISE ZONES AND SIMPLIFIED PLANNING ZONES

Enterprise zone (EZ) and simplified planning zone (SPZ) schemes are intended   **9.42**
to encourage development to take place where it is needed to promote regeneration and economic activity. This objective is achieved through the grant of planning permission, in advance, for forms of development specified in the scheme (some schemes permit all forms of development with specified exceptions), thus avoiding the need to submit an application and providing developers with a degree of certainty. In addition, EZs offer a range of fiscal benefits, typically including exemptions from local authority rates and greater capital allowances for capital expenditure incurred on construction, extension or improvement of industrial and commercial buildings. There are no automatic fiscal benefits from a SPZ scheme. Both forms of scheme have been criticised for encouraging existing businesses in the area to relocate within the zone, rather than attracting fresh employment.

An EZ is prepared by the planning authority and designated by order of the Scottish Ministers.[142] SPZs are promoted by the planning authority.[143] Proposals for an EZ or SPZ are advertised, giving the public an opportunity to lodge representations.

---

[139] TCPSA 1997 s.186(3)–(5). Section 186(3) will be repealed once the Planning (Consequential Provisions) (Scotland) Act 1997 Sch.1(1) para.1 is brought into effect.
[140] CAR 1984 (SI 1984/467) reg.7(2).
[141] TCPSA 1997 s.187. *Baillie Lite Ltd v Glasgow City Council*, 1999 S.C. 606.
[142] Local Government, Planning and Land Act 1980 s.179 and Sch.32, as amended. TCPSA 1997 ss.55

In the case of an SPZ, there is provision for a public local inquiry to be held to consider any objections received, although there is no longer a requirement to hold an inquiry. The Scottish Ministers have powers to require the authority to consider modifications to the proposed SPZ, and to call in the proposals for his decision. An SPZ scheme ceases to have effect 10 years after the date of its adoption or approval. No application for planning permission will be required where a development authorised by a planning permission under the SPZ scheme has commenced within the 10-year period.

The grant of permission by EZ and SPZ schemes is subject to the provisions of the Conservation (Natural Habitats, etc.) Regulations 1994 (SI 1994/2716) (see para.9.48 below). In addition, the grant of permission by an SPZ scheme does not remove the need for environmental assessment (see Ch.5 above).

NATURAL HERITAGE

9.43   In the exercise of all statutory functions, including planning, the Scottish Ministers and planning authorities are required to have regard to the desirability of conserving the natural heritage of Scotland; and to further the conservation of biodiversity.[144]

Natural heritage issues are closely linked to the objective of sustainable development, which is discussed in Chs 3 and 5.[145]

Scottish Natural Heritage (SNH) is the agency responsible for advising the Government and local authorities on natural heritage issues.[146]

Also highly relevant is the precautionary principle, which recognises that preventative action may be justified even where the scientific evidence is less than conclusive. The Scottish Government guidance indicates that the precautionary principle should be applied where the impacts of a proposed development on nationally or internationally significant landscape or natural heritage resources are uncertain, but there is sound evidence for believing that significant irreversible damage could occur.[147]

Development plans must contain natural heritage policies (see Ch.3 above). Impacts on, or benefits for, natural heritage will be a material consideration in the determination of planning applications. The planning authority must consult SNH in relation to certain planning applications, and may not be able to grant planning permission if SNH object to the development, without first notifying the Scottish Ministers (see Ch.5 above). The environmental assessment process includes consideration of the effects of a proposed development on flora and fauna, soil, water, air, climate and the landscape (see Ch.5 above).

There are also a series of statutory natural heritage designations which restrict

---

and 56.

143 TCPSA 1997 ss.49–54 and Sch.5; Town and Country Planning (Simplified Planning Zone) (Scotland) Regulations 1995 (SI 1995/2043). See Central Research Unit, *Research on the General Permitted Development Order and Related Mechanisms* (Scottish Office, 1998) Pt 8; Circular 18/1995, Planning and Compensation Act 1991: Simplified Planning Zones (Scottish Office, 1995).

144 Countryside (Scotland) Act 1967 s.66 and Nature Conservation (Scotland) Act 2004 s.1. *Cairngorms Campaign v Cairngorms National Park Authority* [2012] CSOH 153. See Colin T. Reid, *Nature Conservation Law*, 3rd edn (Edinburgh: W. Green, 2009), paras 1.2.1–1.2.11.

145 The Scottish Government guidance is contained in SPP, paras 193–218.

146 Natural Heritage (Scotland) Act 1991 outlines its role. Website at: *http://www.snh.org.uk* [Accessed 2 February 2016].

147 SPP, para.204.

the development or use of land, some of which have their origins in EU or International Treaties.[148] This chapter outlines the provisions relating to National Scenic Areas, Sites of Special Scientific Interest (SSSIs), Nature Conservation Orders, and Special Areas of Conservation. Other environmental or nature conservation designations have less direct planning consequences, and the sites affected are often also designated as SSSIs. These designations include:

Areas of Great Landscape Value: which are declared in development plans and have no statutory force. **9.44**

Environmentally Sensitive Areas (ESAs): which are designated by the Scottish Ministers after consultation with SNH, under the Agriculture Act 1986.[149] Within ESAs, agreements may be made with farmers and crofters regarding use of environmentally friendly methods in return for financial payments.

Green belts: which are designated in development plans. Their purpose is to prevent urban sprawl (see para.9.57 below).

Local Nature Reserves: which are declared by local authorities in conjunction with SNH under the National Parks and Access to the Countryside Act 1949.

National Nature Reserves (NNRs): which are declared by SNH under the National Parks and Access to the Countryside Act 1949 and the Wildlife and Countryside Act 1981.

National Parks: Two national parks have been created in Scotland: Loch Lomond and the Trossachs, and the Cairngorms. The National Park Authorities have planning roles (see Ch.2 above). The statutory aims for the national parks are to: conserve and enhance the natural and cultural heritage; promote the sustainable use of the natural resources of the area; promote understanding and enjoyment (including enjoyment in the form of recreation) of the special qualities of the area by the public; and promote sustainable social and economic development of the communities of the area.[150]

Ramsar Sites: which are designated by the Scottish Ministers under the Ramsar Convention on Wetlands of International Importance.

Regional Parks and Country Parks: which are designated by local authorities under the Countryside (Scotland) Act 1981.

Special Protection Areas (SPAs): which are designated by the Scottish Ministers to comply with the EC Directive on the Conservation of Wild Birds 1979. SPAs and Special Areas of Conservation (SACs) (see para.9.48 below) are intended to form a European network of protected areas, known as Natura 2000. SPAs are protected by the Conservation (Natural Habitats, etc.) Regulations 1994 (SI 1994/2716) (discussed in relation to SACs below). The boundaries of SPAs must be selected using ornithological criteria, and economic requirements should not be taken into account.[151] However, in drawing the boundaries a discretion has to be exercised, and the scientific exercise to be undertaken does not require that all contiguous or linked qualifying habitats or species populations have to be included, and existing circumstances

---

[148] See SPP, paras 207–214
[149] Circular 17/1997, Environmentally Sensitive Areas (Scottish Office, 1997).
[150] National Parks (Scotland) Act 2000 ss.1 and 9. *Cairngorms Campaign v Cairngorms National Park Authority* [2012] CSOH 153; *Dalfaber Action Group v Scottish Ministers* [2007] CSOH 180.
[151] *R. v Secretary of State for the Environment Ex p. Royal Society for the Protection of Birds* [1996] J.P.L. 844.

such as the presence of skiing facilities can be taken into account.[152] There is uncertainty about the role of economic factors in situations other than selection of SPA boundaries.[153]

Wild Land: development plans are to identify and safeguard the character of areas of wild land as identified on the 2014 SNH map of wild land areas.[154]

World Heritage Sites: which are listed by the World Heritage Committee of UNESCO (see para.9.28 above) and can include natural habitats and features.

There are also statutory provisions relating to trees (see para.9.30 above) and species protection.[155]

National scenic areas

9.45   The national scenic area (NSA) designation had been superseded by the power to designate natural heritage areas (NHAs), but no NHAs were designated and the provisions have now been repealed, and the power to designate NSAs reintroduced.

NSAs are areas of outstanding scenic value and beauty in a national context, designated by the Scottish Ministers as appropriate for special protection (similar to the areas of outstanding natural beauty in England and Wales). In deciding whether to designate an area as an NSA, the Ministers are to take account of whether the area is of outstanding natural beauty; the amenity of the area, including whether it is of historical, cultural or environmental importance, and the nature of any buildings or other structures within it; and any flora, fauna or physiographical features of the area, whether or not to any extent the product of human intervention in the landscape.[156]

When any planning powers are exercised with respect to any land within NSAs, including the determination of applications for planning permission, special regard must be paid to the desirability of safeguarding or enhancing the character or appearance of the area.[157] The character or appearance is preserved not only by a positive contribution to preservation, but also by development which has a neutral effect and leaves the character or appearance unharmed.[158]

To provide planning authorities with an opportunity to review development proposals, planning permission must be obtained for the following types of development within an NSA, which would otherwise have benefited from permitted development rights[159]:

(a)   erection for agricultural or forestry purposes of all buildings and structures over 12m high (permitted development rights have since been removed for all agricultural buildings over 12m high, see paras 9.51 and 9.53 below);

---

152 *WWF UK Ltd v Scottish Natural Heritage,* 1998 G.W.D. 37–1936; *The Times,* 20 November 1998.
153 *Sustainable Shetland v The Scottish Ministers* [2015] UKSC 4.
154 SPP, para.200. Discussed in *Petition of The John Muir Trust* [2015] CSOH 163.
155 See Reid, *Nature Conservation Law* (2009).
156 TCSPA 1997 s.263A.
157 TCPSA 1997 s.263A(2).
158 *South Lakeland DC v Secretary of State for the Environment* [1992] 2 A.C. 141; *Bath Society v Secretary of State for the Environment* [1991] 1 W.L.R. 1303.
159 Town and Country Planning (Restriction of Permitted Development) (National Scenic Areas) (Scotland) Direction 1987, attached to Circular 9/1987, Development Control in National Scenic Areas (Scottish Office, 1987); display of advertisements on or consisting of a balloon within an NSA will require advertisement consent—Town and Country Planning (Control of Tethered Balloon Advertisements in National Scenic Areas) (Scotland) Direction 1984, attached to Scottish Office Development Department Circular 10/1984 Town and Country Planning (Control of Advertisements) (Scotland) Regulations 1984 (Scottish Office, 1984).

(b) construction of vehicle tracks for agricultural or forestry purposes except forestry tracks which are part of an approved afforestation scheme (some of those permitted development rights have since been removed, see paras 9.51 to 9.53 below); and

(c) all local authority roadworks outside present road boundaries costing more than £100,000.

As an additional safeguard, where the planning authority proposes to grant permission for the forms of development listed below within an NSA, it must consult SNH.[160] If SNH advise against granting permission or recommend conditions other than those proposed by the planning authority, the authority must send details of the application to the Scottish Ministers (see "Notification", Ch.5 above). The authority cannot grant planning permission for the development until 28 days (or any longer or shorter period specified by the Scottish Ministers) have elapsed from the date notified to it by the Scottish Ministers as the date of receipt of the details of the application. This period provides the Scottish Ministers with an opportunity to call in the application for their own decision.

This consultation requirement applies to:

(a) schemes for five or more houses, flats or chalets except those within towns and villages for which specific proposals have been made in an adopted local plan;

(b) sites for five or more mobile dwellings or caravans;

(c) all non-residential developments requiring more than 0.5 hectares of land;

(d) all buildings and structures over 12m high, including agricultural and forestry developments;

(e) vehicle tracks, except where these form part of an approved afforestation scheme; and

(f) all local authority roadworks outside present road boundaries costing more than £100,000.

Sites of special scientific interest

SSSIs are areas of land designated as being of special interest by reason of any **9.46** of their natural features—any flora, fauna or geological or geomorphological features.[161] An SSSI notification has effect from the date on which it is given. The notification makes it an offence to carry out a range of operations without the consent of SNH, unless permission has been given by a relevant regulatory authority, or the work is authorised by planning permission (not permitted development rights), or the work is done in an emergency, or done in accordance with a management agreement, or is carried out as required by a land management order. The requirement to obtain consent extends to public bodies carrying out operations likely to damage the features of a SSSI. It is also an offence to intentionally or recklessly damage any natural feature specified in a SSSI notification, unless as an incidental result of a lawful operation.

---

[160] Town and Country Planning (Notification of Applications) (National Scenic Areas) (Scotland) Direction 1987, attached to Planning Circular 9/1987, Development Control in National Scenic Areas. This was not repealed by Planning Circular 3/2009, Notification of Planning Applications (Scottish Government, 2009), see para.22.

[161] Nature Conservation (Scotland) Act 2004 s.3. Previously SSSIs were designated under the Wildlife and Countryside Act 1981.

Where planning permission is sought for a proposed development which may affect an SSSI (this does not require the development site to be within or adjacent to the SSSI), the planning authority must consult SNH and consider any representations made by them in determining the application.[162] Scottish Natural Heritage's views form part of the material considerations in the determination of the application (see Ch.5 above), but are not binding on the planning authority. However, if the authority decides to grant permission contrary to SNH's recommendation, it must notify the Scottish Ministers.[163] Thereafter the authority cannot grant permission until the expiry of 28 days from the date of receipt by the Ministers, giving them an opportunity to call in the application for decision (see Ch.5 above), or issue a direction restricting the grant of permission.

Where a public body is exercising any function on, or so far as affecting, a SSSI, it must take reasonable steps, so far as is consistent with the proper exercise of its functions, to further the conservation and enhancement of the natural feature specified in the SSSI notification, and maintain or enhance the representative nature of any series of SSSIs to which the SSSI notification contributes.[164]

The restrictions on permitted development rights within SSSIs are limited to electricity cables and mineral exploration (see Ch.4 above). Agricultural and forestry development within SSSIs does not require planning permission, but may require to be notified to SNH as an operation requiring consent (only grants of planning permission following an application to the planning authority provide exemption).

Nature conservation orders

9.47   A nature conservation order is made by the Scottish Ministers to prohibit the carrying out of operations on land, to conserve any natural feature by reason of which land is a SSSI, or is otherwise considered by the Ministers to be of special interest, or to comply with an international obligation.[165] The order can apply to a SSSI, land forming part of a SSSI, and/or land which is contiguous to, or which the Ministers consider to be otherwise associated with a SSSI or land forming part of a SSSI.

The consultation and notification requirements applicable to applications for planning permission which may affect an SSSI do not appear to extend to sites which are subject to nature conservation orders. In practice, consultation and notification are likely to occur.

---

[162] DMPR 2013 (SSI 2013/155) reg.25 and Sch.5. Nature Conservation (Scotland) Act 2004 s.15 imposes a general obligation on regulatory authorities to consult SNH when dealing with consent applications for operations likely to damage the features of an SSSI.

[163] Town and Country Planning (Notification of Applications) (Scotland) Direction 2009, attached to Planning Circular 3/2009, Notification of Planning Applications (Scottish Government, 2009).

[164] Nature Conservation (Scotland) Act 2004 s.12.

[165] Nature Conservation (Scotland) Act 2004 s.23.

Special areas of conservation

SACs are designated by the Scottish Ministers under the Habitats Directive.[166] **9.48**
Many SACs will also be designated as SPAs (see para.9.44 above). The boundaries
of SACs must be drawn up on the same principles applicable to SPAs.[167]

The Conservation (Natural Habitats, etc.) Regulations 1994[168] implement the
provisions of the Habitats Directive. The regulations impose an obligation on the
Scottish Ministers and SNH to exercise their functions so as to secure compliance
with the requirements of the Directive, and a more general obligation on every
public body and others to have regard to the requirements of the Directive in the
exercise of their functions.

The regulations apply to every "European site", which include SACs, SPAs, sites
of Community importance designated by the European Commission under the
Habitats Directive, and potential SACs awaiting designation.[169] The Scottish
Ministers must compile and maintain a register of European sites, and the Ministers
and SNH must keep copies of the register available for public inspection at all
reasonable hours and free of charge. The Ministers must notify SNH of the inclusion of a site in the register, or any amendment or deletion to the register, and SNH
must give notice to every owner or occupier of land within the site. SNH must also
give notice to the planning authority, who must keep available at their principal office for free public inspection a register of all the European sites of which they have
been given notice.

Landward European sites are likely to already be SSSIs (see para.9.46 above).
Under the regulations, the existing notification as a SSSI may be amended, including changes to the list of operations requiring consent which must be notified to
SNH. If the proposed operation is likely to have a significant effect on the site (either
alone or in combination with other plans and projects), SNH may give consent only
after having ascertained that the operation will not adversely affect the integrity of
the site.[170] If there is a risk of operations being carried out without SNH's consent,
the Scottish Ministers may make a nature conservation order, with the result that
the operations specified in the order can only be carried out with the consent of SNH
or in accordance with the terms of a management agreement. SNH can enter into a
management agreement with any owner, lessee or occupier of a European site or
land adjacent thereto.

There is an offence of intentional or reckless damage to a European site.

The regulations affect all authorities undertaking or giving consent, permission
or other authorisation for a plan or project, and not just planning authorities. Where
a plan, including development plans, or project is likely to have significant effect
on a European site, and is not directly connected with or necessary to the management of the site, permission can only be granted if the project will not adversely af-

---

[166] Council Directive 92/43/EEC on the conservation of natural habitats and of wild fauna and flora.
[167] *R. v Secretary of State for the Environment Ex p. Royal Society for the Protection of Birds* [1996]
J.P.L. 844; *WWF UK Ltd v Scottish Natural Heritage*, 1998 G.W.D. 37–1936; *The Times*, 20
November 1998.
[168] Conservation (Natural Habitats, etc.) Regulations 1994 (SI 1994/2716) as amended.
[169] Conservation (Natural Habitats, etc.) Regulations 1994 (SI 1994/2716) reg.10 as amended gives the
full definition.
[170] For example, *RSPB v Secretary of State for Environment, Food and Rural Affairs* [2015] EWCA
Civ 227.

fect the integrity of the site.[171] This restriction can be overcome if the project must be carried out for imperative reasons of overriding public interest. These reasons may relate to human health, public safety or beneficial consequences of primary importance to the environment. In some circumstances, the reasons may be of a social or economic nature. Existing decisions have to be reviewed in light of the regulations, unless the development has been completed. This provision does not require an absolute guarantee that the integrity of the site will not be adversely affected. The authority must identify the foreseeable potential risks and put in place a legally enforceable framework to prevent them from materialising.[172]

Where permission is granted by general development order, such as the PDO (see Ch.4 above), the development cannot proceed if it is likely to have a significant effect on a European site and is not directly connected with or necessary to the management of the site, until written approval is obtained from the planning authority. If development has commenced, it cannot continue until written approval is obtained. The planning authority cannot issue an approval unless the project will not adversely affect the integrity of the site. An application can be made to SNH for their opinion whether the development is likely to have a significant effect. Their opinion is conclusive.

Agriculture and Forestry

9.49 Agricultural use and development traditionally enjoyed widescale exemption from the need for planning permission. This exemption is gradually being eroded.

Agricultural use

9.50 A change from any use to agricultural use, or between different agricultural uses, does not require planning permission,[173] although any associated building or other work is considered separately and may require permission (see para.9.51 below). Thus, no planning permission is required for pigs to be introduced on to land, but it is only once this agricultural use has been established that piggeries can be constructed without planning permission.[174] Fish farming is an exception to this rule, as the placing of fish cages in inland waters requires planning permission,[175] enabling planning authorities to exercise control over the visual and environmental impact of fish farms.

Provided the primary use is agricultural, no planning permission is required for ancillary uses, such as the sale of farm produce to the public on a farm. However, if produce is bought in for sale, the retail element may become a separate use in its own right and, therefore, require planning permission (Ch.4 discusses primary and ancillary uses in more detail).

Agricultural uses include horticulture, seed or fruit growing, dairy farming, breeding and keeping livestock for the production of food, wool, skins or fur (which includes fish farming) or for use in the farming of land, the use of land as grazing,

---

[171] Unsuccessful allegations that the appropriate assessment had not been undertaken properly— *Bagmoor Wind Ltd v Scottish Ministers* [2012] CSIH 93; *Skye Windfarm Action Group Ltd v Highland Council* [2008] CSOH 19.

[172] *WWF UK Ltd v Scottish Natural Heritage*, 1998 G.W.D. 37–1936; *The Times*, 20 November 1998.

[173] TCPSA 1997 s.26(2)(e).

[174] *Jones v Stockport MBC* [1984] J.P.L. 274.

[175] TCPSA 1997 s.26(6).

meadow, or osier land, market gardens or nursery grounds, and the use of land for woodlands (where that use is ancillary to the farming of land for other agricultural purposes).[176] The courts have declared that agricultural use includes the use of land for allotments, grazing horses,[177] fox and mink farming, but not for keeping and boarding cats and dogs, installation of an egg-vending machine, keeping of animals in transit, wholesale slaughtering of animals, and the breeding and training of horses for showjumping.[178] Wine making is also an agricultural use.[179]

Building and other work

Where there is an existing agricultural use, and all of the following criteria are met, planning permission is not required for the erection, extension or alteration of a building; the formation, alteration or maintenance of private ways; or any excavation or engineering operations[180]:

9.51

(a) the land must form part of a unit occupied for the purposes of agriculture other than fish farming;

(b) there must be an existing agricultural use for the purposes of a trade or business;

(c) the work must be reasonably necessary for the purposes of agriculture within the unit[181];

(d) the land is not within a historic battlefield (see para.9.29 above)[182];

(e) the agricultural land must have an area of at least 0.4 hectares, comprised in one piece of land, except in the crofting counties where areas of separate parcels of land may be added together;

(f) the work must not involve the erection, extension or alteration of a dwellinghouse;

(g) any building or structure to be provided must be designed for the purposes of agriculture, thereby avoiding erection of buildings used for keeping livestock, but with the appearance of dwellinghouses;

(h) the ground area of any building to be erected, extended or altered, or of any structure (other than a fence) built for the purposes of accommodating livestock, or of any plant or machinery, must not exceed 465sq m: the ground area is calculated by adding the ground area to be covered by the proposed works to the ground area of any building (other than a dwelling), structure, works, plant or machinery built or provided in the preceding two years within the same unit, any part of which is within 90m of the proposed works;

(i) the height of the building, structure or works must not exceed 12m (3m if within 3km of the perimeter of an aerodrome);

(j) no part of the works must be within 25m of the metalled portion of a trunk or classified road; and

---

[176] TCPSA 1997 s.277(1).

[177] Discussed in *Fox v First Secretary of State* [2003] 4 P.L.R. 26.

[178] See the cases cited in Jeremy Rowan-Robinson et al, *Scottish Planning Law and Procedure* (Edinburgh: SULI/W. Green, 2001) paras 5.142–5.146.

[179] *Millington v Secretary of State for the Environment, Transport and the Regions* [2000] J.P.L. 297.

[180] PDO 1992 (SI 1992/223) art.3 and Sch.1 Class 18.

[181] *MacPherson v Secretary of State for Scotland*, 1985 S.L.T. 134.

[182] Inserted by the Town and Country Planning (General Permitted Development) (Scotland) Amendment Order 2014 (SSI 2014/142).

(k)   where the building or structure to be erected or worked upon is or will be used for housing pigs, poultry, rabbits or animals bred for their skin or fur, or for the storage of slurry or sewage sludge, it must be more than 400m from the curtilage of any permanent building normally occupied by people or apt for such use, which does not form part of the agricultural unit or another such unit.

If these criteria cannot be met, planning permission will be required. A certificate of lawfulness of proposed use or development (CLOPUD) can be obtained from the planning authority in circumstances where it is uncertain whether the criteria have been met (see Ch.4 above).

The following works also do not require planning permission[183]: the carrying out of drainage for agriculture or of any other water management project for that purpose but not irrigation work; the winning and working of any minerals reasonably necessary for agricultural purposes within the agricultural unit, provided the minerals remain within the unit and are used for agricultural purposes; works in connection with the improvement or maintenance of watercourses or land drainage works; and the winning and working of peat by any person for their domestic requirements.

Removal of more than five cubic yards of surface soil from agricultural land in any period of three months is an offence, if planning permission is required but not obtained.[184] This offence also applies to land formerly used for agriculture where that use ceased in consequence of the intention to remove surface soil. It does not extend to the cutting of peat or the removal of such quantities of surface soil as is reasonably necessary in the course of cutting turf.

Prior notification

9.52   Even if planning permission is not required for works, it may be necessary to give the planning authority prior notification of those works by an application to determine whether the prior approval of the authority is required. This prior notification requirement enables the planning authority to exert some degree of control even where planning permission is not required.

The prior notification requirement applies to:

(a)   The erection or significant extension or alteration of a building. A building is significantly extended or altered if either the cubic content of the original building is increased by more than 10 per cent or its height is increased. A building can only be significantly altered or extended once without planning permission. Prior approval may be required for its siting, design and external appearance.

(b)   Formation or alteration of a private way—prior approval may be required in respect of the design, manner of construction or route of the private way.[185]

Work cannot proceed until notification is received from the authority that its prior approval is not required, or its approval is received, or 28 days have elapsed since

---

[183]   PDO 1992 (SI 1992/223) Sch.1 Classes 18A, 19, 20 and 21.
[184]   Agricultural Land (Removal of Surface Soil) Act 1953 s.1, as amended.
[185]   Added by Town and Country Planning (General Permitted Development) (Scotland) Amendment (No. 2) Order 2014 (SSI 2014/300).

the application was lodged and the authority has reached no decision. The work must be carried out in accordance with the approved details or, if no approval is required, in line with the details submitted with the application. In addition, the work must be carried out within five years (three years for a private way) of the date on which approval was given or if no approval was given, the date of the application.

There is a right of appeal to the Scottish Ministers against the decision of the planning authority on the application for approval.[186]

Forestry

Similar provisions apply to forestry uses and works. Forestry use includes operations necessary to render timber marketable and disposable, even where the operations are carried on some distance from the plantation. Therefore, planning permission was not required for a change of use to use as a timber storage and transfer area.[187] Forestry works do not require planning permission unless: the land is in a historic battlefield; the work involves the provision or alteration of a dwelling; the height of any building or works within 3km of an aerodrome would exceed 3m; or any part of the proposed development would be within 25m of the metalled portion of a trunk or classified road.[188] There is a similar prior notification requirement for the erection or significant extension or alteration of a building, and formation or alteration of a private way.

9.53

Designated areas

Farming and forestry operations are often affected by some of the statutory designations examined above. For example, within NSAs the permitted development rights for the erection for forestry purposes of all buildings or structures over 12m high, and for construction of vehicle tracks for agricultural or forestry purposes (except forestry tracks which are part of an approved afforestation scheme), are removed.[189] The result is that an application for planning permission will be required.

9.54

Diversification

In the current climate many farmers are considering diversifying from farming. Diversification projects will often require planning permission, for example the conversion of farm buildings to non-agricultural use, such as holiday cottages or industrial units, the stabling of horses for riding or breeding, or the erection of houses. Use of the farmhouse for bed and breakfast may require planning permission, depending upon the number of guests and the attitude of the planning authority. As mentioned above, a shop on the farm will not require permission provided it only sells produce from the farm. In general, permission will be required

9.55

---

186 TCPSA 1997 s.47.
187 *Farleyer Estate v Secretary of State for Scotland*, 1992 S.L.T. 476.
188 PDO 1992 (SI 1992/223) Sch.1 Class 22, as amended by Town and Country Planning (General Permitted Development) (Scotland) Amendment Order 2014 (SSI 2014/142).Town and Country Planning (General Permitted Development) (Scotland) Amendment (No. 2) Order 2014 (SSI 2014/300).
189 In part this has been superseded by changes to permitted development rights.

for a caravan site, except for some small-scale activities.[190] Non-agricultural uses of land (but not buildings), for any purpose other than as a caravan site do not require planning permission, provided the use does not occur for more than 28 days in a calendar year. Moveable structures, such as marquees, may be placed on the land in connection with such use.[191]

Change of use of agricultural land

9.56   There is no longer any requirement for the Scottish Ministers to be notified by a planning authority proposing to grant planning permission for a proposed development involving a change of use of agricultural land falling within class 1, 2 or 3.1 of the Macaulay land capability classification for agriculture.

DEVELOPMENT IN THE COUNTRYSIDE AND ON GREEN BELT LAND

9.57   The high amenity value of the countryside is acknowledged in the constant pressure for housing development. In order to preserve this amenity, development in the countryside is subject to policies both at national and local level.

Previously national policy discouraged isolated development in the open countryside. Current national policy sets out different approaches for areas easily accessible from cities and main towns; remote and fragile areas and island areas outwith defined small towns; and areas of intermediate accessibility.[192]

Green belt is land designated for the purposes of managing the growth of a town or city in the long term. The key objectives of green belt policy are: to direct planned growth to the most appropriate locations and support regeneration; to protect and enhance the character, landscape setting and identity of the settlement; and to protect and give access to open space. Appropriate uses may include agricultural use, including the re-use of historic agricultural buildings; woodland and forestry, including community woodlands; horticulture, including market gardening and directly connected retailing; recreational uses that are compatible with an agricultural or natural setting; essential infrastructure; development meeting a national requirement or established need, if no other suitable site is available; and intensification of established uses subject to the new development being of a suitable scale and form.[193]

MINERALS

9.58   Planning permission is required for mining operations, including the removal of material of any description from a mineral-working deposit, deposit of pulverised fuel ash or other furnace ash or clinker, or deposit of iron, steel or other metallic slags, and the extraction of minerals from a disused railway embankment.[194] The extraction of each shovelful constitutes a separate development, and it will therefore

---

190 PDO 1992 (SI 1992/223) Sch.1 Classes 16 and 17.
191 PDO 1992 (SI 1992/223) Sch.1 Class 15, as amended by the Town and Country Planning (General Permitted Development) (Scotland) Amendment Order 2014 (SSI 2014/142).
192 SPP, paras 74–83. See also PAN 72, Housing in the Countryside (Scottish Executive, 2005), and PAN 44, Fitting new housing development into the landscape (Scottish Office, 1994).
193 SPP, paras 49–52.
194 TCPSA 1997 s.26(1), (5).

be rare for unauthorised mining operations to become legal.[195] There are permitted development rights (see Ch.4 above) in connection with mineral exploration, development ancillary to mining operations, mining development by the Coal Authority and its licensees, waste tipping at a mine, and removal of material from mineral working deposits.[196]

As a result of the unique problems of mining works, such as the length of the operations, frequent suspension for periods of time and resumption, and the harm caused to the land, the normal planning regime is supplemented by special provisions.[197] Issues such disturbance, disruption and noise, blasting and vibration, and potential pollution of land, air and water; impacts on local communities, individual houses, sensitive receptors and economic sectors important to the local economy; benefits to the local and national economy; cumulative impact with other mineral and landfill sites in the area; effects on natural heritage, habitats and the historic environment; landscape and visual impacts, including cumulative effects; transport impacts; and restoration and aftercare (including any benefits in terms of the remediation of existing areas of dereliction or instability).[198] It is common for any permission to be combined with a s.75 obligation (see Ch.6 above), providing for restoration and aftercare of the site, and a bond to cover the cost of these works.

In connection with an application for planning permission for the winning and working of minerals, in addition to the usual notifiable parties, any person with an interest in minerals ordinarily worked for removal by underground or surface working in, on or under the land must be notified of the application as an owner of the proposed development site.[199] The planning authority must display notice of the application in the vicinity of the application site.[200]

Planning authorities have to notify the Scottish Ministers prior to granting planning permission for opencast coal mining where the site boundary is within 500m from the edge of an existing community or sensitive establishment (see Ch.5 above).

Planning permission may be granted subject to a restoration condition requiring restoration of the site after the winning and working is completed, and an aftercare condition requiring steps to be taken to bring the land to the required standard for either agricultural, forestry or amenity use. Unless a condition expressly specifies a shorter or longer period, the winning and working of minerals or the depositing of mineral waste must cease not later than 60 years after the grant of permission.[201]

Where the winning and working or depositing appears to have permanently

---

[195] *Thomas David (Porthcawl) Ltd v Penybont Rural DC* [1972] 1 W.L.R. 1526.

[196] PDO 1992 (SI 1992/223) Sch.1 Classes 53–66, as amended.

[197] TCPSA 1997 s.262; Town and Country Planning (Scotland) (Minerals) Regulations 1998 (SI 1998/2913), Town and Country Planning (Compensation for Restrictions on Mineral Working and Mineral Waste Depositing) (Scotland) Regulations 1998 (SI 1998/2914) and Management of Extractive Waste (Scotland) Regulations 2010 (SSI 2010/60). Circular 2/1999, Town and Country Planning (Scotland) (Minerals) Regulations 1998 (Scottish Office, 1999), and Circular 3/1999, Town and Country Planning (Compensation for Restrictions on Mineral Working and Mineral Waste Depositing) (Scotland) Regulations 1999 (Scottish Office, 1999).

[198] SPP, para.237; PAN 50, Controlling the Environmental Effects of Surface Mineral Workings (Scottish Office, 1996), including Annexes A–D, and PAN 64, Reclamation of Surface Mineral Workings (Scottish Executive, 2003).

[199] TCPSA 1997 s.35 and DMPR 2013 (SSI 2013/155) reg.15.

[200] DMPR 2013 (SSI 2013/155) reg.19.

[201] TCPSA 1997 s.41(6) and Sch.3.

ceased, the planning authority may prohibit its resumption.[202] Once the prohibition order comes into force, any planning permission for the development ceases to have effect. If the operations have been temporarily suspended, the planning authority may require steps to be taken for the protection of the environment during the period of suspension, to preserve the amenities of the area, to protect it from damage and to prevent any deterioration in the condition of the land. A suspension order does not prevent recommencement of development provided notice is given to the planning authority. Prohibition and suspension orders do not take effect until confirmed by the Scottish Ministers and registered in the Land Register or Register of Sasines.

Since 1 January 1997 mineral developments are subject to a review process which requires, in effect, a fresh application for planning permission to be submitted so that the conditions applicable to the development can be updated.[203] This review process is subject to the environmental assessment requirements.[204] Active sites with permissions granted prior to 22 February 1982 have undergone an initial review, and all sites are reviewed 15 years after the initial grant of planning permission and every 15 years from the date of a previous review. At dormant sites, no minerals development can be carried out until a new scheme of conditions has been submitted to, and agreed by, the planning authority. Old mining permissions granted by interim development orders prior to the Town and Country Planning (Scotland) Act 1947, for which application for registration was not made by 24 July 1992, have ceased to have effect.

CROWN LAND

9.59   The Crown exemption from planning legislation was removed in 2006.[205] There are special procedures for urgent Crown development and enforcement in relation to the Crown.[206] Wartime breaches of planning control by the Crown can be subject to enforcement action by planning authorities for five years after the disposal of the land by the Crown.[207] The Crown also has permitted development rights.[208]

DEVELOPMENT BY PLANNING AUTHORITIES

9.60   If the local development plan contains policies or proposals for development on land owned by the planning authority, or views on the occurrence of such develop-

---

[202] TCPSA 1997 s.71(8) and Sch.8.

[203] TCPSA 1997 s.74 and Schs 9 and 10, derived from the Environment Act 1995 s.96 and Schs 13 and 14. Circular 34/1996, Commencement of Section 96 of the Environment Act 1995: Review of Old Minerals Permissions (Scottish Executive, 1996). See Neil Collar, "Mineral Development", 1996 Prop. L.B. 8. *Lafarge Aggregates Ltd v Scottish Ministers*, 2004 G.W.D. 2–37; *G Hamilton (Tullochgribban Mains) Ltd, Petitioners* [2012] UKSC 31.

[204] The Town and Country Planning (Environmental Impact Assessment) (Scotland) Regulations 2011 (SSI 2011/139) reg.33; Circular 3/2011, The Town and Country Planning(Environmental Impact Assessment) (Scotland) Regulations 2011 (Scottish Government, 2011) paras 166-185.

[205] TCPSA 1997 s.241A, added by Planning and Compulsory Purchase Act 2004 s.90(1), which also added PLBCASA 1997 s.73A and Planning (Hazardous Substances) (Scotland) Act 1997 s.30A.

[206] TCPSA 1997 ss.242A and 245A.

[207] TCPSA 1997 s.251.

[208] Town and Country Planning (General Permitted Development) (Scotland) Order 1992 Classes 75–78 (Development by the Crown); 79–86 (Aviation Development by the Crown); 87–90 (Crown Railways, Dockyards etc. and Lighthouses); 91 (Emergency development by the Crown); and 92–94 (Development for National Security Purposes).

ment, the plan must include a schedule which identifies the land, states that it is so owned and refers to the policies, proposals or views in question.[209]

The council as landowner require to submit an application for planning permission for proposed development to itself as planning authority.[210] There is no longer a prohibition on delegating determination of an application for planning permission made by the planning authority or by a member of the planning authority, or an application relating to land in the ownership of the planning authority or to land in which the planning authority have a financial interest (see Ch.5).

There is a requirement to notify the Scottish Ministers where the planning authority propose to grant planning permission for development for which the planning authority is the applicant/developer; they have a financial or other, e.g. partnership, interest; or which is to be located wholly or partly on land owned by them or in respect of which they may have an interest. Notification is only required if the proposed development would be significantly contrary to the development plan (see Ch.5 above).

HAZARDOUS SUBSTANCES AND DANGEROUS GOODS

Previously, the development control system only provided the planning authority with the opportunity to control storage of hazardous substances on land if this storage amounted to development (see Ch.4 above). A new hazardous use could be introduced or an existing operation intensified without any planning permission being required. Since 1 May 1993, hazardous substances consent must be obtained from the planning authority where the aggregate quantity of the substance on, over or under the land exceeds the controlled quantity.[211] The temporary presence of a substance while in transit will be taken into account only if it is unloaded. Deemed consent for the presence of a substance could be claimed as of right until 1 November 1993.

9.61

Hazardous substances consent is obtained by submitting an application in a similar way to an application for planning permission, with owner and neighbour notification and newspaper advertisement. In determining an application, the authority will have regard to any material consideration, including any current or contemplated use of the land to which the application relates, the use and likely use of land in the vicinity, any planning permission granted for land in the vicinity, the provisions of the development plan, and any advice received from the Health and Safety Executive. Consent may be granted subject to conditions specifying the storage or use of the substance and the times between which it may be present.

The control of hazardous substances regime is similar to normal planning controls. There is a right of appeal to the Scottish Ministers against an actual or deemed refusal of consent. The planning authority has enforcement powers in situations where consent is required but has not been obtained, or there is a failure to comply with the terms or conditions of the consent.

---

[209] TCPSA 1997 s.15(3) and Town and Country Planning (Development Planning) (Scotland) Regulations 2008 (SSI 2008/426) reg.9.

[210] PSA 2006 Sch.1 para.1 repealed the previous special notice of intention to develop procedure in TCPSA 1997 s.263, and Planning etc. (Scotland) Act 2006 (Consequential Provision) Order (SSI 2007/176). See *Lerwick Port Authority v Scottish Ministers* [2007] CSOH 156 at [74].

[211] Planning (Hazardous Substances) (Scotland) Act 1997; Town and Country Planning (Hazardous Substances) (Scotland) Regulations 2015 (SSI 2015/181). *Eriden Properties LLP v Falkirk Council*, 2007 S.L.T. 966. Planning Circular 3/2015, Planning Controls for Hazardous Substances (Scottish Government, 2015).

Hazardous substances consent enures for the benefit of the land and is not personal to the applicant. However, unlike planning permission, the consent is revoked if there is a change of control of part of the site unless an application for continuation of the consent is made in advance to the planning authority.

The planning authority must consult the Health and Safety Executive before determining an application for planning permission, where a proposed development is within an area notified to the authority by the Executive.[212] Notification takes place because of the presence within the vicinity of toxic, highly reactive, explosive or inflammable substances (otherwise than on a relevant nuclear site). This consultation requirement applies where the development involves the provision of residential accommodation, more than 250sq m of retail floor space, 500sq m of office space or 750sq m of floor space to be used for an industrial process, or is otherwise likely to result in a material increase in the number of persons working within or visiting the notified area.

Measures required to secure sites for use during the transport or temporary storage of dangerous goods may require planning permission.[213]

---

[212] DMPR 2013 (SSI 2013/155) reg.25 and Sch.5 para.3.
[213] Planning Circular 3/2006, Planning and the Carriage of Dangerous Goods and Use of Transportable Pressure Equipment (Amendment) Regulations 2005 (Scottish Executive, 2006).

CHAPTER 10

PUBLIC PARTICIPATION

Planning is predominantly about controlling development in the wider public **10.01** interest (a rather sweeping statement of the underlying nature of planning, but Ch.1 discusses this matter in more detail). Therefore, it seems fitting to end this book with an examination of the extent to which members of the public can participate in the planning system. Without the interest and input from members of the public, the system cannot maintain the public confidence which it requires to function efficiently. Thus it is to be hoped that members of the public will continue to exercise their rights. An underlying objective of the reforms to the planning system introduced in 2009 is to give local people better opportunities to influence the decisions that affect them (see Ch.1 above).

The UK is a signatory to the Aarhus Convention. Its three pillars are: access to environmental information, public participation and access to justice. The Convention is being incorporated into the UK by domestic legislation such as the Environmental Information (Scotland) Regulations 2004 (SSI 2004/520) (see para.10.08 below). Although the Convention is an international treaty, its provisions are referred to by the UK courts.[1]

As outlined in Chs 4 and 5, the Human Rights Act 1998 introduced a rights-based culture into British law. Convention rights apply to all persons, and are not divided into developer and third party/objector rights. The planning system has always weighed the competing interests of developers and neighbours/third parties. Convention rights are conferred on all landowners, both developer and neighbours. In determining a planning application, the planning authority has to take account of the neighbours' rights as well as the rights of the applicant. In most instances, the decision reached will be the same as it would have been if Convention rights did not apply.

In this context, the terms "members of the public" or "third parties" are used to denote persons other than the applicant for permission/ developer, the planning authority and bodies which must be consulted as part of the determination of a planning application. These persons may be local residents, and might even have been notified as neighbours of the proposed development, members of a voluntary group such as a community council or amenity society, or concerned individuals. The planning system gives all these members of the public various opportunities to make their views known and be taken into account as part of the decision-making process.

The planning system can be divided into two parts: development planning and development management (see Ch.2 above). The rights of members of the public in each part are examined below.

---

[1] e.g. *Sally Carroll v Scottish Borders Council* [2015] CSIH 73.

DEVELOPMENT PLANS

10.02   The development plan is an expression of the views of the planning authority with regard to use of the land in its district. The authority has few powers or opportunities to implement these views itself, and the provisions of the plan serve more as authoritative guidance to those wishing to develop land. The plan does not remove the need to obtain planning permission, even where a development conforms to its provisions, and those provisions form one of the material considerations taken into account by the authority when determining applications for planning permission. As explained in Chs 3 and 5, the introduction of the plan-led system has resulted in a presumption that planning permission will be granted for a proposed development which is in accordance with the provisions of a development plan, unless material considerations dictate otherwise. It is in this role that the planning authority can implement its views expressed in the plan, but only to the extent of granting permission for developments which are in accordance with the plan and refusing the other applications.

In city regions, there will be a strategic development plan (SDP) and a local development plan (LDP); elsewhere there will only be a LDP. Since 2009, any supplementary guidance issued in connection with either a SDP or a LDP is part of "the development plan". Both SDPs and LDPs are subject to periodic review, alteration or replacement by the planning authority, the procedure for which is discussed in Ch.3. At each stage the authority is required to publish notices in local newspapers and on the internet alerting members of the public to the opportunity of inspecting proposals or draft plans and lodging representations. Information displays are often mounted in public buildings such as libraries, and public meetings may be organised. The local media may carry features on the proposals. Neighbour notification is only required where a proposed LDP includes a proposal for development relating to a specific site which, if implemented, would be likely to have a significant effect on the use or amenity of that site or of neighbouring land, which is land conterminous with or within 20m of the boundary of the specific site.

Members of the public should exercise every such opportunity offered to inspect proposals and lodge written representations making their views known. As plans will only be replaced every five years, and will form the blueprint for developments during that time, it is essential that the views of the community are accurately expressed in the plan which is eventually adopted, not least because it will be difficult to resist any development which is in accordance with the plan. Inspection of the proposals will also bring to light any issues which have escaped the glare of publicity, but are still of importance and worthy of comment. The opportunity should also be taken to correct any factual errors. It should be appreciated that the weight given to opposition often correlates to the number of representations received, and it may be a mistake to assume that others will object and that your representations will make no difference.

10.03   Following the initial consultation stage, modified proposals will often be published. These should be inspected to check whether previous representations have been incorporated (if not, they can be repeated) or if representations should be made in relation to fresh proposals. There is no bar to lodging representations at a later stage which could have been made in connection with an earlier version of the proposals.

After the consultation stages, the proposed SDP is submitted to the Scottish Ministers for approval, and the public is given an opportunity to make representations to the Ministers. The Ministers must hold an examination if representations timeously made have not been withdrawn.

If representations remain outstanding in relation to the proposed local development plan, the persons or bodies maintaining those representations are given the opportunity of presenting their case at an examination. This examination is chaired by a reporter, who is an independent professional normally employed by the Directorate for Planning and Environmental Appeals for determining planning appeals to the Ministers. The examination is, therefore, a valuable opportunity to convince a person independent of the planning authority and the plan preparation process of the need to modify the proposals. The planning authority has very limited scope for declining to follow the reporter's recommendations.

The legality of the decision of the Scottish Ministers on the SDP, or the planning authority on the LDP, may be challenged in the Court of Session by members of the public who are persons "aggrieved", using the statutory review procedure (see Chs 3 and 8 above).[2] The treatment of third parties in the courts is discussed below.

DEVELOPMENT MANAGEMENT

Development management is the term used to describe the determination by the **10.04** planning authority of applications for planning permission (see Ch.5 above), and the taking of enforcement action against breaches of planning control (see Ch.7 above). While it is the former which involves most public participation, members of the public should be prepared to participate in enforcement by reporting activities which are suspected either not to benefit from planning permission or not to conform with the terms and conditions of a grant of permission, rather than relying on detection by under-resourced council planning departments.

The high point of public involvement in the planning system comes with applications for planning permission, where members of the public have the opportunity to lodge representations either with a view towards persuading the authority to refuse permission for the development, or simply expressing views which seem relevant, or in support of the development. The following discussion refers principally to objections, as these are the most common form of representation.

The planning authority is required to take into account representations lodged by certain members of the public, such as notifiable neighbours, or those received following newspaper advertisement or display of site notices. However, even if the application is not advertised, any member of the public can lodge a representation which must be taken into account by the authority to the extent that it raises material planning considerations (see Ch.5 above).

Part of the reason for the extent of public involvement in the determination of planning applications lies in the publicity requirements (see Ch.5 above). In submitting the application, the applicant is required to serve notice upon the owners and agricultural tenants of the development site, and the planning authority must notify neighbours. Broadly, only those neighbours within 20m of the site must be notified. In many circumstances notice of the proposed development must be given by newspaper advertisement, and some authorities have policies of publishing advertisements beyond the statutory requirements. Site notices must be displayed if the proposed development would affect the character or appearance of a conserva-

---

[2] Town and Country Planning (Scotland) Act (TCPSA) 1997 s.237; *Uprichard v Scottish Ministers* [2013] UKSC 21.

tion area or the setting of a listed building. Finally, details of all applications must be entered in a register available for public inspection, allowing concerned members of the public to check regularly on new applications.

10.05   Prior to deciding whether to object, or writing an objection, the plans and other papers lodged with the planning authority in connection with the application should be inspected (the official notices and newspaper advertisements give few details other than the description of the proposed development). Planning authorities publish planning applications on their websites; if inspecting the application at the council office, it is advisable to check with the authority by telephone that these documents are available for inspection (the application may still be in the initial processing stages), and, if so, at what location and times. Unless the application is for planning permission in principle, or a change of use, the application should include detailed drawings of the buildings or other structures involved. Careful note should be taken of details such as the height of buildings in comparison to others in the vicinity and distance from surrounding properties, the architectural style, any loss of trees, provision for car parking, and vehicular and pedestrian access. The details of the parties notified should be checked for any obvious omissions, which should be drawn to the attention of the authority. There should be a duty planning officer present who can explain details of the drawings, and also any policies of the authority which will apply.

In addition to inspecting the drawings accompanying the application, it is important to check with the authority the time limit for lodging objections. The official notices and newspaper advertisements specify time limits, but many authorities do not strictly adhere to these limits. It should also be possible to find out the name of the planning officer dealing with the application, who will normally be prepared to discuss it.

10.06   No procedure is prescribed for lodging objections, but the objection should identify the application concerned, either by reference number, if known, or by repeating the description of the proposed development and specifying the address of the application site. It should be in writing, identify the objector and be signed (confidentiality can be requested). Mention should be made of any official notification of the application received by the objector, as this may oblige the planning authority to take the objection into account. Finally, the objections to the proposed development should be listed, together with the reasons for those objections and any supporting information such as plans or photographs.

The grounds of objection will, of course, depend to a large extent on the form of development proposed and the characteristics of the development site and the surrounding area. The planning authority is legally obliged to take into account all material planning considerations and ignore any other issues (even if these issues are raised by parties whose representations must be taken into account). The grounds of objection can, therefore, be compiled from the list of material considerations given in Ch.5. The level of sophistication of the grounds of objection will depend upon the scale of the development proposed and the views of the objector. While it is not essential that each ground of objection affect the objector directly, some objectors may prefer to limit the objection to the matters most relevant to their personal position. For example, an objection may refer to a traffic problem likely to be caused to residents at one end of a street as a result of the proposed development, notwithstanding that the objector will not suffer any traffic problems.

The planning authority will acknowledge receipt of the objection. Some authorities have a practice of sending copies of objections to the applicant, with the offer of an opportunity of responding to the comments made. When the planning officer comes to consider the recommendation to be made in his report to the authority on the application, the planning considerations raised by any objections will be taken into account. A summary of the considerations (but not usually a copy of the objections) will be included in the report circulated to the councillors who will make the decision (unless the decision is made by an officer under delegated powers).

Objectors may wish to act further than simply lodging an objection. Public opposition to the proposed development can be generated by publicity and meetings. As councillors take account of the number of objections, other members of the public can be encouraged to lodge objections, possibly by the use of style letters which can be photocopied and distributed for signature. Appropriate bodies can be approached with a request for their views. The local councillors, and MPs and MSPs, can be contacted and made aware of objections. If the local councillor is not a member of the committee which will decide the application, he can be asked to pass views to the councillors on that committee. If the scale or importance of the development justifies it, copies of the objection can be sent to each of the councillors who sit on the committee (the council will provide names and addresses). However, care should be taken not to burden them with too much detail and to avoid too frequent contact, which may result in loss of their co-operation. It is also advisable to delay such communications until a few days before the committee is due to consider the application, so that the views will still be fresh in the minds of the councillors at that meeting.

It is important to identify whether the application will be decided by the councillors or by an officer acting under delegated powers. Some planning authorities have schemes of delegation which prevent the use of delegated powers if more than a specified number of objections have been received.

It is also worth maintaining regular contact with the relevant planning officer, both to check the progress of the application and to discover any problems which are being encountered which may either assist the objection, or with which the objector may be in a position to provide assistance.

Some applications involve the applicant and the planning authority entering into **10.07** a s.75 obligation (see Ch.6 above). There may be no sinister purpose behind such an agreement, which may be necessary because normal planning powers cannot regulate the development effectively. However, there is concern about the lack of any public participation in the agreement process and the belief that developers "buy" permission by offering planning benefits over and above what is required for the development. If members of the public are concerned, and not prepared to accept reassurance from the planning department, their only option is to enlist the help of councillors to investigate the terms of any proposed agreement. When it comes to the time for a decision to be made, members of the public are entitled to attend the committee meeting, but it is unusual for them to be allowed to address the committee (although the right of address can always be requested). In many authorities a wide range of planning applications are decided by officers using delegated powers.

Following determination of the application, the decision must be notified to all those who lodged representations. If the application has been refused or granted subject to unacceptable conditions, the applicant has three months to lodge an appeal to the Scottish Ministers, unless the decision was made using delegated powers, in which case the applicant has a right to apply to the local review body (LRB) for review of the decision (see Ch.8 above). Any person who lodged a representation in connection with the application will be informed by the planning authority if an appeal/review is submitted and given the opportunity to lodge further representations. Any person aggrieved by the decision of the reporter/Scottish Ministers/LRB may challenge its legality within six weeks in the Court of Session through the statutory review procedure (see para.10.09 below).

If the planning authority grants planning permission for the proposed development, objectors have no right of appeal to the Scottish Ministers. Their only remedy is to petition the Court of Session for a common law judicial review of the decision. The limited value of such a remedy is discussed below. Other forms of challenge, such as a complaint to the ombudsman, will not prevent the development from proceeding, and are therefore of limited value.

The lack of an opportunity for members of the public to challenge the merits of a decision to grant planning permission may seem unsatisfactory, but it must be remembered that until the introduction of planning control in 1947 landowners could do as they pleased with their land. For this reason, it has been consistent government policy that there is a presumption in favour of development, and the planning authority must show reasons why development should not proceed (see Ch.5 above). To allow members of the public a right of appeal against a grant of permission would unduly restrict the rights of landowners, and be contrary to that presumption. Such a right of appeal would also play havoc with developers who often have a tight timescale for a development, and would incur substantial losses if a project was delayed by an appeal lodged by a member of the public. Even if such losses could be claimed against the person following dismissal of the appeal, most members of the public have insufficient assets to make this worthwhile, and the danger of becoming liable for such losses would dissuade members of the public from utilising the right of appeal in the first place. Unfortunately, members of the public must accept that there is no second chance if they fail to persuade the planning authority that permission should be refused, unless there is a legal flaw in the decision which can be challenged in court. The Scottish Government rejected the introduction of third party appeals during the reform process (see Ch.1 above).

PLANNING INFORMATION

10.08   It is important for third parties to access information. Planning authorities are required to keep registers detailing such matters as the progress and decision of applications for planning permission, enforcement action, and the progress with alteration or repeal and replacement of development plans.[3] These registers must be kept up-to-date and available for public inspection, along with copies of the development plan. Copies of the agenda for the planning committee meeting and any reports to committee must be available to the public at least three days prior to any meeting.[4]

The Freedom of Information (Scotland) Act 2002 and the Environmental Information (Scotland) Regulations 2004 (SSI 2004/520) give rights to request

---

[3]   For example, TCPSA 1997 ss.36 and 36A and Town and Country Planning (Development Management Procedure) (Scotland) Regulations 2008 (SSI 2013/155) regs 16, 21 and 22.
[4]   Local Government (Scotland) Act 1973 s.50B.

information from public bodies.[5] The 2004 Regulations part implement the Aarhus Convention.

MEMBERS OF THE PUBLIC IN COURT

Following an unsatisfactory planning decision, members of the public often assume that it can be challenged in the courts. Indeed, any person aggrieved by a decision to adopt/approve a development plan, or by the decision of the Scottish Ministers on appeal, has the right to challenge that decision in the Court of Session through the statutory review procedure, and there is a similar possibility of challenge against a decision of the planning authority on a planning application by the common law judicial review procedure. These procedures are discussed in detail in Ch.8.   **10.09**

However, members of the public rarely appreciate the limitations on what can be achieved through the court procedures. The right of challenge only extends to the legality of the decision, and not its planning merits. It is not enough to show that the decision was wrong. A successful challenge requires proof that the authority (or the Scottish Ministers) incorrectly exercised their powers by taking into account irrelevant matters or by ignoring relevant factors, or that their decision was irrational, or the procedure adopted for making the decision was unfair (see Ch.8 above). For example, provided the authority has taken all relevant factors into account, the court will not interfere with the weight it chose to place on each factor, unless its decision was irrational. Even if the decision is shown to be illegal, the court has the discretion not to grant any remedy, for example if it decides that the same decision would have been reached in any case. Furthermore, the remedy most likely to be granted is the quashing of the decision. This results in the matter being referred back to the planning authority for a fresh decision to be made. Providing the authority avoids making the same mistake twice, it is likely that it can reach the same decision as before. A successful judicial review may, therefore, be a pyrrhic victory.

Ironically, lodging a comprehensive objection to the application reduces the likelihood of a successful judicial review. The full nature of the objection will alert the planning authority to all the material considerations. It will be difficult to prove that some of the grounds of objection were ignored, as opposed to considered and overruled. Thus the objection will prevent the authority from failing to take into account a relevant consideration and therefore remove one of the grounds for judicial review. This line of reasoning should not dissuade objectors from raising all the grounds of objection, as a successful objection will avoid the need for court action. It is easier for third parties to win, i.e. gain refusal of planning permission, in the factual arena of the planning authority, than the legal arena of the Court of Session.

The first edition of this book suggested that if the previous paragraphs paint a bleak scenario, members of the public seeking to challenge a decision should be cheered by the favourable attitude of the Court of Session shown in recent years towards the status (known by lawyers as standing) of third parties to bring such challenges. In the subsequent period, the approach taken by the court was less favourable. In 2011, the Supreme Court clarified the approach to the question of   **10.10**

---

5   The Scottish Information Commissioner's website explains further:
   http://www.itspublicknowledge.info [Accessed 2 February 2016].

standing, to put an end to the unduly restrictive approach which had been taken.[6] (Details of the legal requirements of standing are discussed in Ch.8). Cases of note involving third parties include a group of local residents who successfully challenged the grant of planning permission for a housing development. Reports had been lodged by consultants acting for the applicants and the objectors. These reports contained conflicting views regarding the applicable law. The court held that the Director of Planning should have advised the planning committee on the correct view of the law and approach to be taken. Since his report appeared to favour the wrong approach, there was a real risk that the committee were misled as to the correct approach. The report also materially misrepresented the facts in respect of the reduction between the previous and present proposals. Since the report appeared to place importance on the comparison between those proposals, it was likely that the committee took into account irrelevant considerations concerning the extent of the reduction.[7]

The two cases noted in the first edition are still relevant. In the first, a member of the public (L) had complained to the planning authority that he had not been notified of the submission of an application in accordance with the neighbour notification procedures and reserved his right to object to the proposed development once he had received such notification. The authority informed the applicants of the position and, without informing L, subsequently granted permission for an amended application in which the boundaries of the development site had been redrawn to avoid any obligation to notify L as a neighbour. The Court of Session quashed this decision on the grounds that L had been unfairly deprived of his legitimate expectation of being able to lodge an objection. While neither the applicant for permission nor the authority had failed to comply with the statutory procedures, the procedure adopted by the authority was unfair because it prejudiced L's rights as a member of the public.[8]

10.11   The other decision worthy of note possibly goes even further towards protecting third-party rights in the development management process. An application for planning permission was submitted which described the proposed development as a roadside petrol station and service area. This description was repeated in the notices served on neighbours and in the newspaper advertisements. However, the plans submitted with the application showed a separate petrol station for each of two roadside sites and a 40-bedroom lodge, two restaurants and three car parks. A member of the public applied to the Court of Session for the decision to grant permission for the development as shown on the plans to be quashed. The court upheld the application on the grounds that the inadequate description had deprived him of an opportunity to lodge representations which might, at least in his view, have affected the result.[9] The significance of the decision in this case can only be appreciated from a detailed examination of the facts. The member of the public was a businessman who was likely to lose business to the bedroom lodge part of the development. It seems that the omission of the lodge from the description caused him to assume wrongly that he had no objection to the development, although inspection of the plans would have corrected this mis-assumption. There was some uncertainty whether he could have produced any planning arguments against the development which would have influenced the decision. Perhaps the most telling

---

[6]   *AXA General Insurance Ltd v HM Advocate* [2011] UKSC 46; [2012] 1 A.C. 868; 2011 S.L.T. 1061.
[7]   *Campbell v Edinburgh City Council*, 1998 G.W.D. 17-877; 1998 69 S.P.E.L. 99.
[8]   *Lochore v Moray DC*, 1992 S.L.T. 16; 1991 34 S.P.L.P. 78.
[9]   *Cumming v Secretary of State for Scotland*, 1993 S.L.T. 228.

fact is that he was eventually given full notice of the true extent of the development and given an opportunity to lodge representations before the decision was taken on the application. Despite all of these factors, the Court of Session upheld his right as a member of the public to expect the description contained in an application for planning permission to give full and fair notice of the extent of the development for which permission was sought.

Such a favourable decision cannot be expected at all times, but these decisions emphasise the importance which the Court of Session has placed on third-party rights in planning.

CONCLUSION

Although the Court of Session has on occasion shown a positive attitude towards **10.12** allowing members of the public to challenge planning decisions, the role of the court is limited to reviewing the decision challenged to ensure that it has been reached within the law. Members of the public have no opportunity to challenge the planning merits of a grant of planning permission or the adoption of a development plan. This emphasises the importance of mounting an effective campaign at the earliest stage.

STANDARD SCALE OF FINES

[From April 1, 1996]   **A1.1**

Level	Amount
1	£200
2	£500
3	£1,000
4	£2,500
5	£5,000

[Criminal Procedure (Scotland) Act 1995 s.225]

APPENDIX 2

BAD NEIGHBOUR DEVELOPMENT[1]

CLASSES OF DEVELOPMENT—REGULATIONS 20(2)(C) AND 41(1)(B)

The following are the classes of development specified for the purposes of regulations 20(2)(c) and 41(1)(b)—

(1)   the construction or installation of buildings for use as a public convenience;   **A2.1**

(2)   the construction of buildings or other operations, or use of land—

    (a)   for the disposal of refuse or waste materials, or for the storage or recovery of reusable metal;

    (b)   for the retention, treatment or disposal of sewage, trade waste, or effluent other than—

        (i)   the construction of pumphouses in a line of sewers;

        (ii)   the construction of septic tanks and cesspools serving single dwellinghouses, or single caravans, or single buildings in which not more than 10 people will normally reside, work or congregate;

        (iii)   the laying of sewers; or

        (iv)   works ancillary to those described in sub paragraphs (i) to (iii);

    (c)   as a scrap yard or coal yard; or

    (d)   for the winning or working of minerals, including management of extractive waste.

(3)   the construction of buildings or use of land or buildings for the purposes of a slaughtering animals (including fish and poultry) or the processing of animal carcasses for final disposal or as part of the production of other goods;

(4)   the construction or use of buildings for any of the following purposes—

    (a)   building for indoor games

    (b)   cinema

    (c)   dancing

    (d)   fun fair

    (e)   gymnasium (not forming part of a school, college or university)

    (f)   hot food shop

    (g)   licensed premises

    (h)   music hall

    (i)   skating rink

    (j)   swimming pool, or

    (k)   theatre;

(5)   the construction of buildings for or the use of buildings or land as—

    (a)   a crematorium or a cemetery;

    (b)   a zoo, or wildlife park, or for the business of boarding or breeding animals;

(6)   the construction of buildings and use of buildings or land for motor racing;

(7)   the construction of a building to a height exceeding 20 metres;

(8)   the construction of buildings, operations, and use of buildings or land which will—

    (a)   affect residential property by reason of fumes, noise, vibration, smoke, artificial lighting, or discharge of any solid or liquid substance;

    (b)   alter the character of an area of established amenity;

    (c)   bring crowds into a generally quiet area;

    (d)   cause activity and noise between the hours of 8 pm and 8 am; and

    (e)   introduce significant change into a homogeneous area.

---

[1]   Town and Country Planning (Development Management Procedure) (Scotland) Regulations 2013 (SSI 2013/155) Sch.3.

INDEX